About the Author

Jonathan Waterlow received his PhD (DPhil) from the University of Oxford in 2012. He went on to hold a British Academy Postdoctoral Fellowship at St Antony's College, Oxford, and was a Research Associate at the University of Bristol from 2016-18. He's also been a Visiting Postdoctoral Fellow at the University of Toronto, and studied at the Universities of Edinburgh, St Andrews, and the Herzen State Pedagogical University in St Petersburg, Russia.

He's a founder at Voices in the Dark (voicesinthedark.world), where he writes and podcasts. His personal website is jonwaterlow.com.

PRAISE FOR *IT'S ONLY A JOKE, COMRADE!*

The best book on Stalinism I've read in a long time. With unprecedented subtlety, Jon Waterlow explores the contradictory responses of Soviet citizens to the Stalin regime through a multi-faceted exploration of the ways in which telling jokes helped citizens cope with the pressures of living under a terroristic regime hell-bent on economic and social modernization.

The book will be required reading for those interested in the history of the Soviet Union, but also for anyone interested in understanding the manifold social and psychological functions that laughter can perform. Waterlow integrates solid archival research with an impressive command of the theoretical literature on humour and he writes lucidly and with verve. This is a book of great humanity and insight (with some good jokes thrown in).

> Professor Stephen A. Smith, FBA
> All Souls College, University of Oxford
> Author of *The Oxford Handbook of the History of Communism*
> and *The Russian Revolution: A Very Short Introduction.*

A stunningly original study of Stalinist society, *It's Only a Joke, Comrade!* explodes the sterile binaries of 'consent' and 'resistance' to show that vast swathes of the Soviet population lived in the thickets of language and ideas where official ideology mingled with popular attitudes.

Waterlow's fresh and fluent style crackles with wit and perception as he deftly teases out the veiled assumptions, fears and aspirations that underpinned the workings of (often gallows) humour in the 1930s Soviet Union. Essential reading for anyone interested in daily life under the Stalinist dictatorship but also for anyone interested in how human beings navigate a path through times of extraordinary upheaval, privation and danger.

> Dr Daniel Beer, Royal Holloway, University of London
> Author of *The House of the Dead: Siberian Exile under the Tsars,*
> winner of the Cundill History Prize.

An extraordinary achievement. Jonathan Waterlow has found a unique lens into Stalinist society through this brilliant exploration of humor. Maneuvering through the dark days of the 1930s, ordinary people told jokes that belie the image of a cowed, totally repressed, atomized population. Rather than all Soviet people being divided into pro- and anti-Soviet, affirmation or dissent/resistance, they made up a 'muddled majority' that practiced a critical acceptance of Soviet life. Humor was at one and the same time a safety valve, a form of social communication, and a critique often founded on acceptance of socialist values and disgust at their violation in the experiences of everyday life.

**Ronald Grigor Suny, William H. Sewell Jr.
Distinguished University Professor of History
The University of Michigan. Author of *The Soviet Experiment*.**

Everyone knows that jokes mattered in the Soviet period, and that under Stalin, they could land you in prison. Jonathan Waterlow's fascinating book is, however, a pioneering historical study of the genre, unique in its sensitivity to the social context in which jokes circulated.

Drawing on extensive unpublished material from archives, it captures the contrary functions of these small comic narratives, as instruments of social solidarity and not just of subversion.

It is also, as any book about jokes should be, lively, engaging, and at times very funny. A must read for anyone interested in Soviet or indeed Russian culture.

**Professor Catriona Kelly, FBA,
New College, University of Oxford
Author of *Russian Literature: A Very Short Introduction*.**

This book re-vitalizes our understanding of Soviet society by demonstrating the ways in which humour served as a means of self-expression for Soviet citizens, offering them agency in their attempts to cope with and adapt to the demanding tribulations of everyday life – whether in shopping queues or in the shadow of Stalin's Great Terror. *It's Only a Joke, Comrade!* is not only an original contribution to the historiography of Stalinism, but contributes as well to our understanding of the role of popular humour, more generally, under authoritarian regimes of the twentieth century.

**Professor Lynne Viola, FRSA, University of Toronto
Author of *Stalinist Perpetrators on Trial* and *The Unknown Gulag: The Lost World of Stalin's Special Settlements*.**

People laugh at the very darkest times as well, as Jonathan Waterlow reveals in his brilliant study of humour and trust under the Stalinist dictatorship. Uncovering the dark and often disturbing ironies of history, *It's Only a Joke, Comrade!* challenges our understanding of 'Soviet subjectivity' by telling a compelling human story of people's ability to maintain agency in their daily encounters with the Stalinist system.

Prodigiously researched and lucidly argued, this book will make a major contribution to understanding Stalinist culture and society. It will be read with great benefit and pleasure by both lay and expert readers. Highly recommended.

Dr Matthias Neumann, University of East Anglia
Author of *The Communist Youth League and the Transformation of the Soviet Union.*

We are told that Stalinism was no laughing matter. Waterlow disagrees, revealing how popular humour was integral to how Soviet citizens engaged with the world around them.

Stalinism, a human drama. This important and engaging book reanimates ordinary Soviet citizens, revealing how they laughed and joked, shared and despaired, connected and communicated across one of the most traumatic periods in modern history. Through the medium of popular humour, Waterlow immerses us deep into the lived experience of ordinary folk during Stalin's 1930s.

A revelatory account of how ordinary citizens experienced Stalinism. Essential reading.

Dr Andy Willimott, University of Reading
Author of *Living the Revolution: Urban Communes and Soviet Socialism, 1917-1932.*

Humour is not an emotion usually associated with Stalin's Soviet Union, but Jon Waterlow's outstanding book shows how it was an integral part of the lives of Soviet citizens as they sought to make sense of the reality of life under the dictator. Enlivened by the bitter-sweet humour of Soviet men and women during the grim years of the 1930s, *It's Only a Joke, Comrade!* gives us a powerful insight into the way societies function at times of great stress and into the nature of humanity itself.

Professor Peter Waldron, University of East Anglia
Former President of the British Association for Slavonic and East European Studies.

It's Only a Joke, Comrade! is a superb book – readable, engagingly-written, original and intellectually sophisticated. Jon Waterlow shows us how ordinary Soviet citizens used jokes and humour to deal with the traumatic and often violent changes of the 1930s, and in doing so he makes a series of much broader interventions in debates over the nature of Stalinist society in the 1930s. Particularly interesting is his portrayal of the complexity of Soviet citizens' attitudes to Stalinism, and of the nature of sociability and trust within Soviet society.

This is one of those rare books that not only has to be read by scholars in the field but is also accessible to a wide readership. Indeed it is an essential read for anybody who wants to get beyond standard views of the 'communist joke' and understand what humour really tells us about life under this extraordinary regime.

Professor David Priestland
St Edmund Hall, University of Oxford
Author of *The Red Flag: Communism and the Making of the Modern World*

Also by Jonathan Waterlow

War Crimes Trials and Investigations:
A Multi-Disciplinary Introduction
(with Jacques Schuhmacher)

The 48 Laws of Power in Practice
(with Andrea Domenichini)

IT'S ONLY A JOKE, COMRADE!

HUMOUR, TRUST AND EVERYDAY LIFE UNDER STALIN (1928 - 1941)

Jonathan Waterlow

Copyright © 2018 Jonathan Waterlow
All rights reserved
The moral rights of the author have been asserted

Cover and book design: Jamie C Johnstone
(www.jamiecjohnstone.com)

ISBN 9781999343408

First published in Oxford, 2018

www.jonwaterlow.com

*For my family
and my friends*

CONTENTS

Acknowledgements	xiii
Author's note	xvii
Glossary & Abbreviations	xix
Introduction	1

PART 1: TAKING LIBERTIES

Chapter 1:	Kirov's Carnival, Stalin's Cult	31
Chapter 2:	Plans and Punchlines: 'The *anekdoty* always saved us'	71
Chapter 3:	Speaking More than Bolshevik: Crosshatching and Codebreaking	105

PART 2: JOKING DANGEROUSLY

Chapter 4:	Who's Laughing Now? Persecution and Prosecution	147

PART 3: ALONE TOGETHER

Chapter 5:	Beyond Resistance: The Psychology of Joke-Telling	187
Chapter 6:	In On the Joke: Humour, Trust and Sociability	225
Conclusion		261
Select Bibliography		267

ACKNOWLEDGEMENTS

This is the part of the book I've most looked forward to writing. It's been ten years in the making and I've got a lot of people to thank for helping to get me over the finish line. To anyone I've inadvertently left out, my apologies – and thank you.

First I must acknowledge the financial support of various institutions: the Arts and Humanities Research Council, UK, funded the doctorate from which the book has grown; the Scottish International Education Trust provided financial assistance in my writing-up year, as did a Scouloudi Junior Research Fellowship at the Institute of Historical Research; latterly, a British Academy Postdoctoral Research Fellowship provided the context in which to make the transition from dissertation to book. Additional support for research trips came from the Colin Matthew Fund and Merton College, Oxford.

My high school History teacher, Philip MacKenzie, inspired me and many others, not only through his passion for History, but for life and the living of it. Without him, this book simply wouldn't exist. When I was a rather lost undergraduate at Edinburgh University, often on the verge of dropping out, the encouragement and support of Donald Bloxham, John Gooding, and Jill Stephenson reignited my curiosity in History.

At Oxford, my doctoral supervisors, David Priestland and Nick Stargardt, were consistently supportive and insightful. In the years since completing the DPhil, David has continued to be a constant source of support, intellectual stimulus, and friendship. I can also scarcely overstate the importance of Steve Smith to this project, as reader, mentor, interlocutor and friend. His kindness over the years is truly humbling.

Catriona Kelly and Lynne Viola examined the dissertation which preceded this book; their advice, support and (appropriately enough) sense of humour have all been very important to the project and to me personally. I later had the wonderful opportunity to spend time with Lynne's colleagues and students at the University of Toronto, and I'm grateful for their warm hospitality and insightful feedback on the first chapter of the book.

Back when I began my research, I was lucky enough to be part of the aptly-acronymed Russian Archives Training Scheme (RATS), organised by Polly Jones and Alex Titov. The spirit of the RATS trip – of helping each other and encouraging links both practical and personal across disciplinary and institutional divides – represents the best of academia, and I'm lucky to have been part of it. I must also thank Alex for his repeated help translating some of the more vexing, colloquial and potty-mouthed material (usually to his delight).

Thanks must also go to those friends and colleagues who read, commented on, or otherwise offered constructive advice on the project. First, I must acknowledge Andy Willimott in all these respects and more. I treasure our friendship – thank you for all the support, the laughs, and the ridiculous adventures over the last decade.

I'm deeply grateful to David Brandenberger for his continued generosity of advice, support, humour, and perceptive feedback over the years. His suggestions on how to rewrite the thesis as a book were hugely appreciated and very perceptive; his skills as a translator also came to the rescue many times.

Gleb Albert, Daniel Beer, Brian Carroll, Andrea Domenichini, Dan Healey, Gav Jacobson, Thom Loyd, Gábor Rittersporn and Mal Spencer also read and/or gave valuable feedback on elements of the manuscript. Tim Johnston provided invaluable orientation pointers for working in The State Archive of the Russian Federation (GARF). Thanks, too, to Vladimir Troyansky, who not only checked and improved several of my translations, but also helped me enormously when I first began learning Russian.

Sarah Davies generously allowed me to see her original research notes from the early 1990s. The closure of various archival materials was especially striking in the former Party archive in St Petersburg (TsGAIPD), and Sarah's notes offered glimpses of material I wasn't allowed to see (such instances are clearly noted).

Sasha Arkhipova and Misha Mel'nichenko's work on *anekdoty* has provided the bedrock on which this book stands. Misha's monumental *Sovetskii anekdot: Ukazatel' siuzhetov (The Soviet Anekdot: A Handbook of Plots)* is essential for anyone interested in Soviet jokes and their history. His and Sasha's advice and unparalleled willingness to share materials and archival leads was both welcome and humbling; I am in their debt. Seth Graham was likewise generous, supportive and patient in answering my many questions and also offered valuable feedback when I began this project. I am also grateful to Frederick Choate, who generously made certain diary materials available to me and who took the time to unscramble them from now-forgotten digital formats.

I'm indebted to the staff – the *sotrudniki* – of all the archives in which I worked, particularly – at GARF – to V.A. Kozlov, as well as to N.I. Abdulaeva and her colleagues in the main reading room.

Particular mention must also go to the indomitable G.M. Tokareva at the Komsomol archive; working under her stern but maternal eye was a true pleasure. The warm support and advice of Hennadii Boriak at the National Academy of Sciences, Kyiv, was generous beyond measure, and he made my time researching in Ukraine far easier than it would otherwise have been.

I would also like to thank China Miéville, who was kind enough to answer some unsolicited questions about the idea of 'crosshatching'. He might not recognise the concept as I've used it here, but his novel *The City and The City* had a major impact on my work and thinking.

My comrades-in-archives all helped in countless ways to make the years of research for this book possible, and to keep body and mind (more or less) intact along the way. So, thank you to: Seth Bernstein, Jon Brunstedt, Alan Crawford, Alistair Dickens, Simon Dixon, Courtney Doucette, Jamie Freeman, George Gilbert, Susan Grant, Sean Guillory, JJ Gurga, Simon Huxtable, Alessandro Iandolo, Misha Kogan, Jared McBride, Brendan McGeever, Alex Melnyk, Colleen Moore, Matthias Neumann, Dan Newman, Simon Pawley, Ben Sawyer, Kelly Kolar Sawyer, Sam Sherry, Scott Siggins, Malcolm Spencer, Sasha Steinberg, Mark Vincent, Alexandra Wachter, Peter Waldron, and Zbigniew Wojnowski.

In Russia, Erik Albrecht, Tobin Auber, Ulf Mauder, and Zhenia Plakhotin all supported me in various ways over the years; thank you. Back in the UK, Christian Bailey, Gen Clutton, Joe Dunlop, Selali Fiamanya, Chloe Jeffries, Jaime Kavanagh, Thom Loyd, Gus McFadzean, Miri Peploe, Will Pooley, Phill Pymm, Maris Rowe-McCulloch, Katia Shulga, Rebecca Thomas, Andrew Tompkins, Lara Tyrrell, and David Waterlow all helped to make life a lot more fun and a lot more meaningful. Thank you all.

I would also like to thank several people who've helped me deal with various and sometimes serious health issues over the years: Dr Richard Gipps, don Howard Lawler, and Dr Mark O'Shea. Your professionalism and kindness mean more to me than you know.

Philip McKernan helped me find the courage to stop waiting for permission to put my work out into the world.

Milan Terlunen's careful critique of the book as it evolved was unparalleled; he'll find many traces of his influence throughout the following pages. Thank you for your love, support and countless puns over the years.

Andrea Domenichini, I don't know if this book would exist without you. Thank you for our friendship; thank you for everything.

No one knows what went into this book better than Jacques

Schuhmacher. He worked tirelessly with me on multiple draft revisions and the book would be a lot less clear and infinitely less fun if he hadn't. Words fail me to describe how much I value his support, insight, intelligence, humour and deep loyalty. Our friendship means the world to me.

I couldn't be happier that the endlessly-talented Jamie Johnstone designed this book and its cover. He inspires me every day and I never stop learning from him. Thank you; I love you.

Last but far from least, I thank my parents. I don't know if you'll enjoy this book, but I couldn't have written it without your love and support. I love you dearly – thank you.

Jon Waterlow

Edinburgh,
April 2018

Author's Note

After countless personal conversations and discussions at the various talks I've given on the subject, it's become clear to me that different people find the subject of jokes under Stalin fascinating for a variety of different reasons.

Some are historians or history fans, who not only want to hear the jokes in all their glory, but also want to know the nitty-gritty details about who the regime arrested for crimes of humour, why, and under what legislation. Others are more interested in the social and psychological aspects of joke-telling – what it means to tell and share jokes under an authoritarian regime; how it eased the psychological pain; helped forge trust between contemporaries; and how it helped them to make sense of their lives during one of the most violent and disruptive periods in modern history. Others still wanted to hear jokes about particular events and policies, or the dirtiest jokes directed at Stalin and his entourage.

This book should hopefully please all these readers, but in addition to the outline of the chapters I give in the Introduction, here's where to find what you're most interested in.

For jokes about the leaders, events, policies, and everyday life, see Chapters 1-2. For an in-depth look at the state's persecution of joke-tellers (the nuts, bolts and statistics of policies and prosecutions), check out Chapter 4. And to dig into the psychological and social effects and dynamics of joke-telling under this repressive regime, head over to Chapter 3, and Chapters 5-6 in particular.

A Note on Names and Translations

Jokes, especially wordplay, are a translator's nightmare, and this book is full of them. I've done my best to retain the effect and sense of the originals, but when too much was lost in translation, I provide the original text for comparison.

I've used the standard Library of Congress system for transliteration, except in the footnotes and bibliography when a given work (or author's name) has been published differently. Still, there's always an element of personal preference in transliterating names, so while I've generally stuck to one system ('Trotskii' over 'Trotsky'), sometimes it seemed too much not to make exceptions ('Chaikovskii' might be more accurate, but it looks very different to 'Tchaikovsky', and writing 'Bol'shevik' instead of 'Bolshevik' just felt silly).

When using Ukrainian names, I transliterate from the Ukrainian ('Kyiv' and 'Odesa', rather than 'Kiev' and 'Odessa').

Throughout the book, I've avoided unnecessary transliteration into the Latin alphabet, except when there's some aspect of a joke, song or word that can still be appreciated by readers who don't know Russian. That said, citations of books and articles are transliterated so they can be more easily found in library catalogues.

All translations are my own unless stated otherwise in the notes.

Glossary & Abbreviations

For the sake of convenience and readability, I've left some frequently-used Russian words untranslated:

anekdot(y)	roughly equivalent to 'joke(s)': a short, humorous tale or question followed by a punchline, although the *anekdot* is more consistently associated with political subject matter.
artel'	a cooperative association for craft, artisan and light industrial enterprises.
blat	influence, 'pull', connections.
chastushka(i)	short, humorous poem(s) or rhyming couplets, usually sung.
kolkhoz(y)	collective farm(s).
kolkhoz|nik/nitsa	collective farmer (male/female).
Komsomol	the Communist Youth League.
komsomol|ets/ka	member of the Komsomol (male/female).
kulak	a theoretically rich peasant, whom the regime sought to destroy.
GPU/OGPU/ NKVD	(Joint) State Political Directorate/People's Commissariat of Internal Affairs: the evolving names for the Secret Police.
raion	district.
oblast'	region.
krai	territory.
vozhd'(i)	leader(s) of the regime, with Stalin the most prominent (equivalent to the German word, *Führer*).

Acronyms in Archival Citations

Russia:

GARF Государственный архив Российской Федерации. State Archive of the Russian Federation. References to documents in f.8131, op.31 are to the majority of the criminal case-files I describe in the Introduction.

NA Народный архив. The People's Archive.

RGASPI Российский государственный архив социально-политической истории. Russian State Archive of Socio-Political History (the former Party archive).
References beginning f.M-1 are from the Komsomol archive, which is now part of RGASPI.

RGALI Российский государственный архив литературы и искусства. Russian State Archive of Literature and Art.

TsGAIPD (SPb) Центральный государственный архив историко-политических документов Санкт-Петербурга. Central State Archive of Historico-Political Documents, St Petersburg (the former Party archive).

Ukraine:

TsDAHOU Центральний державний архів громадських об'єднань України. Central State Archive of Public Organisations of Ukraine (the former Party archive).

TsDAVO Центральний державний архів вищих органів влади та управління України. Central State Archive of the Highest Organs of Government and Administration of Ukraine.

HDA SBU	Галузевий державний архів служби безпеки України. Sectoral State Archive of the Security Service of Ukraine (the former KGB archive).

USA:

HPSSS	Harvard Interview Project on the Soviet Social System.

Citations

I follow a standard archival citation model to keep references short and simple:

f.	*fond* (collection)
op.	*opis'* (inventory)
d.	*delo* (file)
l. ll.	*list, listy* (folio, folios)
ob.	*oborot* (verso)

A date in brackets after an archival or other contemporary source reference indicates when a particular joke or remark was made, according to the document in question.

For references to the Harvard Interview Project on the Soviet Social System (HPSSS), I use the following model:

HPSSS 96/A/7, p.23.

This stands for: Interviewee 96, A Schedule, Volume 7, page 23.

Sometimes, two interview protocols with the same interviewee are filed together, with the page numbering resetting at the start of the second interview. In those cases, I include both numbers (the overall number appears as, for e.g., (seq.10)).

The Harvard Project transcripts contain many typographical errors and off-kilter translations (many of the interviewers were not native English speakers), most of which I've silently corrected when quoting from these materials.

INTRODUCTION

Stalinism. The word conjures up dozens of associations, and 'funny' isn't usually one of them. Far more common are words like 'repression', 'dictatorship', 'famine', 'Gulag' and 'terror' – and with good reason. Although Stalin's regime promised a dazzlingly bright future of abundance and equality for its citizens, and initiated enormous cultural, technological and educational reforms that could (and sometimes even did) improve the lives of many, this was all pursued with brutal, uncompromising force.

In the thirteen years between Stalin's rise to power in 1928 and Hitler's invasion in 1941, the Soviet Union became a colossal pressure-cooker in which a self-declared 'backward' country of illiterate peasants was forced through massive programmes of frantic industrialisation, the bloody collectivisation of agriculture, and heady yet ruthless attempts to create a New Soviet Person who would embody Communist values in word, deed and identity.

In short, the population was to be catapulted into the brave new world of Communism… but catapults are hardly known for their gentle landings or precise aim. Millions starved in the collectivisation famines; hundreds of thousands were arrested in the paranoid purging of 'spies' and 'enemies' in the later 1930s; almost everyone suffered some kind of hardship and privation throughout the decade.

How could this story be understood as anything other than a tragedy? Given the millions arrested by the bloodhounds of the NKVD, what space could there possibly be for humour and laughter under Stalin?

But people laugh in the very darkest times, too. They have to. From the dryly affectionate humour of a eulogy to the achingly dark jokes and nicknames that circulate inside concentration camps, via the sardonic grumbling about everyday hardships and the throwaway one-liners directed at authority figures, people laugh in the face of their troubles from the trivial all the way up to the horrifying.

It can be easy to forget that 'funny' and 'serious' are not opposites; serious things can be funny and funny things can be serious.[1] Jokes are stories we tell ourselves about our experience of the world. They can capture, challenge, reimagine, and soothe that experience, holding tension and emotion in a provisional, playful state. If, as philosophers and folklorists argue, myths are the images through which we explain the world to ourselves, jokes are their more playful siblings; challenging rather than dictating; questioning rather than answering; exploring rather than hiding beneath the covers of accepted wisdom.

This book is about how and why ordinary Soviet citizens laughed and joked about their experiences during one of the most dramatic, unstable, unpredictable and traumatic decades in modern history. It is a book not only about the jokes they told (and there were many), but also about what these jokes can tell us about their perceptions, their sense of self and their place in history, and about their social world. Humour helped them to cope and to stave off despair – at least temporarily – and sharing it with others drew them closer together to help ward off the chill of harsh realities. Studying their jokes brings their experiences back to life and contradicts many long-held views of the period as one of fearful atomisation or gullible belief in Stalin.

The 1930s were hard times, materially and psychologically. But it was the clash between the soaring rhetoric of the glittering socialist future and the grinding realities of daily life that fascinated me from the first time I learnt about the period in high school. It seemed to be such a mess of contradictions and extremes: as the foreign correspondent William Chamberlin put it in 1934, after 12 years in the country, the Soviet Union could be 'contradictorily interpreted to the outside world as a menace, a challenge, an inspiration, and a laughingstock'.[2] Surely, I thought, it would seem like that to its own citizens, too, but they were under considerably more pressure to resolve some of these contradictions in order to make sense of their lives. I wanted to know how they did so.

The first time I came across a Soviet joke that made fun of the oppressive system, I felt a dizzying sense of paradox. It seemed both completely natural that people would tell such jokes in so contradictory and frequently irrational a system, yet simultaneously it contradicted everything I'd learnt and read about the period. The book I was reading, after presenting this dash of creative seasoning, immediately returned to descriptions of terror, victimisation, and brainwashing. But I couldn't go back. The joke contradicted the idea that the population had been suffocated or brought under the regime's control. Its playful nature didn't sound much like committed 'resistance' to me, either. I needed to find more jokes to see if this was just an exception, or if there was something much more interesting and complicated going on.

This was no easy task, however. Until the 1970s, historians of Stalinism were mostly concerned with politics rather than everyday life, both for lack of sources and lack of interest. But even when histories of everyday life emerged, colourful as they were, popular opinion was usually treated in black-and-white fashion. Many looked excitedly for dissidents; in response, others looked for positive engagements with the system. Popular opinion was often interpreted, in short, like 'a binary toggle switch which [was] either in the "anti-Soviet" or "pro-Soviet" position, but [which could not] be in-between'.[3] Jokes, when they appeared at all, were instinctively bundled into the 'anti-Soviet' category.

For decades it seemed we were determined to treat these people in the past very differently to ourselves. Nowhere can a population be divided cleanly into ardent believers and implacable enemies of a political regime, but even today Cold War images of society under Stalin still resonate: that it was a neo-Hobbesian nightmare of 'man as wolf to man'; that the population was either terrified into resentful obedience or, for lack of external sources of information, as well as a certain desperate credulity, brainwashed into loving Big Brother. Emblematic of this is the way Stalin's Cult of Personality continues to be wheeled out in every textbook and monograph on popular opinion as an 'explanation' for why the people did not rebel against the system: they believed in Stalin, even if they had their doubts about the system at large. In fact, as we'll see, the reverse was often true.

Although these ideas endure thanks to their appealing simplicity, in recent years scholars more often talk about 'grey zones' on the continuum between the extremes of force and belief.[4] So this is a book about the 'muddled majority'.[5] Neither outright believers, nor self-conscious opponents, most people could internalise certain of the regime's values and norms, yet simultaneously challenge and avoid others (or, indeed, the same ones at different times). People could be critical but not heretical; they could loathe a particular policy because it impacted them negatively, yet simultaneously enjoy others which seemed fair or beneficial. Even though there were certainly outright opponents and committed believers, Soviet citizens at large had not lost their prerevolutionary ability to reach a plurality of conclusions about their government or their own lives, but they *were* now deprived of the same range of public opinions. In this absence, they were forced to reroute critical discourse into other channels – and humour was one of the most important.[6]

But if no longer 'public' in the sense we'd recognise, these exchanges were still eminently social, making this book quite different from recent influential work on 'Soviet Subjectivities', which has, in its attempt to understand what life was like under Stalin, focused on personal diaries or things people said directly to or in front of Power, rather than to each other.

Of course, in any society, sociability is simply compulsory. Humour is deeply entwined in social life, playing a constant and influential role in how we communicate (breaking the ice; charming a stranger; humiliating an enemy; sharing an experience, and so many more). Humour can be social, personal, cold, warm, emotional, intellectual, foolish, candid and concealing – sometimes all at once – which makes it an incomparably rich (if complex) source through which to explore another culture, past or present.

But that's not how it's been used. The most common interpretation of political joke-telling in this and other repressive regimes is to see it as evidence of a culture of self-conscious resistance to state norms, power and ideas, whether that resistance is defined as a social force, or as some kind of personal, internal refusal.[7] Because the regime sought to define and control the rules and limits of behaviour and opinion in every sphere of life, almost anything except absolute conformity might theoretically be considered 'resistance', then.

But were joke-tellers rebellious souls, striking back at a regime they hated, whether in desperation or just in order to remind themselves that they were not blind to reality? Sometimes. But this is far from the whole story. As a few more nuanced works have begun to show, there was a lot more than 'resistance' going on beneath the surface of even the most vicious joke-telling in the 1930s.[8] As we'll see, jokes involved much more than can be understood within a simple oppositional framework;

they were filled with ambivalence, selectivity, sharp insights and a remarkable ability to weave together the tattered threads of rhetoric and reality when adapting to the Soviet world.

Critical jokes do often have the appearance of blunt instruments, but the meaning of any joke depends on context more than its content. Similar or even identical jokes can mean very different things to different people at different times and in different places. They can also mean different things to the *same* people at different times or in different places, and so on. Depending on context, a given joke may produce diametrically opposed results: told to authority, it may well function as an outright attack; but, when told between ordinary, politically powerless individuals, more often it first defuses anger and tension, and then *diffuses* these effects amongst listeners and fellow joke-tellers. Like popular opinion more generally, we need more nuance than a binary switch between affirmation and rejection can provide.

As I said, many historians now talk about 'grey zones' rather than binaries, but while 'grey zones' are an improvement on black-and-white generalisations, they are still something of a cop-out. 'Grey zone' is a euphemism for 'it's complicated', which is certainly true. But I wanted to know *how* it was complicated – how the boundaries of affirmation and dissent blurred together and how contemporaries made some sense of this mixture. It was not a featureless grey fog people got lost in, but a complex interweaving of the official and unofficial which did not result in a undifferentiated sludge, but in a complex and often vibrant living culture. By definition, there are no simple or conclusive answers here, but we can still do more than say it was grey.

Crosshatching

I'd wrestled with this consciously and unconsciously for years, when, suddenly, the image of crosshatching came to me from a novel: *The City and the City* by China Miéville. The novel's conceit is to have two different cities exist topographically in the same place, but which remain culturally, linguistically and socially separate. More importantly, the citizens of each place must learn to 'unsee' and act as though the other one doesn't exist, or face dire consequences from enforcement agents. In most areas, architecture, signposts and other cues make it clear to which city they belonged, but in others – the crosshatched areas – things were unclear and mixed; they seemed to belong to two cultures at once.[9]

Although Miéville's novel uses the crosshatching metaphor in a quite literal sense, the image of those two sets of cultural influences, norms, assumptions – ways of life – blending and becoming a composite whole resonated powerfully with what I found in the historical sources. The Soviet state frequently demanded that its citizens 'unsee' the world which contradicted propaganda, but even if many pretended to do so, contemporaries were really living in the crosshatching of ideology and daily experience.[10]

To explain, crosshatching is a drawing technique in which two sets of parallel lines ('hatching') intersect each other. By varying the density and angles of those lines, they together create nuanced and even breathtakingly detailed images; simple-seeming elements combine and, in their confluence, form meaningful and powerful images.

I use 'crosshatching' throughout this book to describe the repeated but often unconscious mixing of official and unofficial discourses, values and assumptions, the intersections between which continuously generated new understandings of life and how to live it in the 1930s. The metaphor is particularly useful because it helps steer interpretation away from images of head-on collisions and clashes between the official and unofficial, between state ideology and ordinary people's lived realities. Instead, it allows us to appreciate the ways in which these elements were actively involved with each other, rather than assuming them to forever bypass or to cancel each other out.

The vertical lines of official ideology intersected their horizontal counterparts – the alternative popular values, experiences, priorities and memories of ordinary people. Each moment of interweaving was a fleeting but repeated encounter of ideology and lived reality which, through their interaction – their crosshatching – began to form a map by which citizens could navigate.

They mixed, but not into a featureless grey mass; they were mutually constitutive, altering each other and creating something meaningful in their union. And while we can't map out all or even most of these moments of engagement between the official and the popular – not least because each person would have their own particular view of reality – we can still describe the general nature of those engagements and thereby understand particular instances better.

To put it another way, the early Soviet Union existed in a state of provisional reality; the regime handed out maps to its citizens describing a country that had yet to come into existence. To deal with this paradoxical situation, those citizens tried to use the map in conjunction with their daily experiences. In part, the map shaped their perception, but they updated it as they went along, creating two maps on the same page which gradually blended together to create a composite picture of reality. They lived in the crosshatching.

Defining Humour

Cicero, one of history's most famed orators and himself an 'infamous jokester', posed some questions about laughter in his treatise on oratory, written in the mid-50s BCE. 'What is it?' he wondered; 'What provokes it?'. But while he of all people was deeply sensitive to the art and power of humour, he swiftly admitted his ignorance: 'There is no shame in being ignorant of something which even the self-proclaimed experts do not really understand'.[11] Despite millennia of interest in and acceptance of the importance of humour to our experience of the world and our place within it, Cicero's words still apply.

After Cicero, thousands of theories of humour have been put forward, but little consensus has emerged. As I delved into the distressingly unamusing world of humour studies, I quickly realised that for the past century most writers have been trying unsuccessfully to find a single, unifying theory by building on or blending together the same Big Three hypotheses. The Big Three are most associated with Thomas Hobbes, Henri Bergson and Sigmund Freud (although we can find seeds for each in earlier works). They are, respectively, theories of 'superiority' (we laugh at others' faults, which makes us feel good about ourselves),[12] 'incongruity' (we laugh when incompatible images, concepts and contexts are mixed together, and when our passive expectations are upset),[13] and 'release' (we laugh to release tension and distress).[14] None of the Big Three has been dismissed entirely, but each has been deemed inadequate if taken alone, so scholars looking for an ur-Theory have been trying to find the perfect balance between them, while adding smaller ideas of their own to the mixture. But to little avail.[15]

Unlike these later scholars, Hobbes, Bergson and Freud all knew that it was a fool's errand to pursue a universal theory because humour is fundamentally a sociocultural phenomenon which changes with the times and with the people.[16] As Freud put it, 'the kingdom of humour is constantly being enlarged'; to understand it, Bergson wrote, 'we must put it back in its natural environment, which is society'.[17] This is the approach I take, drawing on elements of these and other theories (notably the more focused studies of Neuroscience and Psychology) when they aid our understanding, rather than trying to crowbar the rich variety of Soviet humour into any single framework.

With this in mind, I take as broad a conception of humour as possible for this book, including not only *anekdoty* (largely equivalent to 'jokes' in English, but usually of a political nature; the singular form is '*anekdot*'), but also humorous songs and poems; sarcasm; mockery; banter; gallows humour; inversions of official hierarchies; melodramatic statements; indulgence in the absurd; breaking taboos; and generally undermining the seriousness of officially-expected behaviour, ceremonies and symbols. The boundaries between all these labels are fluid; categorisations break down as quickly as we create them, so they are only ever a rough shorthand. The only rubric necessary is defined by the contemporary context: was something said or performed in a humorous form? Was it meant to be funny? Was it received as funny? And does it tell us something about how contemporaries made sense of Stalinist society and their place within it? If an example checks that last box and at least one other, then it qualifies for consideration.

Nevertheless, it's worth reminding ourselves that not every *anekdot* or sarcastic remark was laden with deeper significance which we can now attempt to unpack, nor that all humour was political during this decade (although the regime saw almost every aspect of life as political, so the boundaries of this definition were hazy). There were certainly jokes that attacked particular leaders for personal foibles rather than in politically symbolic ways: take, for example, a joke in which the fire brigade stands around in front of a burning house, explaining to onlookers that they can't begin to put out the flames until Lunacharskii, the Commissar for Enlightenment, has arrived to make an introductory speech.[18] This is a simple joke about Lunacharskii's constant speechifying at countless events; there's not really much more to be said about it, and generic jokes like this circulated in the Soviet Union as much as in any other country.

Misha Mel'nichenko's comprehensive guide to the genre of the Soviet *anekdot* also reminds us that there were countless jokes about drunkards, sex, deceitful spouses, doctor-patient relations and more.[19] People still played practical jokes on each other,[20] mocked young lovers' bumbling attempts at writing love poems,[21] and dealt with interpersonal tensions with sarcastic and evasive jokes.[22] We shouldn't forget that everyday, non-political humour continued in these years, but it is not the subject of this book.

Some of the jokes in this book probably won't make you laugh out loud, or perhaps won't seem funny at all. The point, though, is that they were considered funny by the people who told them, and by attempting to think ourselves into their (threadbare) shoes and the mindset that made their jokes genuinely amusing, we come a significant step closer to understanding their lives, perspectives, and values.[23] We can follow the thread of humour back into the broader fabric of society.

Humour may be a human universal, as countless theories, histories and anthropological studies make plain, but each culture's humour has its own history, too. In Russia, the political *anekdot* came into its own at the turn of the twentieth century, developing out of an oral culture of storytelling and of more literary 'anecdotes', which didn't have to be funny, but which threw light on issues, events, and notable people.[24] Unlike sung humorous ditties – *chastushki*, plural; *chastushka*, singular – the *anekdot* is more associated with urban contexts, but the 1930s was a period of mass inward migration, so both identities and folk culture were in flux. We'll see plenty of *chastushki* in the towns, rubbing shoulders with the growing numbers of *anekdoty*.

Intertwined with these rather newer forms were the themes, motifs and practice of *smekh i grekh* – 'laughter and sin' – sexual and scatological folk songs, obscene proverbs, and other carnivalesque, exuberantly transgressive speech that dated back to at least the seventeenth century.[25] These traditional elements all appeared in 1930s humour and play a prominent role in Chapters 1 and 3.

Although humour obviously had its local flavours, there was nothing quintessentially Russian about it, which is why political humour in Eastern Bloc countries was (and in modern-day North Korea is) so similar.[26] The political and social context shape the jokes more than the traditional reference points, which was why I, a foreigner with limited knowledge of Russian folklore and born only a few years before the Soviet Union collapsed, could sit giggling in the archives at 1930s *anekdoty*: familiarity with the context was key.

Like culture itself, humour is a constantly evolving product of continuous interactions between the past and the present. All the same, if one focuses too much on the past, humour's relevance and resonance in the present moment can be lost. Tracing the roots of particular joke plots and structures may amuse folklorists, but when you realise it's possible to trace a joke about Stalin all the way back to Byzantium, you begin to realise it doesn't tell you much about Stalinist society to do so.[27] We can certainly boil jokes and stories down to their basic structures, but this removes all the content, context and delivery – precisely the things we need in order for humour to be a useful historical source, and precisely the things which brought humour to life for the people enjoying it.[28] This is like watching a band play while wearing earplugs; you can see the physical form of music being made, maybe even feel some vibrations from the stage, but you're entirely missing the point.

What these long and worldwide folkloric histories of humour do reveal, however, is that we're looking at some fundamental elements of the human condition. Whatever the times and the conditions people find themselves in, humour helps them make sense of the world, meeting core psychological needs. It can serve as a way of coping and making sense of things; creating stories and meanings through testing, challenging, and playing with the dominant pressures and power structures of the moment (themes explored in Chapters 5-6).

More broadly, this is a book about freedom and repression, loyalty and censorship, the will to survive tempered by the pressure to conform. It asks what it means to live under a dictatorship: how do people make sense of their lives in an authoritarian system; how do they talk about it, and whom can they trust to do so? The answers are often surprisingly, even disturbingly, similar to how we cope with life in non-authoritarian societies, albeit with the stakes and pressures greatly reduced. It's therefore chastening but important to realise how normal Stalinism could become to contemporaries. Although we often look to history for 'lessons', we tend to place our focus exclusively on the politics and ideologies, rather than on the generic psychological and social mechanisms that people use to make sense of, and get by under, *any* conditions.

Chapter Map

The book is organised into three parts, flowing from a focus on the content and character of the jokes themselves, to the repercussions of telling them, and on to the psychological and social motivations and effects of sharing them. Put another way, I describe what people said, the dangers of saying it, and why they did so anyway. With that broad arc in mind, I offer a brief overview of the central issues raised.

Chapter 1: Kirov's Carnival, Stalin's Cult

Writing in the late 1930s, the theorist Mikhail Bakhtin argued that carnivalesque behaviour – ranging from joke-telling and mockery to grotesque and vulgar public acts that symbolically dethroned the high and mighty – represented a popular truth of revolutionary potential.[29] Chapter 1 explores the myriad ways Soviet people dethroned their leaders and brought them down to earthy reality, from the quietly subversive to the raucously sexualised and scatological, focusing on the irrepressibly carnivalesque responses to the murder of Leningrad Party boss Sergei Kirov in December 1934.

But this and other cases don't fit Bakhtin's claim that popular laughter 'builds its own world versus the official world, [...] its own state versus the official state'.[30] In his romantic view, this was a counterculture which, despite the unrelenting weight of officialdom, 'remained uninfected by lies'.[31] This was what Bakhtin – who lived under Stalinism – wanted to believe, but a counterculture is always defined by the culture it counters: it can never be pure and 'uninfected'. I make the case instead that humour was more counterpoint than counterculture, an innovative interplay of different elements which were more than merely 'the playful reversal of respectable conventions'.[32]

Even Stalin's portrait might be used for target-practice on a firing range, or his sexual liaisons imagined and mocked, which rather complicates the widely held idea that Stalin's Cult of Personality elevated him above normal politics and criticism. In fact, the Cult's undeniable prominence would actually make him a lightning rod for popular frustration; if the regime made him sacred, the people frequently made him profane.

From hanging portraits of the leaders in suggestive locations to declaring that they wanted to 'take a shit' on Kirov's grave, ordinary people's humour ranged from the subtle to the obscene, but even at its most vulgar, they were not shaping another world placed in direct opposition to the official one. Rather, jokes cast new light on the world contemporaries had no choice but to live in.

Chapter 2: Plans and Punchlines: 'The *anekdoty* always saved us'

For Soviet contemporaries, the pressing realities of poverty, hunger, and the endless demands placed on them by the state simply couldn't be ignored. This was a decade like no other, in which unprecedented modernisation campaigns were implemented at record speed and with brutal force. Robert Conquest popularised the term 'Great Terror' to describe the mass arrests and executions of 'enemies' between roughly 1937-38, but the term has come to reverberate through our understanding of the entire decade. These were certainly frightening times, but the term 'terror' has continued to mislead us into assuming that Soviet citizens were endlessly 'terrorised', or that they lived in constant, silent 'terror' and abject misery throughout these years.

At first glance, humour might seem anathema in such dark days, but, as Chapter 2 shows, in fact this was precisely when it was needed the most. From the Five-Year Plans to the bloody collectivisation campaign, an endless slew of mandatory state loan subscriptions, and the growing suspicion that their blood, sweat and tears might all be for nothing (exacerbated by a truce with Nazi Germany), people's everyday realities clashed painfully with regime promises. Just as contemporaries used *anekdoty* to read the regime's often bloody policies through the incongruous lens of their everyday experiences, they used the blackest humour to cope with the fear of denunciation and the dreaded 3am knock of the NKVD at their apartment door. People were not struck mute by terror during these years; in humour they found ways to deal with the hardships and uncertainties, rather than standing frozen and isolated in the headlights of the NKVD's paddy-wagons. If humour could not save them from the secret police, it could always save them from despair.

Chapter 3: Speaking More than Bolshevik: Crosshatching and Codebreaking

As leaders of a revolutionary regime, the Soviet government wanted to make a fresh start – to clear out the old, unwanted aspects of the past, like religion and traditional family values, and to create in their place a New Soviet Person. Freed from its chains, this figure was supposed to embody the spirit of both intellectual and labourer, to be selflessly devoted to equality, yet simultaneously to exceed all expectations placed upon them. There was much to admire in this ideal and many strove to embody it, taking night classes after an exhausting day of manual labour, or foregoing meals to afford tickets to the theatre. The regime ruled with an iron fist, but it simultaneously stretched out a hand to those who showed themselves willing to become the change the regime wanted to see in the world.

This aspect of Soviet history really only came alive for me when I read Stephen Kotkin's *Magnetic Mountain* and Jochen Hellbeck's work on diarists who tried to fashion themselves into good Soviet citizens. They, along with Igal Halfin, showed how contemporaries actively engaged the system on its own terms, rather than being passively dominated by it. For Kotkin, this meant that people learnt how to act, speak and present themselves to their best advantage by making use of official language, which he called 'speaking Bolshevik'. It 'wasn't necessary to believe' what they said, he suggested, but even by playing the part of good Soviet citizens, they ultimately supported the system.[33]

For Hellbeck and Halfin, on the other hand, this was a conscious and willing attempt by many individuals to *become*, rather than only to play, the role of an ideal Soviet citizen. In their view, contemporaries internalised Soviet ideology to the extent that they in some sense became conditioned and controlled by it: they willingly trapped themselves in the Matrix.[34]

As Gábor Rittersporn notes, however, there's a growing realisation that these studies of 'Soviet Subjectivity' are 'primarily about committed individuals and not Soviet citizens in general'; they are not a 'common denominator', but an interesting minority (and even they wrestled with the endless contradictions of official ideology).[35]

When we look at contemporary jokes, it's immediately apparent that people could and did speak more than Bolshevik. They could certainly criticise the regime in relation to its own promises, calling it out using its own language and values, but they also – often simultaneously – used other, older, more familiar frames of reference, too. Rittersporn has shown how traditional, prerevolutionary practices – what he calls 'folkways' – survived and evolved in the Soviet context, much to the regime's frustration. We see many of these folkways alive and well in Kirov's Carnival (Chapter 1). But although these continued, Rittersporn notes that usually people 'did not see themselves engaging in head-on conflict with the party-state', even if some considered themselves dissenters.[36]

In contrast to the regime's view, for ordinary people this was not a zero-sum game in which one set of values had to triumph over the other. They came instead to interweave their pre-existing values – from personal loyalty to religious conviction; sexist prejudices to ideas of basic fairness – with official ideology. At the heart of this mixing lay a profound desire that rhetoric should reflect reality. They 'decoded' the language of the regime to make it describe reality as ordinary people experienced it. Even when ostensibly speaking Bolshevik, contemporaries also sought to make Bolshevik speak 'real'.

Chapter 4: Who's Laughing Now? Persecution and Prosecution

Whatever the joke-tellers' intentions, many would pay a bitter price. A single joke could lead to the Gulag, a conviction for 'antisoviet agitation', and separation from your family for 10 years or more. Yet the regime's attitudes towards humour were more complex than they first appear. The

Bolsheviks had used satire as a weapon in their revolutionary struggle against tsarism; thereafter they remained convinced that, in the wrong hands, humour was something any regime had cause to fear. They tried to restrict humour to the pages of official satirical magazines such as *Krokodil*, or other carefully-controlled media, which used humour solely to convey the Party line.

Chapter 4 shifts our focus from how joke-tellers perceived the regime to how the regime perceived the joke-tellers. It reconstructs for the first time how the Bolsheviks struggled to control and contain all unofficial humour, and reveals how its perception of humour changed from considering it a blunt instrument to a mind virus which could infect all but the most ardent ideologues. This was a twisted evolution that was largely opaque to the general population, but even if some people managed to keep up with policy, it might already have been too late.

If historians have long known that the Soviet legal system was capricious and unpredictable, the criminal case-files of those convicted for humour reveal that it also practised retroactive 'justice'. A joke that seemed acceptable at the time it was told could be reinterpreted months or years later as evidence of counterrevolutionary intent and could land even devoted Party members in jail. In such a climate of uncertainty and unpredictability, even though joke-tellers might know they were taking a risk, they had little chance of judging the true danger of their actions. Even so, the content of what they actually said frequently turns out to have been less important than who they were.

Chapter 5: Beyond Resistance: The Psychology of Joke-Telling

Joking in these often terrible times was a way to laugh in the face of death, or at least of hardship and tragedy. It could also feel like an act of defiance and even of resistance to the regime, which is the most common interpretation we find in the historiography. But it was much more than this, too.

Humour did not just push back against the powers that be and nor was it only a defiant smile in the face of an uncaring system; it was also creative and adaptive – a sense-making device that reveals much to us about how contemporaries tried to make their way and understand the world around them. In this and other important respects explored in Chapter 5, jokes served a fundamental psychological need.

Studying an extreme case can highlight elements of the ordinary. Everything exceptional, if it endures for long enough, becomes ordinary

– that is, at some level accepted and understood as 'how things are'. People seek to normalise and adapt to their circumstances – so they can find a degree of stability and predictability as they go about their daily lives – but this is not the same as blindly accepting them. Joke-telling could even become a statement of your own existence in this climate of smothering conformity: 'I joke, therefore I am'.

This could be quite practical as well as psychological. Wit and *anekdoty* did not just pick holes in the fabric of the official world and its claims, but actually began to create new ways of looking at it – unofficial rules which could help people get by just a little more comfortably and successfully. These were ways to solve problems and get by *within* the system, rather than attempts to destabilise or to confront it.

In-jokes became a secret language between those in-the-know, and while pointing out what didn't work in the Soviet system, many jokes simultaneously conveyed a kind of clandestine '*know-how*' – hints and tips people shared which explained how to get by to their minimum disadvantage. Barbed as they might be, they were often simultaneously affectionate, expressing a desire that things should work as they were supposed to, rather than writing the system off at large. In this way, they were actively trying to find patterns within the confluence – the crosshatching – of both their own perspectives and official ideology.

Serhy Yekelchyk has pointed out that historians have been largely unable to distinguish between the times when people were mouthing the words and believing the words; between 'genuine belief' and 'widespread dissimulation'.[37] I think this was often unclear and exploratory for the speakers themselves: they were in the process of making sense of the world around them, of trying to discover patterns in the contradictions in order to find ways to get on and get by.

Chapter 5 explores the psychological functions and rewards of joke-telling, and how the extraordinary *became* ordinary for contemporaries over the course of this tumultuous and unpredictable decade.

Chapter 6: In On the Joke: Humour, Trust and Sociability

The influential political theorist Hannah Arendt argued that a 'totalitarian' system, 'like all tyrannies, certainly could not exist without destroying the public realm of life [...] But totalitarian domination [...] is not content with this isolation and destroys private life as well'.[38] Arendt's theory has cast a long shadow through the historiography, but it wasn't just scholars who believed this to be true: many Soviet contemporaries said precisely the same thing.

And yet it struck me that although numerous memoirists, émigrés and others repeated the disturbing tropes of children denouncing parents or spouses denouncing each other, this almost never seemed to be true of them or their close friends.[39] There was a dissonance here which I felt compelled to pursue: the difference between what people said about their own behaviour in contrast to what they said was true of others, or of 'society' more generally. Denunciations among friends and family certainly happened, but this was far from the complete or even the typical picture.

Joke-telling was certainly a risky business, but it was also fundamentally a social act. Therefore, it required a significant measure of trust to share a critical joke. Chapter 6 introduces the idea of 'trust groups' as a way to understand Soviet sociability in the 1930s. In these small associations, people were able to communicate their hopes and fears, and humour was both a stabiliser of those intimate bonds and a potent means to establish them in the first place.

Because the state criminalised political humour, it proves remarkably illuminating to think of joke-tellers as criminals. Like *mafiosi*, they too had to communicate below the radar of the authorities and in the process adopted many techniques of covert signalling and an 'us' and 'them' mentality with regards to society at large. Like an extended mafia family, these trust groups provided means of communication and association that weren't simply independent of the regime, but which did lie beyond its direct control.[40]

Much of the source material we have for joke-telling under Stalinism is evidence of trust failing: surveillance reports and criminal records reveal those moments when individuals misjudged the ever-changing attitudes of the regime towards humour, or the way in which their audience would respond. In this final chapter we turn to a neglected source – the Harvard Interview Project (see section below on sources) – to explore the strategies that made trust groups work, even in an environment of intense repression and widespread distrust. In the process, we discover that even as contemporaries imagined themselves to be the exception that proved the rule, they were actually part of a much wider social phenomenon.

Finding the Jokes

Whenever I told anyone that I was working on ordinary people's humour under Stalin, the first question was always, 'But what are your sources?', usually in tones of mild to severe scepticism. There were no Gallup opinion polls or free press in Stalinist society; people were put in the Gulag for voicing critical opinions, so where could I hope to find *anekdoty*? Others assumed I wanted to study comic films, plays and magazines produced in the 1930s, but while these might amuse and engage the population to some extent, as I discuss in Chapter 4, they were still official cultural productions, not 'from below' expressions of perspective and opinions.

My initial searches turned up dozens of anthologies of *anekdoty*, each promisingly filled with jokes about life under Stalin and the other Soviet leaders. But my excitement soon faded. The anthologies were almost all published in the 1980s and 1990s, clearly copied from each other, and had no convincing source base.[41] Even those few that were published contemporaneously mixed in materials from émigré publications and even from 1920s editions of the official satirical magazine *Krokodil*, despite claiming to represent a living oral folk culture *within* the USSR.

Misha Mel'nichenko has now traced the convoluted evolution of these anthologies, their innumerable knock-offs, and other, principally published sources, as well as performing the Herculean task of triangulating them (some 10,000 jokes in total) to assess whether a given joke really did circulate in the USSR. Thanks to Misha's efforts, we can say with certainty that large parts of the anthologies prove the existence of a vibrant domestic joke-telling culture, but we still lose too much contextual information for them to answer some vital questions: who told a given *anekdot*; to whom; where was it told; what prompted its telling; and what effects did it have?[42] In short, I needed contemporary sources.

A starting point was the accounts of foreign visitors to the 1930s Soviet Union (see Cast of Characters section, below). In trying to understand the Soviet way of life, they quickly homed in on the importance of jokes, which both guided them and helped them to form friendships with Soviet citizens. As outsiders, they didn't face the same risks, but they were sensitive to the insights and function of the jokes they heard. Crucially, they could record and publish their impressions at the time, giving us a contemporaneous sense of joking culture, unlike memoirs or anthologies put together years later and subjected to the filters of hindsight.

The personal diaries of Soviet citizens – some published, some which I found later in the archives – took me another step closer (brief sketches of the diarists who will accompany us throughout the book can also be found below). Diaries are fascinating sources which have received a lot of attention in recent years, but because they're private, personal sources, they give us little sense of how conversation and criticisms unfolded socially. As Malte Griesse rather nicely puts it, 'Lonely perception remains dreamlike; only communication makes it real'.[43] If some people confined their doubt, sarcasm and wit to a diary, others shared this with trusted friends and family members – and the majority of citizens were not lonely, isolated diarists.[44]

I decided to follow the trail left by historians of everyday life and popular opinion. When the doors of the archives creaked open in the early 1990s, these scholars rapidly seized on heaps of documents called *svodki* – summary reports on 'the mood of the people' collected by various official bodies from the secret police to local factory committees. Having repressed all outlets for popular expression, the Soviet regime was, ironically, left desperate to know what the population was thinking: informants, officials, and denouncers all helped fill the gap, and *svodki* were the result. With them, Soviet society sprang to life: we could finally hear people discussing, praising and complaining about the regime.

Svodki certainly have their limitations: they covered subjects which the regime was interested in, rather than providing a sense of wider popular opinion; they focused disproportionately on negative opinions; they were distilled to their most dramatic elements as they travelled up the chain of command; and they acknowledged no middle-ground between opinions labelled 'healthy' or 'counterrevolutionary'.[45]

Critical humour sidesteps most of these issues: because the regime considered it a weapon or virus, it was recorded *by default* as evidence of suspect, negative opinion, regardless of its usually ambivalent and nuanced content, meaning that we can discard the regime's paranoid interpretations and consider the content of the jokes themselves. Compared to the generic, paraphrased opinions in the rest of the *svodki*, the jokes feel infinitely richer, like hearing a (rough) recording of a piece of music, rather than someone trying to describe it to you.

All the same, after months scouring hundreds of *svodki* in the Party, state and Communist Youth League (Komsomol) archives of St Petersburg and Moscow for what crumbs of humour they contained, I was beginning to wonder if I'd ever find enough material to write more than a brief note. Then one day, I struck gold. Following a tip from a colleague, I phoned a director at the State Archive of the Russian Federation (GARF) and asked if I could see a certain database of criminal files. I wasn't really sure what this database was, but it turned out to be a digitised catalogue of 56,000 'supervisory files' (надзорные дела) – extensive reviews of convictions for 'antisoviet agitation' conducted by the USSR's Procuracy.[46] This, I knew, was the 'crime' that joke-tellers were convicted for, so, with shaking hands I typed '*anekdot*' into the search bar. And hundreds of results came back.

For the next few months I read case-file after case-file, immersing myself in the stories of these unlucky individuals, nearly all of which had never been seen before by anyone other than Soviet officials. I thought this would be the closest I could get to the original investigation files, which likely reside in the archive of the KGB's successor, the FSB, whose doors are firmly closed. However, I had chance to work with some original case-files in Kyiv's former KGB archive (HDA SBU), which, under the current regime, is more open to exploring the dark side of the Soviet past; it admits researchers, but doesn't have an equivalent database to that in GARF. There, I realised that the supervisory documents are in many ways richer sources. They not only include extensive material from the original investigations, but also collate materials from various state bodies, letters from the convicts, witnesses and family members, and sometimes even the original handwritten interrogation notes.

Despite these immensely rich sources giving us unprecedented insight into how and where jokes were told, as well as the regime's changing interpretation and punishment of them, there was barely a whisper of the role of denunciation in these cases. The identity of who reported joke-tellers to the authorities was not recorded; if the original informant was one of the witnesses who provided statements about joke-telling, this was never made explicit. It seems highly likely that information on informants was held separately, in the NKVD/KGB archives. The suspicious fire in Tbilisi's KGB archive in the early 1990s conveniently destroyed all files on informants, but not the criminal or investigation files, so we can reasonably assume this division of knowledge held true across the USSR.[47] In any case, I explore the question of mistrust and denunciation in Chapter 6, where it becomes clear that the *idea* of the 'denouncer' was often more important in shaping people's perceptions than any concrete knowledge of who such individuals actually were.

But even as my notes and list of jokes grew, there was still something missing. The case-files tell us in great detail where, when and how people were *caught* for telling *anekdoty* (as well as the state's changing attitude to it, which I recount in Chapter 4), but almost nothing about 'successful' exchanges. What about the untold numbers of people who shared jokes with each other and weren't caught or denounced? Whom did they trust? And what did they think and feel about joke-telling?

Contemporary diaries helped to some extent, but it was another giant database which provided the quantity and quality of detail and insight which I needed to answer these questions: the inelegantly-named Harvard Interview Project on the Soviet Social System (HPSSS). This remarkable project was conducted in 1950-51 by a team of sociologists and comprised 764 interviews with Soviet refugees with the aim of creating a detailed portrait of Soviet society.[48]

Because it was funded by the US Air Force, the Harvard Project was largely ignored by social historians, who assumed that it would surely be riven with Cold War biases. But now its daunting bulk has been digitised, it turns out that the Project was in many ways a thoughtful, perceptive and nuanced attempt to understand what life under Stalin was like, producing analyses that now seem decades ahead of their time.[49] Realising the importance of humour to understand any society, the interviews included specific questions about joke-telling, along with probing enquiries about trust, sociability, friendship and family ties. Again, I immersed myself in these.

Although the interviewees were theoretically more antisoviet than mainstream society, having either chosen to flee the USSR or, having ended up as 'displaced persons' at war's end, were at least keen to secure their refugee status, it's clear from the interviews that they actually held very mixed opinions about the Soviet system. As Sheila Fitzpatrick put it, 'To their perplexed interviewers, it seemed that they were simultaneously pro- and anti-Soviet'.[50]

By combining these varied source bases, all of which have their particular advantages and shortcomings, we can construct a vivid picture of jokes and their telling across the 1930s. It's always a challenge to discern what a population thinks about society and its government, even in those countries where such things can be debated openly. The Soviet case clearly presents a particular challenge, but that is never a reason not to try.

We can't know for sure how many people were sharing political jokes, and even the arrest figures are extremely fragmentary.[51] Nevertheless, there's no reason to think that most people weren't telling or hearing jokes, both because it's an intrinsic part of the human condition, and because we know there was a vibrant cultural practice of political joke-telling which came both before Stalinism and which would see a flourishing renaissance in the post-Stalin years, when the state reduced its strangle-hold on this form of personal expression.

This is primarily an urban study, although the boundaries between town and country where fluid due to mass inward migration. The Soviet Union was – as it liked to remind itself – a vast land of many peoples and we'll meet joke-tellers from Russia, Ukraine, Azerbaijan, Kazakhstan, Belarus and beyond. Clearly, joke-telling was as widespread as it was controversial, with an appeal that crossed all geographical, ethnic and class distinctions.

The period under consideration did not begin and end 'cleanly', but instead starts between 1928-9, when Stalin had taken firm hold of the reins of power and initiated the twin policies of collectivisation and industrialisation. The endpoint is the outbreak of war in June 1941, which presented another set of dramatic upheavals for the Soviet population, which they would again use humour to deal with, but ours is a study of life under Stalinism, not Stalinism at war.

So can the conclusions of this book be generalised to the Soviet population at large? Few things can be generalised about any large number of people, of course, but my sources attest to people of all backgrounds, ages, walks of life, and of both genders, in myriad different situations and with different agendas, turning to humour to help them navigate and understand their lives under the regime. Although statistics will play a role when we look at how the regime punished joke-tellers, this book takes us far beyond numbers and into a world of much richer complexity. From ageing bookkeepers to young mothers; from shock-workers to Party Organisers; and from Red Army soldiers to Soviet schoolchildren, humour was a constant and close companion in the 1930s, and just as it helped reveal to contemporaries how the system actually worked, it reveals to us a great deal about how they found their way and even found themselves in these years of great uncertainty.

***

Cast of Characters

Foreign Visitors' Accounts

William Henry Chamberlin, a correspondent for *Christian Science Monitor*, Chamberlin was a historian and journalist who lived in Russia from 1922-34 and noted dozens of jokes in his diary. After he left the USSR he would publish a book about his time there and dedicated many pages to those *anekdoty*.

Eugene Lyons, a United Press Association journalist who lived in Moscow for 6 years (1928-34) and wrote in some detail about the jokes he heard and reflected on their role as a form of unofficial communication.

Ella Winter, an Australian-British journalist who was sympathetic to the Bolshevik cause, and who recounted her brief visits to the USSR in her 1933 book, *Red Virtue: Human Relations in the Soviet Union*. She, too, couldn't help but include some of the jokes she heard which seemed to sum up life so accurately.

Diarists

Andrei Stepanovich Arzhilovskii (1885–1937), a former peasant imprisoned by the regime for allegedly agitating against collectivisation; he was released after 7 years in 1936, taking a job in a woodworking factory in Tiumen' (Siberia) to support his family. He had a sharp mind and sharp wit, both of which got him into trouble; the pages of his diary fizz with a dry humour, as well as moments of deep sadness, making it impossible to read without a sense of deep empathy for its author. He and the diary were seized by the NKVD in July 1937; he was executed the following month.

Ivan Ivanovich Shitts (1874–1942), a historian and teacher, born in Tambov but who lived and worked in Moscow; he was no fan of the Bolshevik regime and enjoyed collecting critical jokes and stories (which he labelled 'folklore') in his diary. In the early 1930s he smuggled the diary out of the country through diplomatic channels to a friend in France, where it was eventually discovered in the 1980s and published shortly thereafter.

Stepan Fillipovich Podlubnyi (1914–1998), the son of a kulak (an allegedly rich peasant) who hid his origins from the authorities and tried to fashion himself into a New Soviet Person. In his diary he struggles with his past, his identity and his conscience. Podlubnyi's diary and his attempts to become the New Soviet Person has been at the centre of Jochen Hellbeck's work on 'Soviet Subjectivity'.

Konstantin Megrelidze (1900–1943). Not a diarist per se, but he compiled a vast *anekdot* collection. Megrelidze was a professor of Georgian and Russian language, literature, and sociology who moved from Tbilisi to Leningrad in the late 1930s, before his arrest in 1940. He fell under suspicion due to his wife's alleged counterrevolutionary activities, but when the NKVD searched the Megrelidze apartment they uncovered a horde of over 10,000 notecards containing poems, *chastushki*, stories, and dozens of Soviet *anekdoty*. He died while imprisoned in 1943 and, sadly, the collection seems to have been destroyed, but many of the *anekdoty* which most offended the Soviet authorities were quoted in his criminal record. Megrelidze, as his wife testified (and his posthumously published work shows), had been working on folklore and he, like others, considered critical *anekdoty* to fall naturally into this genre of popular culture.[52]

Notes

1. cf. Johan Huizinga, *Homo Ludens: A Study of the Play Element in Culture* (New York, 1949), 45; G.K. Chesterton, *The Collected Works of G.K. Chesterton*, Vol.1, ed. David Dooley (San Francisco, CA, 1986), 159.
2. William Henry Chamberlin, *Russia's Iron Age* (London, 1935), 387.
3. Sheila Fitzpatrick, 'Popular Opinion in Russia under Pre-War Stalinism', Paul Corner (ed.), *Popular Opinion in Totalitarian Regimes: Fascism, Nazism, Communism* (Oxford, 2009), 26.
4. A useful summary of this historiographical trend is David L. Ransel, 'The Scholarship of Everyday Life', Choi Chatterjee, David L Ransel, Mary Cavender & Karen Petrone (eds.), *Everyday Life in Russia Past and Present* (Bloomington, IN, 2015). Most studies of everyday history of the Soviet 1930s identify this mental zone between affirmation and dissent, but do not investigate its nature: e.g. Sarah Davies, *Popular Opinion in Stalin's Russia: Terror, Propaganda, and Dissent* (Cambridge, 1997), 6 ('along the continuum from active consent to active resistance/dissent were a range of heterogeneous positions. [...] In practice, people's views were far more ambivalent and contradictory...'); Stephen Kotkin, *Magnetic Mountain: Stalinism as a Civilization* (Berkeley, CA, 1997), 228 ('Elements of "belief" and "disbelief" appear to have coexisted within everyone...', which was 'an enduring ambivalence', or a state of 'half-belief'); Timothy Johnston, *Being Soviet: Identity, Rumour, and Everyday Life under Stalin, 1939-1953* (Oxford, 2011), xxxix ('the more ambiguous spaces between internalization and rejection'; Johnston's concept of *bricolage* arguably only maintains this ambiguity); Sheila Fitzpatrick, *Everyday Stalinism: Ordinary Life in Extraordinary Times* (New York, 1999), 223 (studied 'popular attitudes to the regime that fall mainly in the range between passive acceptance and cautious hostility'); Karen Petrone, *Life has Become More Joyous, Comrades: Celebrations in the Time of Stalin* (Bloomington, IN, 2000), 204 ('The rest of the population existed on the broad continuum...').
5. To use Ian Kershaw's term: Kershaw, *Popular Opinion and Political Dissent in the Third Reich: Bavaria 1933-1945* (Oxford, 1984), x.
6. cf. M. Mel'nichenko, *Sovetskii anekdot: Ukazatel' siuzhetov* (Moscow, 2014), 14-8; Aleksandr Livshin & Igor' Orlov, *Vlast' i obshchestvo: Dialog v pismakh* (Moscow, 2002), 5-6.
7. Almost every publication on the subject could be cited here, but a representative sample includes: Bruce Adams, *Tiny Revolutions in Russia: Twentieth Century Soviet and Russian History in Anecdotes* (London, 2005); Evgenii Andreevich, *Kreml' i narod* (Munich, 1951); Gregor Benton, 'The Origins of the Political Joke', Chris Powell & George E.C. Paton (eds.), *Humour in Society: Resistance and Control* (Houndmills, 1988); Keith Cameron (ed.), *Humour and History* (Oxford, 1993); Howard Jacobson, *Seriously Funny: From the Ridiculous to the Sublime* (London, 1997); Salcia Landmann, *Der Jüdische Witz* (Olten, 1960); Egon Larsen, *Wit as a Weapon: The Political Joke in History* (London, 1980); Steven Lukes & Itzhak Galnoor, *No Laughing Matter: A Collection of Political Jokes* (London, 1987); George Mikes, *Humour in Memoriam* (London, 1970); Antonin J. Obrdlik, '"Gallows Humor" – A Sociological Phenomenon', *American Journal of Sociology*, 47.5 (1942); James C. Scott, *Weapons of the Weak: Everyday Forms of Peasant Resistance* (New Haven, CT, 1985); Evgeny Zamyatin, *We*, trans. Natasha Randall (London, 2007).

8   e.g. David Brandenberger, *Political Humor under Stalin: An Anthology of Unofficial Jokes and Anecdotes* (Bloomington, IN, 2009), which, although principally an anthology, engaged in some brief (but first-class) analysis and posed numerous potential questions for future research, many of which are addressed in this book; Robert W. Thurston, 'Social Dimensions of Stalinist Rule: Humor and Terror in the USSR, 1935-1941', *Journal of Social History*, 24.3 (1991), which drew some interesting conclusions from a limited source base; and Gábor T. Rittersporn, *Anguish, Anger, and Folkways in Soviet Russia* (Pittsburgh, PA, 2014), which includes a chapter on jokes seen from a folkloric, carnivalesque perspective.

9   China Miéville, *The City and the City* (London, 2009).

10 Many words have been used for these processes – 'appropriation', 'hybridity', or the vague German word 'Eigen-Sinn', to name a few – but ultimately this is all about how people find different ways to deal with what official culture and rules mean for them in everyday life. 'Crosshatching', I think, provides a clearer, more tangible sense of how these elements interact and influence each other.

11 See Mary Beard, *Laughter in Ancient Rome: On Joking, Tickling, and Cracking Up* (Oakland, CA, 2014), 23.

12 Thomas Hobbes, *Leviathan*, ed. Richard Tuck (Cambridge, 2010 [1651]), 43. Hobbes actually only treated humour as a very brief aside and did not, as later writers often suppose, claim to encompass humour as a whole within this theory. In the same sentence that he talked about 'superiority', he wrote that laughter could also signify one's 'Pusillanimity', which would effectively be the opposite of superiority, and even made the far more general suggestion that laughter can also be caused 'by some sudden act of [one's] own, that pleaseth [one]'. This much broader, unspecific proposition, to which Hobbes gave equal weighting, has been overlooked by later theorists, who base their discussions on a selective generalisation of his argument. Hobbes also wrote briefly on laughter some ten years earlier, making much the same points as he would in *Leviathan*, and likewise allowing a range of causes for laughter beyond that of 'superiority': Hobbes, *The Elements of Law, Natural and Politic*, ed. Ferdinand Tönnies (London, 1889 [1640]), 41-2.

Seeds of the superiority theory appeared in Plato and Aristotle, as Seth Graham notes in *Resonant Dissonance: The Russian Joke in Cultural Context* (Evanston, IL, 2009), 15. Plato considered laughter – which he described as scorn born of self-ignorance – to be a dangerous vice, and in his ideal state, comedy would be tightly controlled (*Laws*, Book 7, section 816e; Book 11, section 935e).

13 Henri Bergson, *Laughter: An Essay on the Meaning of the Comic*, trans. Cloudesely Brereton & Fred Rothwell (Rockville, MD, 2008). Arthur Koestler likewise focused upon 'incongruity' theory, but, as Seth Graham notes, this approach can also be traced back to Schopenhauer, Kant, and Descartes (Graham, *Resonant Dissonance*, 15). Blaise Pascal has also been credited with originating the 'incongruity theory', but his observation that 'nothing is more conducive to [laughter] than a surprising disproportion between what we expect and what we see' in fact sits within a wry diatribe aimed at his Jesuit opponents, which not only rests on a much more antagonistic, aggressive picture of humour, but is itself, above all, an acute demonstration of laughter to assert superiority (Pascal, *Les Provinciales*, Onzième lettre (1656-7)). Finally, Mary Beard points out that if we translate the Latin 'discrepantia' as 'incongruity', then there is a case for Cicero having predated all these thinkers by many centuries: Beard, *Laughter in Ancient Rome*, 28.

14 Sigmund Freud, *Jokes and their Relation to the Unconscious*, trans. James Strachey

15. (London, 2001), 146-9; 235-6.
15. A broad selection of such works include: Salvatore Attardo, *Linguistic Theories of Humor* (Berlin & New York, 1994); Noël Carroll, *Humour: A Very Short Introduction* (Oxford, 2014); Simon Critchley, *On Humour* (London, 2002); Christie Davies, *The Mirth of Nations* (New Brunswick, 2002); idem. 'Humour and Protest: Jokes Under Communism', Marjolein 't Hart & Dennis Bos (eds.), *Humour and Social Protest*, International Review of Social History Supplements, 15 (Cambridge, 2007); Arthur Koestler, *The Act of Creation* (London, 1964); John Morreall (ed.), *The Philosophy of Laughter and Humor* (Albany, NY, 1987); Jutta Muschard, 'Jokes and their Relation to Relevance and Cognition or "Can Relevance Theory Account for the Appreciation of Jokes?"', *Zeitschrift für Anglistik und Amerikanistik*, 47.1 (1999); John Allen Paulos, *I Think, Therefore I Laugh: The Flip Side of Philosophy* (London, 2000); Susan C. Vogel, *Humor: A Semiogenetic Approach* (Bochum, 1989); Christopher Wilson, *Jokes: Form, Content, Use and Function* (London, 1979).
16. For Hobbes this is clear in his suggestion of individuals comparing themselves to each other as a key to humour and, more broadly, that he saw it as relevant to his study of human society. Bergson made this explicit throughout his work, and Freud's entire thesis concerns itself with humour as displayed in communication.
17. Freud, *Jokes*, 232; Bergson, *Laughter*, 12.
18. Eugene Lyons, *Modern Moscow* (London, 1935), 270.
19. Mel'nichenko, *Sovetskii anekdot*, 69.
20. HPSSS 51/A/5, p.14; 29/A/3, pp.31-2; 90/A/6, p.22.
21. Lidia Libedinskaia (née Tolstaia), 'The Green Lamp', in Sheila Fitzpatrick & Yuri Slezkine (eds.), *In the Shadow of Revolution: Life Stories of Russian Women from 1917 to the Second World War* (Princeton, NJ, 2000), 298.
22. A.G. Man'kov, *Dnevniki tridtsatykh godov* (St Petersburg, 2001), 131 (12 March 1934).
23. This is not simply an issue of cultural differences, but also of temporal distance: younger generations in post-Soviet Russia would also struggle to intuitively understand many of these *anekdoty*, as a team of sociologists has noted: A.V. Dmitriev, V.V. Latynov & A.T. Khlop'ev, *Neformal'naia politicheskaia kommunikatsiia* (Moscow, 1997), 74.
24. Mel'nichenko, *Sovetskii anekdot*, 7-10.
25. S.A. Smith, 'The Social Meanings of Swearing: Workers and Bad Language in Late Imperial and Early Soviet Russia', *Past and Present*, 160 (1998), 180-1.
26. Ben Lewis, *Hammer & Tickle: A History of Communism Told Through Communist Jokes* (London, 2008); C. Banc & Alan Dundes, *You Call This Living? A Collection of East European Political Jokes* (Athens, GA, 1990); Václav Havel et al., *The Power of the Powerless: Citizens Against the State in Central-Eastern Europe* (London, 1985); Milan Kundera, *The Joke*, trans. Michael Henry Heim (London, 1992); idem, *The Book of Laughter and Forgetting*, trans. Aaron Asher (London, 1996); multiple authors, 'Political Humor from North Korea', <http://www.rfa.org/english/news/korea/koreanjokes-09102008183510.html>, last accessed October 2016.
27. Alexandra Arkhipova, 'Laughing About Stalin: The Formation and Evolution of Soviet Uncensored Jokelore', available on the website of the conference, *Totalitarian Laughter: Cultures of the Comic Under Socialism* <http://slavic.princeton.edu/events/calendar/detail.php?ID=1921>. Also cf. Aleksandra Arkhipova & Mikhail Mel'nichenko, *Anekdoty o Staline: Teksty, kommentarii, issledovaniia* (Moscow, 2010).

28   Vladimir Propp, *Morphology of the Folktale*, trans. Laurence Scott & Louis A. Wagner (2nd edn., London, 1968).
29   Bakhtin was ostensibly analysing the work of François Rabelais, a sixteenth-century French writer of grotesque satires which sent up the Catholic Church and its place in medieval society, but it's generally understood that between the lines Bakhtin was also criticising Stalinist society. See Michael Holquist, 'Prologue', in Mikhail Bakhtin, *Rabelais and his World*, trans. Hélène Iswolsky (Bloomington, IN, 1984); Michael Holquist & Katerina Clark (eds.), *Mikhail Bakhtin* (Cambridge, MA, 1984), Ch.14.
30   Bakhtin, *Rabelais*, 88.
31   M.M. Bakhtin, *The Dialogic Imagination. Four Essays*, ed. Michael Holquist, trans. Caryl Emerson & Michael Holquist (Austin, TX, 1981), 236.
32   Rittersporn, *Anguish, Anger, and Folkways*, 189.
33   Kotkin, *Magnetic Mountain*, Ch.5. Quotation at p.220.
34   See Malte Griesse's critical discussion: 'Soviet Subjectivities: Discourse, Self-Criticism, Imposture', *Kritika*, 9.3 (2008), 610. I discuss Hellbeck's and Halfin's work further in Chapter 3.
35   Rittersporn, *Anguish, Anger, And Folkways*, 8.
36   Rittersporn, *Anguish, Anger, and Folkways*, 214.
37   Serhy Yekelchyk, *Stalin's Citizens: Everyday Politics in the Wake of Total War* (New York, 2014), 3.
38   Hannah Arendt, *The Origins of Totalitarianism* (New York, 1973), 475.
39   Robert Thurston noted this dissonance, but many dismissed his insightful work on Stalinist society with bizarre charges of being an apologist for Stalinist repressions. See Thurston, 'The Soviet Family'.
40   Here I paraphrase Malte Rolf, although he was describing a rather broader definition of 'social'. Malte Rolf, *Soviet Mass Festivals, 1917-1991*, trans. Cynthia Klohr (Pittsburgh, PA, 2013), 8.
41   e.g. Adams, *Tiny Revolutions*; Andreevich, *Kreml'*; Iurii Borev, *Istoriia gosudarstva sovetskogo v predaniiakh i anekdotakh* (Moscow, 1995); 'A.N.' et al, *Russia Dies Laughing: Jokes from Soviet Russia* (London, 1983); James von Geldern & Richard Stites (eds.), *Mass Culture in Soviet Russia* (Bloomington, 1995); Algis Ruksenas, *The World's Best Russian Jokes* (London, 1987); Dora Shturman & Sergei Tiktin, *Sovetskii Soiuz v zerkale politicheskogo anekdota* (London, 1985); Iulius Telesin, *1001 Izbrannyi sovetskii politicheskii anekdot* (Tenafly, NJ, 1986). Mel'nichenko traces this process of 'borrowing': *Sovetskii anekdot*, 35-49.
42   Mel'nichenko, *Sovetskii anekdot*, 27-75.
43   Griesse, 'Soviet Subjectivities', 621.
44   cf. Griesse, 'Soviet Subjectivities', 620-23.
45   cf. V.P. Danilov, 'Vvedenie', V. Danilov, R. Manning & L. Viola (eds.), *Tragediia Sovetskoi derevni: Kollektivizatsiia i raskulachivanie. Dokumenty i materialy v 5 tomakh, 1927-1939*. Tom 1 (Moscow, 1999), 22.
46   The Procuracy (*Prokuratura*) both investigated and tried crimes, and supervised courts and penal facilities under its jurisdiction. It also reviewed all court decisions in both civil and criminal cases.
47   Thanks to Timothy Blauvelt for this information.
48   David Brandenberger, 'A Background Guide to Working with the HPSSS Online', <http://hcl.harvard.edu/collections/hpsss/working_with_hpsss.pdf>, last accessed October 2016.
49   On scholars ignoring the HPSSS, see Sheila Fitzpatrick, 'Revisionism in Soviet History', *History and Theory*, 46.4 (2007), 79-80.

50 Fitzpatrick, 'Popular Opinion', Corner (ed.), *Popular Opinion*, 26.
51 e.g. In September 1935, 33 cases (7 percent of the total) reviewed by the USSR Supreme Court involved 'stories, poems, *chastushki*, *anekdoty* etc' (Arkhipova & Mel'nichenko, *Anekdoty*, 26, which cites S.V. Mironenko & N. Werth (eds.), *Istoriia stalinskogo Gulaga*, Tom 1, *Massovye repressii* (Moscow, 2004), doc. 47). In 1936 a quarter of all those arrested by the NKVD for antisoviet agitation were charged with telling jokes or making threatening statements about the leaders (Brandenberger, *Political Humor*, 19). Roy Medvedev has claimed that 'about 200,000 people' served time specifically for telling *anekdoty*, but he provides no evidence for this (cited in Graham, *Resonant Dissonance*, 8).
52 GARF, f.8131, op.31, d.64008, ll.19-22; K.R. Megrelidze, *Osnovnye problemy sotsiologii myshlenniia*, ed. A. T. Bochorisheli (Moscow, 2007), see foreword for a biographical sketch of Megrelidze's life and work.

PART 1
TAKING LIBERTIES

CHAPTER 1
KIROV'S CARNIVAL, STALIN'S CULT

Stalin and his entourage were the most visible figureheads of the Soviet regime, their faces paraded across the newspapers and their names endlessly recited in tones of soaring adoration on the radio and during the interminable 'agitation and propaganda' meetings people were expected (and compelled) to attend. Naturally enough, then, they also became the foremost targets of citizens' humour, cropping up in contemporary jokes with their trousers (not always) metaphorically down around their ankles.

From shouting famous slogans like 'Thank You, Comrade Stalin!' back at the radio whenever they heard unwelcome news, to sharing perverse and pornographic *anekdoty* about the leaders, contemporaries often mocked their rulers forcefully and with gusto. This chapter is packed with examples ranging from the absurd to the unapologetically crude.

But political humour in the 1930s came in many varieties. While the most famous and well-remembered form was the *anekdot*, there were many less overt and more subtle kinds which allowed contemporaries to poke fun at the leadership without exposing themselves to the same level of danger as reeling off various jokes. They hung portraits of Stalin and his henchmen in suggestively absurd situations; they altered the words on posters and banners to make them sound laughable; or they even switched out the 't' in 'Stalin' for an 'r', making him 'Sralin' – not the 'man of steel', but the 'man of shit', instead.

I call these acts of 'quiet power', because while they could feel empowering to the people who shared them, they remained relatively circumspect, giving contemporaries a degree of plausible deniability if caught. Many took on the style of running 'in-jokes' that became woven into the fabric of everyday life, providing emotional relief for those who chose to see the funny side.

These subversive tactics would, as we'll see, find their fullest expression in the irrepressible carnivalesque impulses provoked by the dramatic murder of Leningrad Party boss S.M. Kirov on 1 December 1934. He was gunned down outside his office by a political nobody and the Soviet world was suddenly turned upside-down – the leadership had become visibly mortal and vulnerable. Ultimately, the regime made Kirov a martyr and used his death to legitimise ever-more repressive measures against the population, but before all that, it set about creating official mourning ceremonials of truly smothering gravitas.

But the people decided they would mark the event rather differently – with a deluge of carnivalesque, absurd, sexualised, violent and dirty humour. I call this Kirov's Carnival – a kind of Soviet Day of the Dead – which throws open to us the wider world of unofficial humour, a world which toys with hierarchies and uses far older, traditional folk culture to lambast, ridicule, debase and defile authority figures.

And no one in authority was safe from this treatment. It's long been thought that Stalin's Cult of Personality somehow elevated him above criticism – even to the level of a demi-god – and that this somehow 'explains' the lack of any widespread popular resistance to the regime. But in ordinary people's critical humour, we find a very different story: in their jokes, Stalin was Public Enemy Number One.

By exploring the many ways ordinary people mocked the leadership and thereby asserted a kind of power over them, from the quiet up to the unapologetically crude, we can begin to probe the pressing question of how making these jokes was even possible in such a repressive regime and why so many citizens thought it worth the risk. We also begin to see that mockery and rejection are not the same thing; that the sacred and the profane are not opposites; and that Stalin wasn't above criticism – he was a lightning rod for it.

But before we work our way up to Stalin himself, let's begin with some of the more circumspect, cautious elements of that humour, which blended subtly into the fabric of everyday life.

Quiet Power

In 1935 at the Urazovskii military training post on the Moscow-Donbas railway line, a portrait of Lenin was nailed up under a coat-rail so that everyone's hats and coats were draped unceremoniously over the great leader's image.[1] This was clearly intentional (why hang a portrait – especially of Lenin – so low?) and each person who hung their outer garments on or in front of the portrait without raising an objection thereby became complicit in the exercise of a subtle, subversive power. This could be replicated in myriad different forms across the USSR – some wags might hang portraits of Stalin in the toilets, for example[2] – or it could be rather more dramatically realised, as it was in the Gorlovskii technical college (техникум), where a portrait of Stalin was found hanging in the shooting range, only half a metre away from the target. Stalin was looking a little worse for wear by this time – his portrait had clearly been repeatedly used for target practice.[3] In all these cases, a tacit, sarcastic disrespect – for Lenin, Stalin, and more generally for the regime they represented – was exhibited in a public space, and yet, in their enigmatic 'silence', these outrages could remain undetected, at least for a while.

Undetected, that is, by the authorities. For ordinary people, however, this was actually an important space in which they could share critical humour which hid in the silence between printed word and social interaction. Here, Soviet citizens exercised what we might call a 'quiet power' through a humour that was principally visual. The pointed juxtaposition; the artfully-placed banner; the misspelled slogan – although these might involve written words, this was a humour hidden in plain sight, consumable within a few seconds, and which was not shared with the aim that it should be widely read and digested. Instead, it was confined to the particular context which made it funny.

The prevalence of acts like this is impossible to determine, of course: the 'quieter' they were, the less likely we are to learn of them later. But given that the archives are simply littered with references to portraits of the *vozhdi* (the leaders) being vandalised, sworn at, or otherwise made targets for popular ire, we can confidently assume that countless further examples of silent subversion involving portraits existed, but that they remained undetected, either because they were less flagrant, or because they went undenounced.

In this way, people were creating small air-pockets in the otherwise suffocatingly repressive conformity demanded by the regime. Given that pressure, a principal attraction of silent subversion was the chance it afforded Soviet citizens to mock leaders and official institutions in public with a relative degree of safety: there was no need to take direct, incriminating action yourself. The creation and survival of these subversions depended not on the silence of the acts, but rather upon the silence of anyone in a position to see and to publicly 'unmask' them.

Like almost all kinds of humour, these acts were therefore inherently social: they were performed in public spaces and their potentially humorous effects then lay dormant until a receptive individual or group identified and 'activated' the joke. In practice, this meant that a given stimulus could become an illicit running joke in a particular workplace or locale – one which could be widely enjoyed, yet with far more personal deniability for participants than if they had either made or laughed openly at an *anekdot*.

This was a kind of covert signalling between people – a practice that the sociologist Diego Gambetta explored in his fascinating book on secret communication tactics inside the criminal underworld of the mafia. Gambetta explored how what he calls 'iconic signifiers' – a style of dress, an inconspicuous logo, certain gestures – and how they facilitate communication between those in-the-know, but which otherwise remain invisible or enigmatic to outsiders. As he puts it, 'the meaning of an icon can be surmised without previous information by anyone who shares the same symbolic universe as that of the signaler'.[4] So unless you've been primed to recognise the symbols, they simply pass you by: it's easy to overlook the inconspicuous logo on the window of a café if you don't know that it means the establishment is under mob protection. In the same way, if you didn't share the same 'symbolic universe' as the people who hung Stalin portraits in the toilets, the act would seem at most inappropriate, or simply a little peculiar: the humour would remain dormant.

But silent subversion could go well beyond portraits and direct jabs at the leadership. For example, the Bolsheviks' love of renaming anything and everything to make it more portentously Soviet could be co-opted for quietly humorous effect by giving farm animals absurdly grand names like 'People's Deputy', 'Mausoleum', 'Soviet', 'Little Pioneer', '*Komsomolets*', 'Commune', or '*Marseillaise*'.[5] Or take the example of the small village of Mare's Puddle, whose inhabitants were encouraged to upgrade its name to give it more gravitas. The villagers pointedly renamed it 'Soviet Puddle' instead.[6]

Graffiti undoubtedly performed a similar role, particularly in semi-concealed locations like toilets, as a Harvard Project respondent recalled,[7] but, unfortunately, evidence of such graffiti rarely survives. Perhaps the inability to attribute it to specific individuals led most informants – who surely spent as much time as anyone else on the loo

– to disregard it. In any case, these relatively minor, simple subversions became part of the scenery of everyday life, providing alternative elements for those who were willing to layer them into their daily experiences and perceptions of the brave new world in which they were living.

Far more openly, at the Leningrad Institute of Municipal Construction, a printed banner was hung announcing the upcoming 'discussion of the [Stalin] Constitution' to be held on 26 June 1936. But the word 'discussion' (*obsuzhdenie*) had been printed without the letter 'b', rendering the event a 'condemnation' or 'denunciation' (*osuzhdenie*) of the Constitution. The announcement remained on display for a good two hours before anyone reported it and it was removed. The culprit was identified as *komsomolets* Ia.A. Klenshtein, whose brother had already been sentenced to four years in a labour camp for counterrevolutionary activity.[8]

Similarly, in preparation for the All-Union Athletics Competition, scheduled to be held at Kyiv's Dinamo stadium, a sign-painter named Golovanevskii omitted the letter 'r' from 'Leningrad' when he painted the placard intended to hang above the main stadium entrance. The resulting word 'Leningad' translates as something like 'Lenin-bastard' or 'Lenin-sod'.[9] The sign hung proudly on display for all of 30 minutes before it was removed, but initial interrogations suggest that Golovanevskii's work was checked and verified before it was hung, so it seems that he was not alone in finding the act entertaining enough to risk severe punishment (he received five years in the camps).[10] There were plenty of similar acts that were a little less provocative, too, like the wall newspaper at a high school in Shirigushskoe, Zubovo-Polianskii raion, which informed readers that 'Students are educated through hooliganism' (воспитываются хулиганством).[11]

There were plenty of other acts of 'hooliganism' which functioned as silently subversive in-jokes that carried a more local (and less enigmatic) flavour. A *kolkhoznik* living near the Belorussian city of Gomel' recalled the local 'custom' of hanging a bag or briefcase of rubbish or even manure on the outstretched arm of the resident Lenin statue during the night; the police had to clamber up to retrieve the offending package the next morning, to much smirking amusement among the locals.[12] As a repeated action, this took on the style of a local running joke, as well as symbolically commenting on what the bright future to which Lenin was pointing was actually like. A subversive commentary on regime policy also appeared on a kolkhoz in Orenburg, where a group of young men (as one of their number later recalled) hoisted up a dead chicken outside the front door of the local council (*sel'sovet*) with a note pinned to the corpse explaining that it had expired trying to lay the final egg required to fulfil the norm.¹³ This kind of thing was not confined to the kolkhoz, either: when prices rose in factory canteens in late 1935 after the abolition of rationing, a mock menu was posted by the door of the Kirov Works lunch hall on 1 October:

> Starter: Kerosine Soup
> Main Course: Fresh moss with *smetana* [sour cream]
> Dessert: A turnip-based sweet¹⁴

In each of these cases, a visual joke was placed in a social space with the clear intention that it be noticed by other citizens – an act of indirect sharing with their contemporaries.

But what was the purpose of these acts, beyond the simple amusement and shared (but deniable) complicity they entailed? A clue can be found in a different but related form of humour: the nonsense rhyme. Many *anekdoty* involved Soviet leaders in unusual or bizarre circumstances in which they lost their dignity, betrayed their stupidity, or were otherwise belittled. Yet sometimes these normally powerful figures appeared in *anekdoty* for no ostensible reason and were not attacked directly by the joke at all, as, for example, in nonsense rhymes like this:

В овраге зарезали кошку,	In a ravine they butchered a cat,
Ленин Сталину сказал:	Lenin said to Stalin,
Ешьте понемножку.	'Little by little, eat some of that'.¹⁵

This is a relatively tame example, but we can find some ditties so thoroughly strange that at first glance we can only infer that their creators and tellers had been enjoying some potent mind-altering substances (consider a *chastushka* in which Stalin rides around on a push-cart with a fish sticking out of his pocket and an onion in his mouth while 'fulfilling the Five-Year Plan' and being chased by his old comrade Molotov on a donkey).¹⁶

There is no real meaning to these *chastushki*, although in the first the frequent theme of hunger is apparent. Such verses gave the storyteller the power to place the mighty, untouchable leaders in ridiculous situations and thereby to challenge their official gravitas and restore a pleasurable sense of agency to the teller. This was the underlying motivation for moving portraits of the leaders into inappropriate positions, too – it was the physical counterpart of the nonsense rhyme. In similar fashion, the placement of misspelled or sardonic messages in public spaces demonstrated the power of popular agency over official ideology, visually warping its meaning through humorous yet (theoretically) discreet or deniable forms. Moreover, Lenin's shit-filled briefcase or the chicken who died trying to fulfil its norm were also in their anonymity acts which could be felt to represent the silent majority.

Sometimes, though, no act of subversion was required at all if you could intentionally 'misread' certain regime symbols as, for example, when a statue of Leningrad Party boss Kirov was erected following his murder: if you stood at just the right angle, his lowered, pointing finger looked very much like a penis.[17] In this and other cases, either you saw it yourself or heard it from someone who trusted you not to denounce them; literally or figuratively, contemporaries could always choose to stand at just the right angle to render regime symbols ridiculous and thereby feel a sense of quiet power over them.

In fact, Soviet censorship practices in many respects became a war against humour, with the uncomfortable juxtaposition of a headline and a picture, or even of two pictures on opposite sides of a newspaper page (e.g. Stalin's portrait and, appearing through the thin paper, a worker swinging a hammer)[18] identified and punished for their counterrevolutionary implications. Intentional or otherwise, this was a battle waged in the spaces between symbol and meaning and was one which the regime could only ever lose.

Common-Sense Superiority

These rather simple, quiet assertions of power over the Soviet leaders must also be understood alongside some of their more complex and overt siblings. The latter did not simply move the *vozhdi* around into absurd contexts like comical pawns, but more strongly and audibly claimed the power to judge and to render them explicitly inferior. This was the power not just of the puppet-master, but of an intellectual better, emphasising the superior, practical common sense of the ordinary citizen, as the following example (involving several Bolshevik leaders) shows, told by one F.E. Nazarov while out hunting with friends:

> Mikoian, Stalin and Ordzhonikidze are sitting in a large room.
> A *muzhik* [a peasant] comes up to them and sees that they're not dipping their pens in their own inkwells, but walk to one another's desks to do so. The muzhik asks them, 'What's all this rigmarole with the ink?' Stalin answers, 'None of your business, I do as I please'.[19]

This is a quintessentially absurdist *anekdot*, with the humour resting on the unexpected refusal to resolve the tension created by the leaders' incoherent actions; the joke ends one step before its natural conclusion by withholding the punchline. But this is also the joke's animating principle: in the eyes of the joke-teller, the Soviet leadership frequently does incoherent, time-wasting or unnecessary things while making no attempt to explain or rationalise their behaviour to the populace.

A variation of this *anekdot*, recorded by Eugene Lyons, the American journalist who lived and worked in Moscow between 1928-34, emphasises the arbitrariness of rule and the stupidity of the leaders even more clearly:

> A foreign delegation was making the rounds of the commissariats. In Commissar Ivanov's offices the delegates found everything beyond reproach, except this: Ivanov had placed a huge spittoon on his desk.
>
> 'Comrade Ivanov,' the delegates ventured, 'what's the idea of this?'
>
> Ivanov flared up and shouted angrily: 'It's my spittoon and I put it where I please!'
>
> At the headquarters of Commissar Stepanov they found a chair suspended from the ceiling. Again the delegation [asked why it was there] and again evoked an irate response.
>
> 'It's my chair and I put it where I please!' he yelled.
>
> When the delegation got to Stalin, it found everything in fine shape. At the conclusion of the interview, however, a spokesman alluded to the strange goings-on in the two commissariats.
>
> 'Oh, forget about that,' Stalin smiled. 'Those men are idiots.'
>
> 'How is it that idiots are at the head of important commissariats?' the spokesman asked.
>
> At this Stalin lost his temper.
>
> 'They're my idiots,' he pounded the table, 'and I put them where I please!'[20]

Continuing this theme, railway electrician V.Iu. Turzhanskii shared the following absurdist *anekdot* with his colleagues:

> A Jew arrives in Moscow and attempts to telephone the circus. Instead he is connected to the Central Executive Committee and when he asks to speak to the head clown, Kalinin picks up the call.[21]

All these jokes move beyond the initial step of asserting power over the leaders and go on to explicitly highlight and ridicule their actions, strongly implying that ordinary people had a comparatively firmer grasp on reality; it was simultaneously an act of mockery and of personal reassurance.

This could be taken a step further, too, and explicitly highlight the costs to the population caused by the idiotic actions of the leadership, as we see in another example recorded by Lyons, in which, at an imagined meeting of the leaders to discuss the achievements of the first Five-Year Plan, Mikoian, the Commissar for Internal Trade, berates the Commissar of Health, Dr. Semashko:

> 'You haven't accomplished anything,' Mikoian chides. 'When you took office ten years ago, there was malaria in the country. Well, there's still malaria. There was typhus in the country – there is still typhus. There was––'
> 'And what has your Commissariat accomplished?' Dr. Sema[s]hko interrupts.
> 'Mine?' Mikoian declares proudly. 'The situation is entirely different. When I took office ten years ago there was bread in the country, wasn't there? Well, there isn't any now. There was meat then – there isn't any now. There was sugar...'[22]

Here the leaders are not simply disconnected from reality, but stand somewhere between being maliciously stupid and stupidly malicious. A final, oft-repeated *anekdot* adds a little more complexity to this picture:

> Kalinin [or Molotov] gives a speech to some *kolkhozniki*, praising the excellent harvest. He is advised to remove his glasses, which are dramatically magnifying the yield.[23]

S.A. Myshakin, a duty officer at L'gov railway station (Kurskaia oblast'), embellished the *anekdot* further, joking that there was a vodka called 'Rykov-glasses' ('*Rykovochki*'), suggesting, in other words, that Soviet leaders like Aleksei Rykov, who did not wear spectacles, could use alcohol instead to similarly multiply their vision.[24] Unlike the harvest, there's more to this *anekdot* than first meets the eye: it implies a popular suspicion that the leaders were engaged in an *intentional* delusion – that a Soviet leader could very well see the reality of devastation and famine in the countryside caused by forced collectivisation, but deliberately chose to employ an artificial, warping filter between himself and that reality.

I.I. Shitts, the historian living in Moscow who'll be accompanying us throughout this book, noted a rather tedious *anekdot* in his diary in February 1929 which described how a tsar (an obvious stand-in for Stalin) demanded that everything in his kingdom be painted red. To save time, money, and the people's anger, he is instead given a set of red-tinted glasses, riffing on the familiar cliché of 'rose-tinted glasses'.[25] In these jokes, the Soviet leaders were likewise being accused of wearing rose-tinted glasses, suggesting a complex popular awareness of official doublethink – an awareness which crops up time and again in 1930s humour directed at those in power, and which prompts us to rethink that Orwellian concept. Orwell suggested it was only the masses who fell prey to doublethink – fooling themselves to try to get by – but in these jokes we can see ordinary people actively identifying and mocking their masters for it instead.

This also prompts us to question another long-standing claim about popular opinion in these years – the 'evil councillors' principle. The representation of Soviet leaders in contemporary humour simply doesn't support the idea – so often wheeled out in history textbooks – that ordinary people could easily forgive and believe in their leaders by blaming all misfortunes on the unsound, scheming counsel of evil bureaucrats and advisers (which is exactly what the diversionary humour of *Krokodil* and other official satirical publications tried to do).[26] Instead, the highest echelons of the Soviet leadership were portrayed in humour as intellectually unstable, foolish, and ready to deceive even themselves. When telling or laughing at these jokes, the ordinary citizen placed themselves in marked contrast to those qualities, as the intellectual and 'common-sense' superior to their leaders.

Humour was a particularly fitting means to do this, readily drawing on the old archetype of the 'fool' who can speak truth to power in barbed yet amusing ways. The specifically Russian version of this archetype is the *iurodivyi*, a 'holy fool' of far greater moral and spiritual purity than the world around him,[27] but the fool is a pan-cultural figure appearing across the globe, from the Native American Lakota's sacred clown, the Heyoka, to Sufism's populist philosopher, Nasreddin Hodja. The 'wise fool' is also familiar to Westerners from such characters as the truth-telling Fool in *King Lear*. Wherever he appears, this figure sees the injustices and arbitrariness of social and political conventions and, despite his capering and apparent silliness, he actually understands more about the world than his contemporaries do. By telling *anekdoty* that poked holes in the fabric of official reality and highlighted the foibles of their leaders, Soviet contemporaries could also play the fool, at least temporarily. All the same, the 'fool' is an officially-sanctioned voice of loyal criticism and in Stalin's Soviet Union, no such licence for comic insight was permitted outside the carefully-controlled pages of publications like *Krokodil*.

Instead, it was in the context of mass celebrations and commemorations that Soviet contemporaries could more meaningfully employ traditional tactics and motifs to engage, challenge, and alter the state's ideological and regulatory demands, and to which we now turn.

Kirov's Carnival

On 1 December 1934, Sergei Mironovich Kirov, the Party boss of Leningrad, was gunned down as he left his office at the Smolnyi Institute by a lone assassin and political nobody, Leonid Vasil'evich Nikolaev. This murder was pivotal in Soviet history: it created a martyr whose death would be used to legitimise the paranoid scapegoating of the later 1930s; it signalled a turn to more repressive times in which critical speech was seen as tantamount to terrorism; and it would spawn countless conspiracy theories about whether Stalin saw a rival in Kirov and therefore had him assassinated.

But Kirov's murder also prompted an outflow of carnivalesque responses from the populace that reveals a great deal to us of their views and resentments, power-relations and perspectives. To understand these Carnival-style responses, we first need to take a moment to consider how mass ceremonial events functioned in the Soviet Union. Official discourse and ideology weren't simply communicated through the pages of *Pravda* and other newspapers, through the radio or the speeches of local activists, nor even just in the observable world of buildings, factories, crests, slogans, passport categories, or the shrine-like 'Red Corners' (containing various forms of propaganda material) that appeared in every workplace. They were also articulated through the more dynamic and participatory form of mass festivals and official holidays which, despite the Soviet obsession with work, increased significantly during the 1930s. As Malte Rolf argues, these festivals were not simply window-dressing, but 'were a method for spreading the regime's new and changing notions of order, for communicating the desired model to all who participated in the parades, whether voluntarily or involuntarily'.[28] They were rituals, and rituals, by definition, have power. As Rolf puts it, 'Festivity was part of politics', and 'Staging power and making it real were reciprocal'.[29]

That was how things were supposed to work, at least. In practice, these mass events didn't play out unaffected by the people participating in them. Alexei Yurchak has described an attitude of knowing world-weariness and even open cynicism on the part of citizens attending mass festivals during the last decades of Soviet power, when practically nobody believed that Communism would ever be achieved,[30] but in the 1930s people were still encountering and engaging with these new festival and holiday activities in a more exploratory, less jaded manner. Indeed, many of the holidays and festivities that would become staples of the Soviet calendar were brand new in the 1930s, so cynical disengagement would for most people take a little longer to develop.

In any case, what's interesting here is not how many citizens went to festivals and parades dragging their feet, but how they made sense of these events within their own life experiences and understandings. While the regime sought a clearly-defined kind of participation from its citizens in these events, in practice individuals could use them as a space in which to articulate their own attitudes, criticisms, or even (to them, if not to the regime) *apolitical* desires to have a good time.[31] Even if people had little desire to applaud the Soviet Union's still-dubious achievements, they could still feel genuinely happy about the chance to take a day off, relax a little, and, most importantly, eat their fill at the specially-stocked canteens and shops. The official aims and popular responses could thereby crosshatch[32] one another in small ways, but it would be too simplistic to interpret this only as the regime using 'bread and circuses' to keep the people happy and docile. Enjoying some food or some entertainment did not and does not mean that people suddenly switch off their critical faculties.

In talking about these critical engagements with Soviet festivals and holidays, I can hardly ignore Mikhail Bakhtin's influential theory of Carnival, which he wrote in the USSR during these same years. In his telling, Carnival is an officially-sanctioned event in which the normal world is temporarily turned upside-down; hierarchies are reversed and social and physical taboos – especially those relating to eating and defecating – are welcomed back into the fold. Like the 'fool', Carnival reveals artifice and inequality in daily life and its structures, but ultimately just serves as a pressure valve to release pent up anger and frustration.

Kirov's murder certainly wasn't treated as cause for celebration by the Soviet leadership, of course, but people's spontaneous responses could not be wholly suppressed: the official proceedings to mark his death – a distinctly solemn mass festival – in popular practice repeatedly spilled over into the carnivalesque, the grotesque, physical, and even scatological, which, in their sum, I call 'Kirov's Carnival'.

As such, consciously or otherwise, contemporaries were drawing on long traditions dating back to medieval Rus',[33] of carving out alternative, subversive spaces within official contexts. These traditions of temporarily inverting hierarchies and exuberantly breaking cultural taboos of etiquette and taste were principally aimed at the Church and its representatives, but we find many echoes of those traditions in the *anekdoty* and *chastushki* of the Soviet 1930s (and the 'common-sense superiority' theme likewise plays on traditional 'folk wisdom' being superior to the formal practices of the state and its leaders).

More importantly, while Bakhtin's theories of Carnival focused on Western Europe, D.S. Likhachev and others working on the traditions of Rus' identified in these practices a more expansive 'world of laughter' that went well beyond the strict temporal limits of Bakhtinian Carnival. For Likhachev, there was a *constant* possibility of entering the world of inversions and laughter; it was a 'worldview' which shadowed the official one and provided an always-accessible 'laughing' alternative that laid bare the artifice and hypocrisy of everyday reality.[34] Likhachev is far more illuminating than Bakhtin in helping us to understand the humour of the 1930s, which was by no means constrained to state-approved times and places. It will become ever clearer over the following pages that much as Soviet citizens could choose to stand at the just the right angle to see Kirov's 'penis', they could always choose to look into Likhachev's 'shadow world' and see things in a different, carnivalesque light. The social and personal effects of doing so were often startling, thrilling, and life-affirming.

Consequently, none of what follows in this section was unique to Kirov among the leaders, but the drama of his assassination concentrated both minds and mockery and brought several more general aspects of contemporary humour aimed at the leaders to the fore. It therefore serves as a revealing focal point for us, too.

Consumption

To the chagrin of the Soviet leadership, anxiously looking over their shoulders even as they wiped away their tears, Kirov's murder prompted an explosion of salacious gossip.[35] Immediate reactions to the news varied widely; if many citizens wept appropriately, a local Party Organiser reported that the announcement of the murder was also greeted with applause in the classrooms of a school in Leningrad's Volodarskii raion.[36] A more vivid response that seemed to exalt in the symbolic 'uncrowning' of the high and mighty was recorded at two technical colleges in the Pukhovichskii raion, Minsk oblast', where 'organised shootings' at portraits of the *vozhdi* took place.[37] In Leningrad's M.

Gel'ts Factory (Petrogradskii raion), shortly after Kirov's death was announced, unknown individuals decorated the toilets with a variety of 'counterrevolutionary slogans', including the conspiratorial suggestion that 'Each Communist is a pawn, dependent on the game-player – Stalin'. Rationing was also addressed on the bathroom tiles, with a prediction that now 'Meat and rolls will be given to the first [rationing] category, but after the second Five-Year Plan, the second category will be sent to Lenin' (i.e. to their graves).[38]

Indeed, rationing and consumption were major themes in people's mocking responses to the Kirov murder, and Soviet leaders were in general frequently upbraided for appearing to be far better fed than everyone else in the Soviet Union. For example, Shinov, a second-year student at the Planovskii Institute in Leningrad's Primorskii raion, responded to the news of Politburo-member Sergo Ordzhonikidze's death in 1937 by gloating that he'd 'died of obesity – they all eat well,' before adding for good measure that the prominent old Bolshevik Valerian Kuibyshev 'died of obesity too'.[39] A.M. Uspenskii, a village teacher in Vladimirskaia oblast', was of a similar opinion, declaring on the day of Ordzhonikidze's death that 'he probably died of overeating'.[40]

So it was therefore part of a broader practice that Kirov's murder – and his podgy corpse – prompted a welter of similar comments: a certain Podoba, working at the Bebel' Factory, asked rhetorically, 'What did Kirov ever do for the workers, besides develop a paunch?'[41] A certain Strelkov reported back to his mates at the Krasnaia zaria Factory on his visit to see Kirov lying in state: 'He was really well fed – he got his rations from the Torgsin, you can tell' (the Torgsin was a limited-access, specially provisioned store).[42] Candidate Party member Serkov of the Molotov Factory asked rhetorically what Kirov's casket would be transported on, bursting into 'venomous laughter' when he wondered just 'how many horses will it take to carry Kirov's coffin?'.[43]

Stalin was singled out as a particular target for this kind of abuse. When a schoolchild in Zubovo-Polianskii raion, Mordovian Autonomous Republic, asked why the *vozhdi* were cremated when they died, a classmate, *komsomolets* Leskin, responded, 'To bake cakes out of the ashes. But they won't burn Stalin because he's [too] fatty (жирный) – he'll be made into soap'.[44] M.V. Pen'kov, a student at the zoological institute in Voroshilovskii raion, Stavropol'skii krai, spotted a piece of (presumably delicious-looking) bread on someone's bedside table lying next to a picture of Stalin. He grumbled to his friends, 'I just bet Stalin gets bread like that – he's stuffed his face' (наел морду).[45] Similarly, a pupil at School 23 in Orel found himself in trouble for explaining livestock shortages by suggesting that 'Stalin ate them'.[46]

The perceived disparity between the lifestyles of the leadership and the majority was clearly a source of significant criticism and ill-feeling. Ordinary people's de facto powerlessness to address this disparity in any practical way therefore motivated a reassertion of power through the humorous inversion of conventional value judgements. That is, even though they were hungry, Soviet citizens mocked the leaders for *having* access to more and better food; they were derided for becoming soft and fat, creating the implicit suggestion that the thinner (or even starving) ordinary people therefore commanded a kind of moral high ground. This rather neatly combined an approval of an ascetic lifestyle familiar from *both* religion *and* the image of the 'professional revolutionary' promoted by the Bolsheviks.

If we examine the practice further, we discover that there was more than straightforward resentment and moral judgement going on here. It was widely claimed, sometimes in the form of humorous rhymes, that a direct consequence of Kirov's death would be a reduction in the price of bread, and that, 'logically', Stalin's death would therefore deliver outright abundance to the masses.[47] Whether in rhyme or in a throwaway comment, this seems to have been a widespread, sarcastic response to the Kirov murder. Here are two representative examples:

В Ленинграде Кирова убили,	When Kirov was popped,
Хлеб без карточек пустили,	Ration cards were dropped,
А если Сталин умрет,	So if Stalin dies,
Жизнь по новому пойдет.	A new life will arise.[48]

[He] was killed – there'll be more bread for us![49]

In part, these imaginings grew from the end of rationing in 1935, shortly after the assassination (although this actually caused prices to rise), but what is really of interest here is the direct link people made between the leader's death and the immediate benefits they imagined for themselves. The citizens making these humorous comments were not just comparing, but were drawing a direct, causal link between their own malnourished conditions and the chubby corpulence of the leaders.

Nevertheless, it's hardly likely that these individuals genuinely believed that the death of one Bolshevik would really leave behind an abundance of extra rations sufficient to feed everyone else. Instead we should consider this sardonic view as an expression of principle. Kirov was used to symbolically represent the institutionalisation of unequal distribution – a small élite consumed far more than their fair share of the food available; Kirov's death was then used to imagine the end of this system, at which point a vast quantity of food would be released into general circulation.⁵⁰ The leaders were therefore portrayed as a group of expropriators, like the bourgeois or noble 'classes' that the Bolsheviks claimed to have overthrown.⁵¹ This rather raises the stakes of the comments from seemingly irrational fantasies to the accusation that the Soviet leadership had simply assumed the role of the expropriators.

It also introduces an important theme that will crop up time and time again in the following pages: humorous criticism was aimed first and foremost at specific individuals, institutions, or policies, but rarely mocked or derided the principles or ideals of the Soviet project at large. This strong tendency seems to echo Likhachev, for he emphasised that humorous criticisms of Church power weren't attacks from outwith the dominant symbolic system, but instead used symbols from within that very system to lay bare its failings and hypocrisies.⁵² In this case, the individual – Kirov – is mocked, yet, simultaneously some of the key tenets of socialist or Marxist ideology are invoked, namely the egalitarian redistribution of materials. In other words, even when calling their leaders fatties, people were making a significant political point: the Bolsheviks stood accused of reneging on their revolutionary credo.

Pointed comments about his chubby frame were just the beginning of Kirov's Carnival, however. As he was no longer sentient, there were fewer ways to humiliate him, and so mockery turned to the symbolic (mis)uses of his earthly remains. This wasn't imagined as solely violent or destructive, however, but was, in grotesque form, closely allied to ideas of food and consumption. For example, when the town of Viatka was renamed 'Kirov' in honour of the fallen leader a few weeks after the assassination, some Komsomol youths were prompted to describe the town as 'Kirov's offal' (потроха Кирова).⁵³ In the woodworking shop of the Putilovets Factory, Anna Liubimova, a temporary worker, fancied butchering Kirov's corpse too: 'He was killed – serves him right. He should be chopped into pieces for not giving out passports and because life under him's so bad'.⁵⁴ On the day of Kirov's state funeral, at a Leningrad factory, a certain Stepanova, a Komsomol organiser, encouraged her colleagues to head to the canteen for lunch because, she claimed, 'We're going to eat Kirov's brains'.⁵⁵ The late Kirov apparently had quite the capacious head, as a worker at another Leningrad factory was reported the same day for declaring that there, too, they were 'having Kirov's brains' for lunch.⁵⁶ Less gruesomely, others took the newspapers reporting on Kirov's death and used them as cigarette paper – both cremating and simultaneously 'consuming' the late leader in the smoke.⁵⁷

In these jokes, Kirov is reduced literally to pieces of meat, degraded to the level of inanimate flesh, chunks of which are then considered separately from the whole (his 'brain', his 'offal'), destroying his physical form. And this treatment wasn't limited to Kirov, either: take, for example, one Emel'ian Vlasiuk who, in a Karelian village, reportedly 'express[ed] the hatred for the Soviet regime among the peasants' when he declared graphically that, 'We will make cutlets out of the Communists!'[58]

This cannibalistic motif challenged socio-political power relations: the act of consumption echoed and inverted images of the *vozhdi* as corpulent consumers lording it over the masses. Given that actual food was in such short supply for the majority of Soviet citizens, they could instead turn to grotesque, cannibalistic imagery in order to conjure a sense of power over the leadership. This returns us to the idea of Kirov's death unleashing new sources of food – but in this case Kirov himself is dinner.

Again, though, this is not an entirely destructive act directed against the regime through the symbol of Kirov. As Bakhtin's discussion of the long history of the consumption trope stressed, this was never a wholly destructive act, but is simultaneously renewing: even though consumption is indeed an act of power over the consumed, which it destroys, it thereby provides life to the consumer (and, later, waste products which are themselves fertiliser for other new life).[59] This is certainly not to suggest that Soviet citizens were consciously composing these jokes and asides with an eye to their symbolic resonance; rather, an age-old trope was deployed because it was particularly in tune with contemporary worries, and Soviet citizens didn't confine themselves to invoking Marxist ideas of expropriation and fair distribution when they criticised shortages and inequalities, but could also turn to a much older, more generic discourse. In so doing, they moved beyond the confines of the 'in-system' mockery Likhachev described in medieval Rus', drawing upon and blending together multiple value systems, both traditional and Soviet.

Toilet Humour

Moving nimbly from the dining hall to the bathroom, scatology (relating to excrement) was a major element of the carnivalesque 'physical' humour used to mock the leadership in the 1930s. In a world turned upside-down, a significant amount of attention comes to rest on what Bakhtin liked to call the 'lower bodily stratum'. Contemporary jokes were rather less euphemistic, however. At the tamer end of the spectrum there were simple imaginings of the leaders going to the toilet: for example, a metalworker in Leningrad reflected in mock sympathy that, 'Our dear Kirov is dead, so now, just think, Stalin and Molotov will even be escorted to the toilet under guard'.[60] A rather more immediate and memorable example was the substitution of an 'r' for the 't' in 'Stalin', rendering him not the 'man of steel' but the 'man of shit', or 'Shitman' (Сралин).[61]

Returning to Kirov, a *komsomolets* responded to news of the assassination with a brief scatological couplet: '*Na Kirova nasrat' i v Moskvu poslat'*': 'Shit on Kirov and send him to Moscow'.[62] Although unlikely to win awards for poetic composition, the sentiment was not unique: at a meeting of the Cheromskii *sel'sovet*, the 25 year-old Anna Glebova announced that, 'Well if I knew where [Kirov]'s buried, I'd take a shit on his grave'.[63]

This kind of bodily humour was likewise used to criticise particular policies, as this rather more convoluted *anekdot* demonstrates:

> An engineer changed his surname, taking for himself the name 'Lenin', and called his daughter *Piatiletka* [Five-Year Plan]. Consequently, when [his] daughter soiled herself, the mother woke the father with the words: 'Get up, Lenin – the Five-Year Plan has shat itself!' (обосралась).[64]

This *anekdot* seems rather strained at first, but there really was a spate of name-changing after the Bolshevik consolidation of power, which led to names even more ridiculous than *Piatiletka* (Elektrosila (Electric Power) or Engelsina, anyone?). Consequently, this joke mocks both the failings of the Five-Year Plan itself and the everyday absurdities created by those devoted individuals who adopted 'revolutionary' names. A final example uses images of bodily waste to pillory collectivisation: a senior veterinarian noted laconically one day at work that, 'Moscow is the heart and the head; the natural waste, the kolkhozy'.[65] (This played on an old saying that Moscow is the 'heart' of Russia and St Petersburg its head, emphasising the traditional role of Petersburg as Russia's cultural and intellectual capital in the nineteenth century.)

The simple shock-factor of faecal images undermining official persons and policies was a potent source of the humour in these examples. The base and material are used to besmirch the high and mighty through an act of debasement and degradation; smearing the mighty leaders with shit exuberantly transgressed elementary social taboos to great comic effect.

According to Bakhtin, this works because such acts manage

to dispel the atmosphere of gloomy and false seriousness [...] to lend it a different look, to render it more material, closer to man and his body, more understandable, and lighter in the bodily sense.[66]

Scatological mockery of Soviet leaders and their policies brought this otherwise inscrutable, alienating world down to a level on which ordinary citizens could reassert their ability to analyse and to judge it. While the leaders normally appeared distant – their lives and official activities opaque – toilet humour could relocate the upper echelons of Soviet society into a reality not only recognisable to the ordinary person, but also clearly beneath or inferior to them. If laughter was a great leveller in itself, as Likhachev stressed,[67] scatological humiliation went further still by inverting inequalities, rather than simply placing everyone on an equal footing.

Nonetheless, however forceful and degrading these jokes, to mock the physical is, from another perspective, simultaneously an admission of weakness: it suggests that the political, social or ideological causes of popular dissatisfaction all lay beyond the reach of the ordinary citizen. The only thing over which they could find some power was in mocking the bodies of the leaders. In doing so, they could gain a sense of illusory power, yet, because they did so in such exaggerated, unrealistic forms, it remained far from a force of any real, practical potency.

Although Bakhtin argued that all scatological imagery is inherently renewing,[68] this is a step too far from practice into theory when dealing with real people rather than literary creations. Scatological humour, however degrading and angry it may have been, was still far from a call to violently attack or destroy the Soviet system or its leaders. These are images of profound disrespect, but not of destructive hatred or implacable opposition. There were many Soviet citizens who got themselves into trouble by openly wishing that Stalin would be murdered after Kirov, for example, but these were not the same individuals who made jokes about the assassination.[69] Those who wished death on Stalin or the other leaders tended not to tell jokes, a distinction reinforced by the jokes themselves, which feature the deaths of *vozhdi* extremely rarely, or only as a pre-existing condition upon which a joke is based.

Instead, we see in contemporary humour a use of grotesque imagery and a laughing, carnivalesque mockery which merrily dances on imaginary graves, but does not advocate murder or, generally, even the removal of its targets.

Dancing on Graves

Even if not advocating murder directly, when a death *did* occur many Soviet citizens were ready and willing to act on the comic desire to dance gaily upon those graves. In this, Bakhtin's ideas of the renewing nature of laughter in response to death were clearly borne out in Soviet citizens' responses to Kirov's murder.[70] In the carnivalesque mode, as normal hierarchies of power are overturned, the masses celebrate, feast, and mock their leaders; Kirov's death prompted many to get into just such a holiday spirit, kindling a kind of Soviet Day of the Dead. They simply couldn't bear to sit through the solemn mourning meetings and prescribed minutes of silence.

In the OGPU Factory in Leningrad, during the five-minute silence held in one of the workshops, the worker and former Party member Chursin farted loudly and, according to the report, 'insolently', disrupting the appropriate solemnity of the event.[71] Less pungently, at the '1st of May' kolkhoz, the *kolkhoznitsa* Anis'ia Ivanova shouted 'Fire!' to disrupt the meeting and clear the room.[72] In the Krasnyi Vyborzhets Factory the five-minute silence was also disrupted. In the machine-repair shop several workers simply laughed throughout the meeting while another, Mikhailov, took an ingot and rolled it about on the floor, creating a noisy distraction. In the rolling mill, the worker D.D. Krikunov was instructed to give the signal for the five minutes' silence by sounding the shop's siren; however, he turned the hand crank so slowly that the siren sounded like a slurring barrel organ, causing many to burst out laughing (Krikunov himself cackled away merrily for the full five minutes).[73]

Getting a taste for holidays, in the machine shop of the Rabochii Factory, Rogovzov, a mechanic, speculated optimistically that 'When Lenin died there was a holiday; Kirov's died – there's another holiday. [So] if all the leaders are finished off, there'll be an eternal holiday'.[74] He wasn't alone in making this extrapolation: at the middle school attached to the Artem mine in Ukraine, a student named Ol'shanskoi mused aloud to his class and teacher that 'We don't have any lessons today because of Kirov's murder, so if they [the leaders] were killed more often, we wouldn't have to study at all'.[75]

Even if there would not be an abundance of future holidays, various citizens were distressed to learn that there would be no parties or dancing to mark the Kirov assassination. One M. Anan'eva, a young worker in the kitchens of the Voroshilov Machine Construction Factory (Leningrad), boldly approached the Party Organiser, Comrade Ulin, and asked to be signed up 'for the party'. Ulin responded in some confusion,

'What party? There's no such party, but a gathering of our factory workers to mourn'. Anan'eva, with apparent sincerity, persisted in some distress, 'But will there really be no dancing?' After Ulin rebuffed her again, she exclaimed that 'I've been to the coffin and cried, [I've been] to the meeting and cried, and now I want to be able to be cheerful and not have to cry *all* the time'.[76]

Others felt the timing of the murder ruled out the appropriate festival feeling: at Factory 3 in Moskovskii raion, *komsomol'ka* Dogaeva grumbled darkly to her colleagues, 'What kind of fool would kill Kirov in winter when it's not possible to have a dance? It would've been better to kill him in summer...'[77] She certainly wasn't alone in her desire to hit the dancefloor: Vadchenko of Leningrad's Factory 7 talked his colleagues down from even going to visit the coffin: 'Idiots are going to go and freeze, but I'd rather go and have a dance'.[78] Perhaps Vadchenko had a specific venue in mind, as other citizens didn't bother to ask permission and simply organised parties themselves: Party member Iakovlev found himself in trouble for hosting 'a party at his home with drinking and dancing' on the official day of mourning.[79] This impulse could be strong and defiant: when another party on the day of mourning, this one at the Volokskii *sel'sovet*, was interrupted by the authorities, one Grigor'ev announced that 'We've been dancing and we'll go on dancing – it'd be all the same to us if Stalin was killed; no one would shed a tear'.[80] And dancing was not the only festive desire to be frustrated: a watchman at a factory in Leningrad, Sergei Patrushin, was infuriated when a shop refused to sell him vodka on the official day of mourning (the sale of all spirits was banned that day), and he burst out, 'What the fuck is this? Even if you kill all of our goddamn *vozhdi*, there should at least be vodka!'.[81]

This friction of interests wasn't always simply a case of people attempting to invert or pervert the nature of the event. It was often only in the process of finding some personal resonance and interest in official state events that contemporaries could find meaning in them. In this case, for many it didn't matter whether Kirov lived or died, but if there was to be an occasion to mark his death, then it only meant something to them if this was in the form of leisure and a party.[82]

And so Kirov's murder prompted a popular and at times irrepressible desire for a carnivalesque celebration – the sanctioned events to mark the assassination were co-opted or inverted in order to relieve or escape from the distress of everyday life. The assassination disrupted normality and opened a door out of routine which people desperately wanted to walk through. In part, we might simply put this down to the desire to have a day off work and to spend it enjoyably. But it can also be seen as a desire for a popular, if transient, assertion of power over the *vozhdi*: the power of the Soviet leadership had been challenged and the leaders had been shown, in dramatic fashion, to be mortal. Reality had delivered in practice what the many jokes directed against the leaders did only in the imagination – it had dethroned and disempowered one of the Soviet leadership.

Sexual Mockery

These corporeal, Bacchanalian practices would hardly be complete without sex, and sexually explicit jokes were another important aspect of the carnivalesque humour directed at the Soviet leadership. However, remarkably few examples of this kind remain in either archival sources or the published collections of *anekdoty* from this time. There's a simple reason for this: cumulative layers of prudish censorship have, over the decades, obscured these 'blue' jokes from view. For much the same reasons, this was true even for the more general, often very creative cultural practice of swearing in Russian ('*mat*') because, as Stephen Smith notes, '*Mat* celebrated gross corporeality, the lower physical faculties, fecundity and decay, nature and excess, things that sat uneasily with Bolshevik asceticism and horror of being engulfed by nature'.[83]

Russian folklorists and literary analysts have long struggled with this problem, and it was only after the fall of the Soviet Union that these layers began to be peeled back sufficiently for scholars of erotic and sexual aspects of Russian and Soviet folk culture to publish or even to gain access to the materials they wanted to work on.[84] Indeed, it was this long-standing '*pruderie*', as he put it, which prompted the leading Russian folklorist of the nineteenth century ('the Russian Grimm'),[85] A.N. Afanas'ev, to collect, publish and thereby preserve those folk materials deemed too rude, crude and lewd to have made it into print before (and even Afanas'ev had to publish this collection anonymously in Geneva).[86] So it was certainly not a Soviet innovation to keep such things out of sight.

It's clear from Afanas'ev's and others' work (notably the famous lexicographer V.I. Dal's collection of some 386 obscene proverbs)[87] that explicit material had, unsurprisingly, long been a significant part of Russian oral folk culture. And this certainly remained true in the 1930s: according to Eugene Lyons, displaying a *pruderie* Afanas'ev would have recognised, the prevalence of this humour was such that a good dose of censorship would be required to publish a volume of contemporary *anekdoty*: 'A good many of them, being thoroughly obscene, would have to be eliminated from such a volume'.[88]

Even in the criminal case-files I worked with – hardly a public venue – if the contents of such jokes were noted down during the original interrogation (itself not guaranteed), once the report was typed up, sexual humour was either omitted completely or hidden behind the euphemistic formula '[s/he] said something which slandered leaders of the Party and government'. Later summaries of case-files echoed this formula, and even modern archival indexes, which sometimes retype summaries of 'clean' handwritten jokes, consistently ignore any sexual *anekdoty* in the same file. Censorious attitudes die hard, it seems. We can only infer, then, that there was a great deal more sexually explicit humour circulating at this time, and must try to reconstruct some of its character from the available evidence.

Most likely due to this censorship and elision, aside from various salacious rumours that Kirov had been murdered for having an affair with the assassin's wife, and that he was a philanderer in general,[89] I didn't find other elements of this kind in Kirov's Carnival specifically, but we do have material relating to other leaders. In these sexual *anekdoty*, aspersions of sexual deviance seem to have been thrown at Stalin in particular, as the following examples demonstrate:

> Stalin 'got to know' a woman and caught lice from her. He went to the doctor for help, but it did no good. Stalin then went to Kalinin for advice and Kalinin suggested, 'Write the word "kolkhoz" where the lice are breeding and they'll soon run off (разбегутся)'.[90]

> Stalin shagged (поимел) some girl and she fell pregnant. Stalin went to the doctor and asked what to do about it. The doctor says, 'Announce it's a kolkhoz and everything will disperse (разбегутся)'.[91]

These variations of the same *anekdot* first land Stalin in hot water for his sexual behaviour, then proffer a solution which mocks his key policy of collectivisation. These *anekdoty* are also plainly related to a more famous, non-sexual version in which, after others fail in the attempt, Stalin alone manages to clear a large animal (often a bull or cow) from blocking the road by quietly threatening to send it to a kolkhoz.[92] William Chamberlin, the American historian and journalist reporting from the USSR in 1922-34, also recorded a more wholesome version in which mice have to be scared out of Stalin's cupboard, and a Harvard Project respondent recalled another relating to the bedbug infestations in the prison he'd been confined to between 1937-9.⁹³ Although censorship denies us further examples, it seems reasonable to suppose that this was not an isolated case and that sexualised, 'dirty' versions of many other popular *anekdoty* circulated alongside their 'clean' counterparts.

Nevertheless, crude and explicit jokes also existed in their own right, as this intrinsically sexual example illustrates:

> Kalinin and Stalin were having a business meeting, but soon began to make jokes and fool about. They wanted some women and they started to tease one another [баловаться]. Kalinin said, 'First I screw you – otherwise you might cheat'. Stalin readily agreed and let himself be buggered by Kalinin. When the old man [Kalinin] grew tired, he asked for a break. Kalinin dressed and went into his study. There, he wrote a decree which made sodomy punishable by eight years in prison. He presented it to Stalin and said, 'Well, if you want eight years of prison, come and get it.'⁹⁴

This particularly graphic *anekdot* is extremely derogatory for two principal reasons. Firstly, sodomy and homosexuality were (and still are) generally considered unacceptable in (former) Soviet states; to portray the two *vozhdi* having homosexual sex was to imply a moral degeneracy of considerable proportions. For some joke-tellers, this *anekdot* might have been told as a direct response to the recriminalisation of sodomy in 1933-4 across all Soviet Republics by inventing a humorous 'explanation' for that legislation.⁹⁵ In so doing, the *anekdot* simultaneously uses the 'unsavoury' subject to mock the leaders, but also implies that they write laws purely for their own, twisted ends.

Secondly, this *anekdot* denigrates Stalin in particular because it portrays him in the 'passive', receiving sexual role. For male same-sex intercourse, the so-called passive role has often been associated with a perverse, weak 'femininity', an attitude which queer theorists, to quote Dan Healey, have regarded 'as a function of the dominant sex/gender system'.⁹⁶ In other words, in homosexual sex traditional gender roles become confused, and the willingness of a man to play the 'woman's part', and thereby relinquish his masculine 'superiority' or 'power', can appear extremely troubling or even threatening to established norms.⁹⁷ This attitude is evident across the board in Soviet medical, police, judicial,⁹⁸ and, notably, Gulag contexts (in the latter, 'male prisoners used same-sex rape and sexual assault to enforce hierarchies of power', which caused the victim to enter a 'caste of "untouchables" [...] who sat at the bottom of the prison social ladder', while those men who took the 'active' role were considered 'normal').⁹⁹ So, in this *anekdot*, Stalin is being dramatically unmanned and depicted as both 'degraded' and as an outright pervert for performing the 'passive' role willingly.

Power is central to the theme and function of this *anekdot*: Stalin is belittled by Kalinin's sexual 'power', his legal power (as Chairman of the Supreme Soviet and hence officially head of state), and indeed his power to trick the *vozhd'*. As with the other examples of sexually explicit humour, the joke-teller derives a sense of empowerment from reducing Stalin to a purely bodily, deviant sexual creature. The wilful disregard for public taboos – sexual disease; illicit liaisons; 'sodomy' – further emphasises the power of the joke-teller, who wantonly and publicly disregards these proprieties. And although Kalinin himself is shown to indulge in anal sex, he largely escapes the stigma attached to it by playing only the 'masculine' role, and then tricking Stalin to escape a role-reversal.[100] Consequently, Kalinin is essentially the figure the joke's audience are expected to identify with; he is the agent who physically dominates and degrades Stalin and then forces him to recognise that degradation.

Sexual mockery of this kind could also take a more casual form. At a convivial gathering to mark a friend's departure to Moscow on a business trip, one M.V. Bulyshev, the director of a mining technical college in the town of Blagoveshchensk, Bashkir Autonomous Republic, noticed there was a portrait of Stalin hanging on the wall, but above it hung a picture of a naked, sleeping woman surrounded by cherubs. Pointing to this unlikely pairing, he joked to the room, 'Look at this – I know the Georgians like boys, but this [the woman] is even better'.[101] This casual slander, playing on a negative stereotype of Georgian men, reminds us how easily sexual slurs could be made in everyday situations, as they are in cultures around the world.[102] (We might also wonder, of course, about the positioning of the portrait and the picture of the naked woman in the first place.)

Stalin wasn't the only leader to be mocked in sexually explicit scenarios, however. By way of comparison, let's consider two examples aimed specifically at Molotov and Kalinin.

> Molotov went abroad and had sex with the wife of some general. When the general later had sex with her, he pulled out his member to discover an old condom stuck to it, bearing the label 'Made in the USSR'. 'That devilish USSR is sneaking around everywhere these days, even up people's vaginas!' he exclaimed.[103]

There's an immediate difference in the way this *anekdot* treats Molotov. He's not actively degraded or mocked; the joke does return him from the political heights to a more crudely material level, but ultimately the humour of this joke comes from the exaggerated vulgarity and the general's naive, nonsensical exclamation. The second example is different again:

> Kalinin received rejuvenation treatment – his genitals were replaced with a dog's and, once he left the hospital, from then on he did everything 'doggy-style' (все производить по собачьи).[104]

The idea of transplanting a dog's genitals to a human and a consequent 'caninisation' of the subject recalls, in reverse, the operation described in Mikhail Bulgakov's novel *Heart of a Dog*, in which a stray dog is transformed into a man.[105] More importantly, the joke similarly reduces Kalinin to the debased status of an animal, but it still doesn't come close to the caustic debasement of Stalin.

The tale of Molotov's sexual liaison does nothing to mock or discomfort him personally and, while Kalinin's canine rejuvenation is certainly a joke at his expense, this is in essence a straightforward, crude imagining designed to ridicule him rather than a character assassination in the style of the Stalin-as-passive-homosexual example. Moreover, the question of power is vital here in two senses: first, in all three *anekdoty* aimed at Stalin, he is not in control of events and ultimately suffers from them, whereas Molotov and Kalinin freely choose to carry out their respective actions: Stalin is deprived of all power, Molotov and Kalinin are not.

Secondly, as Orwell put it, 'the bigger the fall, the bigger the joke[:] it would be better fun to throw a custard pie at a bishop than at a curate'.[106] The pleasurable sense of power gained by the joke-teller in imagining these scenarios is all the greater when mocking Stalin for the simple reason that he had further to fall and the incongruity between his real and imagined positions made these jokes all the funnier.

Carnival as Counterpoint

So what do Kirov's Carnival and all these related forms of humour tell us about contemporaries' engagements with and understandings of their lives in the Soviet 1930s? Carnival and its associated practices are often described as a 'counterpoint' to, and hence separate from, the structures and routines of everyday life.[107] But this separation is misleading: when we look at contemporaries' humour, we can see that

Likhachev was absolutely right to emphasise the constant accessibility of the carnivalesque 'world of laughter'. It didn't require a special occasion for people to stand at just the right angle to see Kirov's 'penis', even if it might be all the funnier to do so when the state was demanding public displays of loyalty or grief.

All the same, if we unpack the term 'counterpoint' a little further, we can understand with much greater nuance not only the relationship between all these carnivalesque practices and the everyday, but also the relationship between contemporary critical humour and the countless official practices dictated by the state.

Although the verb 'to counterpoint' has come to mean 'to emphasise by contrast', in musical composition a counterpoint is a melody (or melodies) played in conjunction with another, and which thereby form a pleasing or notable contrast. In analysing the inversions of Carnival, 'counterpoint' has generally been used in the first sense – to focus on the separateness and contrast of the elements – when in fact the musical sense is far more useful, because it draws our attention to the way a composite whole is produced in the process. The carnivalesque aspects of contemporaries' political humour, which we see particularly vividly in Kirov's Carnival, certainly functioned as counterpoints to official ideology, restrictions and expectations… But for that very reason we must listen to *both* original and counterpoint melodies together, just as Soviet contemporaries had to every day. For them, the 'laughing world' and the official one crosshatched each another, and meaningful patterns – life as they experienced it – emerged from their intersection.

The 'Cult' Problem

Many of the jokes we've examined mock Stalin – not least the vociferous, X-rated attacks on him – and this raises quite a few problems for how we understand the period of his dictatorship. The term 'Cult of Personality' has become synonymous with Stalin's rule, not least due to Nikita Khrushchev's use of the phrase when he denounced Stalin at the Twentieth Party Congress in 1956, initiating a period of 'de-Stalinisation'.

Not unlike Khrushchev, many have, in the tradition of the 'great man' theory of History, sought to explain the Soviet population's quiescence during the tumultuous 1930s by reference to the figure and personality of the *vozhd'* himself. Such analyses propose that the Cult of Stalin had a hypnotic effect on the population and describe its influence as a 'magic spell',[108] or an 'intoxicant',[109] which created a 'blind faith'[110] in the *vozhd'*, hamstringing much potential public outcry or resistance before it had even begun. More recently, these evocative labels have been largely superseded by the term 'political religion', although the underlying assumptions remain unchanged: that people clung to a desperate and usually blind and irrational belief in Big Brother.[111]

But despite the pervasiveness of the Cult in the historiography, close study of the phenomenon remains surprisingly patchy: most conspicuously, there's just one scholarly monograph on the subject, and this focuses only on portraiture and the official production of the Cult, rather than upon its reception.[112] In short, the Cult has often been used as a simplistic 'explanation' for popular quiescence, but has neither been deeply analysed in its own right, nor has the diversity of the Soviet population's contemporary responses to it been explored. But if we do take a look at that variety, the traditional 'explanation' rapidly falls apart.

Saturation

There is no doubt that many Soviet citizens venerated Stalin, but in political humour we can hear many others sharing critical opinions about him and his Cult on a day-to-day basis that rapidly presents us with a very different, more complex image. Let's consider two *anekdoty* which turned up numerous times in the archival sources:

> Stalin summoned a number of economists and told them he wanted to hold a feast for all the people, a feast so great they would revel (пировать) for weeks. He asked the economists how much this would cost, but no one could say. Then one spoke up and said it could be done very cheaply: 'Buy a single bullet and shoot yourself – then everyone will celebrate.'[113]

> Stalin was out swimming, but he began to drown. A *kolkhoznik* who was passing by jumped in and saved him. Stalin started to ask the *kolkhoznik* what he would like as a reward when the latter realised who he had saved. 'Nothing!' he said, 'Just please don't tell anyone I saved you.'[114]

In each *anekdot*, the underlying assumption is that the population at large hates Stalin and would prefer him dead. There's a sense here that Stalin is the principal cause of people's suffering; as another *anekdot* had it, rather elliptically, 'In our country we have such an artist that when he performs, the whole nation weeps'.¹¹⁵ More directly, a Harvard Project respondent recalled a simple pun, altering Stalin's propagated role as Leader and Teacher (*vozhd' i uchitel'*) to Leader and Torturer (*vozhd' i muchitel'*).¹¹⁶ If Stalin was ultimately to blame for their hardships, then citizens could readily imagine that his death would improve their lives.

As this implies, far from being a taboo subject for mockery, or deemed to sit benignly above politics, Stalin was considered and treated in humour as Public Enemy Number One: he was the default object of popular sarcasm, mockery and criticism, and was targeted more often than any other leading figure. As a later Romanian joke described their own dictator's, Ceaușescu's, cult, 'In laughter as in life, he is at the center'.¹¹⁷

In fact, the very saturation of the Stalin Cult became a subject of mockery in its own right. A letter sent to Andrei Zhdanov (Kirov's successor as Leningrad Party boss) makes this point in subtly absurdist fashion, detailing in a long list the ubiquity of Stalin's name by the later 1930s:

> Dear comrade Zhdanov!
> Do you not think that comrade Stalin's name has begun to be very much abused? For example:
>
> Stalin's people's commissar
> Stalin's falcon
> Stalin's pupil
> Stalin's canal
> Stalin's route
> Stalin's pole [sic]
> Stalin's harvest
> Stalin's stint
> Stalin's five-year plan
> Stalin's construction
> Stalin's block of communists and non-party members
> Stalin's Komsomol (it's already being called this)
>
> I could give a hundred other examples, even of little meaning. Everything is Stalin, Stalin, Stalin.¹¹⁸

Although this author went on to encode his message as constructive advice to the leadership, actually warning them of the risk of absurdity such a prevalence of Stalin's name engendered, many others seized on this absurdity directly. For example, a lawyer recalled that, in his workplace in Odesa, on the sign for the toilets someone appended the words 'named after Stalin' (туалет им. Сталина).[119] Less overtly, some Komsomol members in Bashkirskaia oblast' amused themselves by renaming their canteen's dull cabbage broth 'Stalin soup'[120] – an appellation that could sit quite happily alongside the others on the list sent to Zhdanov.

This vein of sarcasm as a response to the overbearing nature of the Cult is neatly summed up in an *anekdot* which recounts how, for an anniversary celebration of Tchaikovsky's work, there was 'a two-hour speech about Comrade Stalin and nothing said at all about Tchaikovsky'.[121] A similar joke described how the centenary of Pushkin's death (1837) would be marked with the erection of a statue which, via several planning revisions, becomes a colossal statue of Stalin holding a small volume of Pushkin's poetry.[122]

More significantly, rather than just mocking the Cult's excesses, by inverting the practice of associating Stalin with every element of life or official policy, he could easily be *blamed* for everything.[123] When the abolition of student grants was announced in October 1940, M.V. Pen'kov blamed Stalin directly, yelling a parody of an official slogan back at the radio announcement in a room of his contemporaries: 'Thank you, Comrade Stalin, for [this] happy life!'[124] Similarly, in Saratov, an unnamed girl was sentenced to five years for being late to work, to which she responded with withering sarcasm, 'Thank you, Comrade Stalin, for a happy childhood', mocking another famous slogan.[125] And, in mid-1940 when the working day was increased from seven to eight hours, Lashina, an accountant in the Northwest shipping fleet, ranted angrily to her colleagues, concluding, in tones of withering scorn, 'Thank you, Comrade Stalin, for stretching out your hand to us, although we have already stretched out our legs,' melding a propagandistic image of Stalin the paternal teacher with a colloquialism meaning 'to kick the bucket'.[126] She was not the only one to respond this way: V.A. Marandzheev, the chief of staff at a musical instrument factory, interjected during a radio broadcast of a lullaby praising Stalin, maintaining the high register of the song for comic effect, 'Hallowed be thy name, Stalin. The workers offered unto Stalin the sacrifice of their 6- and 7-hour working days'.[127]

How can these *anekdoty* and biting one-liners fit with the generally accepted ideas about the Stalin Cult and its importance? Was its influence over people's understanding of and engagements with the regime much less than has so long been claimed? In fact, that Stalin was so often the principal target of mockery doesn't mean that his Cult of Personality was unimportant or unreal. On the contrary, that he so frequently featured in critical humour actually demonstrates how closely he *was* associated with the regime in the minds of the people. But being the symbol and centre of both the Party and the Soviet Union wasn't always a good thing to be when criticism and discontent demanded a ready target.[128]

What it does suggest, however, is that although (as countless historians have argued) the Cult's significance grew disproportionately over the course of the 1930s, many citizens responded to it much as they did to any other official state policy. That is, they received and judged it selectively and critically; it was neither embraced wholesale, nor was it simply dismissed out of hand. Responses depended on changing events, specific policies, and personal experiences. It is in any case rather unrealistic for us to expect to find a static or even a singular opinion of Stalin, even in the mind of a particular individual; people are simply too complex and contradictory for that. Yet when we ask questions about 'popular opinion' we usually want to find a nice, clear answer rather than a mixed one, which is precisely what makes a continuing emphasis on the explanatory power of the Stalin Cult so appealing. But the Stalin Cult cannot simply 'explain' popular opinon to us, even if contemporaries frequently and pointedly used it to help explain their difficult lives to themselves.

First Among Many

When we look at the Stalin Cult, there's certainly a case for what Jan Plamper has called a 'tsarist carryover'[129] in the ways ordinary people related to Stalin – that is, a popular belief that the tsar was fundamentally good and on the people's side, despite all evidence to the contrary. In practice, this 'carryover' was clearly not enough to insulate Stalin from mockery and criticism, but this should hardly surprise us, given the (often obscene) mockery the last Romanovs faced, as Boris Kolonitskii has explored.[130] In short, while there were certainly continuities in how the Russo-Soviet population related to Power across the Revolutionary divide, this by no means equates to a slavish and uncritical adoration and obedience.[131] To understand 1930s receptions of the Stalin Cult, it's far more fruitful to examine the *contemporary* context in which it took shape.

Most importantly, although Stalin's Cult of Personality was the most extreme example, in the 1930s it was far from unique. Other *vozhdi*, including Molotov, Voroshilov, Zhdanov and Kirov, each had their own, smaller cults. Moreover, so did Stakhanovites (award-winning workers), polar explorers, film stars, authors, aviators, and local Party bosses.[132] David Brandenberger goes so far as to identify a 'heroic pantheon' established in this decade, which stood in marked contrast to the 1920s emphasis on collective, mass identities.[133] In other words, official fêting of individuals and their achievements was the norm in the 1930s, up until the disruption of the mass repressions (1937-8) and a consequent reduction in emphasis on individual personalities, *including* a reduction in the saturation levels of the Stalin Cult.[134]

In this context, the Stalin Cult shouldn't be seen as intrinsically exceptional or above normal politics at all, and it certainly wasn't received as such by the population. Yet there *was* one Cult of Personality which appears to have risen above politics in this decade, but although constructed on regime propaganda which sought to draw legitimacy from it, ordinary citizens often used this Cult as a talisman with which to criticise and mock Soviet power and Stalin in particular. This was the Cult of Lenin.

As Lenin's successor, Stalin was in contemporary jokes frequently and unfavourably compared to the late Vladimir Il'ich. In part, comparison was incited by the regime's own propaganda, which elevated Lenin to mythical status, branded Stalin 'the Lenin of today', and placed the two of them together in visual representations of such quantity that you might reasonably wonder if Lenin ever had a moment to himself without Stalin loitering nearby. Yet many people's lived experience, combined no doubt with a degree of rose-tinted hindsight, did not permit such a smooth narrative continuity from Lenin to Stalin: the transition was not called 'The Great Break' for nothing. The rapid, ruthless industrialisation campaigns which dominated the 1930s, the murderous famines created by collectivisation and forcible grain requisition, and the protracted housing shortages caused by mass inward migration to the cities, all meant that the brief period of the New Economic Policy (1921-8), closely associated with Lenin, came to be remembered with (disproportionate) affection as a fundamentally better time.[135]

Needless to say, there are no absolutes to be found when examining folk culture or popular opinion, and Lenin was sometimes lampooned in *anekdoty* during these years and, as we saw earlier in this chapter, subjected to casual, symbolic disrespect. Nevertheless, overwhelmingly he turns up in the cast of characters as the 'good guy', the voice of wisdom, or as betrayed by his successors. This was all directly related to the context of Stalin's rule, too, for in the 1920s Lenin was not represented in *anekdoty* nearly so positively and, after Stalin's death, he took a backseat in the genre until he reappeared once again in the 1970s.[136]

During the 1930s, though, Lenin's importance was accepted and even venerated, as contemporary satirical observations suggest: a seventh-grade schoolgirl summed this up in her History class, saying that 'Stalin is not the *vozhd'*, the *vozhd'* was Lenin. Stalin was just set up as furniture'.[137] Another seventh-grader, one Irina Shapovalova who attended a school in Bashtanskii raion, Ukraine, made a habit of asking pointed and uncomfortable questions in her History classes, including 'Why wasn't Stalin a leader when Lenin was around?', and 'How come when Lenin was ruling mistakes weren't made, but under Stalin there's constant mistakes?'[138] In expressing such critical attitudes at such a tender age, we can safely assume that if Soviet officials later came knocking on these girls' doors, it wasn't to recruit them as official regime historians.

Stalin's status as uninspired placeholder was similarly emphasised by a play on words relating to the shared name of the two leaders' wives, Nadezhda, which literally means 'hope'. Stalin's wife killed herself in 1934 (knowledge about which circulated as rumours across the population), prompting an *anekdot* that got passed around at the Viazemskii Pedagogical Technical College: 'Lenin had hope, and she remains, but Stalin has no hope'.[139]

In another *anekdot*, which appears in a variety of different sources, Stalin's arbitrariness and disregard for Lenin's legacy is likewise expressed with reference to Nadezhda Krupskaia:

Stalin summons Krupskaia: 'So you think you can get away with anything just because you're Lenin's widow? Well, tomorrow I'll declare that Artiukhina is Lenin's widow!'[140]

In this joke, filed away in the literature and language professor Konstantin Megrelidze's *anekdot* collection, Stalin picks Aleksandra Vasil'evna Artiukhina (a Party member since 1910 and the last head of the *Zhenotdel*, the Party's 'Women's Section') to take on the role of 'Lenin's widow', but this varies in other tellings. Klaus Mehnert, a Moscow-born German political scientist, heard it as just 'somebody else', while L.P. Nikolaev, an anatomist and anthropologist, recorded it in his diary as 'Ordzhonikidze's mother-in-law'.[141] In any telling, the point remained that Stalin was quite happy to arbitrarily break with Lenin's legacy and even with reality itself.

The relationship which many contemporaries felt they had to the first two Soviet leaders is most clearly imagined in political humour when they're placed side-by-side, as these final examples illustrate. This short *chastushka* was sung in a school in the Oktiabr'skii raion of Ukraine:

Ленин Ленин дорогой,	Lenin dear, Lenin dear,
Возьми Сталина с собой,	Come take Stalin to you near,

> Сталин кушает и пьет,　　　　　　Stalin eats and Stalin drinks,
> А рабочим не дает.　　　　　　　But to the workers nothing
> 　　　　　　　　　　　　　　　　gives.[142]

The mere existence of *chastushki* like this one could itself be cited as 'evidence' of the damaging effects of Stalin's new policies – hence a peasant from L'govskii okrug wrote to Molotov in December 1930 to note pointedly that 'it's not for nothing that there's a new *chastushka*', and, on that basis, demanded that regime policy be changed.[143] Finally, the following *anekdot* was told amongst friends who worked at a catering trust (буфетный трест):

> The ghost of Lenin visits Stalin. 'How're things?' he asks. 'Everything's fine. The people are with me,' replies Stalin. 'If you carry out the Second Five-Year Plan, they will soon be with *me*,' Lenin replies.[144]

Lenin appears in *anekdoty* like these as an authority figure who removes or reprimands Stalin for his shortcomings, or to whom ordinary people call for help. These examples all come from the mid-1930s, contradicting the historian Nina Tumarkin's suggestion that from 1931 onwards the Lenin cult and the 'nostalgia' it could evoke faded next to the bright lights shone upon Stalin.[145] In official propaganda, Lenin and a eulogised memory of him continued to provide foundation stones for Stalin's Cult; but those stones could simultaneously provide a platform from which citizens could throw criticism and mockery.

***

Just as their forebears had done in medieval Rus' and more recently under the last tsars, ordinary people found ways to carve out spaces for their alternative views within the restrictions of the Soviet regime through laughter, inversions, the assertion of folk wisdom, and the use of bodily, obscene imagery. In the practices of silent subversion we see how these elements could exist quietly but persistently, woven into the fabric of daily life. In Kirov's Carnival, by contrast, we see how they could also spill over into official state events and mix with the regime's own tropes and values. Soviet leaders, from Stalin downwards, were made targets for the frustrated barbs of *anekdoty* and other mockery, but, just as the Lenin Cult could serve to critique Stalin, excursions into the 'laughing world' served principally to counterpoint the official world and its leaders, rather than to reject them outright.

Notes

1. RGASPI, f.17, op.120, d.176, l.135 (February 1935).
2. HPSSS 66/A/6, pp.7-8 (seq.73-4).
3. RGASPI, f.M-1, op.23, d.1106, l.45 (February 1935).
4. Diego Gambetta, *Codes of the Underworld: How Criminals Communicate* (Princeton, NJ, 2011), 154.
5. GARF, f.9425, op.1, d.6, ll.176-7, cited in Gábor T. Rittersporn, 'Perevernutyi mir sovetskogo smekha', I.V. Narskii et al (eds.), *Ot velikogo do smeshnogo... Instrumentalizatsiia smekha v rossiiskoi istorii XX veka* (Cheliabinsk, 2013), 179.
6. Cited in Lynne Viola, *Peasant Rebels under Stalin: Collectivization and the Culture of Peasant Resistance* (Oxford, 1996), 43.
7. HPSSS 451/(NY)1053/A/31, p.11.
8. TsGAIPD, f.24, op.2v, d.2059, l.201.
9. Fitzpatrick cites similar examples ('Kirov*gad* and Stalin*gad*') in *Everyday Stalinism*, 184.
10. HDA SBU, f.6, d.31144FP, ll.1, 15-6, 18, 50 (September 1937).
11. RGASPI, f.M-1, op.23, d.1102, l.126 (May 1935).
12. HPSSS 116/A/9, p.18.
13. HPSSS 62/A/5, pp.24-5.
14. TsGAIPD, f.24, op.2v, d.1373, l.5 (October-November 1935).
15. RGASPI, f.M-1, op.23, d.1102, l.131 (January-May 1935).
16. HPSSS 133/A/10, pp.15-6.
17. Jan Plamper, 'Abolishing Ambiguity: Soviet Censorship Practices in the 1930s', *Russian Review*, 60.4 (2001), 534-6.
18. Plamper, 'Abolishing Ambiguity', 537.
19. GARF, f.8131, op.31, d.7585, l.15 (1936-7). Also cf. HPSSS 64/A/6, p.68. '*Muzhik*' means both a peasant and, more generally a 'man' or 'fellow', with connotations of good character.
20. Lyons, *Modern Moscow*, 270.
21. GARF, f.8131, op.31, d.85131, l.10 (1936). The character is Jewish, it seems, because stereotypically Jews had difficulty pronouncing the Russian 'r'. Hence a request to be connected '*v tsirk*' (to the circus) could be misheard as '*VTsIK*' (the All-Russian Central Executive Committee). The question of antisemitism and the role of the 'Jew' character in these jokes is discussed at length in Chapter 3.
22. Paraphrased from Lyons, *Modern Moscow*, 266.
23. Paraphrased from several examples: GARF, f.8131, op.31, d.16218, l.17 (1937); d.18921, l.12 (1934-7); d.43506, l.16 (1937-40); d.82045, l.9 (1936); d.85221, l.9 (1930-35); also cf. Mel'nichenko, *Sovetskii anekdot*, 328.
24. GARF, f.8131, op.31, d.85221, l.12 (1930-35). This also carries some connotation of a nickname given to weak, state-produced vodka in the 1930s, 'Rykovka' (cf. N.B. Lebina, *Povsednevnaia zhizn' sovetskogo goroda 1920-1930 gody* (St Petersburg, 1999), 33; Lebina notes a couple of *anekdoty* related to 'Rykovka', although she has no sources for these). However, given that the same Myshakin told both the 'glasses' joke and this '*Rykovochki*' variant, he was most likely riffing on the vodka brand *and* the original 'glasses' joke.
25. I.I. Shitts, *Dnevnik "Velikogo pereloma" (mart 1928–avgust 1931)* (Paris, 1991), 90-91 (1929).
26. Letters to the leadership had to navigate a path between blaming local authorities and the principal leaders themselves: see Alexander Livshin, 'Bridging the Gap:

Government-Society Dialogue via Letters', *Slavonic and East European Review*, 91.1 (2013), 70-76.

27 cf. D.S. Likhachev, A.M. Panchenko & N.V. Ponyrko, *Smekh v drevnei Rusi* (Leningrad, 1984), 4-5.
28 Rolf, *Soviet Mass Festivals*, 3.
29 Rolf, *Soviet Mass Festivals*, 1.
30 Alexei Yurchak, 'The Cynical Reason of Late Socialism: Power, Pretense, and the *Anekdot*', *Public Culture*, 9 (1997), 162-5.
31 Themes explored in Petrone, *Life has Become More Joyous* and Rolf, *Soviet Mass Festivals*.
32 'Crosshatching' is a term I explain in the Introduction, which describes not only the mixing of official and popular perspectives, but also how their mutual interactions generated new, idiosyncratic understandings of Soviet life.
33 A description for the people and regions and states of the 'Kievan Rus'' (ninth-thirteenth centuries), incorporating parts of modern-day Belarus, Ukraine, and western Russia.
34 D.S. Likhachev, 'Smekh kak mirovozzrenie', in *Istoricheskaia poetika russkoi literatury. Smekh kak mirovozzrenie i drugie raboty* (St Petersburg, 1997), 342, 344-5; Likhachev, Panchenko & Ponyrko, *Smekh v Drevnei Rusi*. My thanks to Steve Smith for discussing this scholarship with me.
35 Matthew Lenoe, *The Kirov Murder and Soviet Society* (New Haven, CT, 2010), Ch.12.
36 TsGAIPD, f.24, op.5, d.2288, l.105 (December 1934).
37 RGASPI, f.17, op.120, d.174, l.18 (December 1934).
38 TsGAIPD, f.24, op.5, d.2288, l.9 (December 1934). Referring to the principal rationing categories introduced by the regime in 1929 and defined by one's social origin and occupation, workers, of course, being the best-provisioned (cf. Elena Osokina, *Ierarkhiia potrebleniia: O zhizni liudei v usloviiakh stalinskogo snabzheniia 1928-1935 gg.* (Moscow, 1993), Ch.1 and throughout).
39 TsGAIPD, f.24, op.2v, d.2659, l.100 (February 1937). Kuibyshev had died in 1935.
40 GARF, f.8131, op.31, d.80433, l.6 (February 1937).
41 Quoted in Lesley Ann Rimmel, *The Kirov Murder and Soviet Society: Propaganda and Popular Opinion in Leningrad, 1934-1935*, PhD Thesis, University of Pennsylvania (1995), 114. Translation Rimmel's.
42 TsGAIPD, f.24, op.5, d.2288, l.3.
43 TsGAIPD, f.24, op.5, d.2288, l.46.
44 RGASPI, f.M-1, op.23, d.1102, l.130 (May 1935).
45 GARF, f.8131, op.31, d.43506, l.18 (no later than 1940).
46 RGASPI, f.17, op.120, d.176, l.27 (February 1935).
47 RGASPI, f.17, op.120, d.174, l.48 (Tajikistan, April 1935); d.175, l.50 (Cherepanovskii raion, March 1935); d.176, l.176 (Povorino and Novokhopersk, March 1935); f.M-1, op.23, l.155 (Khislavinskii raion, April 1935); d.1106, l.8 (?Moscow, March 1935); TsGAIPD, f.25, op.5, d.43, l.5 (Leningrad, December 1934); f.K598, op.1, d.5387, l.93 (Leningrad, 1935). Thanks to Sarah Davies for this final reference.
48 RGASPI, f.M-1, op.23, d,1102, l.130 (Lopatino, May 1935); also cf. TsGAIPD, f.24, op.5, d.2288, l.105 (Leningrad, 2 December 1934).
49 TsGAIPD, f.25, op.5, d.45, l.6 (Leningrad, December 1934).
50 Various similar views are noted in Sarah Davies, '"Us Against Them": Social Identity in Soviet Russia, 1934-41', *Russian Review*, 56.1 (1997), 84-8.
51 That is, the concept of expropriator is visible here, although words like 'bourgeois' and '*burzhui*' do not appear in these sources, in contrast to the importance of those terms around the 1917 Revolution. cf. Orlando Figes & Boris Kolonitskii,

Interpreting the Russian Revolution: The Language and Symbols of 1917 (New Haven, CT, 1999), Ch.6.
52　Likhachev, 'Smekh', 346.
53　RGASPI, f.M-1, op.23, d.1105, l.68 (December 1934).
54　TsGAIPD, f.24, op.5, d.2288, l.6 (December 1934).
55　TsGAIPD, f.25, op.5, d.47, l.162; also cf. f.24, op.5, d.2288, l.110 (December 1934). Some kind of 'brains' were on the menu that day.
56　TsGAIPD, f.25, op.5, d.52, l.89 (December 1934).
57　TsGAIPD, f.24, op.5, d.2291, l.39 (December 1934).
58　HDA SBU, f.16, op.32, d.54, l.256 (1939). The village is described as 'село, вербской волости', which is probably a misspelling of 'Вепсской волости', if this is indeed a Karelian village as stated in the report.
59　Bakhtin, *Rabelais*, 325. This trope is certainly not confined to Europe, either: e.g. Scott, *Weapons of the Weak*, 186-8.
60　TsGAIPD, f.24, op.5, d.2291, l.1 (December 1934).
61　RGASPI, f.M-1, op.23, d.1102, l.117 (May 1935).
62　TsGAIPD, f.25, op.5, d.45, l.108 (December 1934).
63　TsGAIPD f.24, op.5, d.2291, l.123 (December 1934).
64　RGASPI, f.M-1, op.23, d.1184, l.113 (September 1936).
65　GARF, f.8131, op.31, d.84861, l.5 (1937).
66　Bakhtin, *Rabelais*, 380.
67　Likhachev, '*Smekh*', 351; Likhachev, Panchenko & Ponyrko, *Smekh*, 3.
68　Bakhtin, *Rabelais*, Chs. 5&6.
69　e.g. TsGAIPD, f.25, op.5, d.45, ll.7, 103; d.46, l.3; d.47, ll.29, 31, 62, 175; d.49, l.74; d.52, l.75; d.53, ll.81-2; d.54, l.54 (all December 1934).
70　Bakhtin, *Rabelais*, Ch.2, esp. p.148; idem, *Dialogic Imagination*, 196-8.
71　TsGAIPD, f.24, op.5, d.2288, ll.97, 129.
72　TsGAIPD, f.24, op.5, d.2291, l.48.
73　TsGAIPD, f.24, op.5, d.2288, l.97.
74　TsGAIPD, f.24, op.5, d.2288, l.129.
75　HDA SBU, f.16, op.28, d.12, l.63 (1935).
76　TsGAIPD, f.25, op.5, d.45, l.83 (December 1934).
77　TsGAIPD, f.25, op.5, d.45, l.102 (December 1934).
78　TsGAIPD, f.24, op.5, d.2288, l.98.
79　TsGAIPD, f.25, op.5, d.54, l.9 (December 1934). Also cf. f.24, op.5, d.2291, l.19. On two neighbouring kolkhozy, youths likewise sought to have a dance in place of the mourning meeting: TsGAIPD, f.24, op.5, d.2289, l.126.
80　TsGAIPD, f.24, op.5, d.2290, l.29(ob).
81　TsGAIPD, f.24, op.5, d.2291, ll.100-3. (The report notes he used bad language which was then censored; I am translating from: 'Нам то … хоть убейте всех дьяволов наших вождей, лишь бы была водка'.)
82　cf. Rolf, *Soviet Mass Festivals*, 125-6.
83　Smith, 'Social Meanings of Swearing', 197-8.
84　See the foreword of N. Bogomolov (ed.), *Anti-mir russkoi kul'tury. Iazyk. Fol'klor. Literatura.* (Moscow, 1996).
85　B. Uspenskii, '"Zavetnye skazki" A.N. Afanas'eva', Bogomolov (ed.), *Anti-mir*, 143.
86　A.N. Afanas'ev, *Russkie zavetnye skazki* (St Petersburg, 1994 [Geneva, 1872]), foreword. Also cf. Smith, 'Social Meanings of Swearing'.
87　cf. Smith, 'Social Meanings of Swearing', 180.
88　Lyons, *Modern Moscow*, 261.
89　cf. Lenoe, *The Kirov Murder*, Ch.12.

90 GARF, f.8131, op.31, d.7031 (1936); also cf. HPSSS 60/A/5, p.33; 62/A/5, p.2; and a variation in which everyone in the Kremlin gets body lice: Lyons, *Modern Moscow*, 269.
91 GARF, f.8131, op.31, d.85228, l.2(ob) (1937).
92 Arkhipova & Mel'nichenko, *Anekdoty*, 147-51, 296-9; GARF, f.8131, op.31, d.97733, l.8 (1936); also cf. Mel'nichenko, *Sovetskii anekdot*, 474-5.
93 Chamberlin, *Russia's Iron Age*, 329; HPSSS, 102/A/8, p.64.
94 GARF, f.8131, op.31, d.85229, l.6 (1937).
95 GARF, f.5446, op.18a, d.849, l.3 (date of telling unclear; report dated 26 June 1936); many thanks to Gábor Rittersporn for this reference. On the legislation, cf. Dan Healey, *Homosexual Desire in Revolutionary Russia* (Chicago, IL, 2001), 183-96.
96 Dan Healey, 'The Disappearance of the Russian Queen, or How the Soviet Closet was Born', Barbara Evans Clements, Rebecca Friedman & Dan Healey (eds.), *Russian Masculinities in History and Culture* (Houndmills, 2002), 168, n.20.
97 In another case, one L.V. Fadeev liked referring to Stalin as *baba*, a rather derogatory word usually reserved for women, translating roughly as 'wifey' or 'broad'. He tried to excuse this as an accidental mistranslation from his native Tatar (GARF, f.8131, op.31, d.60588, l.43 (1932-4)).
98 Healey, *Homosexual Desire*; idem, 'The Disappearance', 152-66.
99 Dan Healey, 'Forging Gulag Sexualities: Penal Homosexuality and the Reform of the Gulag after Stalin', conference paper delivered at the British Association for Slavonic and East European Studies Conference, April 2014, 9-10. My thanks to Dan for sharing his paper with me.
100 This is an unusual representation of Kalinin, who is more often portrayed in popular humour as a doddering old man who accidentally finds himself in embarrassing situations (cf. for e.g. Brandenberger, *Political Humor*, 148-50). Perhaps, therefore, his domination of Stalin could be seen as even more derogatory to the latter, given the normally-assumed weakness of Kalinin.
101 GARF, f.8131, op.31, d.43623, l.7 (March 1940).
102 Christie Davies, *Jokes and Targets* (Bloomingtom, IN, 2011), Ch.4.
103 GARF, f.8131, op.31, d.82045, l.10 (1936-7). Particular thanks to David Brandenberger for help translating this one.
104 GARF, f.8131, op.31, d.82045, l.9 (1936-7); also cf. HPSSS 110/A/8, pp.24-5.
105 Mikhail Bulgakov, *The Heart of a Dog*, trans. Michael Glenny (London, 2005). Bulgakov's 1925 novel was not published in the USSR until 1987 (it was published abroad in 1968), but experiments involving genital transplants and 'rejuvenation' treatments of this kind were quite widely publicised during the 1920s, popular knowledge of which most likely informed this joke. (cf. Frances Lee Bernstein, *The Dictatorship of Sex: Lifestyle Advice for the Soviet Masses* (DeKalb, IL, 2011), Ch.2.)
106 George Orwell, 'Funny but not Vulgar', *The Collected Essays, Journalism and Letters of George Orwell*, Vol. III: *As I Please, 1943-45*, ed. Sonia Orwell & Ian Angus (London, 1968), 284.
107 As Rolf summarises, *Soviet Mass Festivals*, 6.
108 e.g. Hannah Arendt, who uses it in discussion of both Stalin and Hitler's personality cults: *Origins of Totalitarianism*, 305, n.1; Adam B. Ulam likewise wrote that Stalin 'cast a veritable spell over the Soviet people', *Stalin: The Man and his Era* (London, 1989), xxiii; Robert Vincent Daniels also recently described Khrushchev as breaking 'the magic spell' with his 1956 speech, *The Rise and Fall of Communism in Russia* (New Haven, CT, 2007), 208; writing during Perestroika, historian Natan Eidelman combined two such concepts to explain Stalin's rule as a 'hypnotic spell',

'Under Stalin's Spell', *Moscow News*, 30 (1988), 2.
109 E.A. Rees, 'Leader Cults: Varieties, Preconditions and Functions', Balázs Apor et al. (eds.), *The Leader Cult in Communist Dictatorships: Stalin and the Eastern Bloc* (Houndmills, 2004), 12.
110 Roy Medvedev, *Let History Judge: The Origins and Consequences of Stalinism*, revised & expanded edition, trans. George Shriver (Oxford, 1989), 617, 620; Dmitri Volkogonov, *Stalin: Triumph and Tragedy*, trans. Harold Shukman (London, 2000), xxiv, also 192. See also: Kh. Kobo (ed.), *Osmyslit' kul't Stalina* (Moscow, 1989), 5-6.
111 For a work of synthesis which exemplifies this approach, see Michael Burleigh, *Sacred Causes: Religion and Politics from the European Dictators to Al Qaeda* (London, 2006), esp. 71-94. On the Stalin cult as political religion in particular, see Lebina, *Povsednevnaia zhizn'*, Ch.2, §2, esp. p.157. See also the collection, Roger Griffin (ed.), *Fascism, Totalitarianism and Political Religion* (London, 2005); Nicola Hille, 'Der Führerkult im Bild. Die Darstellung von Hitler, Stalin und Mussolini in der politischen Sichtagitation der 1920er bis 1940er Jahre', Benno Ennker & Heidi Hein-Kircher (eds.), *Der Führer im Europa des 20. Jahrhunderts* (Marburg, 2010). For an extreme example of taking the comparison between Stalinism/Communism and religion beyond its limits, see Arthur Jay Klinghoffer, *Red Apocalypse: The Religious Evolution of Soviet Communism* (Lanham, MD, 1996).
112 Jan Plamper, *The Stalin Cult: A Study in the Alchemy of Power* (New Haven, CT, 2012).
113 There are many versions of this joke, some involving the purchase of a rope for Stalin to hang himself with instead; I present a generic version based principally on GARF, f.8131, op.31, d.49998, l.21 (1937). See also: *ibid.*, d.40412 (duplicated *delo* number, see the case for Мужило) (1935-40); d.85229, ll.5-6 (1937); d.91956, ll.8-9 (1934); HDA SBU, f.6, d.33754FP, l.88 (1936-7); RGASPI, f.M-1, op.23, d.1107, l.61 (1935); f.17, op.120, d.176, l.115 (1935); HPSSS 1/A/1, p.26. See also Mel'nichenko, *Sovetskii anekdot*, 228-9.
114 I present a generic version based primarily on GARF, f.8131, op.31, d.52823, l.7 (1934); see also *ibid.*, d.43804, ll.12-13 (1937); d.83157, l.23 (1940-41); d.99140, l.3 (1935); HPSSS 2/A/1, p.38; 25/A/3, p.67; 29/A/3, p.88; 54/A/5, p.28; 60/A/5, p.33; 66/A/6, p.67; 149/A/12, pp.94-5; 639/A/30, p.39; Chamberlin, *Russia's Iron Age*, 330. See also Arkhipova & Mel'nichenko, *Anekdoty*, 245-7.
115 GARF, f.8131, op.31, d.88415, l.12 (1937); d.86405, l.4 (1941).
116 HPSSS 7/A/1, p.38.
117 Robert Cochran, '"What Courage!": Romanian "Our Leader" Jokes', *The Journal of American Folklore*, 102.405 (1989), 261.
118 Letter to Zhdanov, quoted in Davies, *Popular Opinion*, 174 (July 1938).
119 HPSSS 149/A/12, p.71 (specific dating unclear; the respondent was stationed in Odesa between 1932-41).
120 RGASPI, f.M-1, op.23, d.1102, ll.115-6 (May 1935).
121 GARF, f.8131, op.31, d.68720 (1940).
122 It is very likely that this joke was told in 1937 as a direct response to the celebration. Mel'nichenko, *Sovetskii anekdot*, 757-9. A still more extreme version ends with a statue of Stalin reading his own works. Sometimes the anniversary is Shevchenko's, most likely reflecting where and by whom the *anekdot* was told, Pushkin being Russia's national poet, and Shevchenko Ukraine's.
123 On the official practice, see Jeffrey Brooks, *Thank You, Comrade Stalin! Soviet Public Culture from Revolution to Cold War* (Princeton, NJ, 2001), Ch.4.
124 GARF, f.8131, op.31, d.43506, l.22 (3 October 1940).

[125] GARF, f.8131, op.31, d.76432, l.1 (Dating unclear, but most likely from between mid-1940 and mid-1941, after the passing of the Labour Law which made it an offence to be late to work (on which, see Chapter 2)).

[126] TsGAIPD, f.24, op.2v, d.4306, l.193 (July 1940).

[127] TsGAIPD, f.24, op.2v, d.4312, l.24 (July 1940). ('Да святится имя твое СТАЛИН. Рабочие принесли жертву Сталину свой 6 и 7-ми часовой рабочий день.')

[128] For the peasantry's extremely negative attitudes towards Stalin in the 1930s, see Sheila Fitzpatrick, *Stalin's Peasants: Resistance and Survival in the Russian Village After Collectivization* (New York, 1994), 287-96.

[129] Jan Plamper, 'Introduction: Modern Personality Cults', Jan Plamper & Klaus Heller (eds.), *Personality Cults in Stalinism / Personenkulte im Stalinismus* (Göttingen, 2004), 20. Also cf. Nina Tumarkin, *Lenin Lives! The Lenin Cult in Soviet Russia* (Cambridge, MA, 1983), Ch.1.

[130] Boris Kolonitskii, '*Tragicheskaia erotika*': *Obrazy imperatorskoi sem'i v gody pervoi mirovoi voiny* (Moscow, 2010).

[131] cf. Jonathan Waterlow, 'Speaking More than Bolshevik: Humour, Subjectivity, and Crosshatching in Stalin's 1930s', Matthias Neumann & Andy Willimott (eds.), *Rethinking the Russian Revolution as Historical Divide* (Abingdon, 2017).

[132] Davies, *Popular Opinion*, 153-4; idem, 'The "Cult" of the Vozhd': Representations in Letters, 1934-1941', *Russian History*, 24.1-2 (1997), 133-4; Fitzpatrick, *Everyday Stalinism*, 30, 71-5; Oksana Bulgakowa, 'Der erste sowjetische Filmstar', Plamper & Heller (eds.), *Personality Cults*, esp. 375-86; Plamper, 'Introduction', *ibid*., 18.

[133] David Brandenberger, *Propaganda State in Crisis: Soviet Ideology, Indoctrination, and Terror under Stalin, 1927-1941* (New Haven, CT, 2011), 180. On the creation of this 'pantheon', see Ch.4.

[134] Davies, *Popular Opinion*, 152; idem, 'The "Cult" of the Vozhd", 133-4; Malte Rolf, 'The Leader's Many Bodies: Leader Cults and Mass Festivals in Voronezh, Novosibirsk and Kemerovo in the 1930s', Plamper & Heller (eds.), *Personality Cults*, 205.

[135] Almost every Harvard Project respondent held such a view of the NEP. For example, HPSSS 4/A/1, p.23; 8/A/1, pp.4, 21, 29; 18/A/2, p.45; 25/A/3, p.49; 30/A/4, pp.29-30; 32/A/4, p.38; 33/A/4, p.30; 80/A/6, p.9; 98/A/7, p.32; 104/A/8, p.21; 110/A/8, p.83; 639/A/30, p.48.

[136] See Mel'nichenko, *Sovetskii anekdot*. My thanks to Misha for discussing this changing representation of Lenin with me.

[137] RGASPI, f.M-1, op.23, d.1102, l.8 (1935). ('…Сталина поставили для мебели.')

[138] HDA SBU, f.16, op.28, d.12, ll.53-4 (1935).

[139] RGASPI, f.M-1, op.23, d.1102, l.167 (1935). Nadezhda Krupskaia lived until 1939.

[140] GARF, f.8131, op.31, d.64008, l.9 (no later than 1940).

[141] Klaus Mehnert, *The Anatomy of Soviet Man*, trans. Maurice Rosenbaum (London, 1961 [1958]); Lev Petrovich Nikolaev, diary entry for 25 January 1937 at <www.prozhito.org>. Also cf. Mel'nichenko, *Sovetskii anekdot*, 203-4.

[142] HDA SBU, f.16, op.28, d.12, l.52 (1935); TsDAHOU, f.1, op.20, d.6642, l.26 (1935).

[143] Quoted in A.Ia. Livshin, I.B. Orlov & O.V. Khlevniuk (eds.), *Pis'ma vo vlast', 1928-1939: Zaiavleniia, zhaloby, donosy, pis'ma v gosudarstvennye struktury i sovetskim vozhdiam* (Moscow, 2002), 144.

[144] GARF, f.8131, op.31, d.99140, l.3 (1935). Only a summary of the joke appears in this file, but it survives in largely consistent versions elsewhere: Lyons, *Modern Moscow*, 272; Mel'nichenko, *Sovetskii anekdot*, 216-7. Also cf. TsGAIPD, f.24, op.5, d.2288, l.9 (1934).

[145] Tumarkin, *Lenin Lives!*, 251-3.

CHAPTER 2

PLANS AND PUNCHLINES:
'THE ANEKDOTY ALWAYS SAVED US'

If ordinary people created Kirov's Carnival as a counterpoint to the official mourning ceremonials for the fallen leader, they could always turn to that same 'laughing world' when dealing with their experience of all the other policies and campaigns affecting them from day to day. There was a particular need for this in the 1930s, a decade like no other. The revolutionaries' dream of grasping the levers of power had become reality and they seized them with gusto. As Stalin and his supporters rose to the top of the heap at the end of the 1920s, they chose to shunt the revolutionary programme into 'full steam ahead', unleashing unprecedented waves of creation and destruction, of progress and deterioration, of excitement and despair.

    Perhaps the only parallel we could draw to this comprehensive, state-orchestrated lurch into modernisation in order to 'catch up' with the world's most advanced industrial powers would be the stunning transformation of Japan after the Meiji Restoration in 1868. There, too, disturbing interactions with external powers prompted a headlong rush to modernise before, the leaders feared, they became an easy victim of the imperialist West. As in the Soviet Union, Japan's rulers initiated the close study of West European technology, bureaucracies, and expertise, as well as inviting advisors and skilled engineers to work with and train a new generation of native experts. In both countries this would also involve destroying elements of traditional culture in service to new ideals but also, ultimately, to the centralisation of power in what were both, despite their very different sizes, traditionally fragmented societies. In fact, the modernisation of Japan would itself provide some of the impetus for Russia and then the USSR to modernise when, in 1905, Japan obliterated the Russian Navy and announced its presence as a major player on the world stage.

Yet, remarkable as it was, the transformation of Japan took place over some forty years; Stalin wanted change delivered in a quarter of the time. The Soviet state would mercilessly pursue this extraordinary goal across the 1930s, and in this chapter I trace the (often bitterly) humorous critical responses of ordinary people to the most significant policies the state implemented.

By proceeding in a roughly chronological order we find hints both of a growing awareness among joke-tellers that they were putting their necks on the line by speaking out in public places, but also of an increasingly bleak outlook, even as they cracked their jokes. Given that Stalin's 1930s are so closely associated with repression and mass arrests, it might come as a surprise to learn that contemporaries were telling jokes at all. In fact, joking and laughter were indispensable responses to the catastrophic human costs of the forced industrialisation drive, the violent collectivisation of agriculture, and even to the repressions of 1937-8. People did not live in paralysed fear during those years, despite what the famous 'Great Terror' label implies, and the jokes many told allow us to move several steps closer to understanding how they interpreted, and on some level dealt with, the hardships, instability, and their fears during the decade.

Due to the creative, reactive nature of citizens' responses, every policy or event could foster a style, tone, or degree of anger unique to each. This chapter explores these key points of friction over the decade, but before we begin, it's important to appreciate how basic, immediate everyday frustrations could eclipse seemingly grander concerns, making all the regime's ideological imperatives laughable by comparison.

Everyday Priorities

Much to the chagrin of Party officials, reports on 'the mood the people' or 'the workers' of a particular institution frequently highlighted that, for most people, the mundane and practical always took precedence over the bright lights of regime ideology. The reports often ranked the most popular concerns raised by workers in a particular factory shop, and these were invariably taken up with questions about shortages – of food, accommodation, of clothing, and more. In Leningrad's Kirov Factory, mere days after Kirov himself had been murdered, calls to have a new shower installed still featured several places above any mention of increasing 'class vigilance'![1]

The very incongruity of bringing propaganda and the everyday together made for comic results. Take, for example, the persistence with which jokes and sarcastic remarks included some reference to the widespread shortages of clothing, particularly of shoes and boots. The jokes not only highlighted the problem, but used it symbolically to counter or reject both regime propaganda about material abundance in general, and onerous demands made of individuals at particular moments.

The more general criticism came in sardonic remarks like that made by one D.I. Pavlov, a technician at a locomotive depot in Riazan', north of Moscow, who pointed at his tattered boots and joked, echoing the register of official rhetoric, 'Look, this is how we have to proceed in this life'.[2] This is hardly sidesplitting, but his colleagues said it was funny when questioned by the authorities; he was mocking the grandeur of the promised future in contrast to the battered vagabonds who were supposed to populate it. A certain S.I. Larin was rather blunter in his description of life on the kolkhoz: '[The *kolkhozniki*] go about the village naked, bare arses shining'.[3]

Kirov's Carnival also included some of these pointed, bitter comments about material conditions. Gener, a worker at the Proletarskii Factory in Leningrad, hadn't bothered to attend the public demonstration of grief and was questioned by his boss regarding his absence. Gener replied flippantly, 'Well, did you give me boots for it? I have only one pair, both for work and for everything else'.[4] Although the humour of his riposte lay in the incongruity between the gravity of the political event and his mundane concern for appropriate footwear, for Gener and others who answered back in this way,[5] a lack of boots could genuinely have seemed more important.

This hierarchy of priorities emerged again at the funeral itself, when Party member Ianison, a joiner, addressed the cadaver sarcastically as he shuffled by the casket: 'I don't have any shoes – let me alone with your funeral'.[6] Biting, cynical words brought the focus literally back down to earth, deflating propaganda and its demands, but it also reveals the way in which many Soviet citizens ordered their priorities. The everyday not only trumped the political, but could even be used to negate it.[7]

All the same, there was no real escape from the demands and restrictions of the regime; even if you didn't attend Kirov's funeral, you ultimately still had no boots. This made the portrayal of insistent practicalities in contemporary humour still more realistic: prosaic realities might deflate official rhetoric, but even within the jokes there was no fanciful victory over those realities. This was made explicit in an *anekdot* told by Ia. D. Movshevich, a cashier at the Krasnyi Partisan artel' in the town of El'ts, Lipetskaia oblast', which he related to his workmates:

> Commissar of War Litvinov was in England and returned to the Soviet Union with an English minister. On the train they argued about the state loans. Litvinov insisted that 'in the USSR we have people queuing up for the loan', but the English minister said, 'you have queues for bread, not for the loan'. Yet when they arrived, he was convinced to the contrary… because Litvinov had called ahead to switch the signs for the bread shop and the loan subscription office.[8]

Movshevich and others could mock the regime for its need to lie in order to achieve the picture it desired, but ultimately the joke-tellers were still hungry and still queueing for bread, whatever the official labels suggested. Contemporary political humour exposed the official, but almost never indulged in happy endings.

Harsh realities were often all too pressing. First among those pressures was hunger, which dominated people's responses to the regime for much of the 1930s. As the student A.I. Mitrofanov made clear, Soviet power's achievements meant little when you were always hungry: he asked his friends 'What has Soviet power given you?'; one answered 'The chance to study', but Mitrofanov shot back with a sardonic rhyme, 'You can read, but can't feed' (*gramotnyi, no golodnyi*).[9] A teacher at the Pestovskii middle school in Leningradskaia oblast', a certain Polianskii, made a similar point to a group of his colleagues, saying that 'They can't feed us on consciousness and transportation – [we need] bread'.[10] With empty bellies, there was little chance that people could or would spend their time engaging deeply with ideology – something encapsulated in a skit by the famous Soviet humorist Il'ia Il'f, which he confided to his private notebooks. In his public role, Il'f helped to defuse popular criticism of the regime through published satirical stories which blamed problems on state-approved targets (see Chapter 4), but in private he could be more acerbic: "'There is no God!" [declared a student]. "But is there [any] cheese?" asked the teacher sadly'.[11]

As well as contesting the importance of regime policies and ideology, contemporaries used humour to express their pent-up frustration and, more implicitly, to try to quell their fears of starvation. The diary of Andrei Arzhilovskii (see Introduction) is brimming with references to hunger, which, characteristically, he tried to contain with irony:

> Just before 6[am] I went out and got in line for bread. My happy fellow countrymen were already standing there, getting used to socialism.

And:

> We have a unique way of relaxing on our day off: I got up at 4:00 and went out for firewood in 30 degrees of frost – I made five trips and covered 10 kilometres, all told. I [then] spent two hours in the breadline.[12]

Less privately, Party member K. Petrova spoke out sarcastically at a meeting in the Kirov Factory (where they so desperately wanted a new shower installed), noting that 'For the workers, rice will now only be [seen] in museums'.[13] Others joked bitterly that their children did not even know what sugar was,[14] or deferred basic foodstuffs to the realm of fantasy: veterinary student P. Afanas'ev recorded in his diary (later seized by his institute's director), 'Bread is already the stuff of fairytales and dreams',[15] while the chauffeur Anebov wrote biting comments in his garage's wall newspaper, including that 'we can only remember cheese and butter in [our] dreams'.[16]

The constant struggle to survive on inadequate wages and the dilemmas it produced are perhaps most vividly captured in a short rhyme told by the worker Semenova at the Kazinskii factory in Leningrad as the end of rationing (and consequent price rises) approached: 'Now we will be either naked and sated, or dressed and dying' (*Teper' my budem ili zhe syt[y] da golye, ili zhe odety i golodnye*).[17] In these one-liners, Soviet people have lost their basic dignity; they are reduced either to animalistic survival (naked and sated), or otherwise starve to death as the cost of retaining a sense of civilisation. Like the description of the *kolkhozniki* walking around with 'bare arses shining', there is a strong sense of humiliation in this (self-)representation, and the acid humour is coloured by a sense of desperation. The targets or 'victims' of jokes which focused on poverty and hunger were really the joke-tellers themselves, who lived in precisely those conditions. Even when the incoherence or pernicious nature of regime policies was specifically emphasised, the target of the humour remained the ordinary citizen as their innocent victim.

The sharply fatalistic edge to these jokes could often shade into a gallows humour that laughed explicitly at the imminence of death, as we can see in a short poem describing the future under Communism, recited by M.M. Makhotin, a senior officer in the Black Sea Fleet.

Солечное отопление,	Heating by sunlight,
Лунное освещение,	Lighting by moonlight,
Райское одеяние,	Clothing as in paradise,
Заочное питание,	Feeding by correspondence,
Гробовое молчание	Silence as in the graveyard,
и всеобщее ликование.	and general rejoicing.[18]

If the future was bright, it was likely only to be appreciated by corpses.

The same feeling was evoked by various jokes about the Bolsheviks' obsession with the word 'tempo'. The term was liberally thrown around to emphasise the speed and urgency required for the Soviet Union to catch up with and overtake the West, and incitements to work harder and fulfil the Five-Year Plans in record time were strewn with mentions of 'Bolshevik tempo'. Bland repetition inevitably led to mockery; as a Harvard Project respondent (a psychiatric doctor) put it, the repetition of all propaganda, however attractive at first, meant that psychologically it 'became repulsive [...] like getting cake three times a day'.[19]

The psychological nausea could be eased by telling a joke, and so a popular *anekdot* I discovered many times in the archives recounts the visit of a *kolkhoznik* to Kalinin, in which the former asks the elder statesman to please explain what 'tempo' means, because he and his fellow peasants still cannot understand its importance to the Party. Kalinin takes him to the window and points at a passing tram: 'You see, if we have a dozen trams at the moment, after five years we will have hundreds'. This, then, was the meaning of 'tempo'! The peasant returned to his kolkhoz and, as his comrades gathered around him, clamouring to learn the meaning for themselves, he looked around for inspiration and pointed to the nearby cemetery, declaring 'You see those dozen graves?

After five years, there will be thousands!'[20]

The bleak fatalism of this and other contemporary jokes shouldn't be equated with any simplistic ideas about Russians being somehow conditioned to suffering (a trope which refuses to die despite its obvious orientalism and condescension).[21] Ordinary people's political humour often contained sharp, critical barbs aimed at Soviet leaders, policies, and even Stalin himself, and so the fatalistic themes of death and self-mockery we see in many *anekdoty* are clearly just two possible ingredients among many. Moreover, although death was always close at hand, laughter was in fact a rejection of death's power to conquer; it demonstrated a consciousness of crisis and misfortune, but did not allow crisis and misfortune to dictate people's response. Jokes not only provided a vehicle for expressing particular feelings and opinions, but simultaneously helped to shape an often sanguine response.

Their humour, in short, remained ambivalent. A punchline did not represent a 'conclusion' in either sense of the word, because humour functioned as a continuing, open dialogue with those pressing, everyday issues. That's why in Arzhilovskii's diary we see that, when he's depressed, he writes in leaden statements of fact: nothing is open for discussion. When he feels more optimistic, he writes with humour and wit about exactly the same issues which had previously depressed him. Humour can incorporate both the depressing and the optimistic because it's a genre of possibility; as the many jokes above suggest, terrible experiences could be reconfigured to provoke pleasurable laughter, or at least to mitigate outright resignation and despair. In this way, humour represents a continued, dynamic engagement with reality and searches for a way forward, even when dealing with the desperate and, in truth, inescapable. A joke was not the final word, but a signal that the conversation was not yet concluded.

We shouldn't forget that this could take the form of flippant throwaway lines, too, which were less politically pointed but still clearly tuned into an underlying irritation with official rhetoric, its proliferation and its implications. For example, John Scott, an American who lived and worked in Magnitogorsk – a landmark site of Soviet construction, portrayed as the crucible of the new society – during the 1930s, recorded in his diary a more lighthearted variation on the morbid 'tempo' joke, this version expressing vexation at most: 'A bearded Soviet engineer who had been in the plane remarked bitterly, "Two hours from Chelyabinsk to Magnitogorsk [by plane], a trip which takes twenty hours in the train – and then we spend four more hours to get from the aerodrome to the city. That's Bolshevik tempo!"'[22]

I.I. Shitts, the Moscow-based historian, also recorded an example of this in his diary, where he described how a fellow historian, Bochkarev, was arrested in Moscow for responding with a rude joke to a question from his students regarding 'tempo'. Instead of answering the question about what the word meant, he apparently responded, 'Well, it looks like you feed your faces with a Bolshevik tempo'.[23] Propaganda and its learned phrases were becoming part of the fabric of everyday life, but the regime did not take kindly to such instances of interweaving, even though it could actually have seen it as a positive sign of an increasing level of acceptance, or at least of proliferation. Instead, the words and symbols of the regime were to remain sacred objects, unsullied by interactions with the prosaic, and defended with harsh zealotry. As would become their trademark, the Bolsheviks' rigidity just created more problems (and more jokes), adding to the already substantial problem-pile of modernisation, mass education, looming warfare, and the creation of the 'new Soviet person'.

There was a counterweight to the sub-genre of morbid humour – one which offered a more wryly ironic view of everyday practicalities. When price rises were announced, a worker at the Rabochii factory in Leningrad responded by saying: 'Let the prices go up – we won't need to go to market and stand in queues [anymore]'.[24] This silver lining is absurd yet light-hearted; it bypasses the potential for starvation and death and instead finds amusement in a more palatable (but just as real) 'fringe benefit' of the situation. In the same way, the worker Trubitsyn greeted price hikes with the words, 'I was a drunkard, but since the price rises for bread I've given up drinking'.[25] Andrei Arzhilovskii also chose to look on the bright side when he noted in his diary that he and his contemporaries were 'enjoying the blessings of the revolution… [queueing to buy] peas which the state sells for 1 r[uble] 30 k[opeks] a kilogram, i.e. at least 20 times more expensive than "kulak" prices… You have to assume that the peas will be really delicious'.[26] And, at a less personal level, the decline of the ruble elicited various jokes of this kind, as William Chamberlin recorded: 'Soviet money is the jolliest with which to travel, because every foreigner laughs when he sees it'.[27]

Then again, almost no Soviet citizens were allowed or could afford to travel abroad under Stalin, so the exchange rate was hardly the most pressing concern. What held most people's attention and became the object of their frustrated humour were problems closer to home, not least government schemes which tried to take what little money they had away from them.

Policies and Punchlines

Evasions and Frustration: State Loan Subscriptions

State-orchestrated modernisation came at a high price, but the regime did not have deep pockets. Nor did the general population, but the regime nonetheless set about rummaging through its citizens' wallets in search of more funds. It created a series of government bond schemes and then harassed ordinary people to sign away a significant portion of their wages to buy them.

In comparison to the vivid human drama of the repressions or the upheavals of collectivisation, these schemes have not held the attention of many historians, but they dominated the daily lives of Soviet contemporaries. The loans could make the difference not only between putting food on the table or going hungry, but also whether you would be daily persecuted at work for failing to sign up. The sense of being under attack was summed up in an *anekdot* circulating in the early 1930s, recorded by William Chamberlin, in which a man is found drowned in the Moscow River, showing 'no signs of violence, except a few bonds [for] the five-year-plan loan' on his person.[28] If this seems like an exaggeration, we should bear in mind that loan enrolment agents were sometimes murdered, such was the desperation and animosity the policy generated.[29] The loans were officially voluntary, but, as with most 'voluntary' activities in Soviet life, they were actually unavoidable, and so a new, unofficial category of 'voluntary-compulsory' was born, accompanied by much rueful eye-rolling.[30]

The loan campaigns were pursued by the Party's representatives in every workplace, who set about publicly and repeatedly cajoling people to subscribe. Many citizens responded with a biting, devil-may-care humour which attempted to deflect the demands. In a Sevastopol' factory, a banner encouraging workers to sign up to the loan was altered overnight to read '*Fools*, sign up for the loan'; this clearly struck a chord, as members of the third shift decided to carry the banner aloft with them into a general meeting later that day.[31] In the Kommunar factory in Minsk, only five workers (of 150) voted in favour of the state loan in mid-1932. The second attempt to pass the motion was not looking much better, and when one worker was singled out to explain why he hadn't raised his hand in favour, he shot back sarcastically, 'On the soup [you feed us], my arm cannot be raised'.[32]

In similarly facetious manner, a certain Marenko, who earned over 400 rubles a month, responded theatrically to the demands: 'I'm not refusing to sign up – no! Put me down for 10 rubles' – a tiny amount in the eyes of officials and therefore entirely unacceptable.³³ A worker at the Serpukhov factory, Fillipov, refused to sign up to the loan at all because, he said, 'I [already] don't have enough money for food, wine and girls!'³⁴ In cases like these, people were attempting to evade unwelcome pressures from officials without placing themselves in explicit opposition to the regime; they used humour tactically to sidestep its demands, rather than meeting them head-on. These were ultimately fruitless gestures, but they still reveal how the implementation of regime policies could play out on the ground.

Other citizens did not just dodge the issue of loan contributions, but actively mocked the scheme itself. An old worker at the Krasnyi Putilovets factory declared 'with irony' that '[we] finish work each month and then give all the wages back to you for the loan'.³⁵ Savchenko, a worker at the Metallist factory in Kherson, refused to sign up to the industrialisation loan in 1929, citing his sanity as reason enough not to: 'I've not gone mad yet! The bottomless barrel never fills; they're forever robbing the workers!'³⁶ As loan campaign after loan campaign rolled out in the following years, Savchenko's sarcasm would seem increasingly justified.

The idea of 'robbing the workers' also tapped into a potent element of Bolshevik ideology, and disputed the new regime's claims to serve the 'working class'. A lawyer (юрист) at Leningrad's Uritskii Factory used his training to do much the same thing as Savchenko, but in a more complex manner, by asking why people should sign up for the loan, given that 'in the second Five-Year Plan we're building a classless society; on that basis, as a result all money will be annulled', and so the loans would become irrelevant.³⁷ A worker at the same factory likewise played Bolshevik ideology off against itself when he refused to sign up 'until the wreckers have been shot'.³⁸ 'Wreckers' were a largely non-existent regime bogeyman on which to blame shortcomings and accidents caused by unrealistic industrialisation targets, but this shadowy figure could also be (mis)used by contemporaries to pursue their own, prosaic aims in the workplace.³⁹ In these ways, official ideology could be neatly crosshatched with the desires of contemporaries to have a few more kopeks each month on which to live; they could criticise official discourse even as they hid within it.

All these comments were spoken directly to Party agitators or in open meetings, which reflects the time they were made: they were all voiced in the early 1930s, when it seemed reasonable to assume that no serious punishment would follow (see Chapter 4). In this relatively more open environment, humour formed part of a collective, quite public recalcitrance or evasiveness, supporting a 'go-slow' attitude that carved out spaces of (temporary) non-conformity. Consider, for example, that around this time workers in parts of Buguruslanskii raion (Orenburg oblast') began regularly turning up to work between one and two hours late. One individual, an accounting clerk (учетник), took this to an extreme, one day arriving a full five hours late and then, with a casual disregard for authority, defended himself with placid humour: 'I overslept a little'.[40]

'Foot-dragging' and 'dissimulation' are two of the key 'weapons of the weak' that the anthropologist James C. Scott identified in his landmark study of what he calls 'everyday resistance', but, as he emphasises, these acts 'typically avoid any direct, symbolic confrontation with authority' and instead function for individuals as a quiet 'form of self-help'.[41] That 'self-help' might, in the end, mean just a few more hours of sleep, but it was also an indirect assertion of popular agency, with humour used, if not to avoid all sanctions, then at least to lubricate the attempt somewhat. As we'll see below, however, the regime struck back with the 1940 Labour Law which criminalised lateness to work, whatever the excuse.

By the end of the decade, moreover, contemporaries' negative reactions seem to have shifted to a far blacker tone than the evasive flippancy of the early 1930s. In 1937, an inspector at the Elektroapparat Factory in Leningrad, Issar, commented that 'I'd be better flogging myself than signing up for these tickets'.[42] A few years later, in response to a loan drive in July 1940, a worker at Factory 198 in Nikolaev, Ukraine, responded to the Party Organiser's cajoling to subscribe more than a third of his wages with the words, 'If you're going to keep demanding, I'll put myself down for a bullet in the head'.[43] At the same time, a plumber in the Nasos factory in Leningrad oblast' responded to the drive with: 'What're you on about? I'd be better hanging myself here on this crossbeam'.[44]

By this time, the impact of the loans on their lives was much clearer to contemporaries, and the jokes and sarcasm had lost their playfulness: the drinks and girls were replaced by the bleak nihilism of the gallows. If humour in general can generate a sense of distance and detachment from the object of mockery, throwing in the image of suicide brought this function to the fore. It represented an imagined, fictitious escape from the weight of reality – an escape from the power of the state, despite the obvious – total – personal costs involved. Of course, this tone was not a consequence of the loans in isolation, but was a response to a decade's worth of forced industrialisation and material shortages, which brings us to the series of Five-Year Plans that dominated these years.

Running On The Spot: The Five-Year Plans

Jokes and humorous remarks made about the Five-Year Plans were a little more generalised and less concerned with evading specific requirements; instead, they reflected how contemporaries experienced the realities of the great industrialisation drive initiated at the end of the 1920s. Although the first Five-Year Plan was officially completed ahead of schedule, critical humour directed against it usually suggested that this and subsequent Plans were impossible or would take twice the time projected. This was summed up in various *chastushki* like one sung by a young fourth-grade schoolgirl at a raion-level competition (*Olympiad*) in front of an audience, whose reactions are sadly unrecorded:

Пятилетка, пятилетка,	Five-Year Plan, Five-Year Plan,
Пятилетка в десять лет,	Five-Year Plan in ten, I bet,
Не пойду я к вам в колхозы,	I'm not heading to the kolkhozy,
У вас в колхозах хлеба нет.	Where you've got no bread.[45]

Another example was (amazingly) recited by a school teacher (later arrested) to her fifth-grade class as a model for their homework assignment – the composition of both Soviet and antisoviet *chastushki*:

Хлеба нет,	Bread gone,
Мяса нет,	Meat gone,
Пятилетка	The Five-Year Plan
В десять лет.	Is ten years long.[46]

Still more succinctly, Konstantin Megrelidze noted the following in his *anekdot* collection: '[What's] the absolute longest joke? The Five-Year Plan.'[47]

The heavy emphasis these examples place on the duration of the Plan in part reflects how, with each Plan immediately succeeded by another, there was little chance to feel any sense of progress, let alone completion. But it was also a satirical comment on the endless incitements to record-breaking speed, to complete each 'Five-Year Plan in Four Years'. To those who had to fulfil the targets, the reality felt more like a Sisyphean labour performed with someone shouting constantly over their shoulder to work faster.

With the pounding drumbeat of Bolshevik tempo ringing in their ears, it was easy to feel as though they were living at two very different speeds. The sense of time whistling past appears frequently in

Arzhilovskii's diary, for example: 'I was just thinking how frantic our pace of life is'; 'Time is marching on, just try to keep up'; 'It's amazing how quickly time passes'; and, drawing parallels to two major symbols of modernity, 'Life is a speeding train'; 'Time rushes on like a fast car'.⁴⁸ Even émigrés like the Soviet defector Viktor Kravchenko were not immune to the sense of rapid progress: despite his opposition to the Bolshevik regime in general, he could not help but recall how it was 'wonderful to feel that we're striding forward in seven-league boots'.⁴⁹

However, for Arzhilovskii and those who actually lived in the Soviet Union in the 1930s, this was a rather abstracted feeling juxtaposed to slow and tedious realities, of long periods of drudgery standing in queues, shivering indoors without firewood, and waiting for housing conditions to improve. Bolshevik 'tempo' might be fast, but it seemed in practice to mean running on the spot with nothing to eat.

Material shortages, especially of food, were placed front-and-centre in mockery directed at the Five-Year Plans. With 'bread gone' and 'meat gone', starvation seemed to be just around the corner, but at the same time the Soviet government was exporting grain to pay for industrial equipment. With this in mind, in 1933 at a factory training school (*Fabrichno-zavodskoe uchenichestvo*, FZU) in Moscow, a student remarked tartly that 'By the end of the second five-year plan we'll all be eating tractors'.⁵⁰

Similarly, Mikhailov, a social scientist at another FZU, complained sarcastically to his colleagues, 'They're sending bread abroad for gold and machinery (машины), but we workers and peasants are starving. I mean, are we meant to eat gold and machinery?'⁵¹ More enigmatically, S.I. Posun'ko, a middle-peasant in Ukraine, kicked up a fuss in a queue for rations, telling the authorities that 'you're building blast-furnaces, but you're going to eat iron' – whether this would be like 'eating tractors', or was a darker reference to eating a bullet, in suicide or otherwise, was left to the imagination.⁵² Others were less oblique: Bublikov, who had just arrived from Vladivostok to serve on the Don-Kuban naval fleet, told his new comrades that by the third Five-Year Plan, 'it'll be continuous coffins' they would be producing.⁵³ By highlighting these unpleasant realities, Soviet citizens could both rhetorically kick back at the regime and demonstrate to one another that, despite official propaganda, they were acutely aware of the state's priorities and could thereby (re)gain a pleasurable sense of their own mental agency.

Once again, jabs at the regime often played on official discourse even as they criticised it. One joke, recorded by foreign visitors and Soviet citizens alike, combined a reference to the Bolsheviks' reforms to the Cyrillic alphabet and a reflection upon the realities of the brave new world's industrialisation drive:

> The letter 'M' is to be removed from the Russian alphabet as superfluous: in the USSR there is no meat, manufactured goods, milk, *maslo* (butter), *mylo* (soap) …[54]

In similarly caustic fashion, I.I. Shitts recorded a joke in his diary in which a group of Jews congratulate Stalin on the occasion of his 50th birthday, but then express the wish that he will complete the next 50 in the record time of two years.[55] And, at a workers' meeting in Vyborgskii raion, Leningrad, as another anniversary of the Revolution approached, a pointed question (deemed 'unhealthy' by the report writer) was posed: 'Why, if we've been building [socialism] for 15 years, do we have no shoes and no clothes?'[56]

In this way, joking about unpleasant truths could also become a kind of public performance, designed to be enjoyed as a group. This was not performance confined or directly conditioned by a particular event as Kirov's Carnival had been, but more general moments of the carnivalesque that arose spontaneously. Consider, for example, how one Comrade Mironov addressed the shortage of consumer goods and basic food provisioning amidst the propaganda of the Five-Year Plan and the abundance it was supposed to create. He performed something like a stand-up routine in front of the workers in the electrical shop of the Krasnyi Profintern factory, provoking laughter and applause for his efforts:

> There's no sugar, no shoes, no firewood. You can only live for a week like that, and all they give us are promises: they promise pork, but there are no pigs; they promise rabbit, but there are no rabbits (laughter). [They promise] consumer goods [ширпотреб], consumer goods, consumer goods, consumer goods, consumer goods… (applause) And once again, nothing.[57]

That this was such a public, open performance is again probably explained by its timing (1932), at which point Mironov and others would know they were taking some risk, but would not have reason to expect the heavy punishments which became the norm for joke-tellers later in the decade (see Chapter 4). Nevertheless, the urge to speak out in this way was impossible to suppress entirely: joking meant sharing, and sharing meant lessening the psychological weight of fears, suffering, and frustration.

If the Five-Year Plans and industrialisation in general were characterised by a paradoxical pairing of speed and a depressing stasis, popular humour was a key mode by which contemporaries could highlight and reflect upon the latter experience and its relation to the former, attempting to integrate them (uncomfortably) with the official propaganda of thundering steam engines, electricity, and record-breaking. As we see in Arzhilovskii's diary, Soviet citizens were experiencing both simultaneously and so naturally set about trying to integrate them. Yet, however hard the conditions in the industrialising towns, in the early 1930s the challenges faced by the population were exponentially harder in the countryside.

Laughing in the Dark: Collectivisation

The forcible collectivisation of agriculture began in 1928 and was mostly completed by 1932, having created a famine which claimed somewhere between 4 and 6.5 million lives.[58] The appalling experiences of the Soviet peasantry in these years have been written about at length, but it has been difficult to recover the voices of contemporaries who struggled to describe and comprehend the destruction unleashed around them. Peasants rarely leave documentary traces from which we can reconstruct their perspectives, but due to the great transmitability of jokes and songs, we can recover some vital fragments of how some discussed collectivisation at the time of its implementation.

The first thing we notice is the pitch-black tone of these jokes. Consider, for instance, the brief *anekdot* told by senior agronomist and candidate Party member, P.F. Pomelova, concerning the collectivisation famine and the outbreaks of cannibalism it caused: 'An agronomist travelled to Ukraine on holiday. A single bone of his skeleton was all they found of him.'[59] Not all jokes were quite so blunt, but rarely were they less bleak.

A rhyming couplet told by craftsman-mechanic Kuznetsov to other workers at a railway station in Krasnoufimsk summed up the lives of collective farmers:

| Колхозники – канареечки, | *Kolkhozniki* are little canaries, |
| Целый год проработали без копеечки. | They work year round with never a penny.[60] |

Unpaid, caged and used in mines to detect gas build-ups, the 'little canaries' had the worst of all worlds, and the one-sided economic relationship between state and peasant, based on forced state requisitioning, was summed up by Sukhovienko, a building technician (техник-строитель) working in Nizhin, Ukraine: 'Breed, breed! The sheep will be yours, and the meat will be ours!'[61] Again, the *kolkhozniki* are simply used and discarded.

The unhappy lives of the *kolkhozniki* were directly and repeatedly attributed to the nature of the kolkhoz system itself, which was portrayed as broken, depressing, but also inescapable. Consider the following two *chastushki*:

Хорошо в колхозе жить,	On the kolkhoz life is good,
Один работает	One is working,
Семеро	Seven
С голоду сидит [*sic*].	From hunger sit.[62]
Если-б не было морозов,	If there was no frost,
Не было бы холоду.	There would be no cold.
Если-б не было колхозов,	If there were no kolkhozy,
Не было бы голоду.	There would be no hunger.[63]

The first *chastushka* draws on a Russian proverb (один с сошкой, а семеро с ложкой / One with the plough, seven with their spoons), which emphasises how the labour of the few feeds the many.[64] Hunger and suffering are the inescapable motifs of both *chastushki*, expressed in a bleakly factual tone. Arguably, these examples are not amusing at all, but I include them with good reason: the *chastushka* is a form intimately associated with humour. Like jokes and *anekdoty*, *chastushki* follow various set patterns or structures; they critically comment on particular events or everyday life; pass judgement upon them; provide a sense of pleasure through the act of telling and hearing them; and, most importantly, are almost always humorous. The question, then, is where has the humour gone in these *chastushki*?

In fact, almost all contemporary jokes about collectivisation and the kolkhozy have a consistently different tone to those we've seen so far. There are no imagined silver linings here. The first *chastushka* clearly shows that life is *not* good on the kolkhoz, but offers no escape – even an imagined one – from those conditions. The first line, echoing propaganda, sits in juxtaposition to a reality described in the following three, and there is no sense that these perspectives are actively struggling with each other. Although the first line is ironic, there is little bite but much bitterness in the poem, with hopeless resignation its underlying tone. The second *chastushka* goes even further by proposing an ineluctable connection between the kolkhoz system and famine, by comparing it to the relationship between season and temperature – a natural and unchangeable relationship, however unwelcome it may feel.

We might also recall the joke from Chapter 1 in which Moscow is named 'the heart and head' of the country, but the kolkhozy are its 'natural waste', or the lewd *anekdoty* in which Stalin deals with his sexual misfortunes by declaring the relevant physical area a kolkhoz. While the Soviet leaders were mocked with the use of scatological and other base images, the kolkhozy were treated more harshly still: they were not soiled, but were the excretion itself.[65] And while in the sexual *anekdoty* directed at Stalin the kolkhoz plays a secondary role, this is itself telling: it had become a shorthand threat, the awfulness of which was so evident that it could scare anything and everything away (a theme which endured in *anekdoty* for decades).[66]

Remember the joke about 'eating tractors' by the end of the Five-Year Plan – a joke that found humour in proposing an absurd solution to a seemingly impossible situation? In contrast, the *anekdoty* and *chastushki* which focus on the starvation created by collectivisation offer no such short-circuiting of logic: the mutton is taken; the canaries are never paid; most peasants lie motionless from hunger; famine comes as surely as frost in winter. These are at their core a bitter lament betraying a fatalistic resignation to hardships which are perceived as inescapable.

But despite the gloomy nature of all these examples, we shouldn't forget that the form in which they were communicated was an important, shaping context that alters the meaning of what initially seem to be straightforwardly pessimistic, depressing words. These *chastushki* would have been sung; the jokes, however bleak, were told to elicit laughter (or why tell them as jokes at all?). These are social, communicative and performative genres, the use of which implied sharing the distressing nature of collectivisation in a way that was more complex than just the grim acceptance of an unpleasant fate. This was not a mute resignation, but rather a continuing conversation in which these troubling themes could be shared and their individual burden thereby lessened, if only mentally.

This may also have some resonance with the historian Sheila Fitzpatrick's focus on the motif of 'how the mice buried the cat'. In her seminal analysis, Fitzpatrick draws on a symbolic image used in Russian woodcuts in the late seventeenth and early eighteenth centuries, presenting a carnivalesque scene in which a large cat – then associated with Peter the Great – is buried by a group of celebrating, instrument-playing mice.

Transferring this symbol to the state-sanctioned, public trials of allegedly corrupt local officials in the late 1930s, Fitzpatrick argues that although the 'cat' – the Soviet representatives in the village – might have died (i.e. were purged), the 'mice' – the peasants – had not had the power to kill it themselves. They could rejoice in burying the cat, but this was not truly 'their' victory.[67] In much the same way, the extremely dark humour about collectivisation demonstrates a powerlessness, but also the survival of a sense of collective opinion and community turned against the state's measures and waiting for the moment at which the carnivalesque burial of the cat might commence (as it clearly did following Kirov's murder).

We catch a glimpse of this spirit in an *anekdot* which Stepan Podlubnyi (the son of a kulak who nevertheless committed himself to becoming the best Soviet citizen he could be) recorded in his diary in late 1936, which he heard while visiting his native village in Ukraine. A Party official goes up to a peasant and says:

> 'When're you going to deliver this grain? Why haven't you delivered it yet?'
> 'Wait till it dries, then I'll deliver it.'
> 'Why dry it? Deliver it first and then it can dry.'[68]

This joke was intended to be shared with an audience familiar with agriculture (thankfully, we can ask the internet), who would know that grain has to be dried after harvest in a complex process requiring careful storage and controlled conditions, or it will spoil within a few days. To transport it wet would destroy it, even if there was access to the necessary drying equipment at the other end. So the joke is clearly at the expense of the interfering and inept representative of state power and, while describing a grim and painful reality, this could still help rural people feel better, together, by elevating themselves above such foolishness, asserting again the common sense superiority we saw in Chapter 1, but here one of a more specific, localised kind. And this was not the only way in which humorous responses were shaped by their context.

Although this fatalistic style was by far the most common shading of humour I found in relation to collectivisation, there was another, less melancholic and more politically-focused variety. The writer and intellectual Arthur Koestler recorded hearing the following *anekdot* when visiting the USSR in 1932, while himself a devout Communist:

> Q: What does it mean when there is food in the town but no food in the country?
> A: A Left, Trotskyist deviation.

> Q: What does it mean when there is food in the country but not in the town?
> A: A Right, Bukharinite deviation.
> Q: What does it mean when there is no food in the country and no food in the town?
> A: The correct application of the general line.
> Q: What does it mean when there is food both in the country and in the town?
> A: The horrors of Capitalism.[69]

Koestler's rendering may seem a little polished, riffing on the factionalism which existed among the leading Bolsheviks before Stalin gained supremacy, but close variations of this *anekdot* appear in Soviet diary entries written in 1929, confirming its contemporary existence.[70]

An accountant working at the freight railway station in Tashkent (ст. Ташкент-товарная), Mariia Morozova, told her colleagues the following, rather similar *anekdot*:

> Stalin asked Voroshilov [a leading Bolshevik and prominent military figure] to teach him how to march properly. They began to practise, and Voroshilov instructed Stalin, 'Turn to the left!', but Stalin responded, 'No, that's a left deviation!' Then Voroshilov said, 'Turn to the right!', but Stalin answered, 'No, that's a right deviation!' So Voroshilov replied, 'Oh to hell with you, walk in a straight line.'[71]

These *anekdoty* attempt to find an ideological 'rationale' for the devastation caused by collectivisation, and instead find humour in the sheer absurdity and disconnection from reality they 'discover' in high-level politicking. The tone of these two *anekdoty* is, due to their distinctly more ideological focus, quite different from the examples we've seen before. In large part, this difference can be attributed to the social backgrounds of the people who shared them. Koestler, as a foreign journalist, was moving in better-educated, better-off circles, and the second *anekdot* was told by an educated, white-collar worker to her office colleagues. Conversely, all the collectivisation jokes and *chastushki* we saw earlier were told by individuals from a rural background, or who were from Ukraine itself, where the famine hit hardest.

In other words, the less political and more emotionally bleak examples were told by people who most likely had first-hand experience of collectivisation and were reflecting on it in that knowledge; Koestler and Morozova would very likely have been puzzled by Podlubnyi's joke about the wet grain. Critical jokes depended as much on the context of their telling (including the teller and the audience) as they did on what was being criticised; because they tried to integrate their targets into lived experiences, the latter inevitably shaped the way the former was engaged.

Timing was also a key factor determining what jokes were told; they were very often an immediate reaction to a particular policy or event. But this was not always the case. *Anekdoty* and other humorous responses to the Five-Year Plans and collectivisation outlived the immediate period when those policies were conceived and implemented. Once a particular witticism had begun to circulate, it would often last for years, repeated at ever greater distances from its point of origin, even though it continued to engage that point directly. In part, this endurance may simply be because certain jokes became 'favourites', but this also had as much to do with the continuing relevance they held for contemporaries. From the evidence available, it does not seem that immediate humorous responses to, for example, the second Five-Year Plan were different from those to the first, or that opinions of the kolkhozy altered very greatly in the later 1930s once the famine had abated. It seems, therefore, that the first wave of jokes prompted by these policies persisted because they both encapsulated some recognisable truth for contemporaries and that this truth remained consistent across the decade. Although the initial surprise or novelty value of the joke might have faded, the abrasion of the policy or event in question persisted in their minds: the problems of and damages caused by collectivisation did not fade away, nor did the state significantly alter its focus on industrialisation. As long as these abrasions persisted, the jokes about them would continue.

Gallows Laughter: The 'Great Terror'

The mass repressions which gripped the Soviet Union in 1937-8, in which three-quarters of a million Soviet citizens were executed and a further million sent to the Gulag,[72] have become synonymous with Stalinism and the Soviet 1930s in general. Given the vast human cost and suffering involved, this is entirely understandable, but it rather complicates the traditional picture of these years as a period of 'terror' to discover that Soviet citizens also made jokes about the repressions as they were unfolding – not least because by joking about it they not only recognised it, but simultaneously exposed themselves to its dangers.

Karl Schlögel's voluminous book *Moscow 1937* provides a

panorama of the capital during the year that became a byword for arbitrary arrest and execution, highlighting that even as those bloody events unfolded, ordinary life went on, from theatre-going to film releases, academic conferences to summer walks in Gor'kii Park.[73] But for contemporaries this was not a discrete set of experiences taking place on a parallel track; in their darkly humorous responses to the repressions we see them grappling with the intersection of violent, frightening excesses with their daily, mundane experiences. These engagements are also illuminating because, unlike interpretations and rationalisations of the 'Great Terror' made with the benefit of hindsight, which we can read in memoirs, contemporary humour bears witness to those mental processes in development and in situ.

The frequent disappearances of friends and colleagues during these years gave everyday life a potentially absurd instability in which dramatic, life-changing events could happen with essentially no coherent, or at least predictable, rationale available to explain them. (Indeed, it was this emotionally-charged absurdity which Mikhail Bulgakov played on so effectively in his most famous novel, *Master and Margarita*.[74]) This feeling was evoked in a sardonic remark made between two workers in the Krasnaia znamia factory in Leningrad: 'Where's the map of the world?' one asked, searching for said item. His colleague, a female worker by the name of V'iuk, known as something of a joke-teller, replied: 'The map's been arrested. The C[entral] C[ommittee] sent it to prison'.[75] It would be interesting, though probably too strained, to infer that V'iuk was symbolically hinting at the reduction of citizens' horizons at this time due to the omnipresent fear of arrest, but at the very least her flippant remark highlights the sense of arbitrary arrests spiralling out of control and into the realm of the thoroughly illogical.

By 1938 the arrests seemed completely indiscriminate, as the photographer Iu.N. Govorov pointed out in an *anekdot* he told to a friend in Moscow, in which he asked: 'Who makes up the USSR? – Many enemies and just one friend of the people'.[76] Clearly, it is Stalin alone who is considered the unequivocal 'friend of the people', while anyone else in the country was in danger of being branded an enemy.

The scale of the arrests led Govorov and others to dish out ironic, bitter praise to the NKVD for their repressive labours. Govorov noted simply that 'NKVD investigators work like Stakhanovites', the Soviet heroes of labour known for their record-setting efforts.[77] A final-year schoolgirl and candidate member for the Komsomol's Central Committee, Ol'ga Iakovleva, reported a career advisor for making a related comment: when asked where she'd like to work, Ol'ga replied 'in the NKVD', but she was advised not to apply because, 'Well, is there anyone left to catch?'.⁷⁸ In a similar tone, Stepan Podlubnyi noted in his diary on 19 December 1937 that, 'The old proverb says that "we all live by the grace of god". Now they tell it differently: "we all live by the grace of the NKVD"'.⁷⁹

The arrest of countless high-ranking Party members made this frightening proposition seem all the more plausible; whom could you trust if so many responsible and powerful figures were now being 'unmasked'? As a former *kolkhoznik* and brigadier recalled sardonically after the war, 'Only people who are in the cemeteries avoid trouble with the secret police'.⁸⁰ This paranoid mindset was captured in a surprisingly perceptive one-liner delivered by a fifth-grade student at School 142 in Kyiv, who fired a catapult at a portrait of Voroshilov in his classroom and declared, when his classmates berated him, 'Today he's a *vozhd'*, but tomorrow he could be an enemy of the people!'⁸¹ In this we see flickers of the carnivalesque urge to flip hierarchies in response to destabilising, transitional moments. Just as Kirov's death engendered a sense of instability and the simultaneous possibility to break with expected norms and, more generally, how rituals of transition between particular states (marriages, funerals, coming-of-age ceremonies) prompt such carnivalesque behaviour, so the mass repressions could stimulate these inversionary, iconoclastic urges. Like the jokes themselves, these were states of possibility and uncertainty.

We can't know the prevalence of these opinions, but the examples we have conflict with the standard narrative of the 'Great Terror' which has long claimed that Soviet citizens tended to believe that the mass arrests were justified up to the point when they or their close friends and family were directly affected.⁸² These jokes and sarcastic comments suggest, on the contrary, that at least some citizens realised *at the time* that mass arrests increasingly included ordinary people who were guilty of no crime, even under Soviet law.

This is neatly encapsulated in a mock theatre programme composed by the director Viktor Tripot and his circle, which featured plausibly- but suggestively-named venues paired with real plays:

- GPU Theatre, matinée: *Pearl Fishers* (Искатели жемчуга); evening: *Fear* (Страх)
- People's Theatre, showing *Guilt of the Innocents* (Без вины виноватые).⁸³

In this parody, the secret police work through fear, under the cover of darkness, belying the integrity of their official, 'daytime' duty to seek out valuable information in the interests of state security. 'The people' are obviously the implied victims of this situation, and are unfairly judged 'guilty' en masse by the authorities.

These responses had some precedents, even if the scale of arrests and repressions did not. I.I. Shitts recorded a joke in his diary in 1930 that referred to the unfolding persecution and imprisonment of 'bourgeois specialists' by the GPU:

> Menzhinskii (of the GPU) upbraids Kuibyshev for the weak development of the economy. Kuibyshev explains this failure: 'If only I had as many engineers as you [now] do'.[84]

William Chamberlin recorded a similar *anekdot* related to this persecution of 'specialists': 'I have three sons. One is an engineer; one is an [agronomist]; the third is also in prison'.[85] These jokes are clearly very similar to those about the mass repressions some seven years later, and as such we can see that citizens were learning how to interpret disturbing, repressive regime actions over the course of the decade, returning to these interpretative 'tools' when they needed them once again.

All the examples from 1937 onwards are coloured by a pronounced focus on instability, in which normal rules no longer seem to apply. Nothing can be relied upon to stay in place: neither a simple map, nor the leaders of the country themselves. The disorientation this caused is reflected in the distinct powerlessness at the centre of these jokes; the humour lies in the loss of all agency in relation to the frightening events described, combined with an incongruous dismissal of their importance.

Consider a particularly bleak example recorded in the diary of V.I. Vernadskii, a famous scientist and the first president of the Ukrainian Academy of Sciences. As he recorded it, the joke ran that prior to Nikolai Ezhov's reign over the NKVD there were already some 10 million people in the camps, but, once he rose to prominence, Ezhov considered a further 15 million arrests to be necessary. It's hard to see where the humour is here, but Vernadskii explicitly identifies it as an *anekdot* and implies that it was funny to him and his friends; this was a black gallows humour which laughed directly at the very frightening and arbitrary scale of the mass arrests.[86] The *raison d'être* of jokes like this lay in the desire of contemporaries to tackle the repressions in a form which, while allowing for a recognition of their irrationality, provided an imagined detachment or superiority over them: although the madman may kill you, at least *you* are not mad too.

This is one of the key functions of humour that focuses on tragic, painful or merely uncomfortable subjects: it creates a psychological detachment by shifting those oppressive elements into a genre which permits us to laugh at them and thereby feel a sense of control and hence a freedom from their power (see Chapter 5). In a seeming paradox, therefore, as the risk of telling jokes increased, so did the urge to tell them. As Vernadskii noted in late 1938, one evening when he and his friends spoke about the 'senseless terror, [which] can ruin your life and [that of your] loved ones', they did so 'in *anekdoty*'; and this despite the fact he personally knew individuals who had been arrested specifically for telling *anekdoty*.[87] Even knowing how dangerous it was, the need to talk about these events could not be subdued, and humour – itself dangerous – was too natural and helpful a way to do this to be ignored.

Although these examples of Soviet contemporaries using humour to engage with the repressions as they unfolded do not significantly conflict with later recollections in memoirs and interviews, they still complicate the persistent idea that Soviet society was mutely terrified and atomised during these years – an impression sustained in part by the use of the ambiguous term 'Great Terror'. While these were certainly some effects of the repressions, they were not the only response; instead of silent fear and isolation, the jokes we find from these years suggest that other people (or the same people at different moments) felt compelled to address the severe instabilities caused by spiralling mass arrests, and, just as importantly, that they did so not only in whispered conversations with family members (as memoirs and diaries usually suggest), but also with colleagues and friends in the workplace.

On Time or Doing Time: The Labour Law of 1940

Although not nearly as bleak or damaging as the mass repressions, responses to the 1940 Labour Law had a similar character, at least in tone. This piece of legislation made it a criminal offence to be late to work or to change jobs on your own initiative, and its influence could hardly be ignored: the criminalisation of labour infractions accounted for two-thirds of all criminal convictions in 1940 following the Law's implementation on 26 June.[88] Much as critical jokes and sarcasm about the state loans had by this point shed their playfulness and become bitter kick-backs at the regime, responses to the Labour Law were resentful and biting.

Samodurov, a worker at the Max Goltz factory in Leningrad, responded to news of the Law by 'asking in surprise: "Just how many prisons will need to be built to fit everyone in who breaks that law?"'.[89] M.V. Bulyshev (he who accused Stalin of 'liking boys' in Chapter 1) likewise characterised the Labour Law as a 'recruitment drive for the camps'.[90] Taking a similar tack, another worker, Petrov, stated at a discussion of the new Law that 'I've already booked myself a place in prison because the law won't stop me leaving this factory if I want to'.[91] This was an interesting position to take, suggesting both a rejection of the Law's power and legitimacy, yet simultaneously resigning himself to the personal consequences it would entail. For Petrov and those like him, personal sovereignty was a principle worth suffering for (although, by using humour to express that position, he inevitably softened the assertion, whether in the attempt to avoid trouble, or because he was tentatively exploring the extent of his own conviction as he voiced it aloud).

Unlike reactions to policies such as collectivisation or the Five-Year Plans, which tended to treat the campaigns themselves as harsh realities to somehow be dealt with, the Labour Law seems to have been taken as a direct attack on 'us', the people. Its aims were not understood separately from its unwelcome effects because it was an explicit threat to all citizens; the sense of being directly persecuted and abused by the state was the predominant theme in their critical responses. Take, for instance, the reaction of a worker at the Voskova-Malkov factory, who grumbled among a group of fellow metal grinders that 'In [this] law the only thing missing is the whip with which to beat the workers'.[92] The electrician Pavel Sherbakovich, the son of a White general (opposing the Bolsheviks in the Russian Civil War), discussed the Law with his fellow workers at a Leningrad production plant, comparing it to serfdom and suggesting that 'our leaders must have been drunk when they signed this declaration',[93] making it clear just how nonsensical he thought it.

At the same time, another law was enacted which extended the standard working day from seven to eight hours, and established a seven-day working week (each person still received one day off, but that day depended on workplace scheduling). The effects of these two restrictive laws could prove all too much, prompting the designer (конструктор) Shatilov to claim that 'I'm voting for an 18-hour working day – it's the quickest way to kick the bucket'. As with the increasing pressures of the state loans (which Shatilov also mentioned before his sarcastically suicidal comment), a rapid death could feel like the only way out.[94]

Not everyone was quite so restrained in their reaction to the Labour Law. So incensed was the lathe-turner A.G. Grigor'ev that he turned to melodrama. This 28 year-old Leningrad native fashioned shackles from some lengths of chain and, attaching these to his wrists and ankles, chained himself to one of the machines in his factory. He proceeded to declaim loudly and demonstratively to his fellow workers, rattling his chains as he did so, that '*This* is what the government's Law (*ukaz*) means!'. Unsurprisingly, he was arrested and an investigation launched.⁹⁵

Grigor'ev's actions were clearly a far more (personally) destructive way to vent anger and frustration at the state's directives than the caustic remarks of Samodurov, Bulyshev or Petrov. While his actions share certain aspects with humour, for it was a performance of the absurd (both the act of the man himself and the implied absurdity of the Labour Law), it also highlights by contrast how much more meaningful and affecting sharing jokes could be. All Grigor'ev's actions really achieved was to get himself arrested, even if his performance might have had some similar effects (or affects) to joke-sharing on those who saw him and who could empathise with his perspective. Yet, unlike joke-telling, Grigor'ev was actively excluding himself from the possibility of being part of that feeling of community, both by placing himself on a stage rather than among his comrades, and by almost begging to be arrested and literally removed from that social context. In part, his arrest was also due to the time at which he spoke: if Comrade Mironov's stand-up routine – even without dramatic props like Grigor'ev's chains – was acceptable but risqué in 1932, by 1940, such public performances were simply beyond the pale (a theme we'll explore in Chapter 4).

Interestingly, from the evidence available it seems that both the Labour Law and the state loans of the later 1930s provoked humorous criticisms that were bleaker and more despairing in tone than those which addressed the mass repressions in 1937-8. This makes sense when we remember that, if one of humour's functions is to distance us from unpleasant realities, making jokes about suicide was hardly to distance yourself from arbitrary arrests and executions. Instead, those throwaway references to putting yourself down 'for a bullet in the head' made psychological sense when dealing with difficulties which, however painful and discomfiting, could be mentally softened by exaggerating them beyond reality. The jokes were responses to and hence were also fundamentally conditioned by particular events and realities. Sometimes this meant inviting the spectre of death directly into the conversation, but if the spectre was already nearby, the urge was instead to laugh in its face.

The Nazi-Soviet Pact: Selling Out

Another spectre stalked the mental landscape of Soviet contemporaries across the 1930s, but it came much closer at the end of the decade: the spectre of war with Germany. Rumours circulated endlessly about this expected conflict, but then, suddenly, everything changed. The Nazi-Soviet Pact was signed in August 1939, and it came as a bolt from the blue. The Pact was announced on the front page of *Pravda*, complete with a photograph of Stalin, Molotov and Ribbentrop all grinning merrily rather than throttling each other as the mortal ideological enemies they had officially been the day before.[96] This sudden reversal was greeted with scepticism and confusion by many.[97]

But confusion was, as ever, accompanied in some quarters by amusement at the sheer incongruity and brazenness of the political manoeuvre. A supply agent and his friend burst into laughter as the news was read out by their regular Party Organiser: 'Look, the same person said the opposite [yesterday] – they didn't even bother to swap [him]', his friend giggled.[98]

The contradiction and hypocrisy was amusing in its very incongruity, but soon enough humour was used to address questions that went beyond bewilderment and confusion. For more than a decade, the regime had been demanding intense sacrifices of the population in order to achieve their heralded goal of forging a brave new world, using repressive measures in often unpredictable fashion to force this world into being. Humour was a crucial coping mechanism for people to bear and to navigate through these daily hardships, yet despite the often powerful criticisms delivered in their jokes, the appeal of the regime's overarching project remained intact. People's very real suffering could still be seen as serving some higher purpose. Yet, when the Pact was announced, it raised serious questions in the minds of the population: Was the regime honest about its declared goal to create a Communist utopia if it was prepared to make a deal with the devil? Were people simply being asked to slave their lives away under false pretences?

These doubts were not new for many, yet signing a Pact with the Nazi regime, for years described as the toxic antithesis of the Soviet project, made such concerns pressing and deeply troubling. Now, many people began to seriously wonder, were the leaders simply brutal and ambitious, brutal and fundamentally dishonest, or, perhaps worst of all, merely opportunistic and unprincipled? Many felt that the people had been sold out, and were merely the pawns of politicians.

A *kolkhoznitsa* from the Bolshevik artel' in Genicheskii raion, Ukraine, considered the Pact to be a case of: 'Molotov and Hitler drinking tea, but they shove us around so that we fight'.⁹⁹ In her view, the two leaders can relax over a refreshing cuppa while ordinary citizens from *both* countries are made puppets. At the Kirov Theatre in Leningrad, one Stelichek made a similar joke:

> If you'd said a year ago that Stalin and Molotov would be working together with Ribbentrop, you would have got 15 years; but now, look at this picture – two Arians and two Party men' [this rhymes in Russian: '*dva ariitsa i dva partiitsa*'].¹⁰⁰

In this imagining, the ideologies of both regimes are invoked ('Arians' and 'Party men') and placed in complement to each other; indeed, Stalin is apparently described as both an Arian *and* a Party man (possibly because Molotov's wife was Jewish, he is here considered a Jew), blurring the boundaries even further between these repressive political regimes.

If these joke-tellers began to see a similarity between the Soviet and Nazi leaderships, it was a natural extension to feel a sense of camaraderie with German civilians, too. While both sets of leaders happily drank tea, ordinary people on both sides would ultimately come to suffer the consequences.

When the Soviet Union began to occupy Eastern Europe from mid-1940, this perception only grew stronger. In the jokes which followed, we find an increasing emphasis on a camaraderie of suffering imagined between the citizens of the USSR and their new, forcibly-acquired comrades. E.T. Khodorovskii, a dough roller at the bread factory in Vinnytsia, Ukraine, declared sarcastically that,

> It's good for our brothers in Western Ukraine and Belorussia now that we've freed them. If a kilogram of sugar was worth kopeks before, now it's worth 100 rubles.¹⁰¹

More succinctly, M.D. Kareeva, a typist at the Central Naval Research Institute, told her colleagues that the seizure of the Baltic states meant that now 'they'll [get to] starve with us'!¹⁰² Both these jokes create a sense of mutual suffering, of all ordinary citizens being joined together because they are, or will be, equally badly affected by the political manoeuvrings of the Soviet (and Nazi) leadership. Along with the jokes about the Pact itself, these responses all propose a sense of collective identity that cuts across national and state boundaries to include all ordinary people, whether Soviet, Baltic, Belorussian, or German – an identity which is placed in contrast to the machinations of their rulers, who are likewise portrayed as a supra-national collective.

Using humour to address these events was a particularly productive way of expressing and even fostering this imagined camaraderie because, as with responses to the mass repressions of 1937-8, it helped to create a sense of detachment from destabilising events and fears, but also lessened the burden of them. And if a burden shared is a burden halved, then even a weight as heavy as this could be ameliorated when it was shared across multiple populations.

Ironically, this was not so dissimilar to the kind of international unity which Marx and Lenin had prophesied in terms of a world proletariat, although clearly not one *empowered* by an awareness of a shared identity and circumstances. Instead, this camaraderie is portrayed only as a kind of mutual suffering and helplessness, of being pawns in the games of political leaders.

Yet, even as critical humour engaged with foreign policy and external affairs, it remained inherently introspective. There was little depth to the characterisations of the outside world; instead, other populations and their leaders were portrayed as essentially analogous to the Soviet case. A hazy understanding of the international arena – a consequence of limited sources of information, combined with an understandable prioritisation of their own immediate difficulties – was employed primarily as a mirror with which Soviet citizens could reflect upon their own lives.

The reported 'evils' of Nazi Germany, which the regime had used as a bogeyman to make the Soviet project seem both desirable and essential to survival, were seen by some as already on full display in the USSR. P.I. Gadalov told his colleagues at the Aleksandrov station depot on the Iarovslavskii railway line that 'fascism has a brother in the communist';[103] Konstantin Megredlidze entrusted to his *anekdot* collection a line which drew a parallel between Hitler's dictatorship and the 'dictatorship of the *vozhdi*';[104] and, when asked 'In which countries does fascism exist?', a second-year university student in Tomsk answered acerbically, 'There is fascism in Germany, Italy, and in the USSR'.[105] Another common refrain was to pointedly observe that life was much better in the USA or in other capitalist countries,[106] or, as a joke circulating in Minsk in 1932 had it, 'a single American billionaire could buy the entire Five-Year Plan'.[107]

In all these jokes, the outside world is used as a reference point by which to judge the disappointments and frustrations of Soviet life; even when it came to truly dramatic international news stories, the difficult experience of daily life in the Soviet Union remained for Soviet citizens the centre of gravity about which all regime policies, domestic and foreign, orbited.[108]

This is not difficult to understand: the pressures of Stalin's demands to modernise the country at breakneck speed, and the merciless and often paranoid way those demands were implemented, made it impossible for contemporaries not to read policies and ideology through their everyday experiences.

In facing the endless State Loans and Five-Year Plans, the huge death toll of collectivisation, and the shockwaves of the mass repressions, humour was a crucial coping mechanism, especially when the regime's actions seemed illogical and destructive. Amidst the contradictions and the suffering, even in the darkest times, where there was humour, there was still life. As Mikhail Gorbachev put it later, 'the *anekdoty* always saved us'.[109]

Notes

1. TsGAIPD, f.25, op.5, d.46, ll.83-4 (December 1934).
2. GARF, f.8131, op.31, d.85474, l.2 (1939-40). ('Вот как приходится ходить при настоящей жизни'.)
3. GARF, f.8131, op.31, d.99015, l.19 (Early 1936 at the latest). ('Они ходят по деревне босые и светят голыми задницами'.)
4. TsGAIPD, f.25, op.5, d.53, ll.120-1. Another worker at the same factory made much the same reply: 'Well did you give me boots?', TsGAIPD f.24, op.5, d.2288, l.13 (December 1934).
5. cf. GARF, f.7676, op.21, d.8, l.84 (1932).
6. TsGAIPD, f.25, op.5, d.45, l.110 (December 1934).
7. Something which certainly continued in the postwar period: cf. Yekelchyk, *Stalin's Citizens*, 139-40.
8. Paraphrased from GARF, f.8131, op.31, d.1587, l.5(ob) (March 1937). Also cf. L.M. Glassman, 'The Bolsheviki as Humorists', *Current History*, 32.4 (1930), 724.
9. GARF, f.8131, op.31, d.43506, l.20 (c.1940).
10. TsGAIPD, f.24, op.2v, d.4017, l.137 (January 1940).
11. Il'ia Il'f & Evegenii Petrov, *Sobranie sochinenii v piati tomakh*, tom 5 (Moscow, 1961), 236 (Il'f's undated entries range from 1925 to his death in 1937).
12. Andrei Arzhilovskii, diary entries for 10 and 18 February 1937, Véronique Garros, Natalia Korenevskaya & Thomas Lahusen (eds.), *Intimacy and Terror: Soviet Diaries of the 1930s*, trans. Carol A. Flath (New York, 1995), 144, 147.
13. TsGAIPD, f.25, op.5, d.46, l.6 (December 1934).
14. Mel'nichenko, *Sovetskii anekdot*, 538.
15. RGASPI, f.M-1, op.23, d.1106, l.121 (c.1934-5).
16. GARF, f.5451, op.43, d.30, l.121(ob) (March 1933).
17. TsGAIPD, f.25, op.5, d.54, l.37 (December 1934).
18. GARF, f.8131, op.31, d.85338, l.18 (1940). Thanks to Steve Smith for help with the translation, which is particularly tricky in this case. The 'Feeding by correspondence' line implies 'virtual' (i.e. non-existent) food.
19. HPSSS 139/A/11, p.44.
20. GARF, f.8131, op.31, d.99140, l.3 (1935); d.16230, l.36 (1935). The archival recordings are a shortened summary of the joke's content. I have reconstructed it with reference to Mel'nichenko, *Sovetskii anekdot*, 498-9. Also see a related witticism by a worker in a Leningrad factory, who noted simply that 'Lenin led us to death by a gentle route, but Stalin does so with a faster tempo!' (GARF, f.5451, op.43, d.13, l.101 [October 1932]).
21. For this tendency to ascribe a vague 'cult of suffering' to the Russian psyche, see Daniel Rancour-Laferriere, *The Slave Soul of Russia: Moral Masochism and the Cult of Suffering* (London, 1995).
22. John Scott, *Behind the Urals: An American Worker in Russia's City of Steel*, ed. Stephen Kotkin (Bloomington, IN, 1989), 114.
23. Shitts, *Dnevnik*, 274 (1931). ('а случалось вам едать большевистским темпом'.)
24. GARF, f.5451, op.43, d.27, l.40 (January 1933).
25. TsGAIPD, f.24, op.5, d.2712, l.35 (November 1934).
26. Arzhilovskii, diary entry for 6 March 1937, Garros et al (eds.), *Intimacy and Terror*, 150-1. 'Kulak' was the name given to 'rich' peasants, whom the regime persecuted and dispossessed as part of the collectivisation drive.
27. Chamberlin, *Russia's Iron Age*, 102.

28. Chamberlin, *Russia's Iron Age*, 330.
29. e.g. GARF, f.7676, op.21, d.8, ll.81-2 (June 1932).
30. cf. HPSSS 111/A/9, p.10; 136/A/11, p.15; 147/A/12, p.4; 302/A/15, p.4; 454/(NY)1350/A/33, p.7; 516/B/5, pp.6-7. The Russian term was принудительно-добровольно. (The term 'free market' was a similar case, given it referred to the extremely expensive small kolkhoz markets permitted to make up for some of the shortfalls in the official shops (Shitts, *Dnevnik*, 200 (1930)).)
31. GARF, f.7676, op.21, d.4, l.46 (1932).
32. GARF, f.5451, op.43, d.12, l.2 (2 June 1932).
33. GARF, f.5451, op.43, d.12, l.32 (3 July 1932).
34. GARF, f.5451, op.43, d.28, l.178 (25 May 1933).
35. GARF, f.5451, op.43, d.12, l.74 (16 September 1932).
36. TsDAHOU, f.1, op.20, d.2988, l.147 (20 September 1929).
37. GARF, f.7676, op.21, d.4, l.44 (1932).
38. GARF, f.1235, op.107, d.434, l.99 (December 1930).
39. Wendy Z. Goldman, *Terror and Democracy in the Age of Stalin: The Social Dynamics of Repression* (Cambridge, 2007), Ch.3.
40. GARF, f.5451, op.43, d.12, l.15 (2 June 1932).
41. Scott, *Weapons of the Weak*, xvi, 29, 350.
42. TsGAIPD, f.24, op.2v, d.2664, l.262. More specifically, this related to a fundraising state lottery.
43. HDA SBU, f.16, op.33, d.57, l.156.
44. TsGAIPD, f.24, op.2v, d.4306, l.163.
45. RGASPI, f.M-1, op.23, d.1265, l.42 (1937).
46. RGASPI, f.671, op.1, d.244, l.36 (1936).
47. GARF, f.8131, op.31, d.64008, l.26.
48. Arzhilovskii, diary entries, Garros et al (eds.), *Intimacy and Terror*, 114, 131, 137, 139, 150 (1936-7).
49. Victor Kravchenko, *I Chose Freedom. The Personal and Political Life of a Soviet Official* (London, 1947), 108.
50. GARF, f.5451, op.43, d.27, l.16 (January 1933).
51. RGASPI, f.17, op.120, d.176, l.236 (1931).
52. TsDAVO, f.288, op.1, d.141, l.4 (1934). ('…вы строите домны, а будите кушать чугун'.)
53. RGASPI, f.M-1, op.23, d.1184, l.104 (1936). ('…будут сплошные гробы'.)
54. I present a generic version based on: GARF, f.8131, op.31, d.83654, l.10 (1936); HPSSS 396/A/20, p.10; Una Pope-Hennessy, *The Closed City: Impressions of a Visit to Leningrad* (London, 1938), 49; Mel'nichenko, *Sovetskii anekdot*, 541.
55. Shitts, *Dnevnik*, 273 (1931). I discuss the significance and role of the 'Jew' character in contemporary humour in Chapter 3.
56. GARF, f.7676, op.21, d.8, l.207 (October 1932).
57. GARF, f.5451, op.43, d.12, l.73 and, with slight variation, f.7676, op.21, d.8, ll.156, 159 (September 1932).
58. Viola estimates 4-5 million, *Peasant Rebels*, 209; R.W. Davies & Stephen G. Wheatcroft propose 5.5-6.5 million, *The Years of Hunger: Soviet Agriculture, 1931-1933* (Houndmills, 2004), 400-1, 415. As Viola notes, however, these numbers remain and will always remain imprecise.
59. GARF, f.8131, op.31, d.52823, l.8 (c.1934).
60. GARF, f.8131, op.31, d.241, l.4 (1933).
61. GARF, f.8131, op.31, d.4393, l.13 (c.1937).
62. GARF, f.8131, op.31, d.41217, l.9 (c.1933); also cf. HPSSS 104/A/8, p.10.

63 TsGAIPD, f.24, op.2v, d.1198, l.194 (late 1935). Thanks to Sarah Davies for this reference.
64 Thanks to Steve Smith for bringing this to my attention.
65 A Harvard Project interviewee recalled that determining whether the kolkhoz (a collective-owned farm) or *sovkhoz* (a state-owned farm) was better was like choosing between a 'pile of manure' divided in two by a wagon wheel (HPSSS 102/A/8, p.65).
66 Arkhipova & Mel'nichenko, *Anekdoty*, 147-51, 296-9.
67 Fitzpatrick, *Stalin's Peasants*, Ch.11, esp. p.310.
68 Stepan Podlubnyi, diary entry for 22 August 1936, in Garros et al (eds.), *Intimacy and Terror*, 298. I have altered the translation with reference to the original.
69 Arthur Koestler, *The Invisible Writing* (London, 2005 [1954]), 72.
70 Mel'nichenko, *Sovetskii anekdot*, 104 (no.117).
71 GARF, f.8131, op.31, d.85228, l.2(ob) (1937).
72 James Harris (ed.), *The Anatomy of Terror: Political Violence under Stalin* (Oxford, 2013), 1. These figures include the end of 1936, but the vast majority relate to 1937-8.
73 Karl Schlögel, *Moscow 1937*, trans. Rodney Livingstone (Cambridge, 2012).
74 Mikhail Bulgakov, *The Master and Margarita*, trans. Michael Glenny (London, 2003), written between 1928-40.
75 TsGAIPD, f.24, op.2v, d.2664, l.203 (1937).
76 GARF, f.8131, op.31, d.19123, l.26 (1938). ('Из кого состоит СССР? – Из друга народа и врагов народа'.)
77 GARF, f.8131, op.31, d.19123, l.26 (c.1940).
78 RGASPI, f.M-1, op.23, d.1236, ll.12-3 (July 1937), cited in P.P. Aleksandrov-Derkachenko (ed.), *Russkoe i sovetskoe molodezhnoe dvizhenie v dokumentakh 1905-1937 gg.* (Moscow, 2002), 274.
79 Podlubnyi, diary entry, Garros et al (eds.) *Intimacy and Terror*, 307. I translate the entry differently, using the original Russian (все мы под богом/НКВД ходим). I follow David Brandenberger's lead in translating this idiomatically: cf. his translation of a different source in *Political Humor*, 113.
80 HPSSS 129/A/10, p.11.
81 HDA SBU, f.16, op.31, d.80, l.45 (1938). It is likely, of course, that this young student was repeating something he had heard at home or elsewhere from adults, an issue I discuss in the next chapter.
82 Orlando Figes retells this conventional narrative in *The Whisperers: Private Life in Stalin's Russia* (London, 2007). See esp. pp.277-85; also cf. Wendy Z. Goldman, *Inventing the Enemy: Terror and Denunciation in Stalin's Russia* (Cambridge, 2011), 2, 76.
83 Quoted in Nataliia Sokolova, 'V zerkale smekha', *Voprosy Literatury*, 3 (1996), 374. This refers to Georges Bizet's *Pearl Fishers* (*Les pêcheurs de perles*, 1863); A.N. Afinogenov's *Fear* (1931); and A.N. Ostrovskii's *Guilt of the Innocents* (1884).
84 Shitts, *Dnevnik*, 191 (1930).
85 Chamberlin, *Russia's Iron Age*, 308.
86 V.I. Vernadskii, *Dnevniki 1935-1941 v dvukh knigakh*, tom 2 (Moscow, 2006), 75.
87 Vernadskii, *Dnevniki 1935-1941*, tom 1, 364 (4 December 1938); 235 (20 February 1938).
88 On the Labour Law, see Peter H. Solomon, Jr., *Soviet Criminal Justice under Stalin* (Cambridge, 1996), Ch.9. Statistics at p.299.
89 TsGAIPD, f.24, op.2v, d.4026, l.204 (1940). (In Russian, this was *zavod im. Maksa Gol'tsa*.)

90 GARF, f.8131, op.31, d.43623, l.6 (1940).
91 TsGAIPD, f.24, op.2v, d.4306, l.130 (1940).
92 TsGAIPD, f.24, op.2v, d.4306, l.142 (1940).
93 TsGAIPD, f.24, op.2v, d.4306, l.158 (1940).
94 TsGAIPD, f.24, op.2v, d.4306, ll.213-4 (1940). ('Этим самым, скорее протянешь ноги.')
95 TsGAIPD, f.24, op.2v, d.4306, l.136 (1940).
96 *Pravda*, 24 August 1939, 1.
97 Johnston, *Being Soviet*, 23-9.
98 HPSSS 74/A/6, p.63.
99 HDA SBU, f.16, op.32, d.54, l.222 (1939) ('…а нас сводят, чтобы мы дрались').
100 TsGAIPD, f.24, op.2v, d.3561, l.210 (1939). Thanks to Sarah Davies for this reference.
101 GARF, f.8131, op.31, d.88374, l.1(ob) (1940).
102 GARF, f.8131, op.31, d.68720 (1940). (Центральный научно-исследовательский институт морского флота.) For similar examples, see Brandenberger, *Political Humor*, 124.
103 GARF, f.8131, op.31, d.95714, l.11 (c.1932).
104 GARF, f.8131, op.31, d.64008, l.9 (No later than 1940).
105 RGASPI, f.M-1, op.23, d.1106, ll.129-30 (1935).
106 e.g. GARF, f.8131, op.31, d. 29139, ll.7-8 (1941-2); d. 34853, l.10 (1935).
107 GARF, f.5451, op.43, d.12, l.5 (1932).
108 A theme explored in a study of rumours circulating in this period: Johnston, *Being Soviet*, esp. xxiii-xli & Ch.1.
109 As recounted in V. Bakhtin, 'Anekdoty nas spasali vsegda', A. Strelianyi, G. Sapgir, V. Bakhtin & N. Ordynskii (eds.), *Samizdat veka* (Moscow/Minsk, 1997), 799.

CHAPTER 3
SPEAKING MORE THAN BOLSHEVIK: CROSSHATCHING AND CODEBREAKING

Forging the brave new world of Soviet Communism required far more than Five-Year Plans and collectivisation. A new world required new people, and Stalin's regime set about moulding the population in the only way it knew how: propaganda supported by direct and often brutal force. In the 1930s, the regime tried to eradicate unwanted 'leftovers' from the past: religion, gender inequality, the traditional family unit… In short, they wanted a new system and 'a new human' to inhabit it.

The New Soviet Person was to be athletic, educated, selfless, and completely dedicated to the mission of creating a perfect Communist world. They would be as well versed in great literature as they were in Marxism, committed to equality yet driven to exceed all expectations placed upon them. The aim was to perfect the self in order to perfect society, and to reforge oneself through ardent, cleansing labour. In the process, Soviet citizens had to learn a new ideological language in order to understand the demands placed on them, from 'shock-work' to 'Bolshevik tempo'. They also had to conceptualise and internalise what their efforts were supposed to achieve: grasping the developmental ladder from 'socialism' to 'communism' was no small task for millions who had for generations been illiterate peasants.

Some twenty years ago, Stephen Kotkin argued that this didn't turn out quite as the regime intended. Soviet citizens learnt how to 'speak Bolshevik', he said, but this was only to use the language and values of the regime to their best advantage, regardless of whether they believed everything they said.[1] If they were critical of the regime, like the medieval satirists Likhachev studied, they did so from within the symbolic world of the official order; they did not attack it by drawing on some other set of norms or values, but by holding up a mirror to that world in order to highlight its contradictions and inconsistencies.[2]

The concept of 'speaking Bolshevik' would go on to inspire many scholars to investigate what it meant to write, read, or even to think Bolshevik, moving our focus away from traditional 'totalitarian' binaries of support and resistance and into more complex grey areas. Nevertheless, two scholars in particular objected to the idea that Soviet people would only engage with Bolshevik ideology in such a coldly calculating manner. Jochen Hellbeck and Igal Halfin argued that citizens might *willingly* inscribe themselves – their identities and autobiographies – into official ideology, particularly within the personal setting of their diaries.[3] For Hellbeck and Halfin, acts of speaking Bolshevik represented going well beyond using regime ideology as a tool, and into playing it like a role you hoped to actually become, either by immediate near-spiritual conversion, or, like the diarists Hellbeck studied, faking it till they made it.[4]

For subscribers to this 'Soviet Subjectivity' school, learning to speak Bolshevik seemed to necessitate forgetting or at least disowning any other language you might have known. If Bolshevik language did not come to think for contemporaries, they nevertheless tried their hardest to think within it. All of which seemed to imply a profound disconnection from the prerevolutionary period – a rupture the Bolsheviks themselves certainly wanted to establish.

Every revolutionary regime by definition claims that it's making a fresh start. The past, they declare, has been torn up and thrown away, and now a fresh page awaits brand new ideas and structures (including some that will rewrite the past from the perspective of this new regime). Having done this, everyone can feel nice and smug that what they have achieved is 'progress', and perhaps in some ways it is.

But no society or culture is ever a 'blank page'. Revolutions don't wipe people's memories, even if they convince the majority of people to leave the past behind them. Every generation is defined by its parents rather more than it might care to admit and, as the cultural theorist Michel de Certeau put it, 'in spite of a persistent fiction, we never write on a blank page, but always on one that has already been written on'.[5] 'Progress', in other words, does not appear from nowhere and will always be just one more layer on top of other, similar layers. So although the Soviet leaders sought to create an entirely new civilisation, way of life, and, of course, a New Soviet Person, they could only attempt to do so on the foundations of the past.

The same was true of the population. Kirov's Carnival has already given us a taste of this: people used older folk traditions and practices to send up the regime and criticise the leadership, from mocking their excessive consumption in a moralising fashion, to making crude jokes about Stalin's sexual proclivities. And in Chapter 2, we saw how everyday realities could not be ignored when they conflicted so abrasively with the grand ideological promises of the regime. Soviet ceremonials mattered little when you were starving and had no shoes to wear. In their jokes, many people were demonstrably and often gleefully speaking more than Bolshevik.

Many of these older cultural registers are woven into the fabric of contemporary political humour; we find them in the implicit assumptions, thematic proclivities and the choice of contexts in which the humorous narratives take place. And because many or even most jokes centre upon the juxtaposition of incompatible premises or viewpoints, before ultimately judging one to be superior (or at least the other to be flawed), we can use them to discern some of the principles, 'truths', or paradigms which, for many Soviet citizens, would (or should) triumph over official ideological values and ideas.

But this was not necessarily a case of the old beating off the new: as Lawrence Levine puts it, 'Culture is a process, not a fixed condition; it is the product of unremitting interaction between the past and the present'; or, to paraphrase Jung, like the meeting of two chemical substances, if there is any reaction, both are transformed – and often in unexpected ways.[6] This chapter identifies some of these older values and paradigms and explores how they crosshatched and interacted with the new Soviet world, shaping an emergent, hybridised worldview in the process.

The second part of the chapter examines a closely related but more complex process of engagement with official ideology (and which has more in common with Likhachev's model). Here, contemporaries again juxtaposed official rhetoric with everyday realities – the chasm between the two could itself be frequently (and darkly) amusing – but they also went a step further. They created a shadow language: they seized ideological words and concepts and reforged them to fit their own experiences and interpretations of life in the Soviet Union. This was more than throwing critical barbs from the sidelines: they were contesting the meaning of official language itself and trying to make it somehow fit reality. They would rather see meaning than madness in the hard world they found themselves in, and so they set about breaking the 'code' of ideological language, to reveal what it really meant in practice. Not only did they speak more than Bolshevik, they also made 'Bolshevik' speak 'real'.

The Old in the New

Jokes are often brief sketches, just a few lines long and with the background and context assumed or evoked rather than elaborated. If you don't know the assumptions, you rarely get the joke, which is why foreign jokes are so often lost in translation. But these assumptions – the backdrop against which the punchline plays out – can tell us a lot. Beneath the surface level of many *anekdoty* lie a series of cultural value judgements, assumptions, and traditional modes of thought that served to create the 'world' in which the events of each joke unfolded. Humour is, in this sense, a multivalent cultural artefact: it contains a wealth of information about the perspectives and points of reference held by the people sharing it and, when we examine these elements in the Soviet context, we quickly discover many values and assumptions drawn from prerevolutionary paradigms and persisting, older standards of judgement that had little in common with the official Soviet world.

But this wasn't a head-on clash between old and new values, between tradition and revolution; it was a more nuanced, often unconscious crosshatching of those elements. We can see something of this in the thousands of letters written by ordinary people to those in power; the writers would attempt to bolster their pleas for help or redress with a mixture of clichés drawn from *both* the Soviet newspapers and traditional proverbs and folk wisdom.[7] For many, distinctions between these paradigms were far from clear-cut; even when speaking directly to the regime, there seems to have been little conscious sense that these value systems were in fundamental conflict.

What lies in the background can be hard to see, so we'll approach it from three different angles. Each of these highlights a particular prerevolutionary paradigm or perspective which was woven into the fabric of political humour, but, more than the fact of its survival, *how* it was woven in and what effects this had, particularly in the case of religious belief, reveals a great deal about how people made sense of their lives in the 1930s.

Sexism and Misogyny

The mass introduction of women to the workforce and significant changes to their traditional social roles seemed to represent the beginning of a new era for gender relations in the Soviet Union. Between 1928-37, some 6.6 million women entered the workforce in industry and service; indeed, of the four million new workers joining the labour force between 1932-37, a full 85 per cent of them were women.[8] By the late 1930s, even if they rarely made it to the top jobs, and never to the Politburo, women were remarkably well represented in skilled professions, making up 63 percent of physicians and 42 percent of the country's economists.[9] Along with these practical changes, the striking and powerful image of a New Soviet Woman strode into 1920s propaganda: she was a 'selfless revolutionary', 'modest, firm, dedicated, sympathetic, courageous, bold, hard-working, energetic' and of equal standing to her male comrades.[10]

But the tide would soon turn against these emancipatory changes. In 1930 the Party's *Zhenotdel* (Women's Section) was abolished and, despite a brief flurry of feminist activism during the first Five-Year Plan, the tone of official propaganda shifted ever more towards the promotion of traditional family values. In June 1936 a new law banned abortion (except in cases where the woman's health was endangered) and made divorce more difficult and expensive to obtain; at the same time, financial incentives were offered to women who had large numbers of children.[11] The change was clear: although women were expected to continue working alongside men, the state muted their political voice and expected them to perform the additional roles of idealised housewives and diligent baby-factories.

These profound but inconsistent changes, both on paper and in everyday life, have been studied in depth by various scholars, but it has been a more complex task to assess how gender relations were understood and spoken about on the ground by ordinary citizens.[12] Because, as we know, humour is a principal means through which people grapple with the new, uncomfortable, and the unstable, it seems reasonable to expect to see the changing role of women in Soviet society tackled in contemporary *anekdoty*. Did men accept the new roles and rights the state had afforded women in the 1920s? And even as the state began to renege on its promises, were these social changes discussed in everyday discourse? Well, the short answers are: 'no', and 'hardly ever'. The representation of women in political humour is extremely simplistic and one-sided, but this itself offers us some important insight into contemporary male attitudes to, and social portrayals of, women.

In political humour, the New Soviet Woman is conspicuously absent in either her 1920s incarnation as emancipated superwoman, or as the 1930s 'equal' but doubly-burdened worker and proud housewife. Women almost always appear in 1930s *anekdoty* as exclusively sexual beings or as sexless *babushki* (grandmothers). The former play secondary roles to male characters or are unprotestingly ravished by them (unlike in traditional erotic folklore, in which women were often powerful *because* of their sexuality).[13] The folkloric *babushka* is, on the other hand, characterised primarily by her age and associated moral authority, rather than by her gender.[14] With this in mind, we'll direct our attention to the figure of the younger woman as a source of contemporary male representations of the female gender.[15]

Here's a typical example of how women were represented in *anekdoty*:

> A young lady was sitting on the boulevard, wearing silk stockings. On her right leg hung a portrait of Stalin, and on the left, one of Lenin. A Jew walked by and stopped to bow. He bowed three times, and the young woman asked him, 'Why did you bow three times, you should've bowed twice – once to Lenin, once to Stalin.' But the Jew replied that he bowed once to each of them, and a third time because he'd spotted the beard of Karl Marx.[16]

This young woman is presented essentially as part of the scenery; the only reason she's not simply replaced by a wall is to facilitate the crude sexual allusion. The historian I.I. Shitts recorded another *anekdot* circulating in 1931 which asked, 'Why have women started wearing long skirts?', followed by the reply, 'It must have something to do with the general transition to closed distribution.'[17] So, to comment on a change in state provisioning, women are portrayed en masse as a (sexual) commodity that's now restricted by state legislation.

Other policy changes could prompt this kind of sexist humour: student stipends were abolished in 1940, causing V.P. Babinskii, a student at the Zoological Institute in Voroshilovskii raion, Stavropol'skii krai, to joke to his friends that 'the girls won't be able to study anymore, so they'll have to open some brothels' to pay their tuition fees.[18] Assuming that Babinskii and his male comrades weren't also planning to go on the game, women's achievements in education are here completely ignored and their only asset identified, once again, as sex. As we saw in the *anekdoty* in Chapter 1, that asset might also be seen as purely negative, with women appearing in those jokes solely to provide problematic sexual scenarios – unwanted pregnancy and pubic lice. In all these jokes, women are present to facilitate laughter aimed ultimately at the system and its leaders, but they suffer casual yet often profound collateral degradation.

Actual sexual intercourse was also drawn in a distinctly misogynistic fashion, as this *anekdot* demonstrates:

> Sometime while Comrade Andreev was People's Commissar of a [railway] line, he was in Tiflis and visited the [station's] bathhouse. There he saw three buttons. He pressed the first one and a boy appeared. Andreev sent him away. He pressed the second button and a young lady came in, whom he proceeded to use [использовал]. When he pressed the third button, an Armenian entered the room and raped Andreev. Since then, railway stations feature only two buttons.[19]

This crudely colourful *anekdot* is pretty typical in how it represents sex and women (as well as an ethnic stereotype that Armenians are partial to sodomy). From the start, the female character – a prostitute, we assume – is made absurd by referring to her as a 'young lady' (the Russian word '*baryshnia*' carries even stronger connotations of noble birth) and is then unceremoniously 'used' by this Comrade Andreev. That sexual penetration is an act of forceful domination is then immediately re-emphasised by the rape of Andreev, an act which has strong similarities with the *anekdot* from Chapter 1 in which Kalinin sodomises Stalin. In both cases, the *anekdot* is not simply homophobic (little surprise in itself, given the country and the time period), but clearly equates the act of sexual penetration with domination more broadly. Kalinin's physical power as the sodomiser was bolstered by his 'moral' refusal to take the 'female' role, hammered home when Kalinin proceeds to outlaw sodomy. Kalinin, in the role of dominant penetrator, is the winner on all counts, whereas Stalin or Comrade Andreev, via the act of penetration, are degraded, dominated, and deceived.

Of course, it's no great surprise to find that the propagandistic representations of the New Soviet Woman did not find true reflection in social reality. But what *is* striking in the humour of these years – years of enormous social change – is the apparent absence of *all* gender tensions, except in instances featuring (homo)sexual domination as a means to mock certain authority figures. The closest we have to examples of humour which addressed changing gender relations deal with the subject of alimony payments. One was recorded by the Western journalist Ella Winter in 1933, and relates to the new Code on Marriage, Family and Guardianship, introduced in 1927. The Code made divorce far easier to obtain; in response, divorce rates soared and the Supreme Court was forced to instigate punishments for men who married purely to get women into bed and then annulled the marriage.[20]

> A man comes to the court and is asked to pay alimony to his wife, a third of his income.
> 'I can't. I'm already paying that to a wife.'
> 'Well, you must pay a second third.'
> 'I can't. I'm already paying that too.'
> 'Well, then you must pay a third third.'
> 'I can't. I'm paying that too.'
> 'What do you mean? You are paying all your wages to former wives? Then what are you living on?'
> 'I'm living on the alimony my wife is getting from five other men.'[21]

The playwright A.N. Afinogenov recorded a few humorous aphorisms on this subject in his personal papers, too: 'If it weren't for the alimony, how would you remember your youth?'; 'Never love so much that you will have to pay alimony afterwards'; and, in a similar vein, 'Before you get divorced, ask yourself: where will you banish your wife to?'.[22]

These witticisms suggest that some changes in traditional socio-sexual relations *were* subject to humorous, satirical comment. But the New Soviet Woman is still missing in action. Instead, while that first alimony joke gently chides the philandering Soviet men who took advantage of the new laws, women are left not only off-stage, but, as in the jokes we just examined, have effectively been turned into a commodity traded between men on a sexual marketplace. This implies a far greater degree of continuity in traditional, misogynistic attitudes than can be accommodated under the umbrella rationale of propaganda simply presenting a distorted view of women's roles in the 1930s. Instead, changing gender roles were seemingly shrugged off by male Soviet citizens, who paid the subject little heed.

This is not simply a source issue: while regime agents might not have recorded jokes made specifically about women's changing roles, the same absence holds true across the other source bases I examined. And even if we assume that misogynistic humour would not have been recorded, we still have the evidence of how women were portrayed in the humour which *was* documented, or, rather, how they were *not* portrayed. The persistent absence of women in jokes reflects a far more deeply entrenched set of cultural assumptions. Women are wallpaper in this, a genre given to contemporary social commentary; they are not considered important enough to merit inclusion in anything but minor or degrading roles. This is itself evidence of a continued, engrained misogyny at odds with the story we see in legal documents and propaganda posters.

If we accept that humour functions in large part to control and resolve frustrations and tensions, the absence of direct comic engagement with changing gender roles likely indicates a male refusal to adapt. In Wendy Goldman's study of women's entry into the workplace in the 1930s, she identifies 'resentment' as the defining male reaction – a 'resentment [expressed] in a sexualised form', which often escalated from verbal slurs to sexual harassment and assault.[23] These reactions closely mirror the indirect, implicit gender assumptions embedded within 1930s *anekdoty* that address women solely through a language of (often aggressive) sexual commodification or domination. However inconsistent the regime's approach to women and their role within society across the 1920s-30s, for male citizens, the entrenched cultural paradigm seems only to have been enflamed rather than dampened or extinguished by legislative and propaganda attempts to reshape gender relations. Whatever the very real changes in the press and on the ground, the jokes tell us a different story about contemporary attitudes and assumptions.

Religious Belief

Hounded yet never entirely crushed in the 1930s, religious belief would burst forth once again during the Great Patriotic War when Stalin, recognising how the nearness of death and hope for an afterlife rather concentrate the mind during wartime, allowed the Orthodox Church a mild reprieve. Just a few years earlier, the 1937 census had shown that over half the Soviet population were prepared to openly declare themselves 'believers', too.[24] Clearly, belief never entirely went away, and in humour we can see that religious assumptions (often passively) continued to inform the interpretational foundations from which citizens critiqued and wrestled with the Soviet world.[25]

Occasionally, the appearance of religion in critical humour took the form of mockery directed at authority figures. For example, when his wages were delayed yet again, a worker in tannery 2 in Odesa loudly declared that, 'Jesus Christ rode on one donkey, but Stalin [rides] on 150 million donkeys'.[26] Christ, in this reckoning, was far less demanding as a leader, and Stalin was happy to treat all citizens of the USSR as pack animals. Rather more explicitly, Shitts recorded an *anekdot* in his diary which portrays a direct confrontation between believers and a *bezbozhnik*, a member of the League of Militant Atheists, an organisation which sent its emissaries out into the countryside to 'convert' the peasantry to atheism:

> In a village, a '*bezbozhnik*' demonstrated at length to the peasants that there is no God. After his speech, he asks the audience whether what he's said makes sense. One of the *muzhiki* [peasants] adopts a Socratic method.
> [He asks] 'Have you seen how horses shit?'
> 'I've seen it'.
> 'And you know what their shit's like?'
> 'Yes'.
> [The *muzhik*] then asks about humans and ascertains that horse shit and human shit are different. 'And do you know why?'
> The *bezbozhnik* can't find an answer.
> 'So then, you son-of-a-bitch, if you don't understand shit, how do you presume to judge God?'[27]

But as the militant *bezbozhnik* campaign wound down, scenes like these diminished in jokes too. By the 1930s, such direct attacks and confrontations involving religious references or assumptions seem to have been rare. More commonly, religion remained in the background of critical humour, but it was no less significant as a result.

Various *anekdoty* featured God or St Peter in positions of power over Bolsheviks' lives and afterlives. A widespread joke involved a leading Bolshevik (his identity varies) attempting to enter Heaven after death, but being refused entry. A stranger then volunteers to help the despondent Bolshevik, loading him into a sack and marching back up to the pearly gates: 'Do you have Marx [or Lenin] in there?'. 'Yes,' comes the reply. 'Well, here's his trash,' the helpful stranger answers, tossing the sack over.[28] The idea of Marx, Lenin, Stalin, or other Bolsheviks (officially atheists) entering Heaven is clearly absurd, but the focus of this joke is actually the denigration of a current Soviet leader as the 'trash' or leftovers of his predecessors.

This is echoed in a *chastushka* that a worker sang in Odesa's Petrovskii factory:

Ленин, Ленин –	Lenin, Lenin
Ты на небе	You're in Heaven
Тут твои детки	Here your bairns
Умирают от пятилетки.	Are dying from the Plan.[29]

This time Lenin has made it into Heaven, but again the motivation here is not to argue for the existence of God or an afterlife, but simply to highlight the people's suffering under the Five-Year Plan. In these jokes and many others, there is a consistent assumption: God remains the ultimate power and arbiter, even though the humour or point of the joke lies elsewhere. The world continued to be God's stage, upon which the Bolsheviks happened, for the time being, to perform.

This hierarchy of paradigms is visible in the sarcastic declamation of M.A. Uspenskii, a village teacher in Nebylovskii raion, Vladimirskaia oblast', who pompously explained the '1 to 5' Soviet marking system to his class: 'God's knowledge is a 5, a teacher's is a 4, but students' is a 3'. Uspenskii's knowledge and understanding of propriety was clearly not up to scratch, however, as he would have cause to reflect following his arrest and conviction for 'antisoviet agitation'.[30] A more developed *anekdot* was preserved by Shitts in his diary:

> In need of some money, a Jew climbs a tall tree and leaves a note there for God, asking for 50 rubles. Down below, he is caught and questioned by an agent who takes him to the GPU to explain why he'd climbed the tree. The Jew explains frankly. Thinking to attract him to the atheist movement, the agent assures him that God will not help, but that Soviet power will: he gives him 25 rubles.
>
> The Jew runs back to the same tree and sends thanks to God for the 25 rubles, but asks that in future He sends the money directly, because they [the authorities] only gave him half, keeping 25 rubles for themselves.[31]

Despite Soviet Power's best attempts to convince, cajole and even to bribe people to renounce God, as this *anekdot* neatly captures, many simply continued to interpret the world and its phenomena through a religious lens.

We can also detect the underlying presence of a religious paradigm in emotionally-charged language. Jokes and sarcasm driven by frustration or anger were often accompanied by curses like 'Devil take you!', branding various Soviet leaders 'Devils', or simply shouting 'To the Devil!'[32] In Leningrad, in the wake of the Kirov murder, a frequent response was to rhetorically dispatch the former city boss directly to Hell: numerous workers in Leningrad factories, and others in an informant's apartment block, were heard dismissing the assassination with a curt, 'To hell with him!' (чёрт с ним).[33] Others, like a certain Petrov in Leningrad's Stalin Factory, took a different yet still religiously-infused tack: 'One's been buried, and thank God!'[34]

None of this proves that the Soviet citizens who used these

expressions were religious believers, but it still highlights a continuity of religious elements in everyday and emotional language.³⁵ Ways of discussing certain important topics – particularly death – were still significantly coloured by prerevolutionary, religious categories and terminology. If 'speaking Bolshevik', with its learned phrases, slogans and values was as important, or at least as constant, in everyday life as historians have often implied,³⁶ then the survival of these overtly religious elements in open speech should not be overlooked in their significance.

If we return to the diary of the student zoologist P. Afanas'ev, who we met briefly in Chapter 2 joking that bread was now the stuff 'of fairytales', we gain a little more insight into the space in many citizens' lives or outlooks which was not left empty by the loss of religion but, on the contrary, was a space which religion never entirely vacated. Afanas'ev grappled with the tension he personally felt in a rather mordant poem:

В материю твою всегда я верил	In your materialism I have always believed
И диалектику считаю за закон	And I consider dialectics a law
Но петь о ней пока я не намерен	But I still don't intend to sing of it
И мне пришлось вернуться до икон.	And I had to return to the ikons.³⁷

The young Afanas'ev, brought up in the Soviet world from birth, expresses a strong, self-consciously rational confidence in the Marxist principles of dialectical materialism. Yet, despite this, he finds those frameworks insufficient to satisfy his emotional and spiritual needs. His internal conflict or need for spiritual reassurance was far from unique, as we can see in the resurgence of religious belief during the war and, indeed, after the Soviet Union collapsed. (Under Stalin, we might also speculate that the very fact religious belief was publicly frowned upon or punished would, ironically, make it attractive to young people seeking to rebel against official expectations.) In the Harvard Interview Project, too, we frequently encounter complex mixtures of formal, outward atheism and a lingering, often unreflective belief in a god, in the importance of faith and of a Church, or simply a strong conviction that religious freedom should be guaranteed in any state.

On the other hand, religion might also fill more prosaic desires left unsatisfied by the Soviet regime. For some rural dwellers, the Church might simply be, as Sarah Davies notes, 'explicitly associated with entertainment': there were so few cultural or recreational activities on offer that going to church, especially for particular events, could help relieve the boredom of the long winter months. The local church might have a talented choir, for example, and so, as one *kolkhoznitsa* summed up, 'I go to church like I go to the club – for entertainment. If you go to the club to see a film you have to pay, while to go to the church is free'.[38] In Leningrad's Krasnogvardeets factory, on 2 May 1937 workers similarly decided to celebrate Easter rather than go on a cultural outing because, they grumbled, the outing required them to chip in some money from their wages![39] Attending Church events did not necessarily imply belief, then, or at least not a belief uninflected by more everyday interests and a keen eye for a bargain.

In the predominantly Muslim territories of Central Asia, the egalitarian principles of Soviet socialism were often enthusiastically taken up, as they fitted quite neatly with existing religious outlooks. However, this by no means led to the abandonment of religious faith, resulting instead by 1940, as Paul Froese puts it, in 'a bizarre blend of antireligious policy sporadically enforced by a local leadership of self-proclaimed Muslims'.[40] In fact, when confessional freedom seemed to be on the cards during discussions of the 1936 Stalin Constitution held across the USSR, in one Muslim area the population not only asked for 12 mosques to be reopened, but had even devised a plan for their mullahs to be funded by the local kolkhoz, neatly blending together traditional Muslim and the new Soviet collectivism.[41]

Orthodox believers also cited the Stalin Constitution to defend their right to worship; but, again, secular and religious elements became rapidly interwoven. In the Mordovian Republic some 500 people actually gathered in prayer to thank God for Article 124 of the Constitution, which granted them confessional freedom, echoing the *anekdot* about the GPU's attempts to bribe a Jew into atheism.[42] Others argued, more practically, that if all repossessed church buildings now belonged to 'the people', then 'the people' could damn well decide to reopen them.[43]

This mixing of values wasn't just about leveraging Soviet promises to protect the faith, though. Like the Muslim communities, Orthodox citizens might actually come to accept particular Soviet policies by blending them with preexisting religious teachings – for example, by criticising or persecuting kulaks (allegedly 'rich' peasants) because the gospels also proclaimed 'Woe to you, the rich'.[44] A Lutheran pastor even concluded a sermon in 1936 with the words, 'We must become Stakhanovites of our belief and religion'![45] Like the pastor, contemporaries could become quite holistic in their approach: multiple value systems were available to them (despite the state's attempts to destroy all but its own), so they picked and chose the bits they liked, or the ones which seemed most useful to them in a particular situation. This was why students, even good Komsomol members, might appeal to saints, say their prayers and use ikons as religions talismans before taking exams, and why over 200 girls, who'd somehow convinced themselves that the 1937 census foreshadowed the Apocalypse, turned up at a first-aid station in their village to request certificates attesting to their virginity, believing this would help secure them redemption.[46] In uncertain times, why not try to stack the odds in your favour?

Tensions obviously still remained, but this was the tension of coexistence and entanglement, rather than a to-the-death struggle. As William Husband eloquently put it in his study of religion in the early Soviet Union, the majority was made up of people like

> the youth who preferred one faith at home and another in public, the peasant who believed in and praised God but resented priests and opposed any new religious expenditures, the worker who had received religious training in childhood but passively and without visible regret became resigned to 'the new way' after the revolution, the so-called protoproletarian who failed to attend church regularly or fulfill Easter obligations but clung tenaciously to the right to celebrate church holidays, [and] the party member who observed both religious and civil rites...[47]

Festivals and holidays were particularly fertile ground for the creative mixing of traditional and Soviet rituals and practices. While the state tried to wipe religious holidays off the calendar by creating its own, many (probably most) people simply took the opportunity to celebrate both. Andrei Arzhilovskii and countless others continued to celebrate Easter, but were just as happy to raise a glass and snack on a *kulich* (the traditional pastry blessed at the Easter service) on an otherwise Red 1 May.[48] And even if you chose only to mark the new Soviet holidays, you might still use the Orthodox calendar to give temporal shape to the year, not from religious conviction, but because the seasonal rhythms were engrained to the point they simply felt 'natural'.[49]

It was in these moments, to quote Malte Rolf, 'that the culture of celebrations dictated by the party-run state first became living culture'.[50] Like Kirov's Carnival, any officially-ordered and -orchestrated event could be adopted and adapted by ordinary people. In the process it changed from something 'forced upon them from the top to an event that had some meaning for the people'.[51] Once again, this was not the officially-sanctioned, brief Carnival that Mikhail Bakhtin wrote about (see Chapter 1), but a more nuanced and continuous blending of sanctioned and unsanctioned elements; they crosshatched and influenced each other, forming something new – something living – in their union. More importantly, this was not only true of festivals, the subject of Rolf's study, but of *all* ideological dictates; as we'll see later in this Chapter and in Chapter 5, culture came alive in the crosshatching.

As for religion specifically, the picture is one of complex and changing *blends* of religious and non-religious outlooks. Confessional faith remained a potential source from which Soviet citizens young and old could draw comfort, insight, and alternative standards of judgement with which to crosshatch the officially-determined world around them. The religious assumptions which persisted in critical humour and in everyday speech, as well as in the practical rhythms of village life, suggest the endurance but also interweaving of these values with the new Soviet world. In fact, the Harvard Project analysts concluded that by the 1950s, 'much of the religious sentiment that remains [in the Soviet Union] has become more secularized and is expressed in the form of social ethics',[52] just as it would across much of Western Europe in the following decades. In the often chilly world (literally and metaphorically) of modernisation and poverty, threads of religion could be woven into the fabric of daily life to provide warmth, comfort, and a sense of greater coherence to the whole.

Historical Awareness

October 1917 was evidently not an uncrossable fissure in the minds of Soviet citizens and, alongside the often passively-retained cultural and social values we've been discussing, they could also draw on their memories and knowledge of prerevolutionary history to critique and to question the new Soviet world. A particularly colourful example was the widespread practice of 'decoding' official acronyms, which we'll examine in more detail below. For now, we'll take just one example, which was to decipher the acronym of the Communist Party itself as 'All-Union Serfdom of the Bolsheviks' (the Russian acronym was VKP(b) and the decipherment ran '*Vsesoiuznoe Krepostnoe Pravo Bol'shevikov*').[53] A child in the fourth grade deciphered it just as 'All-Union Serfdom',[54] and a Komsomol organiser told a student at a medical technical college in Voronezh that it stood for the 'Second Serfdom of the Bolsheviks'.[55] A similar comparison appears in an *anekdot* told by a train conductor while at work in 1938:

> Stalin asks an old man how old he is. The latter answers, 'I don't know,' and asks Stalin in turn, 'How many years were there between the first serfdom and the second? That'll be how old I am.'[56]

In these jokes, the new regime is not only explicitly and unfavourably compared to the old one, they even suggest that Bolshevism was a dramatic regression towards the pre-1861 period, before Alexander II abolished serfdom. Indeed, when the Labour Law was passed in July 1940, E.T. Iakovlev, a mechanic working at Leningrad's Gidrogeopribor factory, remarked waspishly that now quite 'a few historians are going to need to refute [the idea] that serfdom was abolished in 1861.'[57] Recall, too, the antics of A.G. Grigor'ev, the lathe-turner in Leningrad who fashioned shackles and chained himself to his machine, shouting and clanking his manacles to show what the Labour Law meant for ordinary workers (Chapter 2). Grigor'ev was clearly expressing a widespread sentiment, although it was rather safer (and simpler) to draw parallels with serfdom without resorting to the use of physical chains.

This awareness of prerevolutionary history could play an important role in postrevolutionary assessments of your life, rights, and estimation of the new rulers. On the latter subject, the American journalist and historian William Chamberlin recorded an *anekdot*, circulating in the early 1930s, which highlighted the various strengths of former monarchs that were sorely needed in the Soviet present:

> Russia, after the five-year plan, needed three Tsars: Peter the Great to clear up the unfinished building, Alexander II to free the peasants from serfdom, and Nicholas II to raise enough food to make up for the shortage.[58]

A.S. Samoshin told an *anekdot* among his fellow workers at the Tel'man factory in Voronezh that went further still, emphasising what a political revolution really meant in structural terms:

> Under tsarism the tsar was at the top, and at the very bottom were the tramps and market tricksters. But now it's all turned around: the tsar's at the bottom, and the tramps are in charge.[59]

These comparisons might be sharp, but they were also underlaid by a simple nostalgia and generalised equation of the tsarist regime with 'good times'. A short rhyming couplet, which some Komsomol students pointedly wrote in their textbooks beneath a passage on building 'the foundations of socialist economics', made this plain:

| *Byl tsar' i tsaritsa,* | [When] there was the tsar and tsarina, |
| *Byl khleb i pshenitsa.* | There was bread and there was wheat.⁶⁰ |

An underlying, shared sense of older standards – of History, even – provided a benchmark against which the Soviet regime was judged by contemporaries, but these comparisons were not always overtly negative. We can find *anekdoty* in which Stalin is simply induced to admit that he is now 'in [tsar] Nikolai's place', for example.⁶¹ A similar connection between the last tsar and the new rulers was made visually at Factory 67 in Serpukhov, Moskovskaia oblast', in which a poster of the late emperor was pinned up with the legend '*joining the Party*' (вступает в партию).⁶² Nevertheless, even in these cases of comic but not explicitly negative comparison, the very hint that the two regimes were similar meant that the Bolsheviks' claim to be creating an entirely new life and political system was being explicitly repudiated.

All these comparisons demonstrate both an awareness of sociopolitical structures which predated the Revolution and a practice of directly criticising the Soviet regime in relation to them. But contemporaries were simultaneously criticising the regime with reference to its own promises, too: the failure of the Bolsheviks to introduce promised civil rights, particularly after these were set down in the 1936 Stalin Constitution, was criticised *both* in relation to Bolshevik promises *and* far older ideas of emancipation. Similarly, as the mass arrests of 1937-8 unfolded, historical knowledge and Bolshevik values could be harnessed side-by-side in an angry, rather desperate threat that appeared in graffiti scrawled on the toilet walls of Canteen 129 in Leningrad: 'It's going to be the same for all you Communists as it was for the tsarist gendarmes in 1917'.⁶³ Although the Bolsheviks had overthrown a repressive police system, they had now created their own and could potentially fall victim to the same revolutionary desires that had brought them to power.

We should also remember that the *anekdot* and *chastushka* genres themselves represent a continued engagement with prerevolutionary times. These forms had a rich history in oral culture as a way of socially criticising power and authority, and many of the central premises and tropes which characterised them in the 1930s drew on a rich 'language of traditional subjects and motifs'.⁶⁴ As Seth Graham puts it, 'Although the *anekdot* rapidly acquired new, historically specific features in the transformed sociopolitical atmosphere following the October Revolution, it is a mistake simply to draw a thick red boundary at 1917 on the time line of its generic evolution'.⁶⁵

Hence, for example, many 1930s *anekdoty* included animals as protagonists – blending into the venerable genre of Aesopian 'animal folktales' ('сказки о животных').⁶⁶ This format gave the jokes the added sense and power of conveying a moral lesson (or warning) of some kind, and carried a strong egalitarian edge that levelled (or inverted) power structures, which was an underlying theme in Chapter 1. Folk wisdom of this kind usually trumped anything the Bolsheviks had to offer, and was given voice in *anekdoty* by the figure of the *babushka* or *muzhik* – characters defined by a traditional, earthy authority. Even as these forms developed to engage with and sometimes internalise elements of the new Soviet world, contemporaries could nevertheless feel that they were speaking in a language that was in certain important ways their own, or which was, at least, not the regime's.

Antisemitism?

It's time to address the elephant in the room, or, rather, the Jews in the jokes. Antisemitic views were recorded by the regime if they were overheard, and, moreover, in the very same 'mood reports' (*svodki*) which reported 'antisoviet' jokes there was often a separate section which focused specifically on 'manifestations of antisemitism'.⁶⁷ In these reports, the traditional clarion call to 'beat the Jews' ('бей жидов') was diligently noted when the authorities detected it, as were other publicly-voiced expressions of antisemitism.⁶⁸ Antisemitism was not, then, a phenomenon which the regime chose to ignore (though its level of interest was inconsistent); it was instead monitored, yet considered an issue distinct from humour. Was this in fact the case?

Every culture has jokes about its neighbours, and they're often disparaging if not simply xenophobic or racist. The Soviet Union was no different, but, aside from the memorable 'two buttons' joke we saw earlier, in which an Armenian rapes Comrade Andreev, or the throwaway remark about Georgians 'liking boys' in Chapter 1, there are surprisingly few examples of ethnicity-based prejudice in the *anekdoty* I discovered in the archives. We can only assume that, given their prevalence in published anthologies, such material was not usually considered 'antisoviet agitation' by the authorities.

There is one major exception: the character of 'the Jew', who appears frequently in 1930s *anekdoty* recorded *both* by the state and in the diaries and memoirs of ordinary citizens. For a long time I was puzzled by the way so many *anekdoty* seemed to have 'the Jew' as their main character for no apparent reason: the characters didn't seem to be doing anything stereotypically 'Jewish', so why were they there? Antisemitism certainly existed in the 1930s and would escalate during and after the Second World War under the regime's direction. Was I missing the prejudice in the jokes, or was something more complicated going on?

All bar one of the *anekdoty* I found which include 'Jews'[69] present the character in a rather ambivalent manner. Consider these examples:

> Two Jews who lived together had a lot of gamebirds (дичи), chickens, ducks, etc. These birds did not behave – they fought and tried to run off. The Jews decided to pluck the birds, which made them cold and so they huddled together in a big heap. This was, allegedly, the principle on which the kolkhoz was formed.[70]

In this *anekdot*, Jews are ostensibly charged with creating the kolkhoz system – an extremely negative indictment. But they apparently do so by accident, are seemingly not portrayed as representatives of Soviet power at large, and nor do they really benefit from the creation of the kolkhoz system. Here's another one:

> At the beginning of Soviet power, two Jews agreed that one should sell coffins and the other bread rolls. If the regime fed the workers well, the bread rolls would sell; if not, the coffins.[71]

This *anekdot* plays on a stereotype of Jews as cunning merchants. We're expected to laugh at their craftiness in finding a way to prosper in spite of Soviet power, but it would be a stretch to see this as unequivocally antisemitic. The privations and potential suffering of the people are caused by 'Soviet power', not (nor exacerbated) by the Jews as 'profiteers'.

More importantly, 'crafty' characters in Russian folklore are usually seen in a positive light. The Russian concept of *'khitrost"* (cunning, craftiness) lacks the negative connotations familiar to English speakers, and is often a virtue attributed to the heroes of folk stories. This is neatly illustrated in a joke recorded by Eugene Lyons that features a Jew outwitting the state: facing execution for counterrevolution, this Jew is granted a final request. He asks for strawberries. 'But this is November,' the warden apologises; 'there are no strawberries in November'. 'That's all right. I can wait till summer,' the Jew assures him.[72]

A final example to consider here is the *anekdot* we saw earlier in which a Jew bows to the portraits of Stalin and Lenin, and then to the 'beard of Karl Marx'. In that joke, the 'Jew' character is the mouthpiece for the punchline, but he displays no obviously 'Jewish' characteristics aside from, perhaps, an exaggerated obsequiousness which is anyway tempered by wit. The humour of the *anekdot* essentially lies in its smutty allusion and poking fun at the ubiquitous sight of Soviet leaders' portraits placed next to ones of Karl Marx.

So what can we conclude from all this? There are certainly Jewish stereotypes at play here: the Jew as (perhaps) Bolshevik, as merchant, or as exaggeratedly servile. Other reports strongly suggest that antisemitism continued to exist in the general population in these years. And yet these *anekdoty* are not quite so straightforward: like the religiously-infused jokes, they contain stereotypical assumptions, but those assumptions *are not the point* of the jokes. The *anekdot* we saw in Chapter 1, in which, due to his accent – an inability to pronounce the rolling Russian 'r' – a Jew's phonecall to 'the circus' (*v tsirk*) is misdirected to the Central Executive Committee (*VTsIK*) makes this distinction clearer. Although containing a negative stereotype, in this joke as in others, the humour actually lay elsewhere: in this case, when Kalinin answers the phone as 'chief clown'.

In these *anekdoty*, the 'Jewish' characters facilitate the joke, but they are not its targets, nor are they usually essential to its function; their 'Jewishness' is of only secondary importance. And let's take this point further by comparing multiple versions of *anekdoty* to see how interchangeable the 'Jewish' characters were. Consider, for example, the *anekdot* from Chapter 1 in which Stalin tries to make everyone in the Soviet Union happy and is advised that he can do so very cheaply – for the price of a single bullet. Of the seven examples I found in the archives, the person who gives Stalin this 'advice' is a Jew on only two occasions.[73] Otherwise, he is an actor, an economist (twice), Stalin's secretary, or is left undescribed.[74] In another joke, the stranger who helps a leading Bolshevik into Heaven by throwing him over the pearly gates in a sack is on one occasion 'an apostle', and on another 'an elderly Jew'.[75] There is clearly no antisemitic core in this case, given the interchangeability across religious divides which allows a (Christian) apostle to perform the same duty as a Jew. This is given further weight by reference to other source-bases: Arkhipova and Mel'nichenko cite eight variations of this *anekdot*, in which the helpful stranger is a Jew on four occasions, but is also Trotskii, 'one of ours' ('из наших'), a jolly Iaroslavets (a citizen of Iaroslavl', renowned in folktales for their cunning), or even the devil himself.[76]

The *anekdot* in which Stalin is saved from drowning only for his rescuer to regret the deed when he realises who he's saved features, from the four versions I discovered, a Jew only once.[77] Otherwise, Stalin's saviour was a peasant, or, on two occasions, a *kolkhoznik*.[78] In the two sources for a joke in which a couple of friends walk past Lenin's mausoleum and note listlessly that it would have been better had Lenin lived and his ideas died, these men are described once as 'two Jews' and once simply as 'two people'.[79] Exactly the same casting holds true for an *anekdot* in which two figures stand by the Kremlin wondering if the walls are so high in order to keep bandits *in* or out.[80] And, perhaps most telling of all, it was perfectly possible for different witnesses in a criminal investigation into 'antisoviet' *anekdot*-telling to remember the very same joke differently, one recalling a 'Jew' in the central role, another simply 'a peasant'.[81]

Given how easily substituted the 'Jew' could be, the ethnicity or stereotype attached to them obviously carries no importance either for the humour of the *anekdot* nor, or very little, in the motivation of the joke-teller. Instead, the 'Jew' was a literary type – a generic character or fictional convention in the storehouse of tropes and personae ready to be taken off the shelf and made to occupy any number of narrative scenarios.[82] And despite the fact that it was not Jewish citizens sharing these particular jokes, it's clear that the joke-teller and joke-audience are frequently expected to identify with the 'Jewish' character.

In fact, the extensive work of the Odesan folklorist Alter Druianov, who collected thousands of *anekdoty* over the imperial and early Soviet periods in the attempt to preserve Yiddish-language folk culture, shows considerable crossover with its Russian-language counterparts: these were not wholly discrete oral cultures, and the wily, cunning figure of 'the Jew' not only appears consistently in both, but is arguably a creation of Jewish folklore itself.[83] As such, it's not so much antisemitic prejudice that we see woven into the background of these jokes, but like the *anekdot* and *chastushka* forms themselves, it was a familiar means with which to engage the Soviet world in a language other than 'Bolshevik'.

Battles of Significance

Soviet citizens didn't just use reference points and values that predated or were autonomous of official ideology to judge the new regime. There was another, more creative side to this coin: they also took elements of official ideology and judged these *on their own terms*. They forced ideological claims to engage directly with the reality of everyday life as ordinary people experienced it. Substantial discrepancies rapidly became evident, of course, but contemporaries did not stop there: they went on to initiate a dynamic process of contestation, in which they forcibly twisted the meaning of ideological slogans and claims so that, in their reckoning, the words actually came to reflect everyday realities.

To use the language of semiotics, this was a contest over the meaning of official 'signifiers'[84] – a contest over what a particular ideological symbol (a word, picture, or concept) really *meant*. Contestation was, of course, anathema to the Soviet state because it wanted to control and standardise every aspect of its citizens' lives and perceptions. Humour was the perfect means to challenge this, because it constantly challenges our assumptions and pulls the rug out from under us. In humour, we can detect the previously-hidden shadow world of popular language and penetrate beneath the surface layers of 'speaking Bolshevik' to discover additional, ulterior levels of communication.

Before we get going, we should remember for the sake of context that there were also plenty of jokes relating to slogans and official language that tell us little about contemporaries' perspectives and attitudes. That some people might alter the then-famous call to 'catch and overtake' the capitalist West to the sexually-suggestive 'catch and overtake your mum!', which Shitts recorded in his diary, does not tell us a great deal except that official words were never sacred, and that 'your mum' jokes are perennial favourites.[85] Entertaining as these examples can be, they fall outside the scope of this study. All the same, we must bear in mind that a wealth of this everyday and often quite familiar humour coexisted with the more overtly political and (for us) more informative material.

Slogans and Contexts

A simple and widespread joking practice in the 1930s was to repeat official rhetoric in contexts that seriously undermined its claims.[86] Just like the people in Chapter 1 who cried 'Thank you, Comrade Stalin!' when terrible things happened to them, official discourse could easily be made to mock itself, and in the 1930s, the number of disparities between rhetoric and reality made this a near-constant possibility.[87]

For instance, you could repeat the ever-present cry 'Long live Soviet power!' at moments of frustration, as we see in an *anekdot* recorded by Konstantin Megrelidze which attributes the bathetic line to Karl Radek (an Old Bolshevik widely thought to have a sharp and risky sense of humour):[88]

> Radek's monthly allowance was reduced from 30 to 15 rubles [as a punishment]. He responded by telegram: 'Received 15 rubles – long live Soviet power!'[89]

But perhaps the most popular example of this practice was to repeat Stalin's famous 1935 declaration that 'life has become better, comrades; life has become merrier'. This was plainly and painfully untrue for most Soviet citizens, and so it naturally opened the floodgates for repeated ironic use. One B.Ia. Orman, working in a bread factory in Namagan, Uzbek Republic, scornfully repeated the slogan in full when, not for the first time, he was unable to pick up basic foodstuffs.[90] A.P. Lizunov, a labourer at a metallurgical factory in Sverdlovskaia oblast', could not contain his laughter when publicly reciting the famous words: they were so dislocated from reality that they had become a joke in themselves.[91] And Party member Riabov reported a fellow student of the All-Union Academy of Law for mocking the fact that they were now being served low-quality, tinned cod which, in the past, had been used as pig-food. When this cod was on the menu again, he sauntered up to Riabov and said 'You're eating cod again? Indeed it *has* got better, life has become merrier!'[92]

    The slogan could also be called upon to make sarcastic comments about specific policies and events: when abortion was banned in 1936, the old Bolshevik revolutionary, diplomat and Chekist, Aleksandr Iakovlevich Arosev noted in his diary that 'life has become better; life has become solitary'.[93] But perhaps most common of all was a more circumspect expression of sarcastic frustration which we can see in the words of a female factory worker in Leningrad: 'Well, how *merry*'.[94]

    Andrei Arzhilovskii, sardonic as ever, riffed on other ubiquitous slogans about the new and 'happy life'. In his diary, he reflected after a fight had broken out in a queue that 'people just can't seem to appreciate their happy lives' in the Soviet Union, and that, as 'Our factory whistle hoots hoarsely, marking the beginning of a new, happy life in our country[,] it was especially pleasant to stand in line for bread and peas today'.[95]

    Those shortages caused the quality of bread to sharply decline, but sarcastic complaints about it could also be dressed up in Sovietese, as Shitts noted in his diary: 'Our bread is composed of 20% flour and 80% our achievements'.[96] The official obsession with performing and then talking about super-efficient 'shock-work' likewise gave birth to subversive parodies. Not only were NKVD agents labelled 'Stakhanovites' in response to the spiralling numbers of arrests in the 1930s, the journalist Ella Winter noted that in various jokes she heard, 'Thieves, prostitutes, and divorcees, [as well as] officials intrusted [sic] with carrying out the highest measure of social defence (death by shooting), are cited for prosecuting their activities in a shock-brigade manner'.[97] Arzhilovskii played this game, too, repeatedly referencing the lyrics 'I know no other land where one can breathe so free', (taken from a popular song that featured in the hit film *Circus* (1936)), whenever he faced frustration and adversity.[98] As he summed up on 11 December 1936, 'A person breathes free in our country, but starves free, too',[99] bringing the lofty lyrics down to earth with a dull thud.

The media's repeated calls for 'Vigilance!' against spies and saboteurs also provoked sarcastic responses which highlighted the true meaning of the term in everyday life. When the head of the Stalin Metallurgical Plant in Leningrad was instructed to be more vigilant about class enemies, he replied, 'Yes, I've become more vigilant; I don't even sleep at night – I'm guarding my firewood!',[100] pointedly referring to the chronic shortage of winter fuel, and the resulting and widespread problem of theft.

The ubiquity of particular words and phrases practically begged for them to be mocked, but there were many other forms of parody which played more broadly on the lofty rhetoric of official pronouncements. I.P. Tikhonov, the head of a locomotive depot at Novozybkov, was reading aloud the newspaper coverage of the Seventeenth Party Congress, in which a certain Avdeenko claimed that his son's first word was 'Stalin'. Tikhonov broke off his reading to throw in that, 'Well, I hereby pledge to have my son potty-trained by the Seventeenth Congress!', which was greeted with general laughter.[101]

Taking things quite a bit further, at a metal appliance factory in Leningrad during the nightshift of 5-6 December 1934, several young workers were caught writing an increasingly elaborate parody of Soviet propaganda language, mimicking the outpouring of grief then flooding the press after the Kirov murder just a few days earlier. In their parody, the youths' grief was reserved for the 'tragic' loss of a jacket by one of their number, the 18 year-old Kisman:

Government Notice:
With deep sorrow the shop and Party committees and the administration of shop no.1 inform the entire workers' collective of the tragic disappearance of Comrade Kisman's jacket. The villain's hand did not hesitate before removing it from the hangar in the cloakroom. But we will show no mercy to the villains and the enemies of the working class and will still further strengthen [our] class vigilance over our jackets and coats.

The Administration.

Kisman wrote this initial notice himself on the back of a sheet of sandpaper (real paper being in short supply), but it was then expanded upon by his companions, who wrote an official 'Resolution' to accompany it:

> To the Kremlin, 4 December 1934
> The Sally of the Class Enemy
>
> We all mourn for Comrade Kisman's jacket, stolen by the hand of a traitor, an enemy of the working class. But cheer up, Comrade Kisman, for the enemy missed his mark; in place of that jacket, a still better one will be found.
>
> The class enemy never sleeps. We must always be at the ready in order to reduce to dust (развеять в прах) their thieving machinations.[102]

Playing on official rhetoric so accurately that I almost mistook the parody for a genuine 'Resolution' like the countless others sitting in the archives which lifelessly parrot the same words and phrases, Kisman and his mates reconfigured the grandiose ideological world to fit their everyday experiences and thereby produced an unavoidably humorous effect by the glaring incongruity of it all.

Context was king: the persistently vast incongruities between official rhetoric and the real-life conditions in which ordinary people lived meant that even hinting at a given slogan or turn of phrase could immediately provoke smirks and laughter as official claims sank under the weight of reality. Choosing a context in which to do so was just the beginning, though. Contemporaries often went further still and actively reinterpreted official signifiers, creating a clandestine idiom – a shadow language – for themselves in the process.

Shadow Language

Describing how criminals manage to communicate openly without drawing unwanted attention, the sociologist Diego Gambetta, whose theories we encountered earlier in Chapter 1, notes that, 'In fact, anyone who has reason to keep his communications secret resorts to a conventional lexicon', meaning that to avoid attention you need to use everyday words and phrases, but that these can carry a second, secret meaning for those in-the-know.[103]

As Likhachev realised, humour was perfect for creating and sharing these secondary meanings, because laughter, he wrote, 'divides the world in two, creating an endless quantity of doubles, creating a laughing "shadow" of reality'.[104] This 'shadow worldview' could be accessed through the shadow vocabulary[105] which Soviet contemporaries were building over the course of the 1930s. Of course, for multilingual citizens, there was always the possibility of speaking another language to communicate 'secretly' in the open; others could also use the so-called 'court language' (язык придворных) of the criminal underworld, which hid meanings behind slang and letter substitutions.[106] But, as Gambetta warned, both these approaches were more risky than using everyday, inconspicuous vocabulary, because you could never be certain that a nearby, hostile listener didn't know the language in question (and speaking another language could anyway provoke accusations of spying for foreign powers).

The clearest example of shadow language was the widespread practice of reinterpreting the endless acronyms and contractions that littered Soviet life like alphabet soup. Repeating only the letters in sequence could easily hide the meaning particular speakers and listeners actually had in mind. This worked like a double-bottomed suitcase, with the secret message conveyed in an inconspicuous container, lying hidden beneath a false, first layer. Like the local in-jokes of Lenin's shit-filled briefcase or the comically-positioned portraits we saw in Chapter 1, these decipherments could function as a coded body of shared knowledge, passed between trusted parties who were in-the-know.[107]

For example, the initials MTS (Machine-Tractor Station) were frequently reinterpreted to stand for '*Mogila Tovarishcha Stalina*' ('Comrade Stalin's Grave') – a subtext which an 11 year-old at a school in Zhitomir and a 13 year-old student in Kronstadt revealed.[108] A similar but far more widespread decipherment was drawn from the state's own acronym (SSSR in Russian), rendered as '*Smert' Stalina Spaset Rossiiu*' ('Stalin's Death Will Save Russia').[109] This was a remarkably common interpretation which spread in printed as well as spoken form, and abroad as well as at home. In one instance, the NKVD discovered it on a stack of printed flyers stuffed into the window-frames of a train from Moscow to Kharkiv,[110] and at some point in 1935-6 it appeared as the headline on an anti-Bolshevik émigré newspaper printed in Sofia.[111]

This slogan become so well known that it was even used by the Nazis in 1941 on leaflets distributed to the Soviet population by the invading German troops. Alongside a sketch of Stalin being bonked on the head with a hammer and his throat about to be gouged out with a sickle, these leaflets included a tear-off voucher guaranteeing safe passage to defectors!'¹¹² Despite this conspicuous spread of the 'hidden' meaning over the course of the decade, it could still remain an element of a genuinely secretive shadow vocabulary: the acronym could still be used between trusted parties without them spelling it out openly.

Another popular decipherment came from the special shops for Party officials and foreigners, the Torgsin, where payment was in gold or other 'hard' currencies, and the shelves were, in dramatic contrast to the normal shops, actually stocked with goods.¹¹³ Originally the contraction 'Torgsin' meant 'Trade with Foreigners' ('*torgovlia s inostrantsami*'), but in the sarcastic popular version it was decoded letter-by-letter as: 'Comrades, wake up! The workers are dying – Stalin is destroying the people!'¹¹⁴ Variations also circulated, substituting 'Russia' for 'workers', or 'destroying' for 'exhausting' (*iznuriaet*).¹¹⁵ In all cases, there's a clear connection made between the two meanings of the 'Torgsin': these 'decodings' were not arbitrary, but operated as ordinary people's interpretations of the meaning or significance of particular policies or institutions in Soviet life. In this case, the Torgsin is 'revealed' to mean starvation and poverty for all but the powerful few, neatly summing up in everyday speech what the economic historian Elena Osokina called the 'hierarchies of distribution' – of unequal distribution and rationing – which defined so much of Soviet life.¹¹⁶

A similar, but darker, example was the adaptation of '*GOSSTRAKh*' to '*GOSSUZhAS*'. The first is short for 'Government Insurance', but it also contains the word '*strakh*' ('fear'). The unofficial version roughly translates as 'Government Horror'.¹¹⁷ Again, the wordplay directly mocks the institution in question: through the double-reveal of '*strakh*' and '*uzhas*', the government is implied to rest on fear and awfulness, entirely undermining the possibility of it providing some kind of safety-net or security for the population. If we recall the 'voluntary-compulsory' state loan campaigns that people were forced to sign up to from Chapter 2, a moment's amusement could likewise come from folding the paper bond, which was emblazoned with the headline 'State Credit Note', to shorten the word 'State' (*Gosudarstvennyi*) to 'Shitty' (*Govennyi*), thus 'revealing' the actual value of the bond.¹¹⁸

This practice of 'decoding' even included the names of Soviet leaders. Following the Kirov murder, Komsomol authorities learned that members of the Viazemskii pedagogical technical college were advising each other to 'read Kirov's surname backwards', which spelled '*vorik*', meaning 'petty thief'.¹¹⁹ In the village of Parkany, Tiraspol'skii raion, a plaque under a portrait of Voroshilov was vandalised in early 1935: the culprit scrubbed off the leader's name except for the first three letters: '*vor*', meaning 'thief'.¹²⁰ This sort of thing could represent much more to contemporaries than simple wordplay or abuse: the sense of having broken a 'code' by extracting what they considered a wholly accurate description of a leader's character from his name should not be underestimated in its potential to evoke a sense of genuine legitimacy or truth.

Nevertheless, you had to be in on the joke, or at least be *willing* to see it in order to recognise the contraband meanings, even when they were this simple. Voroshilov's own aide repeatedly shortened his boss's name to 'Vor.' in his notes without it occurring to him that this might look pretty dubious to someone else, or that it could even prove dangerous to do so.[121] Like the unintentionally explicit Kirov statue in Chapter 1, where his pointing finger seemed to look like a penis, you had to (choose to) stand at just the right angle to see the funny side.

Even the Soviet crest itself – the principal symbol of the regime – could fall prey to verbal and visual subversion. A simple rhyme of 'hammer and sickle' with 'death and famine' (*Serp i Molot / Smert' i Golod*) made the rounds in various locations (predominantly in Ukraine, where the collectivisation famine hit hardest), its simplicity belying a stark criticism of one of the regime's flagship policies.[122]

This particular play on words also spread in the form of a *chastushka* which became so prevalent that, in a local school in Znamenskii raion, Odesskaia oblast', no sooner had a teacher written the words 'Hammer and Sickle' on the blackboard, than several students 'answered in chorus with the rhyme, "but in the home, death and famine"'.[123] Whether it was a prank or was choruses in the naive belief that the teacher had begun to write out the *chastushka*, this spontaneous group response gives us a hint of just how widespread knowledge of this covert, secondary association could be, especially when packaged in an easily-remembered rhyme.[124]

Being widespread and memorable was one thing, but publicly giving the game away rather undermined the point of a shadow language. Openly revealing these hidden meanings was also not going to be a long-term hobby, as, for example, a switchboard operator at a communications office in Pskovskaia oblast' found out when she responded to the director's request to put him through to the local MTS with the words, 'Giving you Comrade Stalin's Grave'. Her fate is unrecorded, but an investigation was swiftly launched.[125]

The operator's misjudgement was likely an exception, however: what's most striking about the examples we've seen is that, almost exclusively, it was the words or drawings of *children* which betrayed to the authorities the shadow meanings of acronyms and other symbols.[126] Given the depth of political awareness and complexity of the language skills involved, we can assume that the children were just naively repeating things they had heard from adults, most likely their parents, grandparents or neighbours. So, despite occasional slips, these in-jokes most likely did remain in the shadows, hidden inside the double-bottomed suitcase. Many people were arrested or reported for reeling out jokes in these years, but the codebreakers remained more elusive.

Turning the Other Face

The Soviet state, like all authoritarian regimes, hated ambiguity. The official view of the world was to be the *only* view of the world. As the contemporary linguist V.N. Voloshinov put it, rulers like these strive to make ideological words, ideas and symbols 'uniaccentual' – to have only one, clearly-defined meaning which the rest of society isn't allowed to meddle with.[127] Such a totalising ambition is obviously doomed to failure, but, as usual, the Soviet leaders blundered on regardless.

Worse still, because they considered all aspects of life to be theoretically of political and ideological significance, every action, creation or even thought could potentially be subverted by the population. By their own logic, the rulers were unintentionally providing citizens with a potentially infinite store of symbols to contest. This included even seemingly innocent, everyday items like cigarette packets. N.S. Parkhachev, who worked in Kamylovskii raion's health department, told the following *anekdot* to some friends:

> A customer enters a shop and asks the shopkeeper for some cigarettes with a revolutionary name – 'Something like, "What we fought for"' (За что боролись). The shopkeeper replies, 'We don't have "What we fought for", but we do have "What we ended up with"' (на что напоролись), and hands the customer the brand 'Soviet'.[128]

A similar but much darker quip linked the design of 'White Sea Canal' cigarette packets, which featured a map with the new waterway's course highlighted in red, with the notoriously brutal conditions of the actual canal's construction. S.N. Aktimirov, an accountant, pointed out the red line to his colleagues and declared that 'it represents the blood shed by the builders of the canal'.[129] Less directly (and rather more creatively) an ironic interpretation of the 'Victory' brand of matches also circulated in 1937. Although the details of this 'counterrevolutionary interpretation' of the brand-name are not recorded, we can easily imagine that it involved some kind of Soviet 'Victory' being closely linked to destruction, or of everything going up in smoke.[130] One of Aktimirov's colleagues, G.T. Filatov, got in trouble for a similar joke about Party cards. He called them 'ration cards' instead, neatly recasting the symbol of Party membership to better reflect what it signified in the eyes of the majority who were excluded from the Party and its privileges.[131]

Words and symbols can never mean only one thing; each person has their own experience of and associations to them. Everyone to some extent makes their own reality. Voloshinov explored this idea, suggesting that every ideological sign 'has two faces, like Janus',[132] with each 'face' (each meaning) contradicting the other. The 'face' we perceive depends on our perspective. For Soviet citizens of the 1930s, there clearly existed a substantial collection of secondary 'faces' which they might choose to focus on instead of the officially-acceptable ones. I'm certainly not suggesting that Soviet citizens were constantly contesting the 'meaning' of every name, product, or slogan they encountered, but, rather, that such a contestation was always possible, much to the regime's chagrin.

Another Russian linguist, M.A. Krongauz, provides us with a useful model here. He argued that at least in the later period of 'developed socialism', there were two 'languages' used in the Soviet Union: the ritualistic 'Soviet-Russian' and 'Russian' itself. He described this as a 'diglossia': two languages which the people could use, varying the priority they gave to each one at any given moment.[133] Although Krongauz's use of 'Russian' ignores the many other languages spoken in the Soviet Union, he was certainly right that an official, ritualistic language existed adjacent to a colloquial alternative, and that in practice the borders between the two were porous. That's why so many people wrote pleading letters to the authorities that slipped in and out of *both* Sovietese *and* more religious, folkloric language.

For Soviet contemporaries, the world was not filtered through a monolithic, official discourse in which all words, concepts or even everyday objects were defined by the state alone. From the most grandiose slogans, via the omnipresent acronyms and contractions of Newspeak, right down to the lowly pack of cigarettes, many people took these signifiers and created and shared their own alternative interpretations, weaving them into everyday communication. It would be too much to call this a fully-fledged language – it was fundamentally shaped by the official one – but it can at the very least be considered an alternative idiom.

More importantly, they could use both *at the same time*. Even when appearing to 'speak Bolshevik', contemporaries could simultaneously communicate in a shadow language of countless additional meanings. These were creative acts of crosshatching that, unless intentionally or accidentally revealed, remained invisible to the state. This wasn't a pan-Soviet idiom, though: even if Soviet life was standardised in so many ways across the vast expanse of the USSR, it was still too dangerous to share shadow meanings with just anybody (a theme we'll explore more deeply in Chapter 6).

Many covert interpretations were themselves highly localised phenomena, too, because this was about making sense of life as it was experienced at the day-to-day level. Alongside all the decipherments we saw earlier, which just about any Soviet citizen could potentially have understood, there were many, more specific examples. Interpretations like 'KhTZ' (Kharkiv Tractor Factory) as 'Bread Here – Not!',[134] 'MGU' (Moscow State University) as the 'Sorrow of Hungry Students',[135] or 'SVD' (a reference to a film involving a 'Union of a Great Cause') as 'Union of Jolly Affairs',[136] would all have had little relevance or resonance for people who were unaware of that particular factory, student body, or film, and why it might be amusing or particularly revealing to decode the acronyms in this way.[137]

Whether localised or widespread, these contestations of the regime's desire to control the meaning of every aspect of life in the Soviet Union represent a broad popular attempt to reconcile the incongruities between official symbols – from words and values to Party cards and propaganda posters – and the realities which ordinary people encountered in everyday life. This was an inherently critical act, at the heart of which lay a strong desire that words should match reality, and to grapple with and adjust them until they did so.

Therefore, we need to adapt Voloshinov's proposition, because it was actually ordinary Soviet citizens who were (or at least could be) Janus-faced. It was they who could look at the world around them from two different viewpoints – viewpoints which were intimately connected. The distinction is important, because otherwise we ignore the agency and critical ability of Soviet contemporaries. The signifier (the symbol) did not turn a second face to the observer; Kirov's statue didn't rotate to show off its 'penis', and acronyms don't decode themselves. The observer had to look at it a different way, and humour – a genre in which things are constantly being seen from contradictory angles – was the perfect means for them to do so.

This is what Seth Graham, in a beautiful turn of phrase, called 'resonant dissonance'. For the regime, these alternative interpretations were discordant clashes with the official tune it was trying to play. But for the joke-tellers, these were moments when they discovered ways for the official world to resonate with their lived experience. Like Kirov's Carnival, these contestations were ultimately a melodic counterpoint which, in their political dissonance, found personal resonance for contemporaries trying to make sense of their lives.

***

As Anna Krylova put it in her study of female Soviet combatants in the Second World War, 'Far from passively internalizing Soviet ideology, [these women] allow us to study a precedent of a historical subject as a dependable and yet productive mediator of its cultural and social surroundings, even under the constrained conditions of Stalinist society'.[138] This was true of Soviet society more widely, and in humour we find hundreds of snapshots of contemporaries 'mediating' official ideology in everyday life, crosshatching it with their daily experiences and with pre-Soviet values and frames of reference. Memory and practices do not pass through time perfectly unchanged, but they do continue to resonate and affect how people understand and engage with the present (and the future).

When criticising the Soviet regime, people could and did draw from the deeper wells of history and of value systems that long predated the October Revolution. More importantly, when they did so this was not a zero-sum game – contemporaries used them both alongside, and often crosshatched them with, the Bolsheviks' own ideology. They were blending criticism and acceptance in the attempt to make sense of the confusing, disruptive world around them. Many learnt to 'speak Bolshevik', just as we all take on some of the culturally-sanctioned language and values of the times. But this neither meant they forgot older 'languages', let alone that they became trapped in the Soviet one. Continuity and change are not opposites: they are both processes which, in the realm of culture, interact and are inescapably shaped by each other.

This was an inherently social process, in which new, clandestine meanings for official categories were passed between individuals who trusted each other enough to speak in shadow language. This could be exciting, exploratory and personally rewarding, but it was also increasingly dangerous. Ordinary people weren't the only ones working in the shadows: as they told their jokes, the secret police was gradually tightening its net, as the following chapter explores.

Notes

1. Kotkin, *Magnetic Mountain*, Ch.5.
2. Likhachev, 'Smekh', 346.
3. Igal Halfin & Jochen Hellbeck, 'Rethinking the Stalinist Subject: Stephen Kotkin's "Magnetic Mountain" and the State of Soviet Historical Studies', *Jarbücher für Geschichte Osteuropas*, 44.3 (1996).
4. See in particular, Jochen Hellbeck, 'Fashioning the Stalinist Soul: The Diary of Stepan Podlubnyi (1931-9)', *Jahrbücher für Geschichte Osteuropas*, 44.3 (1996); idem, 'Working, Struggling, Becoming: Stalin-Era Autobiographical Texts', *Russian Review*, 60.3 (2001); idem, *Revolution on My Mind: Writing a Diary Under Stalin* (Cambridge, MA, 2006); Igal Halfin, *From Darkness to Light: Class, Consciousness, and Salvation in Revolutionary Russia* (Pittsburgh, PA, 2000); idem, *Terror in My Soul: Communist Autobiographies on Trial* (Cambridge, MA, 2003). Further analysis and critique of these approaches is provided by Andy Willimott, 'Everyday Revolution: The Making of the Soviet Urban Communes', C. Read, A. Lindenmeyr & P. Waldron (eds.), *Russia's Great War and Revolution, 1914-1922: The Home Front* (Bloomington, IN, 2015).
5. Michel de Certeau, *The Practice of Everyday Life*, trans. Steven Rendall (Berkeley & Los Angeles, CA, 1988), 43.
6. Lawrence W. Levine, 'William Shakespeare and the American People: A Study in Cultural Transformation', *American Historical Review*, 89.1 (1984), 48; Carl Gustav Jung, *Modern Man in Search of a Soul*, trans. W.S. Dell & Cary F. Baynes (Abingdon, 2001 [1933]), 49-50.
7. Livshin & Orlov, *Vlast' i obshchestvo*, 19.
8. Wendy Z. Goldman, *Women, the State and Revolution: Soviet Family Policy and Social Life, 1917-1936* (Cambridge, 1993), 310, 312.
9. Barbara Evans Clements, *A History of Women in Russia: From Earliest Times to the Present* (Bloomington, IN, 2012), 213.
10. Barbara Evans Clements, 'The Birth of the New Soviet Woman', Abbot Gleason, Peter Kenez & Richard Stites (eds.), *Bolshevik Culture: Experiment and Order in the Russian Revolution* (Bloomington, IN, 1985), 220.
11. Wendy Z. Goldman, *Women at the Gates: Gender and Industry in Stalin's Russia* (Cambridge, 2002), 282-4.
12. e.g. Goldman, *Women, the State*; idem, *Women at the Gates*; Clements, 'The Birth'; Richard Stites, *The Women's Liberation Movement in Russia: Feminism, Nihilism and Bolshevism, 1860-1930* (Princeton, NJ, 1991); Thomas G. Schrand, 'Socialism in One Gender: Masculine Values in the Stalin Revolution', Barbara Evans Clements, Rebecca Friedman & Dan Healey (eds.), *Russian Masculinities in History and Culture* (Houndmills, 2002).
13. cf. Afanas'ev, *Zavetnye skazki*.
14. This was largely reflected in leading Bolsheviks' humour, too. Amongst the crude caricatures which they passed around during meetings, many of which are now collected in the archives, Vatlin and Malashenko, the historians who've collated these cartoons, note that, 'women appear only as cleaning ladies or secretaries [and] [t]he portrayal of someone as a "broad" was meant to be humiliating'. Alexander Vatlin & Larisa Malashenko (eds.), *Piggy Foxy and the Sword of Revolution: Bolshevik Self-Portraits* (New Haven, CT, 2006), 4.
15. For more on the *babushka* figure, see Jonathan Waterlow, '*Babushka*, Helper, Harlot, Joker: Women and Gender in 1930s Political Humour', Melanie Ilic (ed.), *The

Palgrave Handbook of Women and Gender in Twentieth-Century Russia and the Soviet Union (London, 2018).

[16] GARF, f.8131, op.31, d.80433, l.6(ob) (1928-36). I discuss the significance of the 'Jew' character in *anekdoty* later in this chapter.
[17] Shitts, *Dnevnik*, 289 (1931).
[18] GARF, f.8131, op.31, d.43506, l.20.
[19] GARF, f.8131, op.31, d.82045, l.9ob (1936-7).
[20] Goldman, *Women, the State*, 298.
[21] Ella Winter, *Red Virtue: Human Relationships in the New Russia* (London, 1933), 141.
[22] RGALI, f.2172, op.3, d.8, l.6(ob) (1920s-30s).
[23] Wendy Z. Goldman, 'Babas at the Bench: Gender Conflict in Soviet Industry in the 1930s', Melanie Ilič (ed.), *Women in the Stalin Era* (Houndmills, 2001), 84-5; in the same volume, see also: Sarah Davies, '"A Mother's Cares": Women Workers and Popular Opinion in Stalin's Russia, 1934-41', 89-100.
[24] V.B. Zhiromskaia, I.N. Kiselev & Iu.A. Poliakov (eds.), *Polveka pod grifom "sekretno": vsesoiuznaia perepis' naseleniia 1937 goda* (Moscow, 1996), 98, table 17.
[25] The situation in the countryside was markedly different. There, religious imagery, symbols and ideas were invoked to stand in distinct opposition to the new regime. cf. Lynne Viola, 'Visions of Apocalypse in the Soviet Countryside', *Journal of Modern History*, 62.4 (1990).
[26] TsDAHOU, f.1, op.20, d.3548, l.33 (October 1930). Also cf. Mel'nichenko, *Sovetskii anekdot*, 215-6. Also cf. a related example in which God and Stalin discuss feeding donkeys, noted by one K.A. Zabelin in his diary, later seized by the authorities: GARF, f.8131, op.31, d.84280, l.4 (1933-9).
[27] Shitts, *Dnevnik*, 145-6 (1929).
[28] e.g. GARF, f.8131, op.31, d.70803, ll.23-4 (December 1934) & d.83654, l.10 (1936). On the evolution of this *anekdot*, cf. A.S. Arkhipova & M.A. Mel'nichenko, '"Vot protsenty na vash kapital!" K voprosu o genezise i evoliutsii politicheskogo anekdota' <http://www.ruthenia.ru/document/545661.html>.
[29] TsDAHOU, f.1, op.20, d.3548, l.33 (c.October 1930).
[30] GARF, f.8131, op.31, d.80433, l.7 (up to 1936). ('Бог знает на 5, учитель на 4, а ученики на 3'.) Uspenskii was sentenced to ten years, but this was reduced to four in January 1940 (l.2).
[31] Shitts, *Dnevnik*, 49-50 (1928).
[32] e.g. TsGAIPD, f.25, op.5, d.54, ll.65 & 70 (December 1934); RGASPI, f.M-1, op.23, d.1102, l.115 (May 1935); TsDAHOU, f.1, op.20, d.2987, l.49 (May 1929).
[33] TsGAIPD, f.25, op.5, d.46, l.66; d.54, l.70; d.55, l.13; d.53, l.5 (December 1934).
[34] TsGAIPD, f.25, op.5, d.45, l.6 (December 1934).
[35] Something which could itself prove comic to those who noticed it, as it did to the contemporary humorist Teffi, for example. cf. Viktor Shklovskii, 'K teorii komicheskogo', *Epopeia*, 3 (1922), 61.
[36] Although Kotkin did not imply citizens 'spoke Bolshevik' at all times, the concept has become so widely accepted that it often shades into assumptions of a constant performance.
[37] RGASPI, f.M-1, op.23, d.1106, l.118 (c.1934-5). More strictly, the first line might read, 'In your substance I have always believed', but 'materialism' seems both clearer in English and simultaneously hints at the kind of values in question.
[38] Church being free and having a good choir: TsGAIPD, f.24, op.2v, d.2494, l.119 (1937); quotation from Davies, *Popular Opinion*, 77.
[39] TsGAIPD, f.24, op.2v, d.2494, l.117.
[40] Paul Froese, *The Plot to Kill God: Findings from the Soviet Experiment in Secularization*

41 (Berkeley, CA, 2008), 11. Arthur Koestler's travels in the Central Asian USSR in 1932-3 echo these assessments: cf. *Invisible Writing*, esp. Ch.11.
41 Petrone, *Life has Become More Joyous*, 185.
42 TsGAIPD, f.24, op.2v, d.2494, l.127 (1937); Davies, *Popular Opinion*, 78; Petrone, *Life has Become More Joyous*, 186.
43 William B. Husband, 'Soviet Atheism and Russian Orthodox Strategies of Resistance, 1917-1932', *Journal of Modern History*, 70.1 (1998), 87-8.
44 Davies, *Popular Opinion*, 78.
45 Quoted in Davies, *Popular Opinion*, 78. For further crosshatching of this kind in the later Soviet period, see Nadieszda Kizenko, 'Sacramental Confession in Modern Russia and Ukraine', Catherine Wanner (ed.), *State Secularism and Lived Religion in Soviet Russia and Ukraine* (New York, 2012).
46 Rittersporn, *Anguish, Anger, and Folkways*, 295, 249.
47 William B. Husband, *'Godless Communists': Atheism and Society in Soviet Russia, 1917-1932* (DeKalb, IL, 2000), xv.
48 Rolf, *Soviet Mass Festivals*, 132-4; Petrone, *Life has Become More Joyous*, 19.
49 Rolf, *Soviet Mass Festivals*, 133.
50 Rolf, *Soviet Mass Festivals*, 13.
51 Rolf, *Soviet Mass Festivals*, 126.
52 Alex Inkeles & Raymond A. Bauer, *The Soviet Citizen: Daily Life in a Totalitarian Society* (Cambridge, MA, 1959), 380-1.
53 GARF, f.8131, op.31, d.9963, l.26 (May 1940).
54 RGASPI, f.M-1, op.23, d.1128, l.64 (January 1935).
55 RGASPI, f.M-1, op.23, d.1106, l.86 (November 1935). (*Vtoroe Krepostnoe Pravo Bol'shevikov.*) Also cf. Chamberlin, *Russia's Iron Age*, 79; Mel'nichenko, *Sovetskii anekdot*, 470.
56 GARF, f.8131, op.31, d.88411, l.9.
57 TsGAIPD, f.24, op.2v, d.4306, l.203 (July 1940).
58 Chamberlin, *Russia's Iron Age*, 79.
59 GARF, f.8131, op.31, d.90055, l.7 (1940).
60 RGASPI, f.M-1, op.23, d.1106, l.21 (December 1934).
61 GARF, f.8131, op.31, d.82045, l.9 (1936-7). For a similar example, see d.15983, l.154 (1940-1).
62 GARF, f.5451, op.43, d.28, l.179 (May 1933).
63 TsGAIPD, f.24, op.2v, d.2664, l.210 (1937).
64 Arkhipova & Mel'nichenko, *Anekdoty*, 28.
65 Graham, *Resonant Dissonance*, 18.
66 cf. N.P. Andreev, *Ukazatel' skazochnykh siuzhetov po sisteme Aarne* (Leningrad, 1929). Andreev listed the 'animal folktale' separately from the *anekdot*, but this reflects an already anachronistic distinction by 1929, because his sources were principally drawn from the prerevolutionary period. I discuss this sub-genre in 1930s humour in 'Speaking More Than Bolshevik', Neumann & Willimott (eds.), *Rethinking the Russian Revolution*.
67 e.g. RGASPI, f.M-1, op.23, d.820; d.822; HDA SBU, f.16, op.25, d.2; op.28, d.12; TsDAHOU, f.1, op.20, d.2987; d.2996; TsGAIPD SPb, f.24, op.2v, d.772. Summaries of the most representative letters sent to *Pravda* similarly featured a specific section on the problem of antisemitism, at least at the beginning of the decade: GARF, f.3316, op.16a, d.446.
68 e.g. RGASPI f.M-1, op.23, d.822, l.45 (1928-9); d.1072, l.6 (1934); TsGAIPD SPb, f.24, op.2v, d.772, l.16 (1934); f.25, op.5, d.84, l.46 (1936-7)
69 The only overtly antisemitic *anekdot* I encountered (i.e. that was recorded in the

documents) involved the arrival of various gods into the USSR who were all promptly arrested, except for the Jewish god who rapidly became a People's Commissar with the pseudonym 'Petrov'. (GARF, f.8131, op.31, d.56612, told in 1941.) This joke survives in another variation in which god sends down three emissaries who are each arrested, except for Moses (again, because he is ostensibly Jewish), who becomes 'People's Commissar Petrov' (Adams, *Tiny Revolutions*, 10). A number of other criminal files include reference to antisemitic jokes, but their content is not recorded: GARF, f.8131, op.31, dd.3703, 10093, 33529; HDA SBU, f.6, d.33754FP.

70 GARF, f.8131, op.31, d.86405, l.4 (1941).
71 GARF, f.8131, op.31, d.87767, ll.3-8 (1937).
72 Lyons, *Modern Moscow*, 265.
73 HDA SBU, f.6, d.33754FP, l.88 (1936-7); RGASPI, f.M-1, op.23, d.1107, l.61 (1934-5).
74 GARF, f.8131, op.31, d.40412 (1935-40); d.49998, l.21 (1937); d.85229, ll.5-6 (1937); d.91956, ll.8-9 (1934-5); RGASPI, f.17, op.120, d.176, l.115 (1935) (the latter is a variation on the *anekdot* and does not involve Stalin posing the question).
75 GARF, f.8131, op.31, d.70803, ll.23-4 (1934); d.83654, l.10 (1936).
76 Arkhipova & Mel'nichenko, *Anekdoty*, 58-61.
77 GARF, f.8131, op.31, d.43804, ll.12-3 (June 1937).
78 GARF, f.8131, op.31, d.99140, l.3 (1935); d.83157, l.23 (1940-41); d.52823, l.7 (early 1934).
79 GARF, f.8131, op.31, d.43804. l.13 (June 1937); d.1247, l.18 (1936).
80 GARF, f.8131, op.31, d.83157, l.23 (1940-41) (two Jews); d.34853, l.11 (c.1935) (two people).
81 GARF, f.8131, op.31, d.84619, ll.5, 8 (1935-6).
82 On the cast of characters found in *anekdoty* (from a modern perspective), see E.Ia. Shmeleva & A.D. Shmelev, *Russkii anekdot: Tekst i rechevoi zhanr* (Moscow, 2002), 23. The term 'fictional convention' I take from Carroll, *Humour*, 98-9.
83 cf. Mel'nichenko, *Sovetskii anekdot*, 51. Many thanks to Misha for discussing this and the Druianov collection with me, as well as providing Russian translations of parts of that work (those translations were made for him by Vika Ruvinska).
84 Ferdinand de Saussure, *Course in General Linguistics*, trans. Wade Baskin (London, 1974).
85 Shitts, *Dnevnik*, 191 (1930). (The sexual implication is clearer in Russian: 'Мать твою догнать и перегнать!')
86 cf. Graham, summarising M.A. Krongauz, *Resonant Dissonance*, 92. Also see Peter Sloterdijk's discussion of 'kynicism', in which the solemnity of official ideology is ridiculed and rejected by reference to everyday banalities: Sloterdijk, *Critique of Cynical Reason*, trans. Michael Eldred (London, 1988).
87 A trend highlighted in the bleak satire (written c.1930) of Andrei Platonov, *The Foundation Pit*, trans. Robert & Elisabeth Chandler, & Olga Meerson (London, 2010).
88 cf. Jean-François Fayet, *Karl Radek (1885-1939) Biographie politique* (Bern, 2004), esp. 698.
89 GARF, f.8131, op.31, d.64008, l.26; also cf. Mel'nichenko, *Sovetskii anekdot*, 329.
90 GARF, f.8131, op.31, d.43804, l.13 (1937).
91 GARF, f.8131, op.31, d.6264, l.7 (October 1937).
92 GARF, f.8131, op.31, d.1247, l.10 (1937). ('Ты опять трешку кушаешь, а ведь стало лучше, жить стало веселей'.)
93 A.Ia. Arosev, diary entry for 24 August 1936, at <www.prozhito.org>. ('жить стало не с кем'.) Arosev would be arrested in 1937 and executed in 1938 (he was a

94 former member of the Socialist Revolutionary party).
94 TsGAIPD, f.25, op.10, d.74, l.30 (1937). ('Ну и весело'.)
95 Arzhilovskii, diary entry for 1 March 1937, Garros et al (eds.), *Intimacy and Terror*, 150 (I have slightly altered the translation with reference to the original); entry for 2 February 1937, 141; also cf. 154, 160.
96 Shitts, *Dnevnik*, 90 (1929).
97 Winter, *Red Virtue*, 63-4.
98 Arzhilovskii, Garros et al (eds.), *Intimacy and Terror*, 120, 131, 145. The song is 'Широка страна моя родная' (*Vast/Broad is my Motherland*).
99 Arzhilovskii, Garros et al (eds.), *Intimacy and Terror*, 131. I have altered the translation with reference to the original.
100 TsGAIPD, f.25, op.5, d.48, l.48 (December 1934-January 1935).
101 GARF, f.8131, op.31, d.75960, l.4 (January-February 1934). Perhaps this was a typo and he said the 'Eighteenth', or perhaps it was simply an impression of Avdeenko.
102 TsGAIPD, f.24, op.5, d.2288, l.94.
103 Gambetta, *Codes of the Underworld*, 156.
104 Likhachev, 'Smekh', 369-70. Bakhtin was also sensitive to this 'doubling', but discussed it in more limited terms: Bakhtin, *Dialogic Imagination*, 53, 58, 79.
105 Likhachev, Panchenko & Ponyrko, *Smekh*, 204; Smith, 'Social Meanings of Swearing', 171-2, 187.
106 e.g. (for the personal reminiscences rather than the inaccurate etymological claims) Liudmila Petrushevskaia, 'O chem rech'', Maksim Blant (ed.), *Istoriia glazami Krokodila XX vek: Slova 1922-1937gg.* (Moscow, 2014), 5-8.
107 For further examples, cf. Mel'nichenko, *Sovetskii anekdot*, 222-3. The use of acronyms to conceal sarcastic or ironic twists on slogans was also widely practised within the Soviet penal system: D.S. Baldaev (ed.), *Russian Criminal Tattoo Encyclopaedia*, 3 Vols. (London, 2003-8).
108 HDA SBU, f.16, op.28, d.12, l.33 (February 1935); TsGAIPD, f.24, op.5, d.2712, l.54 (January 1935). The revolutionary Victor Serge also noted that the workers of a particular factory nicknamed a cigarette brand much the same thing, but the original has been somewhat lost in translation (he calls these 'TOS cigarettes', standing officially for 'Tractors of Stalingrad', but unofficially as 'Tomb of Stalin'. It's likely the Stalingrad reference has been added by the translator and that this is, in fact, another MTS joke): see Serge, *From Lenin to Stalin* (London, 1937), 187.
109 GARF, f.8131, op.31, d.73265, l.16 (1943); HDA SBU, f.6, d.18170FP, l.31 (1934-5); f.16, op.31, d.30, l.223 (1938); RGASPI, f.M-1, op.23, d.1106, l.129 (1935); f.17, op.120, d.176, l.27 (1935); TsGAIPD, f.24, op.2v, d.772, l.16 (1934).
110 HDA SBU, f.16, op.31, d.30, l.223 (1938). The train arrived in Kharkiv on 26 November 1938.
111 Undated newspaper, *Za novuiu Rossiiu*, pictured in Arkhipova & Mel'nichenko, *Anekdoty*, 342. The authors date the newspaper as 1935-6.
112 Leaflet reprinted in Arkhipova & Mel'nichenko, *Anekdoty*, 343.
113 The Torgsin existed until 1936, though it remained imprinted in the minds of Soviet citizens as synonymous with unequal distribution. cf. Nataliia Lebina, *Sovetskaia povsednevnost': Normy i anomalii ot voennogo kommunizma k bol'shomu stiliu* (Moscow, 2015), 47-8.
114 HDA SBU, f.16, op.28, d.12, l.49 (March 1935); RGASPI, f.M-1, op.23, d.1128, l.64 (January 1934). (*Tovarishchi Opomnites'*, *Rabochie Gibnut'*, *Stalin Istrebliaet Narod*).
115 TsGAIPD, f.24, op.2v, d.772, l.16 (1934). For further references to deciphering 'Torgsin', see: HDA SBU, f.16, op.30, d.113, l.90 (1937); GARF, f.8131, op.31,

[115] d.70065, l.5 (1934-5); Mel'nichenko, *Sovetskii anekdot*, 217. One further variation appeared in 1936 on a factory wall in Zaporozhskii raion, Ukraine, which replaced 'Wake Up' with 'Beware' (остерегайтесь), at least according to Valerii Vasil'ev, '30-e gody na Ukraine', *Kommunist*, 17 (1990), 82, although he provides no citation for this.

[116] Osokina, *Ierarkhiia potrebleniia*.

[117] GARF, f.8131, op.31, d.12969, l.79 (1939-40); d.39713, l.9 (1940).

[118] HPSSS 451/(NY)1053/A/31, p.16.

[119] RGASPI, f.M-1, op.23, d.1102, l.168 (March 1935).

[120] TsDAHOU, f.1, op.20, d.6642, l.27.

[121] RGASPI, f.74, op.2, d.114, ll.25(ob), 29 (this handwritten travelogue covers ll.13-56 and is stored amongst other official papers relating to Voroshilov's tour of the regions in 1931).

[122] RGASPI, f.17, op.120, d.176, l.153 (March 1935); TsDAHOU, f.1, op.20, d.3198, l.33 (March 1930); d.6210, l.78 (February 1933); d.6642, l.26 (April 1935). The direct equation of one with the other, emphasised by the rhyme, produces a sense of causality that goes much further than most sarcastic humour of the period by damning the regime at large, rather than criticising specific failings.

[123] HDA SBU, f.16, op.28, d.12, l.49 (March 1935). ('а у хаті смерть і голод'.)

[124] An unofficial youth group in Voronezh made much the same connection visually, linking state violence of both word and deed by drawing the Soviet crest with a pen, gun, and skull-and-crossbones incorporated into the design: RGASPI, f.M-1, op.23, d.820, l.8 (1928).

[125] TsGAIPD, f.24, op.5, d.3207, l.58 (1936).

[126] For numerous further examples, see: RGASPI, f.M-1, op.23, d.1102.

[127] In full: 'The ruling class strives to impart a supraclass, eternal character to the ideological sign, to extinguish or drive inward the struggle between social value judgments which occurs in it, to make the sign uniaccentual'. V.N. Voloshinov, *Marxism and the Philosophy of Language*, trans. Ladislav Matejka & I.R. Titunik (New York & London, 1973), 23. This work has previously been attributed to Bakhtin himself, but recent scholarship suggests that, whatever influence Bakhtin may have had on on it, it was indeed written by Voloshinov: Jean-Paul Bronckart & Cristian Bota, *Bakhtine démasqué: Histoire d'un menteur, d'une escroquerie et d'un délire collectif* (Geneva, 2011), 43-5; 413-65.

[128] GARF, f.8131, op.31, d.7038, l.78 (1935-7) (Sverdlovskaia oblast').

[129] GARF, f.8131, op.31, d.8782, l.5(ob) (June 1937).

[130] RGASPI, f.M-1, op.23, d.1265, l.45 (February 1937).

[131] GARF, f.8131, op.31, d.8782, l.5 (1937); also cf. HPSSS 45/A/4, pp.5, 14.

[132] Voloshinov, *Marxism*, 23. Also cf. Bakhtin, *Dialogic Imagination*, 237.

[133] M.A. Krongauz, 'Bessilie iazyka v epokhu zrelogo sotsializma', *Znak: Sbornik statei po lingvistike, semiotike i poetike pamiati A.N. Zhurinskogo* (Moscow, 1994), esp. 236-7.

[134] HDA SBU, f.6, d.33754FP, ll.10; 67 (1936-7). ('*Khleba Tut Zarabotaesh*".)

[135] Noted by the playwright A.N. Afinogenov and held in his personal archive: RGALI, f.2172, op.3, d.8, l.5(ob). ('*Muki Golodnykh Uchashchiesia*'.)

[136] GARF, f.8131, op.31, d.1264 (1937). This apparently referred to an American film shown in the town of Kirov, in which a drunken woman makes reference to the '*Soiuz Velikogo Dela*'. While drinking, I.I. Strugin, a teacher in Slobodskii raion, claimed he was a member of a '*Soiuz Veselogo Dela*'. Jolly or otherwise, this was used by the authorities to accuse him of being a member of a counterrevolutionary organisation.

[137] For further examples, see GARF f.8131, op.31, d.70065, l.6.
[138] Anna Krylova, *Soviet Women in Combat: A History of Violence on the Eastern Front* (New York, 2010), 37-8.

PART 2
JOKING DANGEROUSLY

CHAPTER 4
WHO'S LAUGHING NOW? PERSECUTION AND PROSECUTION

The grim punchline of joke-telling in the 1930s, as recorded in the official documents, was usually 's/he was sentenced to 10 years imprisonment'. In fact, some of the appeal of sharing this kind of critical humour actually derived from the fact that it was dangerously rebellious to do so. Just as breaking cultural taboos in Kirov's Carnival by cracking jokes involving scatology or sex could (and can) appeal on a quite visceral level, so did telling political jokes *at all* in a state which demanded conformity and practised widespread censorship. To an extent, therefore, the regime was actually causing, or at least facilitating, this humour.

But Stalin's regime was not simply 'against' humour. Before the Revolution, the Bolsheviks had used it themselves to undermine the tsarist regime and, after they'd won, they tried to 'direct' this powerful force into channels that served the regime's agenda. They even published satirical magazines like *Krokodil*, produced musical comedies, and regularly featured humorists in the pages of *Pravda* itself. But they did so with a specific purpose, and one that was quite at odds with the kind of grassroots humour we've been exploring. There were real and consequential differences between 'official' and 'unofficial' humour, which was why the famous humorist Il'ia Il'f, who we met in Chapter 3, could produce approved satirical content for Soviet publications, yet was forced to confine his more biting jokes to the pages of his journal.

If the regime was not against humour per se, it was certainly afraid of humour wielded by its enemies, and in the course of the 1930s the leaders came to believe that critical jokes were the telltale sign of the counterrevolutionary. They directly equated *anekdoty* with 'antisoviet agitation', and punished joke-tellers with the notorious Article 58-10 of the Criminal Code.[1] This was the intentionally vague legislation used to suppress all forms of dissent, ranging from everyday bellyaching to outright calls for counterrevolution.

Although the regime tried to project certainty, in practice it was unsure how to grapple with this phenomenon. Unlike cries to overthrow the regime, political jokes were often more ambiguous, but so, too, was the regime's shifting and inconsistent application of the law over the course of the decade. As ever in the early Soviet Union, we are faced not with a monolith but with a shambles – an operational and very powerful shambles, but a shambles nonetheless. If the previous chapters showed us how the joke-tellers viewed the regime, this chapter explores how the regime perceived the population and how it tried to deal with the forces of humour which it had unleashed prior to the Revolution. It reconstructs for the first time the uncertain perception and treatment of humour from the regime's perspective, revealing the conflicting views, interpersonal and institutional rivalries, and the crucial shift in their understanding of humour as a consciously-wielded weapon, to considering it a toxic virus that could rapidly infect the minds of the people.

This confusing process left ordinary citizens almost completely in the dark as to how much risk they were taking by telling *anekdoty*, putting them in a deeply unstable and inconsistent environment. Those who were caught were not necessarily indiscreet or self-consciously attacking the regime; the borders of acceptability were both in unpredictable flux and completely outwith the control of the ordinary citizen. Moreover, by analysing the patterns of arrest for joke-telling across the decade, it turns out that keeping up with policy shifts still wouldn't have guaranteed them safety, due to the regime's unapologetic use of retroactive justice.

To trace these complex developments, we need to examine a mixture of official policy-making materials which dealt explicitly with political humour and critical speech, and sources which tell us how these attitudes played out in practice. In the first case, we'll look at secret communiqués between the Soviet leaders, angry directives sent to local judicial bodies, and reports shaming those who did not follow the developing Party line. In the latter, more complex case, we'll use the criminal case-files of 273 individuals who were arrested and imprisoned for antisoviet humour, including people of all ages and from all walks of life. Unlike reports on the 'mood of the population' (*svodki*) and the other materials used in this book, these case-files include more consistent and in-depth data (e.g. age, social origins, education level, location, etc.). This allows us to make direct comparisons between individuals who were arrested for committing crimes of humour, and the circumstances in which they did so – at the dinner table with their families, in the common rooms of their workplace, or even with total strangers on the train.

In doing so, we are confronted with a surprising picture. In a regime dedicated to forging a classless society long characterised as having zero tolerance for dissent of any kind, who you were often mattered more than what you actually said.

The Years of Joking Dangerously

A Humourless Regime?

Despite the images of unrelenting solemnity we have internalised from reading Orwell or Solzhenitsyn, as the journalist Ben Lewis has pointed out, this was not, in truth, 'an unsmiling regime'.[2] Admittedly, it was still one which could be so po-faced on the subject of humour that it often became unintentionally laughable, as William Chamberlin noted when he came across Komsomol discussions on the functions of humour in Soviet society, which included such exciting articles as 'The Organization of Laughter' and 'The Serious Business of the Smile'.[3] Despite this often rigid, unreflective approach to the subject, the officials who composed and compiled reports on popular 'moods' and who wrote up joke-tellers' criminal case-files *did* explicitly recognise that the people they were writing about were trying to be funny. They freely use the terms '*anekdot*' and 'joke' (шутка), and even noted when something was said 'with irony', or 'with laughter'. In other words, these bureaucrats and NKVD operatives were not inhuman drones consistently missing the joke; they just did not consider the subject material and targets of those jokes to be acceptable.

So what did the regime consider to be acceptable humour? This was not very clear until the 1930s were underway, and was a matter of considerable and self-consciously serious debate until 1931. Beginning in April 1929 in the pages of *Literaturnaia gazeta* ('The Literary Newspaper'), and continuing for almost two years thereafter, the increasingly ill-tempered debate centred upon whether or not humour in general and satire in particular actually had a place in the new, Soviet society.

The leading voice of the 'No' camp was the critic V.I. Blium, who argued vociferously that, while there remained certain prerevolutionary elements in society to be fought, 'ludic' methods (i.e. satire) should now be jettisoned in favour of more 'serious' or 'realistic' options, to be pursued in the press, trades unions, and social organisations.[4] In his view, the revolutionary struggle was over, so there was no longer any need for the 'weapon' of satire. Moreover, like an old rifle used to win the Revolution that was now left sitting around the house, its continued presence was surely a disaster waiting to happen in the new, socialist society. Frustrated and increasingly censored, the author Mikhail Bulgakov summed up Blium's position in a letter he wrote to the government: 'ANY SATIRIST IN THE USSR IS TRYING TO UNDERMINE THE SOVIET SYSTEM'.[5] His angry capitals were hardly an exaggeration.

To settle the issue, in typically bureaucratic fashion, a special state Commission for the Study of Satirical Genres in Art and Literature was founded in 1930, and no less a figure than the first Commissar for Enlightenment (1917-29), A.V. Lunacharskii, was appointed to lead it. The Commission was charged with the grandiose task of analysing 'the satirical genre from the Middle Ages to the present day in both Western and Eastern [European] heritage'. It was granted a significant budget to acquire foreign printed and photographic materials, as well as a free hand to commandeer Russo-Soviet items from the Academy of Sciences library in Moscow, all in order to create a systematised archive of materials relevant to the study of 'questions [relating to] the theory and history of European satire'.[6]

Lunacharskii was an obvious choice to head the Commission: he had been interested in and had published over 30 articles on satire and humour over the years, although Annie Gérin has pointed out that he was hardly the most sophisticated thinker, tending to regurgitate whichever theory he'd read most recently, before flitting on to the next one. But all the same, he was ultimately dedicated to crowbarring everything into a suitably Marxist framework of class struggle.[7]

Lunacharskii outlined the Commission's findings in a speech in January 1931 (still deemed 'correct' enough to be reprinted four years later), in which he made it clear that the Bolsheviks principally viewed humour as a 'tool' (орудие), or 'weapon of class struggle'.[8] He stressed the power of humour as a social regulator, emphasising that throughout history it had been used either by the ruling or the working classes against one another – the rulers to keep the workers in check, the workers eventually to fight off their oppressors.

This was essentially to repeat the definition of '*anekdot*' that appeared in the first edition of the *Great Soviet Encyclopaedia* in 1926, which noted that 'the political *anekdot* [...] acquires great agitational significance during social crises as a special kind of weapon for political struggle'.[9] So far, so familiar, but where Lunacharskii and the Commission departed from Blium and the 'No' camp was in their belief that this was a struggle that would continue for some time to come, as the new regime consolidated its position. As Lunacharskii concluded, 'We must therefore [...] analyse the historical progress of laughter and, thus, sharpen the weapons of our humorists and our satirists'.[10]

This did not mark a change in Lunacharskii's own thinking (he had written some 10 years previously that 'without releasing the sword form one hand, in the other we can now use a [more] subtle weapon: laughter' in the continuing fight against the Revolution's beaten but still lingering enemies),[11] but it did settle the public debate. From this point on, the regime's position on the role of humour in society was – as a delegate at the 1934 Soviet Writers' Congress summed it up – that 'The task of Soviet comedy is to "kill with laughter" enemies and to "correct with laughter"' those loyal to the regime.[12]

The unquestioned assumption both during the debate, and in this rather predictable compromise, was that humour is a weapon and, therefore, is something wielded in violence. As such, even as the regime elected to keep using this weapon for its own purposes, anxieties lingered that its enemies could do real harm with it, too. These beliefs stemmed directly from the Bolsheviks' days in the revolutionary trenches, when they had mocked and ridiculed tsarism. Because they had thereafter seized power with no little support, it was easy to believe that their satirical attacks had played a role in that eventual victory. This was something M.F. Shkiriatov, a hard-line Party functionary, made plain at the Central Committee Plenum of January 1933, during a discussion of Party discipline:

> I would like to speak of another antiparty method of operation, namely the so-called jokes. What are these jokes? Jokes against the party constitute agitation against the party. Who among us Bolsheviks does not know how we fought against tsarism in the old days, how we told jokes in order to undermine the authority of the existing system? [...] This has also been employed as a keen weapon against the Central Committee of the party.[13]

Admittedly, these comments came shortly after Shkiriatov accused critics of the Party line of utilising such nefarious tactics as 'wine and debauchery' – using drunkenness as 'a cover' and an excuse for conducting politically suspect conversations[14] – so this was hardly the most nuanced or composed discussion of political humour. All the same, it was certainly true that the Bolsheviks had long considered political humour to be a potent weapon, and this continued to condition their thinking and use of it during the 1930s.

It certainly characterised the way the leaders used humour amongst themselves. Memoirs and other fragmentary sources give us the sense that the humour they shared was usually simplistic joshing and leg-pulling, but that it was almost constantly underlaid by struggles for power and for Stalin's favour. Similarly, a draft collection of something like 'The Wit and Wisdom of I.V. Stalin', which lies unpublished in his personal archive, is also tellingly composed of cutting put-downs and derisive attacks on his enemies or on ideas which diverged from his own.[15]

In any case, now that the regime had decided to retain the 'subtle weapon' of humour, what did this mean in practice? What counted as 'appropriate' humour in the 1930s and was officially published? This subject would deserve its own book, so we'll confine ourselves to noting the major trends. There were certainly obvious and usually crude satirical attacks of external enemies or the 'leftovers' (остатки) from the old days, like priests or speculators, but this 'weapon' was most often used as a 'corrective', didactic device – teaching through attack, rather than simply destroying. As Natalia Skradol has argued, we can see this in the way Soviet newspapers inserted '(Laughter)' into the transcripts of speeches in order to demonstrate the apparent response of the live audience (who, of course, always responded appropriately) and hence the response expected of readers.[16] And even as the leadership effectively 'kill[ed] with laughter' its enemies – vicious mockery and heartless laughter coloured the plenary sessions preceding the actual executions of the infamous Moscow Show Trials[17] – the performance was simultaneously designed to convey a clear message, thereby 'correct[ing] with laughter' everybody else.

Published humorous stories were also used in this way to send signals to certain groups to change their behaviour, whether that was a specific reprimand in 1935 aimed at Soviet judges for being overly concerned with evidence and detail, rather than the character of the defendant,[18] or, more generally, satirical attacks on inefficient and corrupt bureaucrats – a theme which frequently graced the pages of *Krokodil* in stories and caricatures. The puffed-up local bureaucrat was also mocked for his obfuscating, self-important behaviour in film, as we see, for example, in one of the best-loved musical comedies of the Soviet period, *Volga-Volga* (1938), which is to this day regularly screened on Russian TV.[19] In this whimsical film, the bureaucrat is deflated and made to look absurd in an endless variety of ways, from his own hammy delusions of grandeur to, more prosaically, accidentally stepping on a pig.

Published satirical stories were also used to mark certain policy shifts. Take, for example, the introduction of significant changes to the Soviet education system in 1934, in which much greater emphasis was to be placed on teaching hard facts rather than slogans and abstract ideological concepts. This was signalled in *Pravda* with a short story written by two famous humorists: Il'ia Il'f (whose personal notebooks contained more biting criticisms of the regime than he would ever publish, as we saw in Chapter 2) and his partner, Evgenii Petrov.[20]

The story, 'Conversations at the Tea Table', presents us with a young boy arguing with his parents. The father is an old Bolshevik who finds it difficult to communicate with a son who seems only able to speak in superficial slogans and clichés. The son admonishes his father repeatedly: 'What new things did you learn in class?', asks the father. 'Not in class, in the *group*', answers the son. 'How many times have I told you, dad, that "class" is a reactionary-feudalistic concept'. 'All right, all right. Let's say group. So what were you taught in the group?'. The son replies indignantly, 'We weren't taught, we *studied*'. Their bickering continues until the father attempts to steer the conversation onto safer ground by asking what fun his son gets up to with his friends in their free time. This tack also goes badly, as the son replies in further indignation that, 'We didn't have fun. There was no time'. 'So what *did* you do?' asks the father in some desperation. 'We wrestled (*borolis*')'.

The father perks up at the sound of this, but unfortunately it transpires that this was not the kind of physical wrestling he had in mind, but rather a wrestling with matters of principle. The son and his friends had been 'struggling' (the same word, *borolis*') against 'Lebedevism' in their school… Lebedev, it turns out, is an eight-year-old schoolboy who underperforms in class. His mistakes are interpreted by his insufferably zealous classmates as deviationist tendencies which must forcefully be eliminated; Lebedev, it seems, had become their Trotskii. The story's smug conclusion sees the father get his own back by ridiculing his son's lack of concrete knowledge about historical figures and events. The new education policy was clear: theory without factual knowledge was just hot air and should be mocked (and hence 'corrected') as such.

Whether the authorities acted to change official humorous output in response to audience reactions is difficult to discern and deserves further, in-depth study, but the regime's ideologues certainly spent a great deal of time determining what audience reactions *should* be, and thereafter poring over the reports of informants and digests of readers' letters to newspapers to see if the people were responding 'correctly'. Changes could be made on the basis of the discrepancies they found, although the balance between blaming the cultural product or blaming the audience for not 'getting it' (often next-door to branding those individuals 'enemies') was fluid and poorly defined.

In general, though, David Brandenberger has shown just how closely cultural productions (humorous ones included) had to follow broader, centrally-determined policy campaigns during the 1930s. Films, fiction, histories, plays and concerts all had to follow these dictates or never see the light of day. And, needless to say, these dictates changed repeatedly and without warning: Give us the forces of History in action; give us specific Soviet heroes; don't emphasise any individuals; socialism has been achieved; socialism is in danger; Fascism is our implacable enemy; Germany is our ally against an imperialist world... These political shifts dictated changes in both content and form, as well as how given genres were supposed to serve the regime.[21] Like other official cultural products, official humour was therefore principally didactic rather than responsive to its audience (not least because the audience was always in the process of being reimagined by the state), but it does not follow that it was therefore unamusing to contemporaries as a result.

In fact, there were various points of convergence between official and unofficial political humour, the most obvious example being local bureaucrats, who were targeted by both. Some *anekdot* plots also occasionally turned up in heavily edited form in *Krokodil* and other satirical publications.[22]

However, there are two important reasons why we shouldn't interpret these moments of affinity as instances of state and citizen straightforwardly 'sharing' the same humour. First, these are not points of crossover in the sense of official and unofficial perspectives existing in the same space and having the same meaning: these are more complex moments of crosshatching. An ordinary citizen might laugh at the content of *Krokodil* when a familiar obfuscating bureaucrat was mocked, but they brought their own perspective to the situation too, which was quite different to that of the regime. Contemporaries might well feel that bureaucrats deserved mockery, but their reasons for feeling that way had more to do with how bureaucrats negatively affected their lives, whereas, for the regime, mocking bureaucrats was essentially a way to find scapegoats for inefficiencies and failures, and to punish those who attempted to build up local power bases. In the same way, when Stalin sometimes privately told jokes about mass and arbitrary arrests, he did so from a position of power in order to unsettle his audience. When ordinary citizens told jokes about those subjects, they did so from a position of weakness, counting themselves among the victims.[23]

This brings us to the second reason: state and society used humour for quite different purposes. Even when ostensibly satirising the same subjects, official humour revolved around didacticism, self-exculpation, and blame, but ordinary citizens frequently laughed *at themselves*. While regime satire lambasted the foolishness of bureaucrats or wreckers for failures and shortcomings in the grand march to Communism, Soviet citizens' humour instead focused on the real-life consequences of regime policies, simultaneously mocking the latter *and* laughing at the often terrible predicaments these landed them in, all in the attempt to regain a sense of distance or control – however ephemeral – over those circumstances.

In fact, this was a defining characteristic of unofficial 1930s political humour, perhaps best summed up as *Schadenfreude* directed at yourself. The Soviet writer Z.S. Papernyi (1919-1996), conditioned, of course, by the world in which he lived and worked, went so far as to consider it *the* defining characteristic of a genuine sense of humour. As he put it,

> If, for example, a person buys a lottery ticket for 30 kopecks, wins a Volga [a Soviet car], and is filled with blissful laughter – this is not a sense of humour. But if he has 300 rubles and the lottery ticket with which he thought to win that Volga stolen from him, and he smiles – *this* is the beginning of a sense of humour.[24]

Laughing at your own misfortune lay at the heart of contemporaries' political humour in these years, and, as such, they had much to laugh about. To an extent, this continued a long tradition: Likhachev argued that a defining characteristic of laughter in medieval Rus' was its self-reflexivity, in which jokers 'played the fool' and invited others to laugh as much *at them* as at their message, even as they revealed in their 'buffoonery' potentially uncomfortable truths about the real world.[25] In both contexts, this was because ordinary folk could not effect direct change in the regimes they lived under, but also because those regimes did not permit themselves to be openly laughed at except in officially-designated places, be that during medieval Carnival, or in the micromanaged production of official humour in the Soviet Union.

The most uncomfortable truth about humour in the 1930s, however, was that whatever the debates and directives concerning the official use and production of it, for ordinary citizens who engaged in political joke-telling, it was the views of the NKVD and other organs of state security which mattered most. The approach of those bodies had far more to do with developing interpretations of 'antisoviet agitation' and 'hidden enemies' than it did with academic and artistic commissions and congresses. Although cultural producers and academics concerned with humour were given space to debate and directives to follow, the limits of acceptable critical speech were increasingly defined by rather different agendas as the decade progressed.

From Weapon to Virus

Rumours circulated that the secret police was cracking down on 'antisoviet' humour as early as the late 1920s, as Shitts recorded in his diary.[26] But the real change came in 1935 when humour was drawn into the highly-charged arena of the regime's periodic campaigns to fight off ideological 'contamination' in the Party ranks and in society more generally.[27] After the Kirov murder, a closed letter was circulated to local Party organisations which called for greater 'vigilance' because, the letter insisted, the murder had exposed a nest of hidden enemies within the Party who had escaped the earlier purges.

The idea that good, honest workers had been toiling 'side by side with socially-alien elements' was both disturbing and not to be tolerated further.[28] Too many telltale signs of these 'elements' had been ignored, and at various meetings convened to discuss the closed letter, *anekdoty* were specifically highlighted as one of the signs which betrayed a hidden enemy.[29]

This was mirrored by a change in the state's juridical attitude towards critical speech (including humour). A stream of directives poured out from the Centre that dictated a much broader and harsher application of Article 58-10. The chairman of the USSR Supreme Court, Vinokurov, issued one on 7 March 1935, which demanded a very clear tightening up regarding anything conceivably falling under the umbrella of 'antisoviet agitation'. Article 58-10 cases that had been given only suspended sentences were now deemed incorrect, and actual imprisonment was to be applied; other people tried for simple hooliganism were now also to be retried under 58-10.

More ominously still, in agitation cases reviewed by the 'special collegium' courts (Спецколлегии)[30] in which the trial process could not establish sufficient evidence to secure a conviction, but 'when nevertheless there [were] sufficient facts bearing witness to the soc[ial] danger of the accused, due to their connections to the criminal world, their former convictions, etc., then the particulars of each case were to be forwarded for review by the Special Board (Особое совещание) of the NKVD.[31] In other words, at this time there was a rather panicked concern not to let anyone off for anything that might conceivably be considered 'antisoviet agitation', even when there was no proof of a crime being committed. Suspicion was enough to have you sent to the NKVD, where, of course, due process was often abandoned (and here was already being abandoned in the very act of sending these flimsy cases on to the NKVD Special Board).

More important for our purposes, however, was the directive issued a few days earlier on 2 March 1935 by both Vinokurov and the infamous Chief Prosecutor of the Soviet Union, Vyshinskii, who would preside over the whirlwind of arrests and executions of 1937-8. This directive forbade the quotation of antisoviet statements, including jokes, in all official documents, from police reports right up to court verdicts. This was a serious instruction: a strongly-worded reprimand and public shaming of local bodies which were slow to implement the new practice followed from Vyshinskii on 31 May. Moreover, this proscriptive directive considered the issue serious enough to rank it on the same level as the unwary quotation of state secrets in espionage cases, and permitted only specially-selected, particularly trustworthy lawyers and officials to see the actual words for which a defendant was prosecuted.[32]

By early 1935, then, the regime had complicated its earlier conception of satirical, critical humour as a dangerous 'weapon' wielded in violence by the representatives of a given 'class'. It had now become, along with other expressions of critical opinion, a virus which could, if not rapidly quarantined, spread its malignant influence almost indiscriminately: only a very few trusted officials were deemed politically conscious (i.e. loyal) enough to remain immune. Agency had thus shifted from the joke-teller to the joke itself; intention was no longer a real consideration, because a critical joke was now thought capable of wreaking havoc through careless transmission, regardless of the carrier's (be it the joke-teller's, or the unwary bureaucrat's) aims. In this way, the regime had once again created its own problem: joke-tellers' intentions and audience reactions when sharing an *anekdot* were ignored in favour of the state's own, paranoid reading that this represented the proliferation of a frightening, contagious infection.

Attempts to control and punish critical speech reveal a world of interpersonal and institutional rivalries behind the scenes of Soviet officialdom. Yet even as they struggled to enforce their authority over one another, jokes emerge as a key reference point in their thinking.

Anekdoty were always a crucial part of the rationale (or, rather, fears) which lay behind the punishment of critical speech, as we can see when the issue of quotation resurfaced in May 1936, after the Procuracy complained that the NKVD was not passing on the details of antisoviet statements to them for oversight. Using the issue to defend its autonomy, the NVKD cited its own directive no.00321 (15 August 1935), which 'categorically forbids the direct quotation [приводить дословно] of counterrevolutionary expressions which contain sharp and abusive language, antisoviet *anekdoty*, obscenities, etc. directed towards the leaders of the Party and government'.[33] Moreover, when defending the NKVD's circumspection in recording the actual words of those sentenced under Article 58-10, Assistant Commissar Iakov Agranov crystallised the issue by arguing that to include such speech would transform the official records into 'a catalogue of unprintable jokes'. The documents would themselves become dangerous, and Agranov turned specifically to jokes to emphasise his point.[34] When debating the limits of critical speech and how to control it, humour remained a cardinal point of orientation.

Despite that shared reference point, how things played out on the ground was messy, to the say the least. Although the directives of early 1935 and the 'virus' interpretation would shape the regime's perspective on and treatment of citizens' political humour for the rest of the decade, there was a surprising degree of inconsistency still visible in 1936. This was a year marked by confusions, short-lived reassessments, and top-level bickering over Article 58-10 and its implementation.

On the ground, inconsistencies could arise due to over-cautiousness in recording critical speech. For example, the *kolkhoznitsa* K.D. Aver'ianova was sentenced on 2 June 1936 by the Saratov krai court to two years for having 'at various gatherings and parties of the kolkhoz youth sung counterrevolutionary *chastushki* insulting the *vozhdi*...'. Although she confessed to this, the Supreme Court still overturned the verdict because, they complained, the contents of the *chastushki* had not been recorded in the casefile. Although the offending lines should indeed have been noted *somewhere*, it seems that the new directive on not quoting antisoviet speech meant that sometimes it was either never recorded at all, or that no record of the words was kept on file after the sentence was passed. In this instance, it provided a reprieve for Aver'ianova when her case was reviewed.[35]

Sometimes inconsistencies were not procedural slip-ups, however, and instead reflected high-level powerplays, as when the NKVD refused to pass on details of critical speech to the Procuracy. Here, Chief Prosecutor Vyshinskii's call to quarantine critical speech came back to haunt him, because it allowed the NKVD to elude

Procuracy oversight to some extent. Fearing or at least resenting the rise of the NKVD at the cost of his own authority, Vyshinskii struck back in 1936 by attempting to curtail the indiscriminate force of Article 58-10. In a secret communiqué to Stalin and Molotov dated 16 April, Vyshinskii complained about the number of unnecessary criminal cases brought against citizens who repeated '*chastushki* and songs of antisoviet content', because, he said, those individuals might do so without 'pursuing counterrevolutionary aims', 'there being no [other] grounds to consider them counterrevolutionaries'.[36]

Vyshinskii's apparent change of heart was visible in judicial practice, too, as we can see in a report on the activities of the various special collegia of the USSR Supreme Court in 1936. These reports complained of overzealous prosecutions at the local level, taking as a 'characteristic example' the case of the 21 year-old N.N. Spirin, who had been sentenced by the Saratov krai special collegium on 17 June to two years imprisonment under Article 58-10. During a dance, young Spirin had taken a girl's hat and plopped it unceremoniously on a nearby bust of Lenin. The verdict was overturned upon review, the report noted approvingly.[37] Nevertheless, even if Spirin received this new leniency, there had been no sign of it for *kolkhoznitsa* Aver'ianova, whose sentence was issued a mere 15 days prior to Spirin's. Moreover, she was convicted for *chastushka*-singing, which Vyshinskii had explicitly identified in his letter to Stalin and Molotov as insufficient cause to prosecute. At this point, it seems, inconsistency was the only certainty.

But whatever the inconsistencies and confusions generated by the backstage manoeuvrings and power struggles between the Procuracy, NKVD, and Commissariat of Justice in 1936,[38] this would ultimately prove to be the calm before the storm. The infection doctrine was unmistakably in the ascendant by 1937 as the mass repressions began. More importantly for our purposes, in this ambiguous and volatile legal context in the early- to mid-1930s, it would be absurd to expect ordinary citizens to be able to judge where precisely the borders of acceptable critical speech lay. Many would learn and adjust over time, of course (and many were far more cautious in the first place and did not crack critical jokes), but for some, even if they somehow managed to stay ahead of policy changes, it was, in fact, already too late.

Retroactive Justice

When were people arrested for telling political jokes? A clear pattern emerges from our collection of 273 criminal cases. A single arrest was made in 1933 for antisoviet humour, and between two and five were made the following year.[39] Things began to change in 1935, when up to 14 arrests were made;[40] in 1936 it was 33.[41] This obviously correlates with the directives from above that we just examined, as well as broader patterns: the crackdown following the Kirov murder and the hunt for members of the fictional 'Trotskiist-Zinov'evite' conspiracy that would climax in the notorious Moscow Show Trials. Then there came a veritable explosion of arrests in 1937 (almost 100, tripling the previous year's total)[42] and a concomitant drop following that infamous year (a maximum of 28 arrests in 1938; just 10 in 1939).[43] After this lull, the final flashpoint in our period came in 1941, as part of a general tightening up as the threat of war increased, when arrests jumped to as many as 46.[44]

At first glance, this timeline offers few surprises. Sarah Davies has sketched a detailed timeline of the way Article 58-10 was used across the 1930s, and the peaks and troughs of arrests and sentences largely correlate with the pattern our joke-teller sample provides. She describes a rise following the Kirov murder, reined in during 1936, before gradually building to the explosion of 1937-8; thereafter a significant reduction until 1941.[45] The joke-teller sample only departs from this in the increase of arrests in 1936, rather than a reduction, which, given the inconsistencies and high-level politicking going on in that year, suggests a harsher line existed in practice rather than in policy. Our timeline also reflects the waves of regime repression more broadly,[46] as well as mirroring changes to the leadership and internal organisation of the OGPU-NKVD,[47] and the move in 1938 towards a clearer distinction between political policing and the practice of criminal justice.[48]

However, something has until now been missing from this picture and is revealed by our case study: the practice of retroactive justice. For the regime not only changed the rules unpredictably, but it applied those changes anachronistically too.

If we examine the dates on which joke-tellers in our case study were arrested and compare these with the alleged date of their 'crime', we discover that a quarter of the sample were arrested more than a full year after they had made their joke or humorous comment.[49] Given the speed with which the NKVD frequently swooped down on other antisoviet activities throughout the 1930s, this lethargic response is remarkable. Moreover, the time-lapse makes it highly likely that many joke-tellers spoke in the belief that their words were, if not technically acceptable, then at least unlikely to result in serious reprisals.

If it was possible to tell political jokes or make biting observations during 1931, for example (a year in which our sample contains no arrests), then it was hardly possible for contemporaries to predict that a few years later their words would retroactively be deemed criminal. The regime was doing the equivalent of declaring a ball 'in' at the time it was played, but then, years later, when the rules or court had been altered, retrospectively judging all past shots by the new rules. Inevitably, many shots which had previously flirted with the boundaries were suddenly reclassified as 'out'.

Just as broader discussions about the limits of critical speech always had bearing on *anekdoty*, so the retroactive prosecution of *anekdoty* reflects the treatment of other critical speech. Following the Kirov murder, the Leningrad NKVD was condemned for not noticing alleged warning signs that could have prevented the assassination. In response, as Cynthia Hooper describes, 'the Moscow political police re-examined a number of old denunciations of treasonous activity that they had previously dismissed as trivial', which led in one instance to an increasingly absurd investigation of Kremlin cleaning ladies and librarians.[50]

Retroactivity was not confined to *anekdoty*; moribund denunciations or leading interrogation questions aimed at retrospectively indicting someone could also be readily deployed in numerous contexts as the regime tightened up. But *anekdoty* could also come in handy in this respect: Peter Solomon, an authority on the evolution of the Stalinist legal system, notes that by summer 1937 it was actually 'hard for any justice official to withstand the pressure to join rank and lay political charges wherever possible'.[51] Finding a few stray *anekdoty* in the accused's past easily served this purpose.

This practice of retroactivity and anachronism made joke-telling increasingly dangerous across the 1930s, but it also tells us something fundamental about the Soviet regime's nature and operation. Given that officially-sanctioned humour was designed to teach, it's rather fitting to find this 'lesson' illuminated in the 'Conversations at the Tea Table' story we looked at earlier.

The short story is revealing in two respects: it both signals an official shift in policy through its publication in *Pravda*, and simultaneously sketches the retroactive, anachronistic process the regime initiated whenever such policy shifts were introduced.[52] Despite being genuinely amusing, the tale contains a razor-blade beneath the surface: it signals a change in the official line, but does so by annihilating any trace of the previous one. That the conceited yet hapless child was only singing to the tune of yesterday's orthodoxy is completely ignored; the story is not a motion towards development, but a denunciation of the previous model as incorrect at *any* point in time, even though it had until that moment been, at least in public, inviolable. The unreflective absolutism of this approach is, therefore, scarcely different to (or more coherent than) the schoolchildren's attack on 'Lebedevism'. The story's conclusion conceals a far grimmer reality in which Soviet citizens would not have been merely ridiculed like the schoolboy, but would instead have been arrested for lagging behind official policy. You had to keep pace as the carpet was rolled up behind the advancing vanguard, or otherwise be crushed beneath it.

The Spirit of Certainty

In a fascinating article that focuses on teaching institutions and personnel in the city of Kirov, Larry Holmes suggested that, from the regime's perspective, for much of the 1930s any 'error' in one part of a citizen's life 'required the discovery and, if need be, the invention of analogous activity in all others.' The personal, professional and political were interpreted as a 'symbiosis of errors': if the Party discovered a 'bad apple', it was assumed that they were rotten to the core.[53] This totalising approach was certainly how joke-tellers were treated. If political jokes were a virus, then its carriers were, by the mid-1930s, increasingly treated as contaminated and corrupted vessels.[54]

From this perspective, to share in political humour meant that even the most intimate evidence of loyalty to the regime might offer no security. Recent scholarship has focused on the diaries of citizens who were exploring their identities and their relationship to Soviet power and ideology. These personal documents frequently involved a significant degree of confusion and doubt, as well as often powerful expressions of belief in the Soviet project. But if the state ever got its hands on them, the doubts expressed in these diaries could all too easily become 'proof' of double-dealing and of hiding a second 'face' behind a public mask. Such was the fate of Andrei Arzhilovskii, for example. But there is another, still more depressing layer to this story: even if a diary turned out to be a flawless log of a dedicated true believer, it could *still* be interpreted as 'proof' of dishonesty if the state had discovered (or imagined) 'errors' or 'contamination' elsewhere in a person's life.

Take the case of Boris Iakovlevich Iampol'skii, a 20 year-old native of Saratov who was arrested (along with various others studying or working in the city) for telling antisoviet *anekdoty* in his apartment during social gatherings. The authorities seized his diary, which he had kept for about eight years by the time of his arrest in 1941, and in which, Iampol'skii claimed, it was clear he was a loyal Soviet person through and through ('from brains to bones', as he put it). The authorities actually agreed with his assessment, but nevertheless decided to interpret this document of intense loyalty as an obvious attempt to conceal his 'true face' – they declared the diary a blatant red herring designed to be found by and to mislead the NKVD. As Iampol'skii himself noted later, quite how he would or could have thought up such a devilish trick when he began his diary at age 12 was not a question the investigators bothered to ask themselves.[55]

But although the regime and its agents loved certainty, they clearly acted inconsistently across this decade, so we must pause to ask how they negotiated this seeming contradiction. Part of the answer can be seen in the history and use of Article 58-10 itself. Although it would become inextricably associated with Stalinist repressions in the 1930s, Article 58 actually appeared in the 1926 Soviet penal code, so it would be wrong to consider it as simply 'Stalinist', because it predates Stalin's ascendancy by several years.

Instead, this highlights an important issue: the Soviet regime (and, we might note, the rulers of post-Soviet Russia) rarely changed existing legislation on-the-fly for short-term ends. Instead, they changed the *interpretation* of that legislation – altering the spirit but not the letter of the law, or, alternatively, suddenly enforcing the letter of the law far more strictly than they had ever done before. Crucially, however, the regime never openly acknowledged these changes in attitude and interpretation: at every stage, the official line was that the state was being 100 percent consistent, and they could point to the (mostly) unchanging letter of the law to 'prove' it.

This is clear in the language that Procuracy officials used in the criminal case-files when they were assessing appeals. A conviction might be upheld in a review conducted right up to the early 1950s, but the same individual could then be completely exonerated a few years later.[56] This obviously reflected broader political changes after Stalin's death, but the point here is that the report-writers refused to acknowledge that fact.

Instead, they wrote painstaking summaries of the original investigation before coming to their conclusions, but, whether stating that the individual was guilty or innocent, the language always reflected absolute certainty: 'it is plain from the case-file', 'it is clear'; a plea or a conviction is 'groundless' (неоснованный).

More strikingly still, it's usually impossible to guess the verdict of a review until the very last line: the summary in two reviews separated by a handful of years might be almost identical, yet, while the first would conclude that 'obviously' the joke-teller was guilty, the second would state that the 'content of the *anekdot(y)*' was 'obviously' 'not antisoviet in character' (just remove the 'not', and you would have precisely the formulation used in the original conviction). If exoneration came, the formulation used was likewise sweeping: 's/he is exonerated for lack of any evidence of criminality'.

It was rare for reviews resulting in exoneration to bother with finding reasons or scapegoats for the overturned verdicts – the original convictions were simply labelled 'groundless' and dismissed – but when they did so it was the original investigators who took the fall. In a strongly critical review of the case against Iampol'skii and others for telling *anekdoty* at the former's apartment and passing around lewd poetry, the official analysis, signed by R. Rudenko and dated 23 June 1962, considered this behaviour to be thoroughly 'philistine', but although this was regrettable it was hardly political behaviour. Therefore, Rudenko continued, 'the various *anekdoty* [they] told were "labelled" antisoviet, counterrevolutionary etc.' Such formulations are obviously wrong, the report went on, and were generated 'as a result of the evaluations of these actions by the investigators themselves'.[57]

This is logically incoherent, because no judge or other legal official would have to accept the investigators' 'labels', so at one level this represents straightforward scapegoating of lower-ranking officials. But at the broader level, this interpretation drives home the fact that the regime could, or rather would, only deal in serial certainties. Inconsistencies had therefore to be dismissed as the mistakes of individuals who were unable to see a truth that was always treated as both achingly obvious and eternal. This is ever the disease of authoritarian regimes and a principal reason why they so dislike being laughed at: serial certainties and self-righteousness do not permit the ambiguities generated by humour, yet their po-faced inconsistencies also inherently invite it.

Targeting the Joke-Tellers

Although the judicial and security organs conceptualised and enforced the laws governing the expression of critical opinion in a manner that was opaque, faddish, and near-impossible to predict, there were still patterns visible in how this played out on the ground, and this give us some important insights into the dangers and difficulties of sharing critical humour in the 1930s. Those hazards were defined by the regime, of course, so what follows in the remainder of this chapter simultaneously continues our exploration of the official treatment of humour, but does so with a focus on who the regime seemed to target for joke-telling and, by extension, who was in less danger of negative repercussions. To begin, however, we need to ask where it proved most dangerous to exchange critical jokes, because, in fact, the 'where' was also defined by the 'who'.

Danger Zones: The Where and the Who

Our case study reveals three principal contexts in which joke-telling led to arrest. Almost half (127) occurred in the workplace; a further 46 were in people's apartments in the context of a party or social gathering (a further four cases involved both contexts); and some 52 instances occurred in another public space of some kind.[58] Alcohol was a not infrequent accompaniment to *anekdot*-telling, at least in the context of a party or gathering at someone's apartment. Alcohol can certainly loosen tongues; as a Russian aphorism has it, 'Whatever a sober man has on his mind a drunk has on the tip of his tongue'.[59] However, given that the majority of instances in our case study occurred in the workplace, then unless we assume these raconteurs practised what Soviet report-writers alarmingly called 'systematic drunkenness' all day, every day, it seems that although a familiar companion, alcohol was not essential for *anekdoty* or other humour to be shared openly in dangerous locations.

What's more important to bear in mind is that what made a given location dangerous for joke-telling was the other people in it – hence all three zones in which our arrests took place by their nature involved mixed company rather than (only) tightly-knit friendships.

The workplace was clearly a potentially dangerous place to share humour simply because of the numbers of other people within in it who might denounce a joke-teller to the authorities, or, less proactively, who might be pressured by NKVD agents to produce 'evidence' against a colleague, retrospectively or otherwise. Nevertheless, the relative danger of telling *anekdoty* at work could also be highly variable (every workplace the world over can have its own particular character and norms), and this led to many missteps.

Newcomers to a given workplace could rapidly find themselves in hot water for sharing *anekdoty* or sarcastic remarks that might have been completely safe and even routine at their previous job. For example, Guzynin, a Komsomol member undergoing military service, was drafted to a new unit in 1934 and immediately began joking and telling *anekdoty* with his new brothers-in-arms, no doubt trying to make some new friends. He was swiftly reported to the Komsomol Central Committee; his ultimate fate is unclear.[60] Another Komsomol report notes that, upon his return to base from a series of international voyages, naval recruit Bublikov immediately began reeling out jokes with his new comrades on board a training vessel. Bublikov did this in front of more than 70 people, so he clearly didn't expect his confident banter to have serious consequences. In his absence on those voyages, however, it seems the norms of appropriate conduct had shifted; his case was referred to the NKVD.[61] Guzynin and Bublikov made the same mistake: they *immediately* began telling jokes upon their arrival, allowing themselves no time to take the temperature of the microclimate they'd just entered.

It didn't have to be the content of the humour itself which led to reprimand or denunciation, however, but the context and manner in which it took place. Consider the case of N.E. Koniaev, a student at a Kyiv technical institute, who frequently dropped into the student dormitory, though he wasn't a resident, and asked other students to tell *anekdoty* and chat with him. One witness said that these *anekdoty* were 'bawdy' (похабные) in nature; another complained that Koniaev interrupted other students' work with his frequent visits. Consequently, the outsider Koniaev was reported to the authorities and received a four-year sentence for 'antisoviet agitation'.[62] He was convicted not for telling explicitly antisoviet *anekdoty*, but because telling jokes disrupted diligent (and therefore implicitly loyal) students. Once again, an outsider's attempts to ingratiate his way into a group of his contemporaries was rebuffed by an in-group which, in this instance, appreciated neither his brand of jokes (perhaps fearing that he was an agent provocateur, inviting them to tell compromising political *anekdoty*), nor the fact he used them to interrupt their studies. A dormitory, like a workplace, or any social location with a consistent roster of people, also had its own localised rules of conduct.

If Koniaev's difficulties arose more from his unreceptive audience than the location in which he told his unrequited jokes, it was also a mistake to judge the safety of a given scenario by reference to your audience alone. Take the example of A.F. Klevakin, a schoolteacher who was arrested for telling *anekdoty* in a restaurant. This was obviously a public space and not therefore one in which Klevakin should have assumed he could speak completely freely, especially as he did so in 1937. However, he had cause to feel more at ease than usual; he was sitting with the restaurant's director and, investigators established, the pair had a pre-existing friendship. Confusion could therefore arise in Klevakin's (and the restaurant director's) sense of the social rules under which their exchange took place: despite being in a public location, the pair chose to use their friendship and the added authority of the director's status as their reference point from which to calculate the risk of sharing political *anekdoty*.[63] In cases like this, it was the public nature of the location (meaning the eavesdropping strangers within it) which could always have the final say: both men were arrested.[64]

The railway network – at stations or when travelling by train – also proved quite a hotspot for catching people exchanging political jokes, accounting for a full 46 of our cases. In part this was no doubt because the regime was particularly sensitive about crime on the transport network – be it sabotage, or the proliferation of antisoviet people and ideas – and it even set up a court system specifically to try cases which took place within it.[65] And, of course, if jokes were a virus, their presence in the arteries of the country was completely unacceptable.

But despite this regime concern, railways arguably facilitated the unwary sharing of *anekdoty* because they are a vivid example of a liminal social space: they represent the connections between places, while not quite being places or destinations in themselves.[66] As such, the time spent between definite spaces can lead to a relaxation in the normal rules of social conduct, as the passengers' contextually-defined identities are suspended in a 'non-place'[67] which belongs to and defines no single person more than any other.[68] Chatting openly with complete strangers befriended on a journey can be a liberating experience, especially if we believe we'll never have to see them again afterwards. The democratising atmosphere of sharing a bus or train ride, and the sense of shared common ground it creates, combines with the sense of being outside your normal social spaces and their various responsibilities. Like alcohol, this can prove a potent loosener of tongues. It was likely a mixture of these factors, combined with regime sensitivity, which led to so many arrests on the railway.

The blurred borders between 'public' and 'private' in this decade will be explored more deeply in the next chapter, but for now suffice it to say that the physical composition (open spaces; thin walls) or the function of a given location (trains which move between places; restaurants as a public space in which people meet for principally private interactions) could well influence the danger of sharing critical humour. All the same, the 'where' should first and foremost be understood in terms of *who* was present.

With this in mind, it shouldn't surprise us to note the most conspicuous absence in these official sources: the family. Even though numerous cases in our sample occurred in apartments, it was never family members who betrayed the joke-teller, or at least they never appeared as witnesses for the prosecution. Nor is the family as a social location (that is, the 'home' defined by the people who constitute it, rather than a physical location, given the severe lack of private space during this decade) one in which humour was betrayed to the authorities. We'll explore the huge importance of the family and close friends to everyday life and sociability in the next chapter, but it's worth considering the issue here from the state's perspective, too.

The Soviet state pursued characteristically contradictory goals regarding the family: as we know from its designation of women in the 1920s as emancipated superwomen and then, in the 1930s, as housewives and mothers, the Soviet family was in the latter decade considered a major element of social stability.[69] And yet the spectre of Pavlik Morozov – the boy-hero who denounced his father only to be murdered by his own family – haunted the '30s, too. Whatever the realities behind the propaganda story of young 'Comrade Pavlik',[70] his heroisation illustrates the regime's concern that regardless of the stability provided by the family unit, ultimate loyalty was owed always to the state. By promoting the boy-hero, the regime made it clear that it wanted its eyes and ears inside the family, lest it become a hotbed of dissent and rebellion.

The regime failed in this ambition. As Sheila Fitzpatrick and Alf Lüdtke remind us, the arrest of a family member frequently led to the arrest of other members and friends, which was likely to reinforce a sense of small-group identity rather than foster loyalty to the vengeful state, whether this was motivated by love or simple self-interest.[71] This is not conjecture, either: the sociologists who conducted the Harvard Project likewise concluded that their 'data reveal that the most frequent reaction to the arrest of a family member was an increase in family solidarity'.[72]

But despite its failure to truly penetrate the family unit, the regime – ever contradictory – simultaneously recognised the validity of internal family loyalties, even when these stood in stark opposition to the official view. The countless letters sent on behalf of relatives who were arrested for antisoviet agitation prompted official review processes rather than the arrest of the letter-writer, even though the latter was essentially challenging the state's verdict. Likewise, the relatives who stood in queues for hours or even days to bring packages and messages to their incarcerated loved ones were not arrested for their clear refusal to accept that their relative was now an 'un-person' or an enemy.[73] The family not only remained a social location – whether in love, loyalty, or fear of collateral damage – in which contemporaries could speak more critically, but, surprisingly, this quasi-autonomous status was something which the state seemed at least tacitly to accept.

Locking Up the Joke-Tellers

Now that we have a sense of when, where and why the regime was arresting joke-tellers in the 1930s, it's high time we asked who the people were that fell foul of the system's paranoid understanding of political humour. To be clear, this sample illustrates the kinds of people the Soviet regime persecuted and punished for sharing political humour, which shouldn't be confused for a complete roster of joke-tellers in the 1930s. It would be impossible to compile such a list anyway, because not all the people who told jokes were caught and there is, alas, no 'joke-tellers' section in the archives, so what follows is a case study of who was caught, along with some consideration of why this might be.

Age

The age of the individuals arrested can be broken down in two ways: their age at the time of telling the joke(s) that got them into trouble, and the period in which they were born, which tells us something about the context of their formative years.[74]

Age:		Born:	
0-19:	10	1920-29:	10
20–29:	60	1910-19:	48
30-39:	84	1900-09:	88
40-49:	64	1890-99:	83
50-59:	23	1880-89:	33
60-69:	5	1870-79:	5

In this sample, the largest number of arrested joke-tellers were over 30, and the majority were born prior to the 1917 Revolution. If we compare this age breakdown to the national demographic as recorded in the 1937 census, we can see even more clearly that these joke-tellers aged 30-years-and-over are significantly overrepresented (and because our case study is primarily urban, I include this figure, too).[75]

Age Range	Joke-tellers	USSR (urban)	USSR (urban & rural)
20-29:	24.39%	23.42%	18.57%
30-39:	**34.15%**	**17.14%**	**14.46%**
40-49:	**26.02%**	**10.07%**	**8.95%**
50-59:	9.35%	6.63%	6.41%
60-69:	2.03%	3.81%	4.38%

In the sample, there are proportionately twice as many arrested joke-tellers in their 30s as there were people of that age in the general population. The figure for those in their 40s is not far shy of three times higher. In other words, the regime seems to have been much more likely to arrest people in these age brackets for telling political jokes than it was the younger generation (and those in the upper age brackets do not seem to have been significantly more in danger).

These figures do not tell us about which age groups were actually *telling* the most political jokes, if there even was such a distinction. What the data do suggest, though, is that Soviet youth was much less severely punished by the authorities than older age groups. Indeed, reading the many Komsomol reports on 'unhealthy symptoms' (болезненные явления) among its members during the 1930s, the regime's disinclination to arrest or to harshly punish younger people[76] for crimes of humour is conspicuous.

Although an imprecise indicator, these reports suggest that almost invariably younger people faced only expulsion from the Komsomol, or disciplinary measures that fell far short of judicial proceedings.[77] Even when the dangerous charges of 'Trotskiism-Zinov'evism' were being hurled around the organisation in late 1936, there's still very little evidence of arrests or serious punishment being meted out.[78] In contrast, the equivalent 'mood reports' (*svodki*) which covered the (adult) workplace regularly concluded reports of an individual's misdemeanour with the statement 's/he was arrested'. The absence of this concluding statement in the Komsomol files is probably significant: for *komsomoltsy*, the only commentary to occasionally accompany the brief description of the miscreant and their crime was a reference to the social origins and present occupations of their parents.[79] Moreover, Seth Bernstein has highlighted that even though around 130,000 *komsomoltsy* were expelled from the organisation in 1937, once the purging had subsided the following year, about half that number successfully appealed and were reinstated, and the success rate of appeals in general made during 1938 reached as high as 77 percent.[80] In short, not even expulsion from the Komsomol was necessarily that meaningful a sentence for many young people.

Such conclusions fly in the face of the official government decree of 7 April 1935, which allowed children as young as 12 to be tried under the general penal code, but Harvard Project respondents generally support this reading. One recalled, quite simply, that 'children wouldn't be tried; it's their parents who would be punished' for any juvenile misdeeds,[81] and many parents were acutely aware of the possibility that their children might get them into trouble and so tried not to speak critically in front of them.[82]

More cynically, another respondent, an itinerant supply agent, recalled that he would 'never talk about political subjects in the presence of a 10 year old child,' because this might be passed on. You had to wait, he explained, until the child had grown up: 'He is a child. He does not understand,' but, he went on simultaneously pessimistic and approving, when he 'starts working and becomes himself a slave, he will start cursing the regime at home, like the rest'.[83] A former teacher addressed this issue explicitly, stating that she considered it her responsibility 'to protect their parents'. To illustrate the point, she took the example of a student firing spitballs round the classroom, one of which hit a portrait of either Lenin or Stalin (she couldn't remember which). The respondent took the child aside in order to 'explain to him the danger' for himself and his family by doing this kind of thing, even if it was done by accident.[84]

The obvious yet still somewhat speculative conclusion we can make here is that the regime, as in most countries, considered younger people less culpable for their actions, and that they were potentially more malleable than the middle-aged and could yet be convinced to serve the Soviet project with appropriate diligence. All the same, there were never any guarantees. A former Gulag boss recalled in his memoir a young prisoner who had been arrested for telling an *anekdot* when he was 16 years old and who had received a hefty seven-year sentence for doing so.[85] Once again, while we can detect broad trends, these were never absolute rules.

Occupation

The regime arrested joke-tellers holding a wide variety of jobs: there are cashiers, chefs, translators, doctors, lathe-turners and even a lumberjack in our sample. Nonetheless, despite this variety, some clear trends are immediately visible. First of all, the number of white-collar job descriptions (158) is more than twice that of blue-collar ones (72),[86] strongly suggesting that the regime was more concerned to arrest and punish the former broad category for crimes of humour. This fits neatly with the regime's particular interest in ensuring ideological conformity amongst the more educated parts of society at various moments across the 1930s, whereas blue-collar employees were more likely to feel the state's repressive influence when its focus shifted to the more practical questions of labour discipline and productivity. Ideology and labour were obviously not separate in the Soviet Union, but blue-collar workers were, all the same, often treated less harshly for their ideological shortcomings.[87]

Melanie Ilič's study of the mass repressions in Leningrad in the late 1930s confirms this picture: as she writes, 'white-collar workers [...] were victims of the purges in significantly higher proportions than their overall weighting in the Leningrad population'.[88] In short, if indulging in ideological nonconformity, including critical humour, it was at least a little safer if you were not in a white-collar profession of some kind.

The most common occupation in this sample, with 29 individuals arrested, is 'teacher' – a significant number given that it was hardly the most common profession. We might speculate that their classrooms provided these educators with a ready-made audience and an authoritative platform from which to speak. Teachers may have found the urge to make critical comments irresistible at times, particularly given their profession's focus on critical thought in the context of constantly revised edicts to scramble and contort their way down the zigzagging Party line.

More importantly, however, the regime had a particular interest in monitoring teachers: the children of the Revolution were not to be fooled by their educators if the state had anything to say about it. As such, their overrepresentation in the sample makes perfect sense: if the contagion of antisoviet humour was to be contained, teachers were dangerously effective dissemination points (which was also precisely why the regime sought to use them to spread its own ideology). And we should also remember that teachers were probably in more danger than most people of being reported for making a humorous comment, because they were constantly being observed by a classroom of witnesses who, being children, were unlikely to be the most circumspect about what they heard (or, indeed, the most loyal protectors of a teacher they didn't like).

The second most common occupation is a little different: accountant (24 instances).[89] This was a period of intense economic change driven by rigid central planning, so the regime was doubtless concerned that its number-crunchers be dedicated and ideologically 'conscious' individuals (after all, without the appropriate ideological filters, the numbers were all too often defeated by reality). If the bookkeepers were prepared to joke about the system, the whole Soviet project could seem to tremble in the eyes of officials.

But aside from the regime's own concern with more strictly policing the ideological (non)conformity of white-collar workers, a former Soviet accountant painted a rather bleak picture of his profession's standing across all levels of Soviet society:

> The technical personnel hated us bookkeepers as did the chief of the warehouse and the master workman. They called us internal enemies… Bookkeepers are generally regarded by most people as proper crooks (порядочные жулики). Some of them even regarded bookkeepers as bastards (сволочи). The regime regarded bookkeepers as a counterrevolutionary but necessary element.

Indeed, he added, if you tried to tell someone in the Soviet Union that you were an honest man *and* a bookkeeper, 'he would say that it was impossible'.[90]

Accountants aren't exactly known for their popularity in any society, but in the Soviet Union this distrust could well have resulted from the outright necessity of cooking the books in order to at least appear to fulfil the unrealistic demands handed down from on-high. The accountants were 'proper crooks' by necessity, but that necessity nevertheless made them objects of deep suspicion for the state and their fellow citizens alike. This meant that speaking critically was dangerous for bookkeepers not only because the state was watching, but because they were probably more likely to be denounced (for personal or professional reasons, stemming from financial issues).

At first glance it's not surprising that of our 273 arrestees, over three-quarters of them (209) were not and had never been members or candidate members of the Party or Komsomol. Leaving aside the Komsomol members, given the potentially more lenient and complex treatment for crimes of humour which the regime applied to them, 39 critical joke-tellers in our case study were existing or former Party members. Their own perspectives on their joke-telling and arrest will be discussed in the next chapter but, in short, these rested on a sense of their own trustworthiness and a certain licence they assumed this granted them to speak freely. In the Soviet Union, however, all licences, literal and metaphorical, were issued by the state, and the state did not agree with these Party members' self-assessments.

Although non-Party citizens certainly thought Party members were the state's favourites, the regime's propensity to purge the Party ranks means that it's really, if counterintuitively, more surprising that there are so *few* Party members in this sample, even though purging did not automatically involve criminal proceedings. In much the same way, a certain degree of authority in the workplace also seems to have increased the danger of arrest for crimes of humour.

The last significant group in our case study is individuals who were 'bosses' or directors of some kind (27). As with teachers, these were influential figures who were supposed to ensure discipline, practical and ideological (and were likewise subject to disgruntled denunciation by their subordinates), and so the regime was less than pleased if these individuals indulged in crimes of humour. Overall, the fact that even top judicial personnel were, from March 1935, denied access to the virus of 'antisoviet' humour hammers the point home that the regime did not consider Party membership or having a position of authority in the state apparatus sufficient to grant someone licence to share *anekdoty*. Rather, it seems to have made them more vulnerable; if infected, their position would surely spread the virus even further.

Education

The regime disproportionately arrested people with a higher than average level of education for telling political jokes in the 1930s. Some 182 of our 273 (or 66.7 percent) had some kind of formal education or at least basic literacy. This number may be even higher because just nine individuals were recorded specifically as uneducated or illiterate; for the remaining 82, there was simply no information recorded about their education. If we therefore discount those 82 unknowns, then the literacy rate among our joke-tellers jumps to a startling 95.3 per cent. In order to measure the significance of this figure, of course, we need to compare it to the 1937 census. Given our sample is almost exclusively male and aged between 20 and 59, the following comparisons are made against the equivalent criteria in the census, and I continue to discount the 82 unknowns.

According to the 1937 census,[91] 86.12 percent of males in this age group were classed as literate or were (or had been) enrolled in some level of formal education, which makes our sample appear only moderately better educated. However, at this time you might be considered 'literate' just for the ability to read a few words and sign your name, so if we examine specific education levels, we get a more realistic sense of joke-tellers' educational level compared to the population at large. Some 52 (or 27.23 percent) in our sample had gained or were studying to gain the middle (среднее) education level – almost three times the national figure (8.21 percent). Similarly, 44 (23.04 percent) had or were studying for a higher (вышее) educational qualification, whereas the national figure was just 1.69 percent.[92]

What can we take away from this bundle of numbers? First, just as the regime was more concerned with punishing the more skilled, white-collar workers, it likewise turned an unsympathetic eye on those with a higher than average level of education who shared critical *anekdoty*, perhaps because they feared the potential for this to grow into a meaningful political force. Given the weight the regime put on the power of critical humour, this is certainly plausible, but I think the issue is better understood from a different angle: by asking the question 'Who was the regime willing to let off?'.

The answer, as regards education (remembering that this would vary over the course of the decade), seems to be those individuals with a lower level of education – those who could be judged to 'not know any better', in other words. Like the Komsomol youth and blue-collar workers, under-educated people could be granted a certain indulgence because they were not deemed to be as culpable or unreformable as other members of society. Which leads us directly to the most glaring revelation in the sample data.

Gender

The most striking statistic, which leaps rather than emerges from our case study, is the enormous disparity between the sexes. Of the 273 arrestees, only 15 (or 5.49 percent) were female. This dramatic imbalance is not reflected in the myriad *svodki* sources, in which women joke-tellers appear just as frequently as men, nor in the recollections of memoirists and Harvard Project interviewees.

Therefore, what we see here is perhaps the regime's strongest prejudice in its perception and prosecution of joke-tellers. This entirely fits with the regime's broad approach to women throughout the decade, during which it increasingly cast women as the cooks and mothers of the masculine revolutionary masses. Tellingly, by 1939, the journal *Obshchestvennitsa* was instructing women that they 'should try to create at home for their husbands all the conditions for fruitful work and cultured relaxation'. One can scarcely imagine anything more bourgeois.[93] As Mary Buckley points out, even that journal's title meant, by the later 1930s, not 'a public spirited woman' or 'female activist' as it had in the 1920s, but something more like 'member of a wives' movement' – the mere 'helpers' of the New Soviet Man.[94]

Despite the undeniable increase of women in the industrial workforce, as Thomas Schrand argues, the 'improvement of women's status [was] only possible because of a corresponding and equivalent improvement in men's status; the gap between the two genders and the hierarchy within which women and men are ordered remain[ed] the same'.[95] This consistent gap between the sexes also applied to the degree of danger the regime attributed to the political views of men and women; while both sexes might now be considered political beings within the new

Soviet society, women were not considered to be as politically informed and consequently not as politically *dangerous*.

The regime's attitude towards women's humour was in this way identical to the official, sexist interpretation of female peasant rebels as representatives of the uneducated, benighted past, who were seen as driven by emotion rather than reason.[96] In both cases, when women expressed unorthodox political views, these were written off as hysteria, stupidity, or other 'explanations' drawn from the school of the 'wandering womb'.[97]

We might consider this a form of positive discrimination, in that it apparently granted women a greater licence to speak freely without danger of reprisal. But, for better or worse, this was not quite the case. The fact that women joke-tellers frequently appear in the *svodki* reports created by various regime bodies suggests that the authorities were not simply ignoring women's humour, but only that the buck stopped much earlier. Their humour was being noted, reported, but then did not progress to the judicial stage, where it would have produced more criminal case-files. In other words, women did not escape censure at the local level (which could still have serious impacts on their lives and opportunities), but either the local officials or the higher security organs held a consistent outlook that women were of lesser political significance, or rather, as Lynne Viola puts it, a woman 'was not held directly responsible for her actions, even in cases when she was subject to reprimand or punishment'.[98] Like children, the unskilled, and the uneducated, Soviet women were apparently considered politically immature and beyond full responsibility for their 'backward' views.

It bears emphasising that when women expressed those 'backward' views in political humour, their jokes were indistinguishable from those shared by men. In a blind test based on either *svodki* materials or the few criminal cases available to us, it would be impossible to tell the gender of the joke-teller. As the dozens of examples appearing in this book show, women told political jokes that were just as cutting, vulgar and cruel (qualities stereotypically associated with brash, aggressive masculine humour) as those of their male comrades. The sole exception was that women seem not to have shared sexually explicit jokes of the kind we examined in the previous chapter, but this is hardly a surprise given those jokes unreflectively degraded and humiliated women. From the regime's point of view, however, the only difference which mattered here was not the content of the jokes, but the gender of the joke-teller.

A rather tragic story shows these implicit attitudes in action. On 2 March 1935 at a technical college (*pedtekhnikum*) in the town of Lodeinoe Pole, Leningrad oblast', I.A. Litvinov, an 18 year-old student and Komsomol member, was found hanged in the institution's attic. The previous month he had sung a song in the college which poked fun at heroes of the Soviet Union and, as a consequence, he was ejected from first the Komsomol and then the college itself.

Desolate and depressed, Litvinov informed both the college director and the Party Organiser that he was having suicidal thoughts, but they took little interest. When his body was found on the evening of 2 March, an investigation was launched; the director was sacked and the Party Organiser reprimanded for ignoring the warning signs. And yet the investigative report also noted that Litvinov was not the first to have sung this song within the college walls: a female Komsomol member had also done so, but she received only a reprimand. Yet although she was treated quite differently for committing the very same 'crime', the report makes no comment on this discrepancy, mentioning it only to illustrate the general dangers of 'antisoviet' songs circulating among Soviet youth. It was, it seems, deemed quite reasonable that this young woman had been treated far more leniently than the unfortunate Litvinov – it was not even worth mentioning.[99] Once again, it seemed that who you were mattered more than what you said.

Imagined Conspiracies

If the regime, or at least its agents at the local level, could rarely imagine women's jokes to be worthy of punishment, their imaginations could be wildly overactive when it came to the question of conspiracy. Just shy of three-quarters (203) of our sample cases involved no other accusations against the joke-tellers – that is, they were prosecuted solely for their crimes of humour as interpreted through the prism of Article 58-10. For the other quarter, the secondary charge was most often being part of a counterrevolutionary group, which was prosecuted under Article 58-11.

In reality, the regime was either cynically inventing or, in a state of paranoia, misperceiving these conspiratorial groups. In most cases, it's abundantly clear that the additional charges of participating in a 'counterrevolutionary organisation' meant, in practice, simply exchanging jokes with a group of friends or acquaintances. This informal association with others was frequently interpreted by regime officials as directly analogous to an organised, underground group which threatened Soviet power, and in these cases all group 'members' were bundled into the same case-file and tried within the explicit framework of a counterrevolutionary conspiracy.

A. Ia. Levinovskii, a student in Saratov sentenced alongside

Iampol'skii (the loyal diary-keeper we encountered earlier), described this process from personal experience when his case was reexamined in 1962. 'There was no antisoviet group – it "sprang up" in the course of the pretrial investigation' as the investigators decided to treat routine issues, such as confused and inconsistent statements delivered by the accused (who were questioned at night for many hours at a time), as 'evidence' of a hidden conspiracy.[100] The practice of inferring conspiracy from confusion became routine in the later 1930s and led various joke-tellers to also be charged under Article 58-11 – a charge so flimsy that it was often dropped on appeal far sooner (even by decades) than the 58-10 charge.

It would not be surprising in this context to find that the regime suspected the existence of counterrevolutionary groups with nationalist agendas among those non-Russians whom they arrested for joke-telling. Unfortunately, however, our case study, due to its random nature, cannot offer clear answers on this score. Because 133 individuals (or 48.7 percent) from the sample are Russians and a further 53 have no nationality specified (more than likely meaning they are also Russian), the remaining 87 cases are too widely spread across differing nationalities to provide meaningful data.[101] For the same reasons, the data cannot provide answers as to whether national minorities were more harshly treated for telling *anekdoty*, or whether, perhaps, if prosecuted by regional courts, they might even have been treated more leniently by their local judges. Unfortunately, until more regional research is done, and by scholars who know more languages than I do, such questions will remain open.

***

The regime 'sanctioned' humour in both senses of the word: it chose both 'to punish' and 'to permit' critical humour, but there was a great deal of inconsistency in how and when it did so. And although official and unofficial humour were distinct but not wholly discrete, the regime would always have the final word on what constituted 'acceptable' humour and what merited punishment.

A Soviet citizen's class background was always of cardinal importance to the state, determining a person's social position, opportunities, wage-scale and much more besides. During the mass repressions, it could provide either a measure of protection to an individual, or more ammunition to the authorities. Yet, despite the undeniable power of class labels under the regime, in the case-files that criterion actually proved to be one of the most inconsistently recorded. Instead, when it came to political humour and critical speech more generally, there were several different dynamics simultaneously at play across the decade: the waves of repression at different points; retroactive justice; sexism; ageism; and the regime's particular concern to silence people in certain jobs or positions of authority. Although there were never any guarantees, when it came to sharing political humour, who you were often mattered more than what you actually said.

If political jokes were to be treated as a virus at the level of policy-making, on the ground the regime's concern seems to have been more circumscribed, focused on preventing it circulating amongst citizens who were in a position to spread it further, by dint of their occupation or level of authority. Conversely, the authorities seemed to varying degrees less concerned if women, the young, uneducated, or blue-collar workers became infected, whether because these groups were considered 'curable' through the panacea of political education, or simply because officials at the local level did not have such a paranoid, medicalised view of humour when it was shared by salt-of-the-earth workers, in whose name the regime ruled, or by women and the uneducated whose political views they did not take seriously. Whatever the reasons – and we can only speculate – it's clear that policy did not translate smoothly or consistently into practice.

In this context, until the second half of the decade ordinary citizens had little chance of accurately calculating the risk they took when sharing *anekdoty*, and by then they might already be 'infected' or 'infectious' in the regime's eyes. This is not to say they were simply unaware that they were dancing along the borders of acceptability, but only that it was often impossible to calculate the potential severity of the consequences.

But we don't want to internalise the regime's perspective that ordinary people's political humour always and only represented an offensive act. The sense of danger and transgression – of flipping the bird to authority – inherent in sharing critical *anekdoty* was always a fundamental part of its appeal, but contemporaries told and enjoyed such jokes for many and much deeper reasons than this alone. For them, joke telling could serve important social and interpersonal functions, forging and maintaining bonds of trust in unstable times, as the final two chapters explore.

Notes

[1] This was Article 58-10 in the Russian Republic's Criminal Code. Elsewhere, the designation varied, but the law was the same. e.g. Belorussian Republic: Article 72a; Georgian Republic: also Article 58-10; Tajik Republic: Article 61; Ukrainian Republic: Article 54-10; Uzbek Republic: Article 66.

[2] Lewis, *Hammer and Tickle*, 92.

[3] Chamberlin, *Russia's Iron Age*, 327.

[4] V. Blium, 'Vozroditsa li satira?', *Literaturnaia gazeta*, 6 (27 May 1929), 2. ('от "игрового" к "неигровому" способу борьбы'.) For more on this debate, see Brandenberger, *Political Humor*, 15-7.

[5] Letter dated 28 March 1930, in M. Bulgakov, *Dnevnik. Pis'ma, 1914-1940* (Moscow, 1997), 226.

[6] Lunacharskii's plan for the Commission: GARF, f.3316, op.23, d.614, ll.1-2 (May 1930). The budget was 3,200 rubles (1,000 in foreign currency).

[7] Annie Gérin, 'On rit au *NarKomPros*: Anatoli Lounatcharski et la théorie du rire soviétique', *RACAR Revue d'art canadienne/Canadian Art Review*, 37.1 (2012), 41-52.

[8] A.V. Lunacharskii, 'O smekhe', *Literaturnyi kritik*, 4 (1935), 5, 9.

[9] Cited in Graham, *Resonant Dissonance*, 16-7. Translation Graham's.

[10] Lunacharskii, 'O smekhe', 9.

[11] A.V. Lunacharskii, 'Budem smeiat'sia', in *Sobranie sochinenii v vos'mi tomakh*, (Moscow, 1963-7), tom 4, 77 (first published in *Vestnik teatra*, 58, 23-8 March 1920).

[12] V.Ia. Kirpotin, in *Pervyi vsesoiuznyi s"ezd sovetskikh pisatelei, 1934: Stenograficheskii otchet* (Moscow, 1934), 380.

[13] Quoted in J. Arch Getty & Oleg V. Naumov (eds.), *The Road to Terror: Stalin and the Self-Destruction of the Bolsheviks, 1932-1939* (New Haven, CT, 1999), 89.

[14] Getty & Naumov (eds.), *Road to Terror*, 85.

[15] M. Agatov, 'Aforizmy, obrazy, iumor, narodnye poslovitsy v proizvedeniiakh I.V. Stalina', RGASPI, f.558, op.11, d.1534. On the leaders' humour, see Jonathan Waterlow, 'Sanctioning Laughter in Stalin's Soviet Union', *History Workshop Journal*, 79 (2015), 200-1; 205-6.

[16] Natalia Skradol, 'Laughing with Comrade Stalin: An Analysis of Laughter in a Soviet Newspaper Report', *Russian Review*, 68.1 (2009), 29.

[17] Stenograms of the Plenum: RGASPI f. 558, op.11, dd.18-9; also cf. Natalia Skradol's somewhat uneven analysis: '"There is Nothing Funny About It": Laughing Law at Stalin's Party Plenum', *Slavic Review*, 70.2 (2011).

[18] Il'f & Petrov, 'Delo studenta Sveranovskogo', *Pravda*, 15 May 1935. The significance of the feuilleton as a signal was made all the plainer when the Moscow City Court issued a statement of support, printed in *Pravda* the following day.

[19] On humour in *Volga-Volga*, see Evgeny Dobrenko, 'The Singing Masses and the Laughing State in the Musical Comedy of the Stalinist 1930s', and Seth Graham, 'Varieties of Reflexivity in the Russo-Soviet *Anekdot*' (p.178), both in Lesley Milne (ed.), *Reflective Laughter: Aspects of Humour in Russian Culture* (London, 2004).

[20] Il'f & Petrov, 'Razgovory za chainym stolom', *Pravda*, 21 May 1934.

[21] Brandenberger, *Propaganda State*.

[22] See Mel'nichenko, *Sovetskii anekdot*, 44.

[23] I discuss this point in more detail in 'Sanctioning Laughter', 200-1; 204-7.

[24] Zinovii Papernyi (ed.), *Nesmotria ni na chto. Ot Chekhova do nashikh dnei. Istorii,*

anekdoty i smeshnye sluchai (Moscow, 2002), 176.
[25] For a short précis of this argument, see Likhachev, Panchenko & Ponyrko, *Smekh*, 4; for more detail, see Likhachev, 'Smekh'.
[26] Shitts, *Dnevnik*, 115.
[27] On these campaigns, see David Priestland, *Stalinism and the Politics of Mobilization: Ideas, Power, and Terror in Inter-war Russia* (Oxford, 2007).
[28] Report on preliminary results of Party meetings' study of the closed letter in Leningrad: TsGAIPD, f.24, op.5, d.2682, l.5 (6 February 1935).
[29] TsGAIPD, f.24, op.5, d.2682, ll.5, 9, 17 (February 1935); d.2685, l.7 (March 1935).
[30] 'Special collegium' courts were established in 1934 to deal with cases deemed most harmful to the state. See David R. Shearer, *Policing Stalin's Socialism: Repression and Social Order in the Soviet Union, 1924-1953* (New Haven, CT, 2009), 127.
[31] Directive no.13, GARF, f.9474, op.16, d.76, l.9. Akulov had issued a similar directive to all Procurators at the Republic and krai/oblast' level back on 23 January 1935, although this focused more on 'terrorist' acts and agitation, which at least theoretically was a little more circumscribed in its meaning: directive 13/36/00728, ibid, ll.109-11.
[32] GARF, f.8131, op.38, d.6, ll.31, 75. The 'supervisory reviews' which I read of the original case-files were of a suitably high level in the organs of criminal justice that they included the offending jokes, but even there these were sometimes hidden behind euphemistic formulations.
[33] GARF, f.5446, op.18a, d.849, l.2 (26 May 1936). Molotov sided with the NKVD, scrawling 'Agreed' across the page. Many thanks to Gábor Rittersporn for this reference.
[34] Quoted in Paul Hagenloh, *Stalin's Police: Public Order and Mass Repression in the USSR, 1926-1941* (Washington DC, 2009), 216 (spelling adjusted to British English; 'catalogue' is translated from 'сборник').
[35] GARF, f.9474, op.16, d.79, l.52.
[36] Document 50, Werth & Mironenko (eds.), *Istoriia stalinskogo Gulaga*. An English translation of this document appears in Oleg Khlevniuk, *The History of the Gulag: From Collectivization to the Great Terror* (New Haven, CT, 2004), 91-5. Vyshinskii did not mention *anekdoty* here specifically, but they were always treated directly alongside and analogously to *chastushki* and songs 'of antisoviet content', so we can infer that this surprising statement applied to political humour in general.
[37] GARF, f.9474, op.16, d.79, l.52.
[38] See Hagenloh, *Stalin's Police*, 214-6.
[39] Two are clearly dated as 1934; three additional arrests occurred between 1934-5.
[40] Three of these occurred between 1935-6; the total may even have been 17 if we include the three arrests dated 1934-5 (see previous note).
[41] This may be higher if we include the three arrests between 1935-6, and a further three between 1936-7.
[42] 97 are specifically dated 1937; we might add the three dated 1936-7, and another five dated 1937-8.
[43] 20 cases are specifically dated 1938; a further five occurred between 1937-8, and three between 1938-9. The latter three might be added to the six which explicitly occurred in 1939, as well as a single further arrest dating from 1939-40.
[44] 44 are specifically dated 1941; two arrests were between 1940-1.
[45] Sarah Davies, 'The Crime of "Anti-Soviet Agitation" in the Soviet Union in the 1930s', *Cahiers du Monde russe*, 39.1-2 (1998), 149-168.
[46] cf. Table 5, 'Secret Police (GPU, OGPU, NKVD) Arrests and Sentences, 1921-39', in Getty & Naumov (eds.), *Road to Terror*, 588.

47 Vladimir N. Khaustov, 'Razvitie sovetskikh organov gosudarstvennoi bezopastnosti: 1917-1953 gg', *Cahiers du Monde russe*, 42.2-4 (2001), 357-374.
48 Solomon, *Soviet Criminal Justice*, 230-1.
49 Specifically, 65 cases. Discounting the 11 instances where the dates are not clear enough to evaluate, this is 24.8 percent of the sample.
50 Cynthia Hooper, 'Trust in Terror? The Search for a Foolproof Science of Soviet Personnel', *Slavonic & East European Review*, 91.1 (2013), 38-44, quotation at 38.
51 Solomon, *Soviet Criminal Justice*, 242.
52 For another example, consider the Il'f & Petrov story 'Otets i syn' ['Father and Son'], which derides the way a child's opportunities could be hampered by their parents' past by taking a real-life story as their model (an admittedly short-lived switch in policy), *Pravda*, 10 September 1935, 4 (also cf. response in *Pravda*, 11 September 1935, 4); or, a story by E. & A. Shatrov which aimed in the post-1937 USSR to ridicule acts of denunciation in line with the end of the mass repressions: 'April', Ivor Montagu & Herbert Marshall (eds.), *The Crocodile Album of Soviet Humour* (London, 1943), 58-64.
53 Larry E. Holmes, 'A Symbiosis of Errors: The Personal, Professional and Political in the Kirov Region, 1931-1941', Lewis Siegelbaum (ed.), *Borders of Socialism: Private Spheres of Soviet Russia* (Houndmills, 2006), 213.
54 Holmes argues that the 'symbiosis' broke down after 1938, but the regime's interpretation of political humour in this manner was re-energised by 1940-41, as our timeline shows.
55 GARF, f.8131, op.31, d.15983, l.3.
56 See Waterlow, 'Sanctioning Laughter', 210-11.
57 GARF, f.8131, op.31, d.15983, l.132.
58 28 cases occurred in unspecified locations; four in prison; two in a camp; two in a hostel; one was printed; one in a diary.
59 e.g. HPSSS 1492/A/34, p.21. Cited in Brandenberger, *Political Humor*, 8. ('Что у трезвого на уме, то у пьяного на языке'. This was far from a new coinage: it appears in Vladimir Dal', *Tolkovyi slovar' zhivogo velikoruskogo iazyka*, tom IV (2nd edn., St Petersburg & Moscow, 1882), cf. entry for 'читый', 608.
60 RGASPI, f.M-1, op.23, d.1107, ll.61-2 (1934).
61 RGASPI, f.M-1, op.23, d.1184, l.104 (1936).
62 GARF, f.8131, op.31, d.70065, l.4 (1934-5).
63 GARF, f.8131, op.31, d.6410, l.4 (1937).
64 cf. another case (with its own peculiarities) based on talking too freely in a restaurant: GARF, f.8131, op.31, d.10670 (1938-40).
65 Resolution of the TsIK '*o lineinykh sudakh*', with discussion and development: GARF, f.3316, op.23, d.123.
66 For a sociological study of train travel, see Gayle Leatherby & Gillian Reynolds, *Train Tracks: Work, Play and Politics on the Railways* (Oxford, 2005). On the mixture of public and private social space, see esp. 7-8, 30-31. See also: Certeau, *The Practice*, 112-4; Matthew Beaumont & Michael Freeman (eds.), *The Railway and Modernity: Time, Space, and the Machine Ensemble* (Oxford, 2007), 'Introduction', esp. 23.
67 I borrow this term from Marc Augé, but without invoking his theory at large. *Non-Places: An Introduction to Supermodernity*, trans. John Howe (2nd edn., London, 2008), cf. viii, 28.
68 At least within a particular wagon class.
69 Goldman, *Women, the State*, Ch.8 & Conclusion; Igor' Kon, *Klubnichka na berezke: Seksual'naia kul'tura v Rossii* (Moscow, 2010), 272-3.

70. On the ever-changing 'meaning' of Pavlik Morozov in the Soviet Union and its conflict with family policies, see Catriona Kelly, *Comrade Pavlik: The Rise and Fall of a Soviet Boy Hero* (London, 2005), esp. 148-9, 261-4.
71. Sheila Fitzpatrick & Alf Lüdtke, 'Energizing the Everyday: On the Breaking and Making of Social Bonds in Nazism and Stalinism', Michael Geyer & Sheila Fitzpatrick (eds.), *Beyond Totalitarianism: Stalinism and Nazism Compared* (Cambridge, 2009), 285-6; Cynthia Hooper makes the same point in 'Terror of Intimacy: Family Politics in the 1930s Soviet Union', Christina Kiaer & Eric Naiman (eds.), *Everyday Life in Early Soviet Russia: Taking the Revolution Inside* (Bloomington, IN, 2006), 77.
72. Raymond A. Bauer, Alex Inkeles & Clyde Kluckhohn, *How the Soviet System Works: Cultural, Psychological & Social Themes* (New York, 1960), 68.
73. cf. Fitzpatrick & Lüdtke, 'Energizing the Everyday', 285-6. See also Thurston, 'The Soviet Family', 565-6. Most review files I use in this case study were prompted by letters from family members protesting the convict's innocence.
74. The first column omits 27 instances where the specific date of the crime was not clear enough to attribute an age bracket and the second column omits 6 instances where the birth year of the individual was not recorded.
75. To find the percentages from the sample, I discounted the 27 unknown or unclear examples, making these figures percentages of 246. The census figures are taken from Iu.A. Poliakov (ed.), *Vsesoiuznaia perepis' naseleniia 1937 goda: obshchie itogi. Sbornik dokumentov i materialov* (Moscow, 2007), 81-4. Note that the combined urban and rural figure on p.84 of this book, as well as the total of 'unknowns' are incorrectly counted: they should be 160,121,646 and 72,054 respectively, and I calculate the age-group percentages in accordance with this correction.
76. Until 1936, Komsomol members were aged between 14 and 23; thereafter, between 15 and 26. cf. Matthias Neumann, *The Communist Youth League and the Transformation of the Soviet Union, 1917-1932* (Abingdon, 2011), 5 & 5, n.37.
77. For numerous reports of this kind see RGASPI, f.M-1, op.23.
78. RGASPI, f.M-1, op.23, d.1172, ll.1-17 (August-October 1936).
79. Usually, no further information on the consequences for the parents was recorded, but we can assume these were unlikely to be positive.
80. Seth Bernstein, *Communist Upbringing under Stalin: The Political Socialization and Militarization of Soviet Youth, 1934-1941*, PhD Thesis, University of Toronto (2013), 207-8. Many thanks to Seth for sharing his work with me.
81. HPSSS 7/A/1, p.28.
82. e.g. HPSSS 41/1/4, p.40; 46/A/4, p.18; 51/A/5, p.53; 114/A/9, p.23.
83. HPSSS 74/A/6, p.30.
84. HPSSS 91/A/7, pp.15-6.
85. Fyodor Vasilevich Mochulsky, *Gulag Boss: A Soviet Memoir*, ed. & trans. Deborah Kaple (New York, 2011), 170.
86. The sample also includes 32 unknown or unclear job descriptions, 4 unemployed persons, 3 prisoners, and 3 housewives (the latter not fitting very clearly into the white/blue-collar dichotomy).
87. Priestland, *Stalinism and the Politics of Mobilization*.
88. Melanie Ilic, 'The Great Terror in Leningrad: Evidence from the *Leningradskii martirolog*', Harris (ed.), *Anatomy of Terror*, 322-5, quotation at 322.
89. Бухгалтер/счетовод.
90. HPSSS 114/A/9, p.12.
91. All census data used here come from Poliakov (ed.), *Vsesoiuznaia perepis'*, 77-80 (male population numbers) and 114-5 (male literacy and education figures).

[92] If we combine the total numbers of people studying for either middle or higher education levels, this would be 9.9 percent of the male population aged between 20-59. In our sample, such individuals represent 50.26 percent. For reference, if we remove the 15 women from our sample for this comparison, the figures would be: 'literate' or some level of education: 169 (95.48 percent); middle education: 48 (27.12 percent); higher education: 40 (22.6 percent).

[93] Quoted in Schrand, 'Socialism in One Gender', 202.

[94] Mary Buckley, 'The Untold Story of the *Obshchestvennitsa* in the 1930s', *Europe-Asia Studies*, 48.4 (1996), 569; 572.

[95] Schrand, 'Socialism in One Gender', 205. Schrand here refers to the 'double helix' metaphor employed by Margaret and Patrice Higgonet in 'The Double Helix', Higgonet et al. (eds.), *Behind the Lines: Gender and the Two World Wars* (New Haven, CT, 1987).

[96] Viola, *Peasant Rebels*, Ch.6.

[97] The notion of 'hysteria' for centuries involved the idea that a woman's uterus could be displaced and thereby cause all manner of emotional and medical pathologies.

[98] Viola, *Peasant Rebels*, 182; Sharon A. Kowalsky makes a similar argument in *Deviant Women: Female Crime and Criminology in Revolutionary Russia, 1880-1930* (DeKalb, IL, 2009), esp. Conclusion.

[99] TsGAIPD, f.24, op.2v, d.1185, ll.225-6.

[100] GARF, f.8131, op.31, d.15983, l.165. ("'возникла'".)

[101] The other nationalities in the sample are as follows: 31 Ukrainian; 15 Jewish; 10 Belorussian; 8 Polish; 4 Georgian; 3 Mordvinian; 2 Chuvash; 2 Estonian; 2 German; 2 Tatar; 1 Armenian; 1 Greek; 1 Kazakh; 1 Latvian; 1 Lithuanian; 1 Shapsug; 1 Swedish; 1 Zyrianin.

PART 3
ALONE TOGETHER

CHAPTER 5
BEYOND RESISTANCE: THE PSYCHOLOGY OF JOKE-TELLING

The Soviet Union was striving in the 1930s to tell a story of incredible progress in all spheres, of catching and overtaking the capitalist world, and, above all, of building a fundamentally new, better and happier society. This story imposed some kind of regularity or rationale on the chaotic world of 1930s Stalinism, but when everyday reality didn't fit that pattern – which was most of the time – people had to search for other ways to make sense of their frequently difficult lives. We all need some measure of consistency in our lives, to recognise patterns of cause and effect, how to get from situations A to B, of norms and expected behaviours, so that we can act (or choose not to) with some sense of what the results will be. This was impossible in the 1930s if contemporaries referred to the official narrative alone, and even that habitually contradicted itself.

If the previous chapter revealed the unpredictable dangers of sharing jokes, this one turns to the numerous psychological, emotional and mental motivations and benefits the risky act of joke-telling could have for ordinary Soviet citizens as they tried to make sense of their lives under this capricious and unpredictable regime. Why did they do it, and what did it do for them?

That telling jokes about difficult and frightening subjects was a coping mechanism is obvious. But how (and how effectively) does this mechanism work? Writers and commentators of all kinds – from historians to sociologists, journalists to memoirists – have explained the psychological motivation for sharing political jokes as 'resistance' to the repressive regime – small acts of defiance and rejection, hinting at a more generally oppositional mindset. Many have gone so far as to claim it was the political jokes that ultimately toppled the Eastern Bloc.[1] But the more I researched humour, the less convinced I was by this way of looking at things.

There is a different, and I think much more interesting, story that *anekdoty* tell us about life under Stalin. When we look closer – at the content, character, and, crucially, at the function of these jokes – we get a very different picture, or at least a far more nuanced one. There is so much more going on in contemporaries' political jokes than a simple push-and-shove rejection of the regime. Certainly, the regime's paranoid interpretation of political humour as either a dangerous weapon or mind virus meant joke-tellers became opponents in official eyes. But few seem to have been motivated in such a direct, uncomplicated manner. To be clear, my point is not to delegitimise 'resistance' as something joking sometimes felt like or was punished as, but to explore how much *more* it could be, and the powerful adaptational effects – psychological and practical – it had, which have been almost entirely overlooked until now.

In her study of women in medieval comic literature, Lisa Perfetti argues that 'mocking jokes' that women make 'in their own minds' or share between themselves 'allow them control over mental space, when control over social space is not so easy'.[2] This was vitally important to their experience of themselves and their social lives, but we would not then claim that it liberated these women from the myriad constraints and prejudices of the culture they lived in. In the same way, enmeshed within a system that carefully circumscribed their social, political and cultural freedoms, ordinary Soviet citizens likewise tried to carve out a mental space for themselves when they lacked control over their standing and opportunities in the official world. These were important, (inter)personal processes, but, like Perfetti's medieval women, there were significant limits to what they achieved.

But what *were* they trying to achieve in jokes or other transgressive acts, anyway? Activities like telling political jokes, trading on the black market, and exchanging favours certainly meant breaking the rules in the Soviet 1930s, but in practice transgressions like these were more often workarounds – ways to solve problems and get by *within* the system, rather than attempts to destabilise or to confront it. The Harvard Project identified quite a few of these 'informal adjustive mechanisms' which, the analysts stressed, were 'mechanisms [that] originate in most instances in the efforts of individual citizens to solve their own problems within the framework of the system', rather than representing an attempt to pervert or entirely circumvent it.[3]

People do not use black markets as a means to overthrow the official economy; they use them because black markets take up the slack created by the failings and restrictions of the 'white' one. Jokes played the same kind of compensatory role at the emotional and psychological levels but also, as we'll see, at the practical level they provided invaluable advice and insights on how to navigate these unstable years. The influential anthropologist James C. Scott argues that ordinary people's 'petty acts of noncompliance' and a 'disbelief in elite homilies' can represent 'a spirit of practice that prevents the worst and promises something better'.[4] But in humour we see more than this: not only did it create and strengthen interpersonal bonds and help diffuse emotional tensions, but it helped contemporaries to work within and yet also *around* the system in ways that were far more concrete than Scott's *promise* of something better. Soviet people did not settle for a promise; they had more than enough unfulfilled promises from the regime to deal with, so in their practice of joke-telling they sought to make things better, right here, right now.

In humour, the molten world is seized and briefly cast into particular shapes according to the will and the perspective of the joke-teller and their audience. The power to do this – the power of the storyteller – creates an exciting sense of interpretative authority to set the world into shapes which are more realistic, recognisable and truthful for the speaker. When we study these shapes, we see various issues which exercised people's emotions and attention, but we can also discern fragments of life advice, proverb-like guides or '*know-how*' for navigating life in disruptive times, and these offer us rich glimpses of how contemporaries gradually made out (or made up) ways to make sense of and find their way within the system.

To explain and adapt is also, in the end, to normalise. Sheila Fitzpatrick, a giant in the field of Soviet social and cultural history, subtitled her study of everyday Stalinism 'ordinary life in extraordinary times'. This chapter sets out to explore not how something distinctly 'ordinary' coexisted with the extraordinary conditions of 1930s Stalinism, but how the extraordinary *became* ordinary for contemporaries over the course of the decade. People will adapt to just about anything given time (which is not to say they will be happy about it); in the 1930s, humour was a crucial way by which they did so and this chapter explores the seeming paradox that by mocking the difficulties and discrepancies they encountered in their lives, contemporaries were simultaneously adapting themselves to those conditions.

Nevertheless, we must remember that joke-telling could certainly be part of the tool-box of the belligerent non-conformist who actively refused to participate in Stalin's brave new world. Consider the dramatic case of E.N. Stradomskii, which I discovered in the archives. His rap sheet makes impressive reading. He was sentenced to three years at the age of 21 for slandering the Party. He escaped, but was caught and given a further three years in 1934. While serving his sentence, he gained another year for petty theft within the camp. On his release in 1938, he refused to do any 'socially useful work' and proceeded the next year to loudly slander NKVD agents and other state organs in a club; he was arrested and sentenced to six years in the camps. Having acquired a further two years on top of that sentence for purloining and altering his official documents, he proceeded to 'systematically spread' antisoviet *anekdoty* amongst other prisoners and, in 1941, began frequently to refuse to work in the camp.[5]

Clearly, for Stradomskii, humour was just one part of the arsenal with which he fought the Soviet system's power over his life tooth and nail, and he was convicted principally (and repeatedly) for his recidivist actions. This is a quite remarkable tale, but the case of Stradomskii and his six convictions,[6] or Grigor'ev in Chapter 2, who chained himself to his machine and ranted and raged against the government, stand in stark contrast to the great majority of joke-tellers in our case study, who were convicted only once, and only for humour. People like Stradomskii were few, and most joke-tellers seem to have told their joke, laughed, shrugged, and then got back to the business of working and surviving within the system. They chose a different path to Stradomskii, practically and psychologically. So let's see where it led.

The Gallows Humour Effect

Perhaps the most striking characteristic of Soviet citizens' humour during the 1930s is its black tone, which often shades deeper still into a darkly ironic gallows humour – something which a group of sociologists explain as follows:

> Gallows humour may serve to manage the impression of courage in the presence of others and to elicit information regarding the situation and the feelings of others. In these circumstances failure by the target to laugh may serve to indicate that he or she is deeply

afraid and may create more concern in the source. On the other hand, hearty laughter by others may serve to indicate less danger and fear, thereby increasing the resolve or morale of the relevant parties to the interaction.[7]

In other words, humour can function as a vital coping and categorising mechanism: it identifies and, through mutual engagement with others, moderates difficult circumstances. The essential element in this definition is not humour in general, however, but the social function of *laughter* specifically.

Most scientific analyses of laughter understand it to be a pre-verbal tool of social communication: it conveys 'basic, primal signals, designed to alert, to communicate, to connect, and to disseminate' information as to whether a situation is safe or not.[8] Most influential in this respect is the 'false-alarm' theory,[9] in which laughter is understood to be a signal that things are OK, that whatever may have seemed threatening is in fact benign, and therefore everyone can relax. Each person's laughter thereafter both releases tension and simultaneously enables everyone else to do likewise.

The laughter produced by gallows humour is therefore essentially a trick we can play on ourselves: by laughing at something which is *not* in fact benign, we are able to create – even if just for a moment – that welcome sense of release and relief. This is by no means guaranteed, of course: even if laughter is elicited by a gallows humour joke, it is only a small step from the trick of positive, relieving laughter to a manic variety that signals quite the opposite, that everything is *not* OK.[10] Nevertheless, in either case, laughter performs an important psychological function, the social aspects of which we'll explore in the next chapter.[11]

But laughter is not the whole story here: it's part of the reason for making gallows humour jokes, but how do the jokes themselves function? What is it that produces the pleasantly misleading 'false alarm' laughter in the first place? As Freud notes, many theorists have emphasised that the enjoyment generated by humour is frequently due to 'the rediscovery of what is familiar'; recognition, in short, is pleasurable.[12] Quoting C. Groos, he continues: 'recognition is always linked with feelings of pleasure. The mere quality of familiarity is easily accompanied by the quiet sense of comfort which Faust felt when, after an uncanny encounter, he entered his study once again'.[13]

This pleasure essentially lies within the power *to be able to* recognise, and therefore to categorise.[14] And by categorise, I mean to restore a sense of 'understandability' to something unfamiliar. As the social anthropologist Mary Douglas put it, this is why some situations seem to *call* for a joke: when expected 'norms' are upset – from a major protocol broken, to a name forgotten, a trip on a paving stone, to a near-death experience – we have a common instinct to make a joke about it and to thereby return to normality.[15] In the Soviet 1930s, this could be as simple as suggesting the leaders must be wearing rose-tinted glasses to explain their refusal to engage with realities the population endured every day, or as weighty as making jokes about the mass repressions as they unfolded (see Chapter 2). The unknown and that over which we can effect no change can easily be frightening; if we can't recognise their parameters and decide how we can interact with them, we become powerless.

'Gallows humour' gets its name because death is for many of us the most intimidating example. But, by reinterpreting things within the genre of humour, *because it is a genre in which things are not expected to make logical sense*, we regain a feeling of comfort (even pleasure) from the power which that process of re-cognition provides. This is gallows humour in a nutshell: it is a process of mutual reassurance through mutual deception; it doesn't explain the unknown and frightening – it explains them away.[16]

By rendering something 'understandable' in this way, we can gain a pleasurable yet illusory sense of control over it, and, without being drawn too deeply into the fascinating world of psychological experiments in this area, it's important to note just how fundamental this is to the human condition. Psychologists have discovered, for instance, that we are far less stressed and anxious when we gain a sense of control over things which are negative or painful, even when this is as limited as knowing when something negative will happen, rather than if it happens unpredictably. This has been demonstrated in rather direct fashion when, during various experiments, test subjects were randomly electrocuted and their levels of anxiety (amount of sweating; heart rates) measured. Unsurprisingly, the subjects became extremely agitated, yet when the same shocks were administered at regular and predictable intervals, their anxiety levels were much reduced.[17] In other words, better the devil you know than the one you do not: at a very deep emotional and physiological level, simply being able to recognise the nature and predictability of something negative can reduce anxiety and suffering. This is an illusion of control, but it is a powerful illusion with very real effects.

In its starkest form, literally making a joke on the way to the gallows allows an individual to transpose their situation into the realm of the absurd and thereby laugh in the face of death itself. Even Jewish prisoners in Nazi concentration camps could still be 'overcome by a grim sense of humor' and share 'songs, poems, [and] jokes' in the shadow of a death that could arrive at any moment, as Viktor Frankl recalled in his memoir, and which Vasilii Grossman captured with devastating brilliance in fiction.[18] In this light, it's no surprise that humour in the Gulag was also widespread.[19]

The direct threat of death itself was not necessary for this form of gallows humour to arise, however. The diarist Stepan Podlubnyi recalled just such a reaction which he shared with his mother as they sat in their apartment with an official summons from the secret police lying before them:

> 'This might be the last evening that we will sit like this together. Perhaps we'll be torn apart and will know nothing more of each other', said Mama. Terrifying. Awful, but said as a joke, laughing. Ah, here goes! We are toys in fate's hands, as the old proverb says.[20]

Even as Podlubnyi and his mother acknowledged their lack of power over events and the possible destruction of their lives, they still found emotional release and even comfort in treating it all as an absurd joke. It seemed too awful to take seriously, and pretending this was really so allowed them to share a momentary respite.

The same process held true at more prosaic levels. For example, the cafeteria at the Kirov Pedagogical Institute was so inadequately provisioned that one of the teachers commented acidly that 'the Institute's cafeteria is not a cafeteria but a parody of one'.[21] Here, again, something genuinely unpleasant yet inescapable – food shortages – was reinterpreted as something inherently *comic* – something to be laughed at rather than to feel victimised by.

Such a response did not uniquely characterise people's reactions to Soviet power and ideology, of course. The same principle can be seen in John Scott's description of workers at Magnitogorsk beginning the day in extraordinarily cold temperatures (in which workers regularly perished) by 'whistling cheerfully, kidding each other and swearing at the cold'.[22] All three actions are social, performative, playful and designed thereby to improve your own and the group's spirits in the face of the unchangeable – in this case, the extreme climate rather than the Soviet regime. In either case, though, it was possible – if difficult – to use these tactics to choose not to feel like a victim of such powerful forces.

Gallows humour could also take on rather more creative, multilayered forms, as we can see in a joke about the mass repressions of the later 1930s told by a certain Stepanova, a female shop assistant in Leningrad:

> In Germany they have one car for each worker, but we have two cars *each*. The [NKVD's] 'Black Crow' and the ambulance.[23]

This joke specifically highlights the extremely frightening, spiralling arrests carried out by the NKVD and, with the ambulance reference, directly connects this to the regime's liberal use of violence against its citizens. The feeling that the secret police were lurking around every corner is also implied by the idea that they had enough manpower to provide a Black Crow and an ambulance for each and every citizen.

But the humour of the joke – the means by which contemporaries might return to 'normality', like Faust to his study – lies not simply in laughing at this disturbing scene as something too awful to take seriously as Podlubnyi and his mother had done, but rather in the twisting of this frightening scenario into a mock-victory over the alleged economic success and material comfort (much gossiped and grumbled about at the time) enjoyed by the population of Nazi Germany. Declaring that something is good when the opposite is self-evidently true is a simple device of rhetorical humour, but the real impact of the joke for contemporaries lay in the spotlight it shone onto the ridiculous persistence of one-upmanship practised in the official media.

In sum, these two short sentences manage not only to return contemporaries for a moment to an illusory safety from under the pall of arbitrary arrests and torture, but simultaneously to puncture the absurdity exhibited daily in the Soviet press, in which failures and shortfalls were re-presented as victories with a brazenness only slightly less than we find in this joke. By relocating these contradictions into the genre of humour, the fact that they made so little sense became a recognisable (in the sense described above) and therefore manageable phenomenon.

In much the same way, people could joke about the propaganda exhorting the population to 'catch and overtake' the West despite most citizens' abject poverty. As Shitts recorded in his diary, 'When it's pointed out that there are no overshoes or boots, and a shortage of shoes, people jokingly console themselves that "it's easier to overtake barefoot"!'.[24] As we know from dozens of jokes in the preceding chapters, the gallows humour effect frequently operated in this way in Stalin's 1930s: the distressing and unchangeable were in humour reconfigured by using the regime's own slogans to emphasise the absurdities of the disparity between propaganda and reality. In this sense, official discourse was made to mock itself – it, too, seemed to call for a joke, and in the 1930s, the disparities between rhetoric and reality made this a near-constant call. 'All of this,' as Arzhilovskii put it to his diary, 'is begging to be written down in a satire.'[25]

Many of these jokes also functioned by providing absurd 'answers' to difficult and painful questions. This is why, for instance, so many jokes aimed at the Soviet leadership focused on the latter's faulty perceptive skills, lack of common sense, or general foolishness: not only did this help make contemporaries feel superior to those in power, but it directly provided an 'answer' to the questions 'how can they be doing this? How can they let this happen?'. By suggesting that the leaders wore magnifying or rose-tinted glasses (see Chapter 2), or even just that a given law must have been 'made while our government was drunk',[26] provided a farcical answer. Such 'answers', of course, do not really explain any of these issues, but they do provide a fleeting emotional sense of resolution. An absurd answer can be better than no answer at all, because it allows for a pretence of solving an intractable or painful problem, thereby releasing some of the angst and tension surrounding it.

The Road Best Travelled?

But what about dark-humoured jokes which seemed to deny the very possibility that contemporaries had any power at all to alter their situation or mindset, betraying instead a grim sense of resignation to their difficult circumstances? These jokes – of which there were many – point to something more than the gallows humour effect.

A.I. Sobolev, a technical controller at a radio recording plant in Moscow, greeted the announcement of the June 1940 Labour Law (criminalising lateness and preventing people from freely changing jobs) with the sarcastic observation that:

> Toilers [трудящиеся] of the USSR have the right to work, relaxation, and to prison.[27]

In 1938, S.I. Shamiakin, a kolkhoz chairman, told the following *anekdot*:

> Two men, a foreigner and 'one of ours' [наш], are taking a walk. The foreigner asks the other, 'What classes are there in the USSR?' The latter answers, 'There are three classes – the serving, the sobbing, and the waiting'.[28]

And one A.I. Suchkov had a few too many drinks at a social gathering in his own apartment and told the following *anekdot*, later reported to the authorities by an evidently-unamused guest:

> To live here is like being on a bus – half are sitting [in prison], and half are shaking.²⁹

The entire population in these *anekdoty* are distinguished only by the degree of suffering the regime subjects them to; if you had not already been arrested, you were 'waiting' or 'shaking' in expectation of it.

Other *anekdoty* went further still, emphasising the impossibility of speaking out in criticism or protest. There is a Russian idiom which means 'to keep mum' or 'keep silent', translating literally as 'to fill your mouth with water' ('набрать в рот воды'). And so a joke passed around Komsomol students in Azovo-Chernomorskii krai ran, 'The water level's dropped in the Moscow river; the people are keeping silent'.³⁰ Another suggested 'We have a drought in the Soviet Union, because 180 million are keeping silent'.³¹

This all seems like a capitulation to the winds of fate – the abdication of any responsibility or imperative to try to change things by interpreting yourself to be outside the realm of conceivable action. In this way, jokes could arguably enshrine a sense of powerlessness, while simultaneously providing some comfort: it could be a relief to accept that escape was impossible, because then there was no pressure to try. As in the last joke, it's not quite clear whether the millions who were keeping mum were being forcibly silenced, or whether they had decided to fill their own mouths with water. Resignation could easily involve filling your mouth with something else, of course: in defence of his boozing, the chairman of a struggling kolkhoz, Viarinen, shrugged off responsibility with the *chastushka*-like phrase: 'I've been drinking and I'm going to drink more; it's all the same – you end up behind bars' (*Ia pil i budu pit'; vse ravno – pridetsia sidet'*).³²

These jokes make it explicit, but many of those we examined earlier also reverberate with a feeling of resignation and powerlessness. Even when *anekdoty* involved victories over the oppressive regime, these were usually just the bodily, base 'triumphs' we saw in Kirov's Carnival, imagined through physical or sexual degradation. This speaks of frustration and powerlessness, like a child stamping a foot, or throwing something against a wall. They know it will have no effect, but it feels good all the same. In fact, the basic emotional responses we associate with childlike behaviour will continue to provide a useful point of reference as we examine contemporaries' struggles to make sense of their restricted and repressive lives, but in this instance we're seeing something a little different.

Even if these jokes seem at first glance to represent a bleak fatalism, a passive resignation to harsh but unchangeable realities, is that truly what they were? Not really. While this may have been true sometimes for some people, even if black humour might ultimately *lead* to acquiescence, the path which led there was not one of simple resignation or despair. As they faced the endless difficulties and disappointments of the 1930s, Soviet contemporaries had a choice: like the multiply-convicted Stradomskii (or still more radical opponents), they could walk the path of direct opposition. Alternatively, they could take the path of despairing resignation, melancholy though it would be. Or they could square their shoulders and walk down the path of humour.

As we know, Stradomskii's path led to the revolving door of the prison camps, but, counterintuitively, *both* the other paths – crying or laughing – led to just one destination: accommodation and acquiescence. Nevertheless, the road you take changes the journey and affects the state you're in when you arrive. The mental equivalent of taking the scenic route rather than the bland or stressful motorway can dramatically change how you feel about the destination when you get there. Taking the path of critical humour meant you could arrive at accommodation feeling that you had not passively accepted illogical and unwelcome realities – you had challenged and grappled with them, proving, if only to yourself, but likely to friends and family as well, that you were not a blind or unthinking automaton.

It's been common to describe joke-telling in these years as 'laughter through tears',[33] but this was not truly the case. It was laughter *instead* of tears: those who shared jokes made a choice (if not consciously, then instinctively) to laugh rather than to cry; they were whistling in the dark rather than allowing fear or despair to take control. This does not mean they did so every time (no doubt tears were often shed), but laughter was a practice and an option – Likhachev's 'laughing world' was always available to them[34] – and we should not confuse these two distinct emotional responses.

To joke about immutable circumstances is not to change them, but rather to change how you feel about them. We might best understand this as a kind of Stoicism, for while contemporaries did not have the power to fundamentally change their circumstances or the regime itself, they always had the power to change the way they understood and responded to them.[35] This was both a conscious and unconscious process of adjustment: by telling jokes, they could consciously reassure themselves that they were not fools unable to see the deficiencies of life in the 1930s, but this humour was simultaneously, if unconsciously, helping them to accommodate those deficiencies. Nevertheless, if their agency was limited in a practical or material sense, at the mental and interpersonal level, things were quite different, as we'll now see.

I Joke, Therefore I Am

As the cultural historian David Hopkin points out, for anyone inventing or telling a story or a joke, 'It is not just a reflection of their personality, or of their circumstances; by telling the story they act to shape their circumstances. The performance is a demonstration of their agency'.[36] When we are the storyteller, we decide how a story is told, including how we describe and relate the stories of our own lives and circumstances.

This can be an empowering feeling, and all the more so when it involves some kind of transgression – something which jokes specialise in by upsetting expectations and revealing the fragility and artificiality of everyday rules and conventions. Similar taboo-breaking would be talking about sex in a society which represses the open discussion of it. In those conditions, as Foucault put it, 'the mere fact that one is speaking about it has the appearance of a deliberate transgression. A person who holds forth in such language places himself to a certain extent outside the reach of power…'.[37] Even if the moment is fleeting and the possibility of punishment significant, exuberantly breaking the rules and transgressing norms can feel remarkably liberating.

In Stalin's Soviet Union, acts of even minor misconduct possessed this allure of the forbidden: whether spontaneously planting a kiss on a bust of Stalin, giggling at Kirov's 'penis', or loudly farting during an official meeting, it was exciting just to exuberantly misbehave and escape the smothering constraints of expected behaviour.[38] We also saw this in Chapter 2 in the way many people reacted to the interminable demands to sign up to state loans: they used sardonic ripostes as an avoidance tactic, even though there was no possibility they would actually succeed in dodging it.

But their sarcasm *was* effective in another sense: for just a moment, they could taste the power and freedom of refusing the demand, and do so with (they hoped) just enough claim that they weren't being 'serious' that they would not end up in serious trouble.

Flippant humour and casual disobedience were common companions. In July 1937, for instance, an investigation into the lack of 'agitprop' (agitation and propaganda) work undertaken during the hot summer months by the supposed activists living in hostels on Leningrad's Fontanka and Moika rivers, was rebuffed by a female resident, who responded facetiously, 'In summer we self-agitate' (мы самоагитируемся).[39] Similarly, at the nearby Kulakov factory, non-Party workers Ponomareva and Alekseeva were found reading a book on the lives of saints. Before the illicit nature of the book was discovered, they tried to escape the situation with belligerent sarcasm: in response to

Party Organiser Gavrilova's question, 'What kind of book is that?' they shot back, 'A little one'.[40]

But transgressive humour did not need to be explicitly political in the sense of criticising regime policies or figures, or even of defying minor officials. It could also take the form of a brief, throwaway flippancy. One day in 1936, A.I. Shilo, an X-ray technician at a hospital on the Turkestan-Siberian railway, was out shopping with friends for placards and portraits to celebrate the new Stalin Constitution. When his friend asked the shopkeeper, 'Do you have anything about the new Constitution?', Shilo butted in with the crude rhyme, 'Do you have anything about *prostitution*?'[41] In another shop, a doctor by the name of G.F. Narozhnyi sarcastically enquired, 'Are you going to get anything good in, or will it all be Soviet trash (дрянь)?'[42] And, in a rather dramatic final example, Nechai, a shop head at a radio factory and an award-winning shock-worker, entered a room where a brigade meeting was taking place and loudly quipped, echoing the language of alarmist propaganda, 'I've come to drink the workers' blood!'. Although some tried to defend his outburst as a simple joke, all were later convinced to reinterpret his words as 'the act of a class-alien person'.[43]

These very basic, spur-of-the-moment jokes broke for a moment the 'fourth wall' of the Soviet drama scripted by the state. Indulging in behaviour inappropriate to the 'role' of a Soviet citizen allowed people (both teller and, at least sometimes, their audience) a momentary release from the straitjacket of 'acceptable' behaviour – restraints they felt acutely, for citizens were expected to act as though they lived in a world enormously different from they one they saw daily before their eyes. All the same, these performative, often petulant transgressions are also distinctly childish. Children, Soviet and otherwise, enjoy simple, public acts of wilfulness which produce a jolt of guilty pleasure as they throw off rules and restrictions placed – in their view arbitrarily – upon them from above, and it's illuminating in this context to consider why.

Kids everywhere enjoy a guilty thrill from defacing their schoolbooks or desks with rude or illicit words and symbols. In the USSR, not only did they end up betraying the shadow meanings of official acronyms (see Chapter 3) by spelling them out for all the world to see, but they also enjoyed drawing a symbol particularly disturbing to the regime: the swastika.

Indeed, from 1935 official censors worked themselves into a nonsensical frenzy when they began to see swastikas everywhere, be that in the tangle of Comintern General Secretary Georgi Dimitrov's forelock in a published photograph of him, to, in an official portrait, the stitching pattern across a button on Stalin's jacket.[44] In 1937 the Central Committee of the Komsomol had its own paranoid meltdown when they began to imagine that Young Pioneers' badges in parts of Leningrad – featuring a burning flame and the hammer and sickle – actually looked like the symbol of the USSR was being burnt at the stake. They also somehow began seeing swastikas in the design, not to mention Trotskii's silhouette embedded in the Pioneers' kerchiefs.[45]

Doubtless picking up on this tension surrounding the symbol, the children themselves spread it around in rather more open ways. During their break-time, fourth-graders at a school in Solombal'skii raion, Arkhangel'sk, used chalk to draw swastikas on their hands and proceeded to stamp them on their classmates' backs.[46] This game seems to have been a favourite across the country, reported amongst students at the Tomsk Transport Institute in Siberia and Leningrad's Chemical-Pharmaceutical Institute.[47] The symbol was also daubed around as graffiti and on scraps of paper that circulated throughout Leningrad's middle schools (one unlucky student was caught with a stack of a hundred sheets, ready to distribute them).[48] Along with her friends, a particularly enterprising student at a school in Kyiv oblast' named Liza Zabrodskaia even carved a swastika into a potato and, taking some ink, set about stamping swastikas all over the school.[49] V.D. Bol'shakov, an 18 year-old shoemaker in Moscow, crafted himself a rather more impressive rubber stamp (presumably from materials available at the shoe factory where he worked) and began stamping the Nazi symbol on the inside lining of the shoes he made, until he was caught doing so in 1936 and was arrested.[50]

But the thrill of drawing this contraband symbol wasn't limited to children and youths. In the carnival atmosphere of the May Day celebrations, no doubt lubricated with more than a little alcohol, swastikas sprang up, scrawled in chalk, on equipment or on the walls of public buildings.[51] And it wasn't only in the midst of drunken festivities that adults got involved in this pastime: take, for instance, an accountant and former Red Army soldier, P.N. Dyshlis, who doodled two small swastikas on the front of a newspaper – on an article written by Stalin, no less – while waiting his turn at the barber's. A fellow customer discovered these scrawls and reported him. And yet, despite eventually admitting that he drew the swastikas, Dyshlis apparently could not explain to the NKVD why he had done so.[52] In fact, it's quite possible that he did not consciously have a particular end in mind.

Just like the children giggling as they stamped swastikas around their schools, a conscious agenda or understanding of the symbol and the act of drawing it was not really important. When living an extremely prescriptive life, the very thrill of creating an illicit image – of having the *power* to create one – could be intensely attractive and psychologically rewarding. As the theorist Michel de Certeau put it, 'The child scrawls and daubs on his schoolbooks; even if he is punished for this crime, he has made a space for himself and signs his existence as an author on it'.[53]

The same principle holds true for all the acts of humorous transgression, whether ostentatiously or quietly performed, that we've explored throughout this book. Even the most throwaway and childish examples represented far more than just the simple pleasure of breaking taboos: at the core of these jokes was an assertion of self, a push for personal agency within a state which had assumed the right to speak for every citizen. Although *anekdoty* usually contained multiple layers of meaning and allusion, they all represent an attempt by contemporaries to assert their agency to interpret and to judge for themselves the strange world around them.

George Orwell once suggested that 'every joke is a tiny revolution', but I think they were rather more important than that.[54] Every joke was a statement by those who shared them that 'I exist', 'I am here', and 'I can think' – people signing their existence on the repressive world around them and creating a place for themselves within it. This was not 'childish' in a pejorative sense, but was, rather, a quintessentially human urge that we see in hand-prints etched onto cave walls 30,000 years ago, to graffiti tags in cities from Pompeii to modern metropoles.[55]

Not Doing The Maths

Doing or saying provocative things without deeply considering their broader implications requires a certain amount of mental gymnastics. We've already seen some elements of this: self-deception is an integral part of the gallows humour effect, and it will also emerge as a surprisingly dominant factor in the next chapter when we examine the crucial issue of trust between friends and families. Self-deception and creating states of exception for yourself were also essential ingredients in making joke-telling an adaptive rather than a consciously anti-regime practice.

Blat provides us with an excellent parallel here. These were informal and very much unofficial networks of favours and exchange that were an indispensable survival mechanism in the 1930s and one in which everyone was involved to some degree. And yet, while acknowledging the ubiquity and importance of *blat*, many Harvard Project respondents simply refused to recognise that they had been engaged in the practice themselves, even if they 'related what were essentially *blat* episodes in their own lives […] in other parts of [their] interview', as Fitzpatrick notes.[56]

Most respondents appear to have considered *blat* to be unsavoury, unfair and even a criminal activity, and yet happily misrecognised their own favour-pulling as perfectly legitimate workarounds in difficult times. Just as we might feel enraged if we get passed over for a job because another candidate is friends with the employer, most of us are more than happy to take advantage of the personal connection when it works in our favour.

Breaking particular rules (or laws) is not the same as denying their general legitimacy, however. As the sociologist David Matza puts it, 'norms may be violated without surrendering allegiance to them';[57] instead, we can create numerous exceptions for ourselves without recognising that these could be interpreted as a rejection of the official rules.

Stuart Henry explored this phenomenon in his study of what he calls Britain's 'hidden economy', which bears more than a passing resemblance to *blat*. Henry focuses on individuals stealing goods from their employers, but who reinterpret these as 'perks' before selling them on cheaply to friends and acquaintances. By relabelling theft as 'perks', and justifying it with claims that 'everyone's doing it', a new kind of 'personal morality' is created in which the thief reasons that s/he is 'doing things to help other people' and, therefore, 'part-time crime is actually *more* moral than most legitimate business'.[58] On the other side of the exchange, people who buy or accept the illicit goods may '*choose* to remain ignorant of the fact that it's been stolen'.[59] The direct equivalent in the Soviet Union was the indulgence of practical (e.g. *blat*) and mental (e.g. humour) coping mechanisms, yet simultaneously *choosing* (perhaps unconsciously) not to perceive these activities as problematic or directly oppositional.

These were workarounds or 'life-hacks', but they were also essentially a refusal to put two and two together, a refusal to recognise and draw conclusions from the inconsistency between your social values or ideals, and your actions. This was why Andrei Arzhilovskii could complain repeatedly to his diary about the endless thefts going on in his area, and yet still make numerous references to his own pilfering: 'I stole some firewood,' he admitted; 'It's become part of my routine'.[60] Like Arzhilovskii, people could refuse to 'do the maths': they circumvented rules in order to survive or improve their lives a little, but rather than interpret their rule-breaking or criticisms as direct clashes with the regime, many (perhaps most) were crosshatching these elements with the official world. Criticism was interwoven with a desire that regime promises would come true; rule-breaking, like a black market, was a compensatory mechanism that shored up rather than undermined the creaking edifice of the official world.[61]

While contemporaries could regularly misrecognise their own rule-breaking as something rather different, political jokes in this period repeatedly shone a spotlight on the regime's failure to uphold its own rules, norms and values. Malicious gossip about your neighbours always contains 'an implicit statement of a rule or norm that has been broken', as James C. Scott puts it.[62] In political humour we see the same process in action, but in this case it is the state rather than a neighbour being upbraided for not conducting itself in accordance with the 'rules' – the rules it had itself made. Here, for once, Party members got in on the joke, too.

Loyal Criticism

If the regime felt political joke-telling constituted direct opposition, joke-tellers themselves seem to have understood it rather differently, which helps to explain why 39 individuals (14 percent) of our case study of 273 people prosecuted for crimes of humour, were existing or former Party members. This minority's significance is weightier than the sum of its parts because these were supposed to be, quite literally, the Party faithful.[63] So why were Party members, of all people, sharing *anekdoty*?

Those who openly told political jokes in front of their subordinates may simply have been flaunting their authority, (mistakenly) believing it would protect them from repercussions.[64] Others, like candidate member A.N. Solov'ev, defended their actions by emphasising that they were only sharing *anekdoty* with fellow Party members[65] – as he put it, only 'in a close circle of Communists' (в тесном кругу коммунистов). In both cases, these Party members seem to have believed joke-telling to be a perk or badge of their authority – a licence to speak more openly than others, or as an exclusive mode of social interaction between each other. And, as Solov'ev pointed out, even Party organisers were at it: during the train journey on which he told the jokes that led to his arrest, 'in that carriage in 1934, when all the Partorgs were travelling, all of them were telling c[ounter] r[evolutionary] *anekdoty*'![66]

Similarly, in an appeal written directly to Stalin in October 1940, I.G. Galkin, a Party member since 1917 who was arrested in 1937 for telling antisoviet *anekdoty*, makes this point more forcefully still. 'After all,' he wrote, 'one cannot deny the fact that all Party members know various *anekdoty*...', going on to claim that his accusers – also Party members – were blatantly involved in sharing the jokes, too; they had simply obscured their participation when they dobbed him in.[67] The danger varied with the political climate, but the habit seems to have been widespread, and even if they knew they were being risqué, Party members were clearly not regime opponents and did not consider joke-telling to make them so.

It bears repeating that across the board most of our arrested joke-tellers seemed genuinely perplexed that their humorous comments were considered proof that they were antisoviet people. When convinced communists found themselves in this position, confusion could also become a source of deep personal pain. Consider the case of Maksim Fedorovich Kul'chitskii, who had been a member of the Communist Party of Western Ukraine and had worked as an underground revolutionary in Polish territory (later incorporated into the Ukrainian Republic) from 1922. Then, in the early 1930s, he had studied for a doctorate (*aspirantura*) at the Institute of Red Professors in Khar'kiv, where he would teach the History of the Party, before taking a job in the archival administration of Stalino in 1935. Yet despite these glowing credentials, Kul'chitskii was arrested in 1936 for telling antisoviet *anekdoty* (and was treated with additional suspicion due to his time abroad).

This came as quite a shock: 'When leaving archival jobs, old folk usually drop right into the cemetery, but I (I was just 38 years old), was arrested', he wrote later, showing a flash of the dry humour that had got him in trouble. But although he admitted to telling several jokes, for Kul'chitskii these in no way indicated or constituted an antisoviet attitude. Writing in 1958, aged 60 and conscious of his own mortality, he beseeched the authorities not to let him die with the stigma and dishonour of his conviction still hanging round his neck.[68]

You didn't need to be a hardened revolutionary like Kul'chitskii to feel similarly misunderstood when branded an opponent of the regime simply for telling a political joke. When A.P. Lekher wrote to the MVD (the NKVD's successor) in September 1953, requesting he be rehabilitated for telling *anekdoty* and spreading 'pornographic poetry' in 1940-41, he specifically focused on how he had (mis)understood his position as a Komsomol member at that time.

> If you look up the protocols of my interrogations in 1941 [you will see] the following: 'I am a *komsomolets*, I love my homeland, but [if] there is something I do not like then I am not afraid even to tell the NKVD'. Yes, I was not afraid of the NKVD [...] because I was an honest person serving the homeland and the government, but, being a *komsomolets*, I did not realise and was unaware that in expressing my critical views I was committing a crime against Soviet power...

He complained further that his comrades did not correct him in this matter, but simply denounced him for the sake of 'political capital'.[69]

Lekher's own investment in the regime's principles and promises impelled him to call it out when it (repeatedly) fell short. He did not see this as opposition, but as a duty and, as a loyal critic, using humour seemed as reasonable a way to do so as any other – perhaps even a gentler method than most. Lekher and these other Party members were not regime opponents. When they shared political jokes between themselves they were dealing with the tension and abrasion they felt in daily life, caught between how things were meant to be and how they actually were. Sharing political jokes was not automatically anti-regime; on the contrary, as with Lekher, it was actually part of a broader desire to bring rhetoric and reality into closer alignment. Just as the Soviet Writers' Congress had determined that the role of humour in the USSR was in part 'to correct with laughter' people failing to live in alignment with regime values, for loyal critics, *anekdoty* were a reciprocal attempt to correct the system.[70]

Wishing it Would Work

But it wasn't just Party people who were, in their own minds, being critical but not heretical. Despite the vitriol and pain that we see in many 1930s *anekdoty*, at their core we often find a simple yet powerful wish that things would just work as they were supposed to. The Soviet regime was, after all, propagating a very attractive vision of what life could be like. Even the Harvard Project respondents, who largely defined themselves as opposed to the regime, nevertheless considered the ideal society to have a cradle-to-the-grave welfare system, total employment, state-owned heavy industry, and that economic activity should be centrally planned. In fact, even while not explicitly favouring an autocratic system, these former Soviet citizens actually seem to have expected one and, rather than wishing for something else, simply hoped that it would be a benevolent and paternal force.[71]

As the perplexed Project analysts mused, although 'there is […] a very high level of dissatisfaction with an exceedingly wide range of Soviet institutions and practices', there was just 'no direct and simple line leading from dissatisfaction with the conditions of life and hostility toward the regime to active disaffection from the whole form and practice of the Soviet system'.[72] Even when rhetorically writing it off, these recent émigrés, many of whom had fled the regime and were now keen to present themselves as its opponents to secure their refugee status, were not rejecting the Soviet system outright, but were still at some level wishing it would work. This was all the more acute for those left behind, who still had to make their way within the system.

In Chapter 3 we saw how Soviet contemporaries turned to prerevolutionary ideas and values to criticise the regime, but they just as often (and even simultaneously) mocked it for not living up to its own ideals and promises. The *anekdot* which I came across most frequently in the contemporary source materials highlights this attitude directly:

> 'Why did Lenin wear shoes, but Stalin wears boots?'
> 'Because Lenin avoided dirty puddles, whereas Stalin tramps right through them.'

Variations included the punchline 'Because Lenin knew where he was going', or featured Stalin dragging the population through a river, drowning them in the process.[73] A timekeeper at a factory in Dedovsk, Moskovskaia oblast', told a similar *anekdot* to her colleagues: 'Lenin, lying in the mausoleum, told Stalin, "Turn me face down so that I won't have to see everything you're doing".'[74] Bringing things even closer to home, another joke declared that 'Lenin is in our hearts, but Stalin on our nerves.'[75]

These *anekdoty* could just be taken as further evidence that Lenin was venerated and the Stalin Cult far from sacrosanct (see Chapter 1), but there's more going on beneath the surface. Here, as in the majority of 1930s *anekdoty*, it is Stalin and his disregard for practicalities and consequences which are mocked, not Lenin's original aims nor, by extension, the Soviet project at large. All those physically degrading and grotesque jokes about the leadership we saw in Kirov's Carnival can also be taken as evidence of people's frustration with the current leaders – and Stalin in particular – for their chronic failure to make Lenin's system work as it was supposed to.

An ex-factory foreman previously based in the Donbas region, interviewed by the Harvard Project, was giving voice to a widespread attitude when he replied to the question, '[Do] you think it is better to blame Stalin and the Soviet leaders than the system itself?' He answered unhesitatingly, 'Yes, of course. The system would not have been so bad [without them]. It depends on how the system is run. It depends on whom.'[76] So it was that contemporaries could declare, like one Nikolai Ryzhkov did at a local election in the Ukrainian village (село) of Portsuk – without detectable irony – that '[We] are for Soviet power, but without the Communists!'[77] In the same way, others might deface their ballot papers with a plea 'For the dictatorship of the proletariat without the Party'.[78]

A large part of the problem was simply that this young regime promised so much, and that it did so in hyperbolic terms. As James C. Scott puts it,

> the very process of attempting to legitimate a social order by idealizing it *always* provides its subjects with the means, the symbolic tools, the very ideas for a critique that operates entirely within the hegemony.[79]

This was certainly the case in the early Soviet Union, as Tracy McDonald has shown for the rural context, where 'Peasants could call the regime on its "official transcript", on state promises for honesty, order, and good government'.[80] The 'official transcript' is Scott's term for 'how things are officially supposed to be' – the public narrative, in other words. And although contemporaries drew upon 'symbolic tools' from non-Soviet sources, the regime was itself providing them abundant Soviet-brand ones, too.

We find this same impulse driving unofficial youth groups in these years, who banded together in frustration to pursue the idealistic goal of putting official ideology into practice.[81] And beyond the idealists, every time someone declared in unpleasant situations that 'life has become merrier!', or decoded an acronym to reveal what it meant in practice, they were calling the regime out in the same way. This was not only an attempt to highlight the gaps between rhetoric and reality, but a plea for a closer synergy between them – to reconcile the discrepancies between genuinely appealing promises and the continuously disappointing experiences of everyday life.

Compared to the Harvard Project respondents, much more was on the line for contemporaries still living in the Soviet Union. We can see this obliquely in the most commonly-recalled *anekdot* in the Project's interviews (it cropped up so often that the interviewers soon recorded it in abbreviated form) which struck a quite different attitude towards the regime and its ideology than the jokes circulating within its borders:

> A peasant complains to Kalinin, 'Look, we have no clothing, we're going around half-naked'. Kalinin replies that he can't help at the moment, but tries to ease the peasant's pain by telling him, 'Look, in Africa they go about completely naked and think nothing of it'. The peasant answers, 'They must have lived under Communism longer over there'.[82]

Rather than criticise its failings, this joke calls Communism itself into question – something much easier to do for those observing from a comfortable distance. But it was not so easy for people living in the Soviet Union to so fundamentally devalue the world they were living in. Unless they were prepared to write off their lives as wasted and thereafter despair, live as a social hermit, or to become a rebel (the latter possibilities being extremely difficult positions to hold in such a regime anyway), contemporaries simply had to adapt and find meaning within new and often harsh realities.

This also highlights an important distinction between political humour in the 1930s and that of the post-Stalin years. Come the Brezhnev era, in short, political humour increasingly betrayed a widespread disbelief in Communism itself;[83] the sense of possibility which flourished amidst the steam and smoke of massive industrial, economic and demographic change in the '30s withered in the long postwar period. Communism gradually became a joke in itself, but in the 1930s far more people were loyal (if exasperated) critics who wanted to consume the finished dish, and were berating the chefs who failed to deliver it.

Political jokes, like *blat*, were not head-on collisions between contemporaries and the regime, nor can they be reduced to a binary of popular practices versus official ideology. But simply wishing things would work was not enough, either: contemporaries needed to develop compensatory mechanisms – practical and psychological – to live through these times and navigate the myriad difficulties and disjunctures threatening to trip them up on a daily basis.

Know-how

The 1930s were extremely disorientating: logic and legislation were in unpredictable flux; political instruction was inconsistent and poorly delivered; retroactive justice could whisk your feet out from under you; and the threat of war hung thickly in the air. Inventing stories to explain a world beyond our ken and control is a fundamental human practice, and so, naturally enough, Soviet contemporaries used gossip, rumours and myths to make some sense of this mess. Myths and rumours have gained increasing attention in recent years, as historians finally realised that, as Robert Dale puts it, 'even when they bear limited resemblance to reality', myths in particular can nonetheless tell us a great deal about how contemporaries 'made sense of their society, both at the time and subsequently'.[84] Or, as the philosopher Alan Watts put it, 'A myth is an image in terms of which we try to make sense of the world'.[85]

Maybe so, but jokes can reveal much more besides. While myths tend to create often elaborate backstories for why things are the way they are, jokes play with those elements while simultaneously pushing (self-) justifications aside to focus on what things are really like in practice. Jokes and witty comments are, after all, very similar to parables or proverbs: they're punchy, self-contained, and often ironic stories or pithy phrases designed to convey lessons about how the world works.[86] (In fact, various Russian folklorists consider aphorisms, parables and the like to either derive from or give birth to *anekdoty*; added to which, in traditional Russian folk culture, proverbs were often humorous, or at least pretty wry, too.[87]) These fragments of 'wisdom' and insight worked as a 'sense-making device' – a term which the sociologist Andrea Mayr has used to describe prison argot: it's an 'insider' idiom which grows to enable the powerless to share their own, unofficial understandings of the world they cohabit alongside, and yet apart from, the official.[88]

The argot-like shadow language of acronyms and secret meanings known between people who trusted each other to share them (see the following chapter) was not used solely as a throwaway game to elicit a momentary smile or knowing look, but could also convey significant information about how the Soviet system actually worked. Contemporaries were simultaneously developing an informal rulebook, compiled from experience and disseminated surreptitiously, as a 'guide' to life during this turbulent period. This by no means implies it was a successful guide, but it nonetheless reveals to us some of the constructive, communal attempts by contemporaries to find ways of more safely and effectively navigating the 1930s. I call this body of unofficial understandings and advice '*know-how*'.

We encountered some examples of *know-how* in Chapter 2, like the neat summary of collectivisation as 'The sheep will be yours, but the meat will be ours!';[89] the direct connection of the hammer and sickle with death and famine, '*Serp i Molot / Smert' i Golod*';[90] or the rhyme which simply equates tsarism with good times: '[When] there was the tsar and tsarina / there was bread and wheat'.[91] Decoding acronyms could offer similar insights, as A.G. Man'kov noted in his diary in mid-1933, describing the reality of the secret police, then called the OGPU: 'O God! Please Unshackle us!' (*O, Gospodi! Pomogi Ubezhat'!*), and, in reverse, 'Flee – if they catch you, they'll have your head' (*Ubezhish' – Poimaiut, Golovu Otrubiat*).[92]

Then again, being caught was just part of living in this regime according to another dark aphorism, which proclaimed that 'He is not a citizen of the Soviet Union who has not sat in jail'.[93] Others focused on the inequality of distribution, riffing on the old adage that 'He who does not work, shall not eat', making it instead, 'He who does not steal, shall not eat'.[94] Going a step further, and losing some precision in the grumbling, a Harvard Project respondent claimed it was truer to say that 'He who does not work, does eat, and he who does work, does not eat', explaining that it was the lazy 'NKVD people and Communists' who ate well but did no real work.[95] Just like proverbs, in these brief jokes a general 'truth' is summed up concisely, pointedly and memorably. These were contraband truisms crystallising popular interpretations of the Soviet regime.

There were, however, more complex variations within this proverb-like genre which moved beyond the mere statement of 'fact', and offered specific advice on how to avoid trouble and to get ahead within the system. These were jokes which provided not only a sense of 'know-how', but also of 'how to'. Let's begin with a simple joke recalled both by a Harvard Project respondent and contemporaneously by the journalist Eugene Lyons, which describes a man sighing heavily on a tram, who is then immediately reprimanded by his wife: 'Don't talk about politics!'.[96] Simple as it is, the punchline actually offered invaluable advice in a time when a visible lack of enthusiasm could easily lead to trouble.[97] And, if your spouse wasn't on-hand, you could always take a look at the safety notice posted next to the tram windows: as a teacher-turned-chemist interviewed by the Harvard Project put it, this provided the best advice for anyone living in the USSR: 'Don't stick your head out'.[98] Conveying much the same information, an old Russian proverb gained renewed life and significance in these years: 'The quieter you are, the further you go' (or, indeed, 'the further you go, the quieter you are').[99]

A slightly more flippant but no less informative joke tells of a worker who hears there's a great deal of construction work going on in a particular part of town, but he protests that he walks by the area every day and has seen no evidence of the work. He is sharply reprimanded: '[Stop wasting] your time promenading instead of reading the newspapers and learning what's going on in the country'.[100] Just as contemporary films painted planned-but-unfinished buildings into the Moscow skyline, ordinary people were likewise better served to act as though the visions proclaimed in the papers already existed.[101]

William Chamberlin jotted down an *anekdot* which made no bones about offering (sardonic) life advice. Riffing on one of Stalin's speeches in which he had proposed 'six conditions' required for the successful operation of industry, the joke provided six conditions for safely navigating life in the USSR:

Don't think. If you must think, don't talk to yourself. If you must talk to yourself, don't talk to others. If you must talk to others, don't write. If you must write, don't print. If you must print, deny it the next day.[102]

These jokes were not all warnings, either. They could be spur-of-the-moment tips, as when factory workers in Leningrad cajoled their colleagues to 'Go to lunch. They're burying Kirov today; lunch will be good!'[103] This was both useful and true, but, like the rest of Kirov's Carnival, it was entirely unacceptable to officials determined to mourn the fallen leader with smothering gravitas. Others contained the equivalent of 'life-hacks' nested within sarcastic political comments: one recalled by a young Crimean sailor ran, 'You know what the difference is between [the newspapers] *Pravda* and *Izvestiia*? [...] *Pravda* has to be torn lengthwise and *Izvestiia* downwards [in order] to be rolled into cigarettes – that's the difference'.[104]

A more famous and long-lasting joke cautioned against trusting those publications: playing on the literal meanings of *Pravda* (truth) and *Izvestiia* (news), this one ran, 'There is no truth in *Pravda* and no news in *Izvestiia*'. This and other examples neatly straddled the boundary between *anekdot* and cautionary advice, for we can find various instances in which contemporaries merely stated as bald fact that there was often no 'truth' in *Pravda*,[105] while others self-consciously reeled it out as a joke,[106] highlighting how smoothly *anekdoty* could shade into practical life advice and social commentary, and vice versa.

Other jokes could be more specific about the kinds of things that would constitute 'sticking your head out'. Shitts recorded one of these, in which a schoolteacher explains to her class a criminal case against two wreckers and invites those in favour of executing the crooks to raise their hands. All but two of the children dutifully lift their hands. Confused, the teacher asks, 'Children, what're you doing?' One of the recalcitrant pair, a young boy, 'answers naively: "But I don't want them to be shot", to which his neighbour, no less naively, explains: "Mariia Aleksandrovna, they're new – they don't know that raising your hand is obligatory"'.[107]

Another example, cautioning against speculation, recorded by the journalist Ella Winter, was also set in a school:

> A visiting school teacher was examining a class in mathematics. 'If I buy a case of apples for 25 roubles and sell it for 50 roubles, what do I get?', he asked.
> 'Three years in jail,' chorused the class.[108]

It's especially fitting that these jokes were set in schools: simple yet damning truths were placed in the mouths of babes – a typical storytelling technique – but this also reflected the fact that children, as we've seen, were more likely to make the mistake of announcing that the emperor had no clothes, or to reveal the double-meanings of official acronyms. More revealing still, these jokes dramatised the fact that people had to *learn* how to act and what (not) to say under the regime, because it was often far from self-evident. Like children at school, everyone had to be socialised according to the norms of this new society. As Christina Kiaer and Eric Naiman have put it, 'in linguistic terms, ideology was transformed from a native to an acquired tongue, a language of which there were no native speakers'.[109] But if they were learning to 'speak Bolshevik' in the real classrooms, many adults were simultaneously learning to speak sense between one another.

Perhaps most telling of all, when invited to discuss the role of *blat* in Soviet life, many Harvard Project respondents immediately recited a contemporary proverb to explain it, which ran '*Blat* is higher than the Sovnarkom' (the Soviet Council of People's Commissars).[110] The readiness with which so many recited this phrase suggests not only the importance of *blat* itself, but just how widespread a 'proverb' like this could be: it was an attitude, a disposition, but also a piece of advice crystallised and disseminated. In fact, the importance of *blat* to daily life in the 1930s generated other new expressions and phrases to describe how things actually worked. Using *blat* could be described as obtaining something 'through connections' (по знакомству), 'On the B-Line' (по букву 'З'), or even through another decipherment of MTS, which ran '*Malen'koe Tovarishcheskoe Sodeistvie*', meaning 'A little comradely help'.[111]

Taken together, a great number of life-lessons and satirical observations were developing and being shared during the 1930s: contemporaries were creating a fugitive body of *know-how*, a shared knowledge of not only fallacies within regime ideology, but also, more importantly, of strategies, tips, or guides as to how you could still navigate and live through the difficulties and dangers of contemporary life. And so, although they were usually withering and scornful, these *know-how* jokes were not simply throwaway grumbles made by people who opposed the regime. The Harvard Project discovered that, in fact, the more antisoviet the disposition of their respondents was, the *less* they relied on rumours as trustworthy sources of information; conversely, 64 percent of the least antisoviet group said that they *did* rely on those unofficial channels. In other words, it seems that the more you were prepared to work within the system, the more you turned to informal means of communication for your information (and, the Project authors added, this was surely still more prevalent, given that their sample was probably more antisoviet than the population at large).[112] Getting by required some measure of *know-how*.

The Patterns in the Crosshatching

To work within the system meant finding ways to make sense of it. Rumours, myths or even gallows humour were attempts to explain the confusing and inescapable by explaining them away – by dreaming up a backstory or other details which briefly, mentally, resolved the anxiety surrounding a particular subject. Psychologists call this process 'illusory pattern recognition'.[113]

As Robert Trivers explains,

> lacking control increases something called illusory pattern recognition. That is, when individuals are induced to feel a lack of control, they tend to see meaningful patterns in random data, as if responding to their unfortunate lack of control by generating (false) coherence in data that would then give them greater control.[114]

Seeing patterns in the world around us, to imbue seemingly random things and events with meaning for which there is little (if any) objective evidence, is an inherent part of the human condition. The need to generate stories to explain why things are the way they are is seemingly hardwired into our brains. Consider, for example, experiments conducted on people suffering short-term memory loss which revealed that, when asked, these individuals automatically (i.e. not entirely consciously) invent plausible stories to explain their current situation. They do not quite realise they are making things up, but they feel compelled to find reasons for the current situation because they sense there *must be* such reasons.[115]

This impulse is certainly not confined to those suffering from memory disorders. At the macro level, entire religions and philosophies have evolved to provide reasons for our existence; and at the everyday level, the same psychological need can make us interpret a series of misfortunes as some kind of 'punishment' from the universe or a deity, or a run of good luck as somehow merited by our good character. In all cases, we reflexively seek out a *reason* for situations and events.[116]

Because it provides meaning and 'explanations', pattern

recognition produces pleasure; in fact, a great deal of the literature on humour focuses on moments of 'recognition'. The unexpected or incongruent elements suddenly sharpen into focus, which is the core of what makes us laugh and enjoy sharing jokes. But even when not producing mirth, understanding the way everyday life works, its conventions, norms, hierarchies and where we fit within them provides a powerful feeling of reassurance – of our place in the world – as the influential sociologist Pierre Bourdieu argued.[117]

And so, absurdist punchlines, completely unrealistic fantasies and the transposing of frightening things into the realm of the comic via gallows humour all served to provide illusory 'reasons', which could, at least temporarily, ease people's anxieties. Rumours worked in much the same way, if more crudely: almost every political, economic or other change in these years immediately prompted rumours that war was coming and *this* – whatever 'this' happened to be – proved it. Even if war as an 'explanation' for events was frightening, it still allowed contemporaries to feel they understood what was going on. This habit tells us something about how acutely people feared and anticipated the return of war, but it also demonstrates the general reflex to slot disturbing events into recognisable patterns and stories. It helps to contain them in familiar moulds, and containment is psychologically next-door to control. As a famous satirist put it, 'Right at the bottom, at the tip of the root, is the fear of the dark and the cold, but once you've given darkness a name you have a measure of control. Or at least you think you have, which is nearly as important'.[118]

But if gallows humour and rumours were examples of illusory pattern recognition – of dismissive self-deception – then examples of *know-how* were much more. They were still instances of pattern recognition, but they did not explain things away: they provided insights and guidance on life in the Soviet Union. In other words, these were not illusory patterns, but patterns which joke-tellers were discerning in the crosshatching of official and unofficial discourses, in the confluence of regime rhetoric and lived reality.

Scholars have sometimes described Soviet contemporaries as learning 'little tactics of the habitat', both mental and practical, as a means to get by as best they could, but the 'tactics' are generally described as isolated examples of opportunism and ad hoc exceptions to normal behaviour.[119] Michel de Certeau coined the phrase and himself emphasised that what he had in mind were 'opportunities seized "on the wing"' that were never consolidated into a culture or practice ('whatever [the tactics] wins, it does not keep').[120]

Know-how, in contrast, was cumulative and had a much longer shelf-life. Captured in the form of jokes and aphorisms, these mini-guides for navigating the Soviet 1930s could circulate and give rise to shared norms and behaviours, rather than being a series of one-off opportunities grabbed on the fly and developed and reflected on no further. People were learning how best to play the game, not just furtively grabbing a piece from the board and making off with it. In time, as life became more predictable, and especially after Stalin's death, this *know-how* settled in humour to become the comfortable cynicism of the familiar, which Alexei Yurchak describes in his work on the late Soviet Union.[121]

As the philosopher James P. Carse puts it, 'It is, in fact, by knowing what the rules are that we know what the game is'.[122] The elements of *know-how* we can detect in humour represent contemporaries sharing their awareness of those rules – not the official rules or laws of the state, but the rules of the 'game' of trying to live as best they could within this disruptive and restrictive regime. Whether practical tips or pointed social commentaries, in a frequently contradictory and unstable setting, they tried to find patterns to provide sense and coherence to the world around them, and to find their own place within it.

Foreigners who went to see Soviet civilisation for themselves faced a similar challenge and responded in similar fashion. As Choi Chatterjee notes, the material abundance the wide-eyed visitors associated with modernity was sorely lacking and they quickly had to learn how to navigate their way through the complexities of everyday Soviet life, forming their own *blat* networks and connections, and thereby generating 'a sort of oral lore' of survival skills which they passed on to their fellow Westerners.[123] As Sheila Fitzpatrick recalls, whether for foreign visitors or Soviet citizens, by the 1960s it was a commonplace to speak in terms of 'two starkly contrasting versions of the Soviet world: how it was supposed to be (*v printsipe*) and how it actually was (*v praktike*)'.[124] But, at least in the 1930s, it would be a mistake to think that 'practice' and 'principle' were entirely separate, or that they represented a simple binary.

'Practice' – life as it was experienced by most people – was what happened in the crosshatching where 'principle' met daily realities, where ideology hit experience and experience hit back, each affecting the other. It's not especially useful, though, just to acknowledge that reality is therefore 'messy' or a 'grey zone', but to realise that it was here that contemporaries actively looked for patterns in the crosshatching. The patterns they found were often illusory, but they still tell us a great deal about both the images through which they made sense of the world, and the psychological need they had to do so. And those patterns were not all illusory, either: *know-how* jokes sketched often very acute pictures of how rhetoric and reality blended in practice.

***

The noted Soviet writer and critic, Viktor Shklovskii, wrote as early as 1922 that

> the abundance of Soviet *anekdoty* in Russia is explained not by a particularly hostile attitude to [Soviet] power, but by the new phenomena of life and the contradictions of daily living (*byt*) that are perceived as comic.

Thereafter, he continued, people 'get used to [a given phenomenon]'; the new becomes the norm and the *anekdot* is no longer amusing.[125]

Shklovskii was half right. Humour certainly helped to normalise many aspects of life in the new Soviet world, but *anekdoty* did not simply fade away once those elements bedded in. Abrasions continued to be felt in the friction between ideology and reality and, in any case, the familiar or 'normal' does not automatically become unfunny.

On the contrary, professional comedians' stock-in-trade is pointing out the absurdities and inconsistencies in, and the mechanistically unreflective way we go about, our daily habits and conventions. Shklovskii lived until 1984, so would himself bear witness to the Brezhnev years in which stability and predictability, far from killing off *anekdoty*, would actually provide endless fuel for an *anekdot*-telling culture whose breadth far exceeded that of the 1920s and '30s.

Even if he was proved wrong on that score, what Shklovskii's 1922 article shows us is that from the earliest days of Soviet power, *anekdoty* were recognisably helping people to cope and to adapt, rather than simply or only to resist and reject the new regime and the new life it was striving, haphazardly, to create. *Anekdoty* included tension, judgement and rejection, but they were ultimately sites of negotiation and adaptation far more than they were mental bulwarks against the regime and its ideology. Humour reveals that there was so much more than a simple push-and-pull relationship between people and state, and the more important 'resistance' to consider is, I think, people's resistance to living a life without coherence or stability, one which they couldn't influence, or which was impossible to navigate safely.

Humour helped to meet this fundamental psychological need,

sometimes by containing, sometimes by explaining (perhaps fancifully), and sometimes by solving the hardships and contradictions which people faced in the 1930s. As they criticised the world, they also created a picture of how they saw it. Humour did not just pick holes in the fabric of the official world and its claims, but tried to weave threads of everyday reality and experience into the design, to give it texture, substance and significance. They had to accommodate the regime, but they also accommodated themselves to it – and this was not simply a case of progressively giving ground, but a dynamic, continuing interaction.

That's not to say people were consciously or consistently pursuing those ends: humour is by nature provisional, playful and ambivalent; it never 'means' just one thing and can simultaneously involve quite contradictory ideas and sentiments. It helped ease the way to accommodating the inescapable; it could frame a powerful wish that things work as they were supposed to; it could be exuberantly, defiantly transgressive… but it could also be self-deceptive in its significance. We shouldn't forget that a person might tell a joke in the same way they might throw a stone into a pond: just to see how big a splash it made. In the process, however, they might ease their sense of powerlessness under the Stalinist system. What joking did for people was not necessarily the same as what it (consciously) meant to them.

A stimulating new theory proposes that all humour ultimately derives from 'benign violations', in which the violation of a norm must simultaneously be appraised as non-threatening in order for it to be funny (rather than offensive or disturbing).[126] To account for the Soviet 1930s, however, we need to extend this theory to include the possibility of wilful self-deception. Soviet contemporaries often laughed at things which were not benign or unthreatening, but which were, on the contrary, very frightening or oppressive, and usually impossible to escape. Their laughter did not signal that these were truly 'benign' targets of mirth, but was instead an exercise in shared self-deception which allowed them to treat these things, at least for a moment, *as if* they were benign. In this way, humour can act as a powerful placebo: it is a trick which helps us to heal ourselves; rationally, it should make no difference, but subjectively and individually it can make all the difference in the world.

And they did not joke alone. The story of joke-telling in Stalin's 1930s is one of people trying to get by as best they could, to find a measure of coherence and understandability in tumultuous times under a capricious and violent government, to sign their existence on the world around them, but also, and perhaps most importantly, of sharing their experiences and their knowledge with the people they trusted. Joke-telling was always in part performance, and the gallows humour effect in particular relied in significant part on hearing reassuring laughter in response to the punchline. But how could people know or discover whom to trust, and what did it mean for sociability and friendship in these years to share these dangerous jokes around?

Notes

1. Seth Graham describes such attitudes in *Resonant Dissonance*, 7-8.
2. Lisa Perfetti, *Women and Laughter in Medieval Comic Literature* (Ann Arbor, MI, 2003), 240.
3. Bauer, Inkeles & Kluckhohn, *How the Soviet System Works*, 91.
4. Scott, *Weapons of the Weak*, 350.
5. GARF, f.8131, op.31, d.11121.
6. Stradomskii's file states that he was sentenced five times, but this appears to be an error given the detailed breakdown of his convictions which I summarise from the same document.
7. Thomas R. Kane, Jerry Suls & James T. Tedeschi, 'Humour as a Tool of Social Interaction', Antony J. Chapman & Hugh C. Foot (eds.), *It's a Funny Thing, Humour* (Oxford, 1977), 14.
8. Peter McGraw & Joel Warner, *The Humor Code: A Global Search for What Makes Things Funny* (New York, 2014), 92.
9. For a brief outline of this 'evolutionary' theory, see V.S. Ramachandran, 'The Neurology and Evolution of Humor, Laughter, and Smiling: The False Alarm Theory', *Medical Hypotheses*, 51.4 (1998), 352.
10. On these different kinds of laughter, see McGraw & Warren, *Humor Code*, 90-2.
11. On the inherently social nature of laughter, see Anthony J. Chapman, 'Social Aspects of Humorous Laughter', Anthony J. Chapman & Hugh C. Foot (eds.), *Humour and Laughter: Theory, Research and Applications* (London, 1976), 173; Robert R. Provine, *Laugher: A Scientific Investigation* (London, 2000), 44-7; Robert R. Provine & Kenneth R. Fischer, 'Laughing, Smiling, and Talking: Relation to Sleeping and Social Context in Humans', *Ethology*, 83.4 (1989), 295–305.
12. Freud, *Jokes*, 121.
13. C. Groos, quoted in Freud, *Jokes*, 121. The reference is to *Faust*, Part I, Scene 3. McGraw and Warren also suggest that familiarity and the appreciation of humour appear to be linked, as opposed to humour inversely correlating to incongruity: *Humor Code*, 7.
14. Groos mentions this element of 'power' (Freud does not believe it should be a relevant factor), but not in the sense I suggest here. 'Power' for Groos is in the sense of a more straightforward mastery, whereas I'm proposing a union of the 'recognition' and 'power' factors as part of the same pleasure-generating process, which might also reconcile the conflict between Freud's and Groos's views. (cf. Freud, *Jokes*, 121-2.)
15. Mary Douglas, *Implicit Meanings: Selected Essays in Anthropology* (2nd edn., London, 1999), 153-4.
16. Lawrence W. Levine describes a similar rationale in *Black Culture and Black Consciousness: Afro-American Folk Thought from Slavery to Freedom* (New York, 1977), 298-366, esp. 342-4. This kind of self-deception in humour is central to Thomas Hobbes's brief thought on the subject. Although Hobbes makes this point only in relation to insults or mockery of individuals, the outcome is the same as gallows humour more generally: ultimately, these are acts of self-deception designed to make the speaker feel more secure: 'And it is incident most to them, that are conscious of the fewest abilities in themselves; who are forced to keep themselves in their own favour, by observing the imperfections of other men. And therefore much Laughter at the defects of others, is a signe of Pusillanimity. For of great minds, one of the proper workes is, to help and free others from scorn; and

compare themselves onely with the most able.' (Hobbes, *Leviathan*, 43.)

17   Robert Trivers, *Deceit and Self-Deception: Fooling Yourself the Better to Fool Others* (London, 2013), 22; Daniel Gilbert, *Stumbling on Happiness* (London, 2007), 20.

18   Quotes from Viktor E. Frankl, *Man's Search for Meaning: An Introduction to Logotherapy*, trans. Ilse Lasch (4th edn., Boston, MA, 1992 [1946]), 29, 52 (Frankl mentions humour numerous times throughout his description of life in the camps); Vasily Grossman, *Life and Fate*, trans. Robert Chandler (London, 2006), 532. See also Steve Lipman, *Laughter in Hell: The Use of Humor During the Holocaust* (Northvale, NJ, 1993); Lynne Rapaport, 'Laughter and Heartache: The Functions of Humor in Holocaust Tragedy', Jonathan Petropoulos & John K. Roth (eds.), *Gray Zones: Ambiguity and Compromise in the Holocaust and Its Aftermath* (New York, 2005).

19   See Simon Belokowsky, 'Laughing on the Inside: Gulag Humor in Terms of a Gulag Society' (forthcoming). My thanks to Simon for sharing this paper with me.

20   Podlubnyi, diary entry for 15 November 1932. Lacking access to the original, I work here from two translations, the German one providing the full diary entry: Hellbeck, *Revolution on my Mind*, 184; and Jochen Hellbeck (ed. & trans.), *Tagebuch aus Moskau 1931-1939* (Munich, 1996), 103.

21   Quoted in Larry E. Holmes, *War, Evacuation, and the Exercise of Power: The Center, Periphery, and Kirov's Pedagogical Institute, 1941-1952* (Lanham, MD, 2012), 3 (1941).

22   Scott, *Behind the Urals*, 16.

23   TsGAIPD, f.24, op.2v, d.3721, l.186 (1939). ('Черный ворон и скорая помощь'; more strictly, this is a 'black raven', but the connotations are of a scavenger, better captured in English by 'crow'.) For variations, see Brandenberger, *Political Humor*, 114-5 & n.16. Shitts also recorded a version of this in his diary in 1931, which suggests that the joke returned whenever arrests increased (Shitts, *Dnevnik*, 316.).

24   Shitts, *Dnevnik*, 157 (1929); also cf. HPSSS 54/A/5, p.28.

25   Arzhilovskii, diary entry for 1 February 1937, Garros et al (eds.), *Intimacy and Terror*, 140.

26   TsGAIPD, f.24, op.2v, d.4306, l.158 (July 1940).

27   GARF, f.8131, op.31, d.10093, l.3 (1940).

28   GARF, f.8131, op.31, d.88855, l.4 (c.1938). ('... имеются три класса – сидящий, рыдающий и ожидающий'.) The first word is literally 'the sitting', but because 'to sit' is also used in Russian to describe doing time in prison, I've translated it here as 'serving'. Although it bears some resemblance to the 'categorising' *anekdoty* described in Chapter 6, this joke emphasises only a general powerlessness in the face of the state. For a similar example, see Chamberlin, *Russia's Iron Age*, 329.

29   GARF, f.8131, op.31, d.3703, l.66 (1938).

30   RGASPI, f.M-1, op.23, d.1102, l.137 (April 1935). (Loosely translated from: 'В Москве-реке воды стало мало, потому что жители воды в рот набрали молчат [*sic*]'.)

31   GARF, f.8131, op.31, d.10087 (1940).

32   TsGAIPD, f.24, op.2v, d.1838, l.96 (1936).

33   The phrase was seemingly coined in chapter 7 of Gogol's *Dead Souls*. It was the title for some collections of *anekdoty*: e.g. a volume from the Minsk publishing house Literatura (cf. Seth Graham, *A Cultural Analysis of the Russo-Soviet* Anekdot, PhD Thesis, University of Pittsburgh (2009), 206-7); John Kolasky, *Laughter Through Tears: Underground Wit, Humor and Satire in the Soviet Russian Empire* (Bullsbrook, 1985). Freud also identifies it in his study: *Jokes*, 232. Even Lunacharskii used the term to describe the laughter of the powerless in his

34 See Chapter 1.
35 See, for example, Seneca, *Letters from a Stoic*, ed. & trans. Robin Campbell (London, 1969); Marcus Aurelius, *Meditations*, trans. Gregory Hays (New York, 2002), esp. Book 4, nos. 1, 49. An excellent modern introduction to these principles is Ryan Holiday, *The Obstacle is the Way: The Ancient Art of Turning Adversity to Advantage* (London, 2014).
36 David Hopkin, *Voices of the People in Nineteenth-Century France* (Cambridge, 2012), 26.
37 Michel Foucault, *A History of Sexuality Vol.1: The Will to Knowledge*, trans. Robert Hurley (London, 1998), 6.
38 Kissing Stalin: GARF, f. 8131, op.31, d.87767, l.5 (1936); other examples, see Chapter 1.
39 TsGAIPD, f.25, op.10, d.75, l.36.
40 TsGAIPD, f.24, op.2v, d.2059, l.80 (June 1936).
41 GARF, f.8131, op.31, d.82045, l.9 (emphasis added).
42 GARF, f.8131, op.31, d.88415, l.13 (1937).
43 GARF, f.5451, op.42, d.262, l.63 (1933).
44 Plamper, 'Abolishing Ambiguity', 537-9.
45 A.K. Sokolov (ed.), *Obshchestvo i vlast' 1930-e gody. Povestvovanie v dokumentakh* (Moscow, 1998), 308-9 (November 1937).
46 RGASPI, f.M-1, op.23, d.1265, l.50 (June 1937). The report identifies one child and one instance in particular, but when questioned the schoolchildren claimed this was not a new game.
47 RGASPI, f.M-1, op.23, d.1106, l.129 (December 1935); TsGAIPD, f.24, op.2v, d.2685, l.2 (February 1937).
48 TsGAIPD, f.24, op.2v, d.2487, l.57 (February 1937).
49 HDA SBU, f.16, op.30, d.113, l.90 (1937).
50 GARF, f.9474, op.16, d.97, l.120 (1936).
51 e.g. TsGAIPD, f.24, op.2v, d.1837, ll.161, 162 (May 1936).
52 HDA SBU, f.6, d.35430FP, ll. 2, 6, 9, 11, 39-44 (the newspaper itself is included in the case-file and is dated 31 December 1937).
53 Certeau, *The Practice*, 31.
54 Orwell, 'Funny, But Not Vulgar', 284.
55 Yuval Noah Harari, *Sapiens: A Brief History of Humankind* (London, 2015), 1; Mary Beard, *Pompeii: The Life of a Roman Town* (London, 2008), 22, 49-50, 59, 115-7, 146-7, 168-71, 183-4, 237-40, 258-9.
56 Sheila Fitzpatrick, 'Blat in Stalin's Time', Stephen Lovell, Alena Ledeneva & Andrei Rogachevskii (eds.), *Bribery and Blat in Russia: Negotiating Reciprocity from the Middle Ages to the 1990s* (Houdmills, 2000), 170. See also: Alena V. Ledeneva, *Russia's Economy of Favours*: Blat, *Networking and Informal Exchange* (Cambridge, 1998), 62-6.
57 David Matza, *Delinquency and Drift* (New York, 1990), 60; also cf. Certeau, *The Practice*, 32.
58 Stuart Henry, *The Hidden Economy: The Context and Control of Borderline Crime* (London, 1978), 58-9, 50-1, 78.
59 Henry, *Hidden Economy*, 56. Emphasis added. This is much the same as the practices which Certeau describes in France that are called '*la perruque*' (literally: 'the wig'), although while he describes the complicity from others that it needs to function, he doesn't address the element of self-deception that is also required. (Certeau, *The Practice*, 24-8.)

60 Arzhilovskii, diary, Garros et al (eds.), *Intimacy and Terror*, quotation p.144. Critical references to others' theft: pp.114, 129, 130, 144, 146 ; references to his own theft: pp.128, 130, 133, 146, 148, 150-1, 154.
61 On the black market working 'in symbiosis' with the legal economy see Elena Osokina, 'Economic Disobedience under Stalin', Lynne Viola (ed.), *Contending with Stalinism: Soviet Power and Popular Resistance in the 1930s* (Ithaca, NY, 2002), 200. Also cf. Rittersporn, *Anguish, Anger, and Folkways*, Ch.8.
62 Scott, *Weapons of the Weak*, 282.
63 Only seven of this number had an obvious reason to feel genuinely dissatisfied, having been formally excluded from the Party, in some cases multiple times: GARF, f.8131, op.31, dd. 6058, 16218, 16276a, 63848, 86702, 87490, 99157.
64 e.g. GARF, f.8131, op.31, dd.86944, 71260, 88855, 1197, 6960, 75465.
65 GARF, f.8131, op.31, dd.52823, 1247, 13043, 88855, 71260. Solov'ev was one of two candidate Party members in our sample, meaning he was effectively a probationary Party member, but his explanation holds true for how full members tried to explain and excuse their joke-telling.
66 GARF, f.8131, op.31, d.60571, l.6.
67 GARF, f.8131, op.31, d.5553, ll.24(ob)-25.
68 GARF, f.8131, op.31, d.83654, ll.2, 9, 23-4, 30-31. Quotation at l.23.
69 GARF, f.8131, op.31, d.15983, ll.57(ob)-58. ('политический капитал'.)
70 Kirpotin, *Pervyi vsesoiuznyi s"ezd*, 380; see Chapter 4.
71 Bauer, Inkeles & Kluckhohn, *How the Soviet System Works*, 139-40.
72 Bauer, Inkeles & Kluckhohn, *How the Soviet System Works*, 261-2.
73 I present the most generic version of this *anekdot*. GARF, f.8131, op.31, d.1587, l.5 (1936); d.29139, l.7 (1941-2); d.43506, l.17 (c.1940); d.85131, l.10 (1936); d.85221, l.8 (1930-5); RGASPI, f.M-1, op.23, d.1102, ll.65-6 & 137 (1935); f.17, op.120, d.175, l.88 (1935); d.176, l.137 (1935); TsDAHOU, f.1, op.20, d.6210, l.10 (1933); HPSSS 61/A/5, p.50; 517/A/26, p.24; 96/(NY)1493/A/35, p.47. For further variations, cf. Mel'nichenko, *Sovetskii anekdot*, 204-5.
74 Cited in Goldman, *Terror and Democracy*, 83 (I have slightly adjusted the translation).
75 HDA SBU, f.16, op.28, d.12, l.26 (February 1935); GARF, f.8131, op.31, d.89832, l.9 (c.1936); also cf. Mel'nichenko, *Sovetskii anekdot*, 235-6. ('Ленин живет в сердцах – а Сталин в печенках'. Literally: 'Stalin [lives] in our livers', which carries a figurative sense of 'to plague'.)
76 HPSSS 99/A/7, p.47.
77 HDA SBU, f.16, op.32, d.54, l.255 (October 1939). It is clear from the surrounding context that although this comment is recorded as 'Вы' ('you'), this was a typographical error and should be 'Мы' ('we').
78 HDA SBU, f.16, op.31, d.77, l.519 (1938).
79 Scott, *Weapons of the Weak*, 338. Also cf. Scott, *Domination and the Arts of Resistance* (New Haven, CT, 1990), 54-5.
80 Tracy McDonald, *Face to the Village: The Riazan Countryside under Soviet Rule, 1921-1930* (Toronto, 2011), 77.
81 Gábor T. Rittersporn, 'Formy obshchestvennogo obikhoda molodezhi i ustanovki sovetskogo rezhima v predvoennom desiatiletii', Timo Vihavainen (ed.), *Normy i tsennosti povsednevnoi zhizni: stanovlenie sotsialiticheskogo obraza zhizni v Rossii, 1920-1930-e gody* (St Petersburg, 2000); for similar groups in the later Stalinist period, cf. Juliane Fürst, 'Prisoners of the Soviet Self? – Political Youth Opposition in Late Stalinism', *Europe-Asia Studies*, 54.3 (2002).
82 I present a generic version, based on: HPSSS 1/A/1, pp.26-7; 3/A/1, p.29; 5/A/1, p.17; 8/A/1, p.23; 25/A/3, p.68; 66/A/6, p.68; 127/A/10, pp.36-7; 149/(NY)1486/A/34,

p.39; 433/(NY)1240/A/32, p.44. Also cf. Lyons, *Modern Moscow*, 267; and Mel'nichenko, *Sovetskii anekdot*, 364.

[83] cf. Yurchak, 'Cynical Reason', esp. 162. Also see Graham, *Resonant Dissonance*, which focuses on this later period.

[84] Robert Dale, 'The Valaam Myth and the Fate of Leningrad's Disabled Veterans', *Russian Review*, 72.2 (2013), 284. On rumours, see Johnston, *Being Soviet*.

[85] Alan Watts, 'Our Image of the World', lecture available at <https://www.alanwatts.org/>.

[86] The *anekdot* in its twentieth-century form itself had much shared ancestry, oral and literary, with moral tales told for primarily didactic purposes rather than to amuse. cf. E.K. Nikanorova, *Istoricheskii anekdot v russkoi literature XVIII veka. Anekdoty o Petre Velikom* (Novosibirsk, 2001), Foreword.

[87] cf. D.S. Komissarov (ed.), *Persidskie narodnye anekdoty* (Moscow, 1990), 9-10; Likhachev, 'Smekh', 357.

[88] Andrea Mayr (quoting D.Wieder), *Prison Discourse: Language as a Means of Control and Resistance* (Houndmills, 2004), 154.

[89] GARF, f.8131, op.31, d.4393, l.13 (c.1937).

[90] RGASPI, f.17, op.120, d.176, l.153 (March 1935); TsDAHOU, f.1, op.20, d.3198, l.33 (March 1930); d.6210, l.78 (February 1933); d.6642, l.26 (April 1935).

[91] RGASPI, f.M-1, op.23, d.1106, l.21 (December 1934).

[92] Man'kov, *Dnevniki*, 74 (24 July 1933).

[93] HPSSS 4/A/1, p.15.

[94] RGASPI, f.671, op.1, d.257, l.27 (1935). Others could riff on this slogan to portray the inequalities they saw in the distribution of food in relation to labour: 'He who does not work not only eats, but also drinks wine; but he who works, gobbles down the chaff [мякину жрет]'. (TsGAIPD, f.24, op.2v, d.1846, l.123 (1936). Thanks to Sarah Davies for this reference.)

[95] HPSSS 60/A/5, p.13.

[96] HPSSS, 104/(NY)1492/A/34, p.21; Lyons, *Modern Moscow*, 273.

[97] Other Harvard Project respondents recounted just such advice from their friends when it came to sharing *anekdoty*, in fact. e.g. HPSSS 133/A/10, p.75.

[98] HPSSS 59/A/5, p.18. (I have anglicised this and replaced the rather incongruous 'motto' with 'maxim'.)

[99] GARF, f.8131, op.31, d.95714, l.10 (1932); f.3316, op.16a, d.446, l.162 (1930); HPSSS 61/A/5, p.13.

[100] Adapted from several examples: Lyons, *Modern Moscow*, 268; HPSSS 11/A/2, p.31; Mel'nichenko, *Sovetskii anekdot*, 513.

[101] See, for e.g., *Kosmicheskii reis* (1935) and *Novaia Moskva* (1938).

[102] Chamberlin, *Russia's Iron Age*, 330. Stalin's 'six conditions' were outlined in a speech on 23 June 1931, and thereafter in *Pravda* on 5 July 1931.

[103] TsGAIPD, f.25, op.5, d.47, ll.5, 42; f.24, op.5, d.2288, ll.48, 114 (December 1934).

[104] HPSSS, 7/A/1, p.3.

[105] RGASPI, f.326, op.1, d.133, l.39 (October 1928); f.M-1, op.23, d.1184, l.98 (1936); NA, f.389, d.15, l.79. Also cf. Mel'nichenko, *Sovetskii anekdot*, 614.

[106] Chamberlin, *Russia's Iron Age*, 329; HPSSS 5/A/1, p.44; 95/A/7, p.29; 451/A/22, p.42. Variation that there is no truth in *Izvestiia* and no news in *Pravda*: HPSSS 96/A/7, pp.29-30; 302/A/15, p.29.

[107] Shitts, *Dnevnik*, 264 (1930). Again, this episode is presented as being halfway between a joke and a tale.

[108] Winter, *Red Virtue*, 17.

[109] Christina Kiaer & Eric Naiman (eds.), *Everyday Life in Early Soviet Russia: Taking*

the Revolution Inside (Bloomington, IN, 2006), 6.

[110] e.g. HPSSS 7/A/1, p.5; 9/A/1, p.19; 13/A/2, p.16; 27/A/3, p.46; 29/A/3, p.23; 66/A/6, p.23; 110/A/8, p.20; 131/A/10, p.4; 133/A/10, p.13; 142/A/11, p.12; 147/A/12, p.19. 'Sovnarkom' also seems to be interpreted in some of the HPSSS interviews as just 'People's Commissar'.

[111] HPSSS 14/A/2, pp.63-4. For other decipherments of 'MTS', see Chapter 3.

[112] Inkeles & Bauer, *The Soviet Citizen*, 163-4.

[113] On which, see Jennifer A. Whitson & Adam D. Galinsky, 'Lacking Control Increases Illusory Pattern Perception', *Science*, 322 (2008), 115-7.

[114] Trivers, *Deceit and Self-Deception*, 23-4.

[115] The psychiatric term for this is 'confabulation'. For an overview of this complex condition, see William Herstein, 'Confabulations about Personal Memories, Normal and Abnormal', Suzanne Nalbantian, Paul M. Matthews & James L. McClelland (eds.), *The Memory Process: Neuroscientific and Humanistic Perspectives* (Cambridge, MA, 2011).

[116] This need to create narratives, regardless of objective evidence, or lack thereof, is a major theme explored in Nassim Nicholas Taleb, *The Black Swan: The Impact of the Highly Improbable* (London, 2007).

[117] Bourdieu used the term 'habitus', a 'structuring structure', as he put it, producing 'pleasure' for the person able to recognise and categorise the people, lifestyles, class, and other elements of the social world around them. Pierre Bourdieu, *Distinction: A Social Critique of the Judgement of Taste*, trans. Richard Nice (London, 2010), 166, 169.

[118] Terry Pratchett, *A Slip of the Keyboard: Collected Non-Fiction* (London, 2014), 95.

[119] See Mark Edele's critique, 'Soviet Society, Social Structure, and Everyday Life: Major Frameworks Reconsidered', *Kritika*, 8.2 (2007).

[120] Certeau, *The Practice*, xix. James C. Scott made a similar point: writing of everyday peasant resistance, he suggested that 'the fight is less a pitched battle than a low-grade hit-and-run guerrilla action.' Scott certainly saw these 'guerrilla' tactics as constituting a more consistent practice, but he does not in the end go much further than Certeau in defining it beyond being some broad kind of resistance to regime encroachments (Scott, *Weapons of the Weak*, 241). Also see Jonathan H. Bolton's superb essay, 'Writing in a Polluted Semiosphere: Everyday Life in Lotman, Foucault, and de Certeau', Andreas Schonle (ed.), *Lotman and Cultural Studies: Encounters and Extensions* (Madison, WI, 2006), esp. 320-33.

[121] Yurchak, 'Cynical Reason'.

[122] James P. Carse, *Finite and Infinite Games: A Vision of Life as Play and Possibility* (New York, 1986), 8.

[123] Choi Chatterjee, 'Everyday Life in Transnational Perspective: Consumption and Consumerism, 1917-1939', Chatterjee et al (eds.), *Everyday Life*, 371.

[124] Sheila Fitzpatrick, 'Afterword', Chatterjee et al (eds.), *Everyday Life*, 399.

[125] Shklovskii, 'K teorii komicheskogo', 63. See also Mel'nichenko, *Sovetskii anekdot*, 24-5.

[126] A. Peter McGraw & Caleb Warren, 'Benign Violations: Making Immoral Behavior Funny', *Psychological Science*, 21.8 (2010), 1141–49. This is also the principal thesis of McGraw & Warner, *The Humor Code*.

CHAPTER 6

IN ON THE JOKE:
HUMOUR, TRUST AND SOCIABILITY

These were the years of joking dangerously. We've seen how risky it was for Soviet citizens to tell jokes in the 1930s: the regime considered humour to be a weapon or a virus – to them, it was all toxic, counterrevolutionary propaganda. A simple one-liner could land you in the Gulag for 10 years or more. But not only were the punishments draconian, they were enforced unpredictably and retroactively. Nobody – not even the Party faithful – was safe from this, creating a climate of profound uncertainty and fear, leading many historians to internalise the regime's perspective and to assume that there was no space for critical humour in the Soviet Union, and that the only people who told jokes were therefore staunch political opponents.

But the compulsion to tell jokes remained irresistible to many. As we saw in the previous chapter, from gallows humour to creative (even essential) *know-how* jokes, many people who did not consider themselves opponents continued to tell jokes in spite of the risk. To vent their frustration over impossible work quotas and unfulfilled promises; to cope, creatively, with intense social and economic upheaval; and even, at the most fundamental level, to assert their own existence in a system that wanted to prescribe everything you could do or be.

Although the previous chapter highlighted the psychological

motivations and rewards of joke-telling, these must still be reconciled with the real and unpredictable dangers involved. If contemporaries couldn't know for sure what punishment they faced at a particular point in time, they certainly knew they were always taking some risk when sharing critical jokes. Nevertheless, *anekdoty* were not just whispered, but were shared surprisingly openly at home, at work, and even with complete strangers on the train.

If joke-tellers were not simply reckless or foolhardy, they evidently believed that they could get away with their jokes, that their sentiments would be shared by their audience, or, at least, that their listeners would not immediately report them to the NKVD. Until now we've primarily dealt with individuals who misjudged this situation and ended up in the arms of the secret police. They were reported by their friends, colleagues, and bystanders: the evidence from the archives is evidence of trust failing.

But there were so many others who also shared jokes but managed to successfully evade the clutches of the NKVD. They did not survive because they were less antisoviet than the already ambivalent joke-tellers whose criminal files now rest in the archives. Some of them, at the end of the war, managed to either flee to, or end up as displaced persons in, the West, where they were interviewed by the Harvard Project's team of sociologists. The team sought to make sense of what life under Stalinism was like, providing an unprecedented insight into their lives under and attitudes towards the regime. Those interviews take us into a world in which people shared much the same jokes as those who were left behind, but in the process they reveal to us how – even if they did not quite realise it themselves – they avoided denunciation and arrest.

Taken together with the archival sources, diaries, and contemporary accounts from visitors to the Soviet Union (who, even if they could publish their reflections in safety thereafter, also had to navigate this complex world without endangering themselves or their Soviet friends), the Harvard Project interviews allow us to answer the heavy questions facing anyone who felt compelled to tell jokes under Stalin.[1]

Whom could you trust to share these jokes? What did it mean to do something so risky – what were the effects, social and personal, of sharing this contraband, provocative material? And, of course, what did it mean to hear in response others laughing knowingly, ruefully, in sympathy, or in agreement?

Because joke-telling was always fundamentally a *social* act, answering these questions tells us something crucial about Soviet society at the grassroots level. This was not a society of Winston Smiths. The isolated protagonist of Orwell's *Nineteen Eighty-Four*, who effectively lives in a cell and whose life rapidly unravels once he forms a close relationship with another person and begins voicing his doubts to her, is a compelling and fascinating creation, but he and his story are still an exaggeration of Soviet life. Life in 1930s Soviet cities could scarcely have been more different: for all the suspicion and doubt that undeniably existed, people did not live in solitary confinement, but in cramped, overcrowded, communal housing and, as we'll see, they seem generally to have remained open with, and even to draw closer to, their families and friends.

If there is one regime perspective that we *can* fruitfully adopt, it is the idea that joke-tellers were criminals. By comparing their situation to that of organised criminals or *mafiosi* – groups who are forced to find ways to communicate and work together without being detected by the authorities, and with the constant fear of betrayal hanging in the air around them – we come a significant step closer to understanding how critical communication took place in the 1930s.

Knowing who and how to trust made all the difference. In exploring these issues, I introduce the idea of 'trust groups': the small associations of two or more people who could speak openly and critically with each other during these years. Like political jokes themselves, trust groups were in part defined by the regime; trust was essential because of the increasing danger of speaking critically. But within them the official and unofficial, Soviet and pre-Soviet, political and personal values did not simply clash, but crosshatched each other in complex and revealing ways.

Tracing the outlines of these trust groups helps us not only to understand the possibilities for open and critical speech in the 1930s, but also the social relations which enabled these potentially dangerous exchanges to occur. This challenges not only long-standing historical interpretations, but also, as we'll see, what contemporaries themselves thought about 'society' outside of their own trust groups. The myth of Pavlik Morozov, the Soviet boy-hero immortalised by the regime for denouncing his own parents, hung heavy in the air. Or at least, in the air outside your own trust group.

The social sharing of jokes illuminates the existence and nature of an unofficial sociability. First, this was because it was a risky undertaking: unless someone simply lost their temper and their good sense, telling a joke involved an important judgement of trust. It was therefore also actively to demonstrate and to perform that trust to their audience, which, if successful, could foster significant interpersonal bonds between the people involved. Second, because jokes often rely upon mocking a 'them' to the benefit of an 'us', the content of these jokes can tell us a great deal about how these trust groups understood themselves and their relation not only to Soviet power at large, but also to other parts of Soviet society. Soviet citizens were not atomised, but nor did their interpersonal relations remain static: they forged new bonds and networks, new relationships of various kinds to suit, or at least to help deal with, the new conditions of the 1930s.

This whole book is a study of life *in extremis*, but although ordinary citizens had to face exceptional difficulties and hardships, they did so in ways that were often deeply familiar, both to them and to us. In the face of major emergencies and natural disasters, we often reflexively assume that 'civilisation' or 'society' will break down and mob violence and self-interest will prevail – a theme we see endlessly repeated in disaster and post-apocalyptic movies, as well as in the fearful reactions of governments and police forces. In reality, as Rebecca Solnit has explored in a fascinating book, when disasters or major emergencies occur, people actually band together to form transient communities of mutual care and assistance. So, although we, or perhaps those in authority, fear that the veneer of 'civilisation' is all too thin, in truth, as an inherently social animal, our default response when push comes to shove is to support one another, at least while the 'normal' rules are suspended.[2]

The Soviet 1930s were not quite a natural disaster, but it's certainly useful to think of the period as a state of sustained emergency. This is by no means to suggest that a spirit of generalised altruism existed across the population, but networks of mutual assistance – material, practical, emotional – demonstrably existed and continued to shape how contemporaries survived and experienced the decade. Humour, once again, offers us a key to understanding how.

Trust Groups

Humour plays an important role in every society as an icebreaker and social integrator, and although our focus here is on political humour, there's no reason to doubt that other, non-political jokes also continued to function this way in the 1930s, although even this small-talk brand of humour could in these times take on a political edge. It is telling, for instance, that Stepan Podlubnyi would shift in his diary from recording his fears of being unmasked as a kulak's son to immediately describing how he consciously tried to play the joker at work to throw his colleagues off the scent. Telling (non-political) jokes hid his own fears and 'bad' background, but simultaneously made him feel better-integrated with his peers.[3]

That said, sometimes humour remained a solo affair, as when Podlubnyi, Arzhilovskii, and others recorded their sardonic asides and wry commentaries in a diary. But even these jokes are made to an imagined audience – a sympathetic listener or friend intimately familiar with your life and the society in which you live. In other words, diarists might record a joke only for themselves, but it's only funny because they imagine the effects of saying it out loud.

Humour is often said to function as a kind of 'safety-valve' for pent-up tension or stress, allowing us to let off steam when it all gets too much. True enough, but this process is both more interesting and more complex than a simplistic, mechanical venting of excess pressure. Humour and laughter are deeply social. They can 'oil the wheels of our social encounters', level or invert hierarchies, or simply form 'part of the rhythm, the ebb and flow of conversation and communication'.[4] Freud even argued (persuasively, if at doleful length) that the linguistic structures of humour are essentially identical to other storytelling or rhetorical techniques. Joke-telling, in short, is a part of social communication as important and potentially complex as any other.[5]

We laugh more in company, too, which increases our enjoyment of both the jokes and the experience of sharing them (this is also the reason, for better or worse, that TV comedies filmed without a live audience have 'canned laughter' added, to help ease viewers into laughing too). More intriguing still, a series of psychological studies revealed that when test subjects listened through headphones to humorous stories, even if they were unknowingly listening to completely different recordings, they shared just as many laughs, knowing looks and smiles with each other as when they really were hearing the same material.[6] If simply believing that we are treating something as a shared joke can affect our feelings, actions and interactions, what did it mean to share jokes about life under Stalin?

Danger was both part of the attraction and a key ingredient in the social effects of making these jokes, meaning that the question of trust was always inescapably important. So saying, even without the oppressive threat of denunciation and arrest, trust is a crucial part of all human relations, as Katherine Hawley sums up in a handy introduction to the concept:

> Trust is at the centre of a whole web of concepts: reliability, predictability, expectation, cooperation, goodwill, and – on the dark side – distrust, insincerity, conspiracy, betrayal, and incompetence.[7]

A complete lack of trust is intolerable for almost all people and, in the often violently unstable and disruptive context of the Soviet 1930s (which Geoffrey Hosking goes so far as to call a 'land of maximum distrust'),[8] contemporaries had to develop new kinds of trust in order to regain some of that web of reliability, predictability and cooperation which allows life to function both practically and emotionally.

Although some scholars have begun to explore the nature of trust in the Soviet Union, they've focused almost exclusively on questions of if and how people trusted the Party or state (or vice versa), rather than if and how they trusted each other.[9] Mirroring the direction of much sociological literature in the area, these scholars have largely ignored the question of citizen-citizen trust relations, seeming at least implicitly to internalise the idea that this was a country of solitary Winston Smiths forced to trust in Big Brother for lack of any viable alternatives.[10]

What this approach does not examine is the trust that citizens might give freely to one another, or the idea that this trust could be motivated by factors other than immediate necessity, security, or fear. People need trust, but they also need each other. Distant leaders or faceless institutions are never enough.

Intimacy and Experience

At one level, the many jokes we've looked at in the preceding chapters allow us to access the critical voices of many Soviet people, and to better grasp how they understood the world around them. But, beyond those wry asides committed only to the pages of a diary, these were not jokes cracked in isolation, whispered to yourself in the dark. They were always social acts. Which begs the question: whom did contemporaries feel they could trust enough to share a joke with them?

The impression gained by visitors to Soviet cities in the late 1930s, like the British writer Una Pope-Hennessy (and repeated by journalists, political scientists and historians for decades thereafter), was often that this was a society defined by the fear that 'every man is a menace to every other man', and that Soviet citizens 'have not even the closely-knit autonomous family as a refuge', because those old bonds had been 'broken' by the state.[11] Plenty of research in the past few decades suggests that this 'atomisation' thesis significantly overstates things, but this was certainly a period in which, to use Yoram Gorlizki's phrase, the level of 'ambient trust' in society was extremely low.[12]

Counterintuitively, the very risk involved in sharing critical humour and other speech actually contributed to the urge to share it. As Joan Emerson, a sociologist, explains, 'It is in situations where pressures for discussion and prohibitions exist simultaneously that [humorous] negotiations to ignore the prohibitions are most likely to arise'.[13] In Stalin's 1930s, it was the ubiquitous disjunctures between rhetoric and reality which provided a continuous supply of such pressures. But negotiating a way to talk about them was not just to open a safety valve and let off steam. Humour did more than momentarily assuage a sense of powerlessness or despair: in Emerson's words, such humorous exchanges represent 'negotiations [which] constitute private agreements to suspend general guidelines and thus have crucial significance for the stabilizing or subverting of social order'.[14] In other words, humour performed in a social, shared context creates a sense of camaraderie, mutual suffering, or endurance which establishes a bond between people: it's the social glue of everyone being 'in the same boat'.

Humour in society can thus function as both a creator and a stabiliser of social bonds. As we see in gallows humour, as well as the mental salve of restoring a degree of understandability to negative or frightening issues, this is a creative and social process. And that's because, as the philosopher Ted Cohen emphasises, for humour to function at all, a kind of 'intimacy' is required between speaker and audience: they must hold certain knowledge and reference points in common in order for a comic remark to be coherent and hence funny (which is why foreign jokes or others requiring extensive prior knowledge so often fall flat).[15]

Thanks to the regime's attempts to impose general a uniformity in politics, culture and society, there was, ironically enough, an abundance of these shared reference points available, representing a vast storehouse of cultural shorthand ready to be activated in humour across the Soviet Union, from state acronyms to the saturation of the Stalin Cult. Moreover, as Emerson hinted, the process of sharing and laughing at a given joke reinforces this 'intimacy', as those involved agree to stand together (even for a moment) to share a particular point of view and, if the subject is a weighty one, share the burden of it in the process.

Although many people felt compelled to do so in less than secure circumstances – as we can now see in the pages of their criminal files – in which misjudgements were made and trust failed, this obviously doesn't mean that no one had trustworthy friends with whom they could share critical jokes.

A former teacher recalled to her Harvard Project interviewers that sharing *anekdoty* and other sensitive material – personal or political – could only be done safely 'in [a] circle of good and trusted friends'.[16] When asked if people told political jokes, another respondent, a painter, answered, 'Yes, lots of them'. When asked 'to whom?' he went on blithely, 'Oh, I could tell them to those I worked with. I knew them all. It was all a joke'. But he then rapidly moderated his lighthearted tone: even if it was 'all a joke', he emphasised that he would never tell them to 'anybody whom I did not know well, under no circumstances'.[17] More succinctly, another respondent, a student from a working-class family, noted that *anekdoty* came only 'from friends and we passed them along to friends'.[18] Trust was always imperative.

This was true of rumours or gossip, as others attested,[19] just as it was for all other kinds of unorthodox, critical conversations. If you wanted to criticise official news stories or comment on current affairs, a former political instructor noted that, although 'It was dangerous,' he could still do so with his 'best friend. He trusted me and I trusted him, so we could talk like that with each other'.[20] Similarly, an Azerbaijani butcher recalled 'If I knew you well, we can talk, for friends do not betray each other', which was quite a statement coming from a man so worried that 'walls have ears', that he felt compelled to get up mid-interview to close the door after it fell slightly ajar.[21]

Contrary to what Una Pope-Hennessy reported from her visit to the Soviet Union, perhaps the most secure trust group of all was the family. As a former Soviet accountant who had worked in Western Siberia recalled,

> In a family you will talk about anything, even about kidding Stalin [*sic*], anecdotes, songs and jokes, and if these means of expression and release did not exist in the family it would be indeed very hard for the population.[22]

An economic planner and sometime schoolteacher expressed a similar view:

> I think a typical example would have been [...] [t]he family which in spite of all the influence from the regime has kept its inner friendship, closeness and warmth, a family, the members of which confided [in] and trusted each other.[23]

For another respondent, a worker who spent most of the 1930s in various jobs in Siberia, the family was the *only* trust group in which he considered it safe enough to exchange jokes; they called any jokes they heard elsewhere 'indiscreet *anekdoty*'.[24] A Ukrainian engineer, echoed this sentiment: 'We told political jokes only in our family. With other people we only listened'.[25] Another respondent, a Russian white-collar worker previously based in Azerbaijan, noted the benefits of this familial security, both financial and, via humorous exchanges, personal:

> [We] united for financial reasons and spiritual comfort. We all had fun together, telling jokes and anecdotes against the regime... joke telling got to be quite a pastime.[26]

Even respondents who, as did a former medical student and then sanitation specialist from Azerbaijan, claimed that in general Soviet 'family members had no trust in each other', might nevertheless insist that they could speak openly and critically with their own family: 'Yes, [I could speak openly] with my mother and my family only. But with others, no, because I could not trust them'.[27]

He was not alone in this contradictory view, in which your own family was always the exception,[28] and this itself illustrates how widespread social distrust could actually exist side-by-side with strong trust relations made at the individual and small group level. The latter, after all, are easily taken for granted; incursions by the state and the difficulties of everyday life easily consume our attention rather than the reassurance of family and friends. This would be like expecting people to dwell on the glasses they wear rather than on the intrusive and intimidating reality they can see through them. The lenses – our social relations – continue to shape how we perceive, but we easily forget them until the moments when they are taken away or damaged.

If for many Soviet citizens friends and family constituted their principal trust groups, this was in many (likely most) cases due to the natural feelings of love and loyalty for your own family. But people do not grow up and become socialised in their family alone. People grow up in wider communities which can also produce powerful bonds formed from shared experiences and deep knowledge of each other's lives and origins. The historiography has often emphasised that the fear of revealing your background, if it was less than perfectly proletarian, meant that Soviet citizens frequently isolated themselves from each other through conscious acts of 'imposture', massaging their autobiographies to suit regime values. But although there are many examples of this practice (Stepan Podlubnyi concealing his kulak background being just one), this clearly doesn't hold true for families and friends who had known each other their whole lives and therefore knew all about each other's 'bad' backgrounds. More importantly, rather than leading to fear and betrayal, that knowledge seems, on the contrary, more often to have brought people closer together and to have fostered bonds of trust based on the security of knowing who each other really was and where they came from.[29]

One Harvard Project respondent, a young Ukrainian man who had begun to study medicine in the 1930s, highlighted how shared backgrounds and generations-long friendship between some families could sustain trust bonds, especially if those families felt detached from mainstream society due to, as he put it, their 'old middle intelligentsia' roots. As he explained, 'We often told anecdotes to each other and there never was one of us arrested, nobody betrayed anybody'.[30] In cases like these, preexisting bonds clearly weren't nullified by the Revolution.

A teacher (a chemist by training) elaborates this point for us, emphasising that the basis for friendships had to include the certainty that one would not denounce the other, before focusing specifically on long-standing cross-family relations as her primary example:

> How many children were children of friends of the family, and these friends of the family actually went back to the grandparents. Their parents were friends of my parents and grandparents and, in some cases, were friends of my grandparents before the Revolution. For us, nationality and social position were not important, although they were important for some people. It was only that we had to be sure we wouldn't be denounced. The majority of my friends were mainly Christians.[31]

The reference to religious belief is another hint at the way shared circumstances and outlooks continued to naturally bring people together, even if its position as an afterthought here suggests that it wasn't a core or necessary reason for this woman's friendships.

Describing her friends, a young woman from an intelligentsia family who was a teenager during the 1930s emphasised that they all had 'similar experiences from earlier times; therefore we couldn't join the Communist Party. We had similar home backgrounds, similar points of view. We went to church… My friends were those of a similar family background and home education'.[32] Their shared backgrounds, in their own view, both excluded them from Party membership, but also clearly bonded them together. Religion is again an element in this, although it is only one piece of the broader mosaic of their shared upbringing.

A young man who would graduate from a Moscow military institute of foreign languages in 1948 made this still more explicit and, despite his comments falling a little beyond our temporal focus, they bear repeating. He recalled that he and three friends (another Russian, a Ukrainian, and a Jew) were a tight-knit group within which they could speak freely and critically, explaining that, 'we were all young and we came from intellectual families. This was our common element and we had common aspirations.'[33]

Although the Harvard Project respondents who reflected in most detail on these bonds seem to have been drawn from an educated, urban milieu, it would be misleading to infer that the same principles wouldn't apply to people from rural or less educated backgrounds. Much has been written about the persistence and importance of family, village and regional ties after mass migrations to the towns in the 1920s-30s. Like immigrants moving en masse to another country, they often lived together and continued to provide an underlying network of support and mutual assistance.[34]

A Belorussian woman, who'd been a literature and language student at a pedagogical institute before the war, made a similar point about family ties, noting that, 'Well, usually if the parents were friends, their children would become friends, too.' But she went on to broaden the list of possible foundations for trusting friendships to include hobbies and shared interests:

> [I]f a few people liked the same things, they would become friends. For example, I made friends with many people who liked to ski. Of course, when we did get together, we didn't always go skiing but we would talk as well.

Such friendships, formed outwith official, regime-sanctioned institutions like the Komsomol, were 'frowned on by the regime', as the respondent herself noted, 'but we did it just the same'.[35]

All these testimonies suggest that while the stakes were higher in the context of Stalin's 1930s, the foundations underlying trusting interpersonal relationships – shared backgrounds, interests, and experiences – were often distinctly unexceptional, even banal. Even though the uniformity of life in the Soviet Union created its own catalogue of shared reference points which could be drawn upon (in humour and otherwise) to forge or sustain an 'intimacy' between citizens, these were frequently crosshatched with preexisting or distinctly non-Soviet elements the like of which we'd expect to find in just about any society.

And yet, the picture we've held for so long of life in the early Soviet Union has consistently denied that it *could* be like that of any other society. This belief has often shaped what we've been able to see: instead of a sprawling web of sometimes intersecting trust groups, we've tended in effect to look at each one as an exception – an islet stranded in a sea of distrust. On the other hand, this belief shaped how many Soviet citizens saw their society, too: even as Harvard Project interviewees recounted their own strong, trusting relationships with friends and family members, the very same people could claim that such bonds were impossible for the rest of society.[36] They, too, considered themselves the exception that proved the rule, rather than symptoms of a broader condition.

To understand this better, we can find an illuminating parallel in the way people commonly respond to natural disasters and states of emergency (and it requires little stretch of the imagination to think of the 1930s as a period of sustained emergency, with its brutal repressive measures and impossible economic demands). As Rebecca Solnit argues, in extreme conditions, cynical received wisdom about society or human nature often persists even when it's repeatedly contradicted by personal experience:

> The image of the selfish, panicky, or regressively savage human being in times of disaster has little truth to it. Decades of meticulous sociological research on behavior in disasters, from the bombings of World War II to floods, tornadoes, earthquakes, and storms across the continent and around the world, have demonstrated this. But belief lags behind…[37]

Just as the idea persists that disasters and emergencies provoke disorder and savagery despite all evidence to the contrary, similar fears of self-interest and denunciation endured in the minds of many during the early Soviet period, even as they themselves acted and interacted with others in ways which entirely contradicted these bleak prognoses.[38] Even if a careful discernment was required in deciding whom to trust, and even if many people continued to think of themselves and their friends as existing in states of exception, society was not shattered.

If theories of total social atomisation have largely been superseded, when historians and sociologists have described informal and unofficial social structures in the 1930s (such as *blat*, patronage, or the black market) they've predominantly focused on how these provided material or status benefits. These are similar to and often intersect with trust group relations, in that they all necessarily required a degree of trust between those involved, but we shouldn't forget that these citizen-citizen connections could be based upon and provide less tangible or utilitarian incentives.

To take the example of *blat*, while individuals might trade reciprocal favours or exchange material goods to which the respective parties had privileged access, this didn't have to be a relationship defined solely by economic benefit. Many *blat* relations can essentially be summed up as getting things 'through a friend of a friend', which should tip us off to the fact that *blat* often began between *friends*, a relationship far more likely to be founded on factors like shared interests, backgrounds, or experiences, just as it would in any society.

As the chemist-turned-teacher quoted above noted, in addition to judging someone trustworthy, meaningful bonds between people also depended on whether 'we could get along with each other; whether they were pleasant companions'.[39] We shouldn't forget, in other words, that people could and did join together for essentially non-economic reasons, to serve the basic human need to share their experiences, passions and problems with others, rather than only if it served their immediate, material needs. Friendship could bring such material benefits, but that did not mean they were the sole or principal reason for it. As Solnit notes, even in the most desperate times, 'We need ties' with others for prosaic and material reasons, yet 'along with purposefulness, immediacy, and agency [they] also give us joy'.[40]

These reasons for friendship, or reasons at least for mutual trust, were also perfectly reasonable prompts for people not to inform on one another for telling political jokes or expressing unorthodox views. The reason for the existence of trust groups did not have to be mutual protection from the oppressive state, even if they could and did provide that. People naturally seek affinities and bonds with each other which, contrary to the Soviet regime's single-minded paranoia, could revolve around entirely apolitical subjects and activities. So although the regime might see a conspiracy in the existence of any and all unofficial social groups, when such a group was called the 'Association of Girls, Vodka, and Snacks', for example, it seems pretty safe to assume that its members had something other than political subterfuge on their minds,[41] just like the friends who enjoyed skiing, or countless others who got together simply to shoot the breeze and relax in good company.

Trust in Jokes

Regardless of the foundations of trust, political humour became a key reference point for contemporaries: when asked about trust in general, numerous Harvard Project respondents turned immediately, unprompted, to *anekdoty* as their litmus test for whether trust existed between particular people. A young woman who'd been a student at a workers' university (*rabfak*) in the later 1930s recalled that, 'I always had feelings of trusting people,' before citing the example that in her student dormitory, 'An anecdote would not [leave] the room'.[42] A Ukrainian woman of expansive opinions, who was a music teacher and sometime seamstress, said much the same, recalling that, 'All our friends lived on the same level, half-naked, half-starved; we thought that opposition to the Soviet power brought us together. We told each other anecdotes'.[43] Drawing the same connection, but working from jokes to trust, a young man who grew up in northern Kazakhstan, who was a schoolchild and shepherd until war broke out, recounted a couple of *anekdoty* to his interviewer before moving directly to recall that he had 'two buddies. We were very open between each other. We knew each other very well; we told each other things we told no one else about our personal life and even as regards politics. I was never as open with my brothers as with them'.[44]

As this last comment suggests, both personal and political intimacy were subjective and highly variable; not every family was a bastion of trust, and nor were shared experiences or circumstances guaranteed to foster trust between everyone involved. Growing up or going to school with someone does not automatically mean you become friends, and just because you can trust someone in the sense of being able to predict how they'll act in a given situation, this doesn't mean that you would or should entrust them with your secrets. Indeed, despite the importance of shared backgrounds or family connections, the preceding chapters plainly show us that many people attempted to forge bonds outside of these structures, too. As a Harvard Project respondent, a former economic planner and now priest, noted:

> Such cases where people were afraid to talk in the family were very rare, because even outside of the family people did talk openly, maybe not as openly, but they did.[45]

If the often more overtly antisoviet Harvard Project respondents were capable of establishing extra-familial trust groups without being arrested, the rest of the population undoubtedly could too. The question, though, is how?

The Joking Mafia: Forging New Trust Groups

Humour was not necessary for trust groups to exist, but it's a particularly useful indicator of them, both for us, looking back through time, and for contemporaries who could make judgements of trust based upon it. This connection went much deeper, however: humour could often be a vital factor in the *creation* of trust groups. But how could you discover if someone else was sympathetic to your critical views? Even if you shared common routines or interests, a process of signalling and discovery was required for trust to grow.

This was where humour came into its own. As a former army officer of peasant background put it, 'the only way you could notice' if other people shared your doubts in the Soviet system, 'was through anecdotes and through jokes'.[46] In part, this was because humour carries with it a potential escape clause: if you use a joke to test another person's willingness to accept or engage with an unorthodox or critical view, then, if they don't react positively, you can deny that the proposition was at all serious ('It was just a joke!').

As the chill winds of repression blew across the Soviet Union in the later 1930s, this get-out clause would be of no use if it came up against the stony faces of the NKVD, as we saw in Chapter 4. Therefore, and with increasing importance as the decade continued, sharing humour outside pre-existing trust groups was a delicate operation – it was a process of *intimating trust*.

As such, each and every joke we've seen so far represented a decision by the speaker to trust their audience. Each sought a bond of intimacy partly assumed (or hoped) to already exist, and partly enhanced and developed by the agreement to participate in the joke – to recognise some 'common ground'.

The risk, or even just the guilty sense of it, involved in sharing critical humour means that we can usefully think of joke-telling as an exchange of trust tokens. A joke was offered as a token of potential trust; laughter was the complementary token, the exchange of which marked the creation or buttressing of intimacy between the people involved. This could work because simply communicating our trust can make other people more trustworthy;[47] there is a moral compliment involved in signalling that you trust another person, which is often received with pleasure, as well as a sense of responsibility not to disprove the positive character assessment. There are certainly limits to this general rule and the betrayal of trust was, as we know, far from uncommon in the Soviet 1930s.

Diego Gambetta's work on how organised criminals – Italian *mafiosi* – communicate is particularly useful in understanding how and why these risky social interactions worked and could result in genuine trust. Although we might not consider joke-telling the mark of a criminal, the Soviet regime certainly did, and it thereby placed contemporaries in a remarkably similar position. As Gambetta notes, 'Criminals face severe constraints on communication imposed by the action of the law,'[48] and so they're forced to develop both covert methods of communication and ways of identifying (and thereafter cultivating) trust bonds between one another that are not only left unprotected by civil institutions, but would actually be punished by them if revealed. Just like *mafiosi*, Soviet people could use official words and acronyms like a double-bottomed suitcase, carrying hidden, subversive meanings recognisable only to those in-the-know (see Chapter 3).

To establish trust in these circumstances, Gambetta explains, 'There are instances when there is an advantage to opening up one's closet for others to see the skeletons….'.[49] Sharing dangerous information which could be used against us is socially potent *because* it is incriminating: volunteering compromising material ('*kompromat*', in Soviet terms) about yourself is not only a demonstration of trust in your audience, but also functions as a signal that we ourselves are trustworthy. As Gambetta deftly sums it up, 'by giving our secrets away we show at once that we trust [the other person] not to misuse the information and that we are not planning to betray them. Otherwise we would not give them ammunition to retaliate'.[50] To share a political joke with someone other than a close confidante in Stalin's 1930s was – ironically – to make a serious statement: I trust you, and the proof is that I'm trusting you not to denounce me for telling this *anekdot*.

This was, Gambetta emphasises, 'an *exchange* of compromising information: all participants are worried about each other's loyalty, and they all disclose compromising information about themselves to one another'.[51] In this way, a 'bilateral' trust bond was established and could, over time, be solidified through further exchanges, the reciprocity binding the joke-tellers together, not only through the experience of sharing perspectives, but because the material being exchanged was dangerous to both.[52]

This is something Emerson notes of critical humour more generally, too, rather than it being something confined to the underworld of mafia communications. As she notes – specifically in the context of humour – not only does the opening of discussions about prohibited subjects 'establish a presumption of trust' between those involved, but this trust has significant, shared consequences, for 'Not only can they trust each other in routine matters, but they share complicity for rule violations which potentially can be extended'.[53] To mix our metaphors a little, the comforting feeling of being in the same boat when sharing difficult circumstances could also mean committing yourself to going down with the ship.

All the same, if this was *why* sharing political jokes could create new trust groups, it still had to be a delicate process. Simply bursting out with a joke about Stalin's sexual proclivities or the absurdities of the Five-Year Plan would be deeply unwise. People who did so were too reckless to seem trustworthy, and an overeagerness to exchange *anekdoty* could raise suspicions that you were an agent provocateur.[54] Instead, the exchange of smaller trust tokens could begin in a shared glance, a raised eyebrow,[55] or, as numerous Harvard Project respondents described, in pointed silences laden with critical subtext.[56]

Intonation could also direct attention towards secondary meanings or connotations without the speaker seeming to say anything controversial. For example, when war broke out, the phrase 'Victory will be ours!' (Победа будет за нами) became a commonplace on the radio, but a shift in emphasis could convey a very different meaning. An old woman on a kolkhoz reportedly mimicked the slogan so that it sounded like 'Victory will be behind us!' (i.e. will be impossible).[57] Instances like these were far less likely to be detected and punished by the regime; in a written transcript they would appear largely if not completely innocuous. These were signals which, like acts of silent subversion (see Chapter 1), could take place and be shared yet not be explicitly referred to by those present.

A former language student recounted a story from his time in the army during the war:

> [W]hen two pilots, Pirogov and Barsov, deserted [a] major came in[to the room] and announced loudly [...] that two Soviet pilots had deserted and he did it with a wicked smile and of course everybody understood [his sentiments on the matter].

When asked if officers were not afraid of doing such things, the respondent added that, 'This depends on how it was done. If he had added a comment – for example, "these are good guys" – this of course would have been dangerous, but if you announce simply a fact, even if it is done with a laugh, nothing was done against it'.[58]

Although a slightly greater degree of leniency may have been possible in the army during these years, this was not an isolated behaviour. Another respondent, at the time (1937) a student at a technical institute, described engaging in a similar method of communication with four fellow students who sat together in a room and talked about Soviet economic policies, but each 'contributed only facts to the discussion and no one drew conclusions. But to everyone it was clear what was meant'.[59] Simply by choosing what to highlight (corruption, difficulties, failures), larger conclusions could be evoked but left unspoken.

After testing the waters in this way, contemporaries could decide to take the plunge and offer a less ambiguous, more dangerous piece of *kompromat* – they could tell a political joke and truly open up their closet to reveal the skeleton of critical thinking. This was always to take a risk, but taking that risk was precisely what made trust possible.

Sites of Sociability: Beyond Public and Private

'We never spoke Soviet at home', a young woman who worked as a field nurse during the war told her Harvard Project interviewers; 'We spoke pure Russian'.[60] 'Pure Russian', in context, essentially meant 'we spoke "ordinary"', rather than the ideologically-charged language of the regime, but what did the respondent mean when she said 'at home'? We know from Chapter 4 where it proved most dangerous for contemporaries to share critical humour, so where was it possible to do so with some degree of safety?

By the Brezhnev period, this was much clearer – the term 'kitchen conversations' (кухонные разговоры) had become a general euphemism for critical and even dissident exchanges. Thanks in large part to increased housing provisions and the far less draconian punishments for sharing critical speech, the late-Soviet kitchen of the so-called *khrushchoby* (the name was itself a joke, playing on the word for the identikit Khrushchev-era apartment blocks ('*khrushchevki*') and the word '*trushchoby*', meaning 'slums') became the focal point of private, unorthodox life.[61] But this was impossible in the 1930s, thanks to chronic and general overcrowding in the towns. Even at the end of the decade, only 25 percent of workers (theoretically the most privileged class) had non-communal apartments.[62] It would take a good deal of imagination and not a little delusion to consider such environments 'private'.[63]

But, like most dichotomies, 'public' and 'private' are more convincing on the page than in real life. Katerina Gerasimova has already dispensed with the binary and suggests that 'home' spaces in the Soviet Union are best characterised as a state of 'public privacy', emphasising that all personal elements of people's lives were lived out and understood as being under the gaze of other citizens.[64] All the same, while this formulation is rich in interpretational possibilities, it hardly describes a situation in which political jokes could be safely exchanged. Perhaps, given the nature of these communal and crowded living conditions, we're simply asking the wrong question, or, rather, the 'where' in 'where was it safe to share *anekdoty*?' needs to be understood differently.

In the 1930s Soviet Union, as we noted in Chapter 4, space

or location were not the determining factors in how contemporaries interacted with each other. A given location came to be defined by the people in it more than by some fundamental characteristics of its own, whether real or imagined. The social meaning of particular locations was shaped and maintained by Soviet citizens themselves. There is a difference, in other words, between a physical space and the social interactions and attendant levels of trust which can occur within it. Or, as Leif Jerram puts it,

> We talk of gay space, male space, sacred space, and so on; but a space cannot possess the quality of being gay, male, or sacred. A sports hall that is used for Pentecostal meetings on a Sunday afternoon may shift from being a 'male space' to a 'sacred space'....[65]

In the same way, trust groups created distinct social contexts within a given space which existed in the perceptions of the individuals present. Thicker walls and a closed door could certainly make a difference to whether people would, in the 1930s, risk engaging in critical speech, but the decisive factor was the *who*, not the *where* (if the walls were thin, one could always whisper, after all).

A workplace trust group was described by a former economic planner, who recalled that '[relations between office co-workers] were very good, very good indeed,' adding that 'We talked quite freely, told jokes, and not once was there any denunciation'. The familiarity and sense of camaraderie engendered by working together every day could forge significant bonds of trust within a workplace, but although this was a possibility, it could never be a rule. As the respondent explained, this trust group did not include the director: whenever he appeared, the group 'never talked of anything else but our work. There were no smiles and no jokes with him....'[66]

Consistent proximity was not in itself enough to create a trust group, then; the director was not included despite also being a regular presence. And we should note that his rank by no means automatically excluded him: Wendy Goldman's recent monograph and John Scott's Magnitogorsk diary both clearly show that relations between ordinary workers, white- or blue-collared, and their managers varied enormously.[67] Instead, these were judgements of trust made on individual, personal bases, even if Party membership or other positions of authority could stack the odds heavily against a person being deemed trustworthy where critical, open speech was concerned.

Although family and close friends emerge as the most secure trust groups in these years, it's telling that Harvard Project respondents always described them in terms of the individuals involved and their feelings towards them; location was scarcely mentioned, and it was never their focus. Crammed into tiny living spaces, the physical 'home' was largely irrelevant in determining the degree of openness possible. Even when families had a room to themselves (which was far from guaranteed), the walls were, as we noted, usually very thin, being either artificial divisions of prerevolutionary dwellings, or cheaply-made new housing blocks. Conversations in these conditions, except in the lowest tones, were never private.[68] While this obviously doesn't deny the possibility of the 'home' space – the apartment, room, or corner of a room – genuinely being the location where open, personal, and critical discussions took place, the more important element remained the trust possible between not only the family unit, but their immediate neighbours, too.

And although some made mistakes – whether in the moment, or because the regime would redraw the boundaries of acceptability later on – contemporaries were not insensitive to this. We know from the criminal prosecutions for jokes told on the job that the workplace was not in itself somewhere trust groups could expect to retain the security of their borders, yet for these failures to have occurred, a great many people must have believed at the time they spoke that it was safe to do so.

The workplace setting could certainly carry additional risk of being overheard due to the sheer number of other, potentially unknown or insufficiently known people within it. Yet, even if a particular shop, office or table had been the site of a previous betrayal or denunciation, it could still become a place of greater trust, *depending on who was present at a given moment*. Contemporaries were not all thoughtless or insensitive to the proprieties of critical exchange during these years; when they spoke this way in the workplace, it was because it did not seem a completely unreasonable thing to do. The misjudgement that some *did* make was to ignore the fact that social contexts were not anchored to a given location: they could and did change; they could and did move.

When people didn't keep this in mind and focused instead on a physical location, things could rapidly go wrong. At a water plant in the town of Verkhneural'sk, Cheliabinskaia oblast', one G.F. Kaftaikin, an accountant, and a number of his fellow administrators got into the habit of exchanging jokes and humorous comments in an office. Kaftaikin even drew a swastika on the wall at one point. If he and his fellow joke-tellers thought the office represented a safe space – safe enough even to leave a physical mark inside bearing witness to their 'antisoviet' behaviour – they were sorely mistaken. The criminal case-file refers to various 'witnesses' to these acts who were, we can assume, colleagues present in the office during these activities, who then testified against these jokesters.[69] Similarly, we should recall the cases of Bublikov and Guzynin from Chapter 4: the former returned to a naval base after serving abroad, and the latter transferred to a new Komsomol unit. Both immediately began telling jokes to their peers, assuming that because they'd done so either in the same or in an analogous location before, that they were safe to do so now. Instead, they were both arrested; the audience and the social context had changed, even if the nature of the location had not.

Location could certainly entail an important gradient in the level of intimacy possible, but it never had the final word in defining these principally human interactions. The decisive factor was always the individuals who were present. However thin they may be, walls do not have ears; only the people behind them do.

We Joke, Therefore We Are

Who did these trust groups think they were? Because trust groups are relational constructs, they didn't exist in isolation from wider society, like free-floating bubbles insulated from the world around them. On the contrary, members of each group were bonded to a significant degree by the sense of their own identities as distinguished from other parts of society. And while political jokes could operate as a social signal to establish and thereafter maintain unofficial bonds, they were simultaneously conveying an opinion or a fragment of an unorthodox worldview. It was always more than a case of merely handing over some *kompromat*; it was also to share a common standpoint and point of view.

As several scholars of Russian folk humour have put it, when sharing a joke 'the laughers are in a sense "conspirators", seeing and understanding something which they had not seen before, and which others cannot see'.[70] The conspiratorial intimacy of sharing jokes fostered not only trust, but also bound people together; they were simultaneously agreeing to suspend whatever differences they might otherwise feel between each another, consenting to position themselves at a shared standpoint – an 'us', usually placed in opposition to some kind of 'them'. And, therefore, when we study the content of what they said, we're not looking at straightforward interpretations of, or statements about, the nature of Soviet society: instead, these were active, performative processes of identity affirmation.

'Us' and 'Them'

Many of the *anekdoty* from these years paint a picture of a society grounded in the distinction between the joke-tellers – who portrayed themselves as members of an underprivileged majority – and various minority groups cast as the regime's favourites. This could be as simple as mocking the leaders for being fatties, as we saw in Kirov's Carnival, but it could also paint a more nuanced picture. These jokes mocked, berated and generally sent up the chosen ones, but in defining 'them' – the privileged – ordinary citizens simultaneously defined themselves. They claimed the power of the storyteller to reveal a less than flattering image of the regime's favourites, and thereby asserted what they, the majority, were *not*.

Much as we saw in the jokes which used a kind of common-sense superiority to mock the Soviet leadership (Chapter 1), rank-and-file Party members were also pilloried for their (alleged) stupidity and/or blind conformity. The craftsman M. Chernyshev told such a joke in Khabarovsk, in the presence, it transpired, of an NKVD operative:

> A man was walking along a street in Moscow when his hat fell off onto the road. A passerby told the man, 'you've dropped your "head" [голова]', to which the man answered, 'I work in Sovnarkom, and in Sovnarkom you can do without a head'.[71]

A similar joke, shared by a member of the swastika-daubing group mentioned earlier, takes the point even further:

> A Communist underwent an operation during which his brain was removed; they said he didn't need it [anymore], because he had a Party card instead.[72]

Throughout the 1930s, jokes like these portrayed Party functionaries as idiotic, ignorant, and incompetent. Contemporaries were thereby affirming that they themselves were *not* slavishly or unthinkingly obedient, and that they were not unhelpful or unfeeling bureaucrats. They were also clearly more intelligent: these scything jokes demonstrated the kind of common sense and critical thinking which Party members readily did without, or which they even had removed as they rose up the ranks of power and privilege.

Komsomol members, like young activists everywhere, were also resented by many contemporaries for their agitational work and goody-two-shoes attitude.[73] As an economic planner in the Ukrainian

Commissariat for local industry recalled, 'the older workers who disliked the [*Komsomoltsy*] and who were not in the party themselves... [always referred] to them as those *komsoi*'. This, she explained, was 'a reference to a [nasty little] fish which ruins your stomach' – a fish, fittingly enough, which people had not had to eat until the scarcity of the Soviet period.[74] Likewise returning to Bakhtin's 'lower' bodily world, a group of overachieving students in Frunzenskii raion, Leningrad, who'd had their pictures printed in the newspaper *Krasnaia gazeta* on 2 June 1937, each received an anonymous letter of 'counterrevolutionary content', along with a selection of pornographic postcards![75] These children of the Revolution were, in the eyes of most, irritating fools who needed to be taken down a peg.

Other regime favourites were treated somewhat differently, though no less abusively. The boiling sense of frustration and resentment at the singling-out and celebrating of a few – and therefore atypical – individuals was particularly evident in the way Stakhanovites were treated in humour. These heroes of labour were made objects of derision by citizens resentful of the often huge monetary rewards and privileges which the state bestowed on them.[76] Like the regime leaders, they too might have their portraits unceremoniously torn from the walls of the workplace,[77] or Stakhanovite youths might be set upon during a Revolution Day gathering by other, non-Stakhanovite youngsters.[78] But this scorn also appeared in creatively bitchy comments, such as blaming any defective work on 'the Stakhanovites',[79] or, as in 'several factories' across Leningrad, when ordinary workers took to using the word 'Stakhanovite' as a vulgarity[80] – a simple but very effective way to devalue the label and to place themselves, the joke-tellers, in a superior position by contrast. Another approach was to slightly alter the word 'Stakhanovites' (*Stakhanovtsy*) to 'Drinkerites' (*Stakanovski/Stakanovki*), emphasising the life of hedonistic indulgence which leading Stakhanovites were seen to enjoy.[81]

We shouldn't interpret people's use of Bolshevik or Soviet terms to discredit officials or regime favourites as a sign that they were becoming trapped in (and therefore somewhat subjugated by) official discourse or values, however. People of colour who reclaim the word 'nigger', or homosexuals who take up the word 'gay' are not somehow 'speaking White' or 'speaking straight', respectively. They are actively changing the meaning and effects of the word. It may not overturn the system or its overall inequalities; arguably, it recognises those very inequalities and prejudices, yet at the same time these acts still redefine particular 'us' and 'them' relationships and, when shared in a trust group, can serve to create elements of a 'shadow language' like those we discussed in Chapter 3 – a covert shorthand with ulterior meanings and quietly subversive subtexts which stalked the official ones.

Redefining elements of official language in this way also knitted trust groups more tightly together, forming elements of a shared, confidential 'idioculture' – something Gary Alan Fine describes as 'a system of knowledge, beliefs, and customs which are particular to a group to which members can refer and employ as the basis of further interaction'.[82] Within these exchanges, trust group members were subtly building systems of knowledge – another kind of *know-how* – which ran counter to the official one, and sharing in this conspiratorial intimacy of in-jokes and allusions fostered social bonds and a shared sense of identity ('We joke, therefore we are').

In any case, where resentments against Stakhanovites flared up, as they did in Leningrad's Krasnogvardeets Factory in 1935, it was clearly driven by jealousy of privilege, but also by the suspicion that membership of the Stakhanovite 'club' really came down to personal favours (something also hinted at by the 'Drinkerites' label, which evokes the image of a drinking society made up of these mini-elites). When two workers, Stepanova and Pozdniakova, were awarded Stakhanovite status at the factory, rumours quickly circulated that these two 'Drinkerites' had been promoted only because they lived with two machine-tool installers apparently in a position to arrange the accolade. The grumbling increased before, at official meetings, it spilled out into open accusations of nepotism. Finding no support from the Party Committee, all four of the accused resigned.[83]

The arbitrariness of such appointments was emphasised in a joke circulating as early as 1928, which described Stalin as the USSR's 'leading chemist', because, to paraphrase, he alone could make officials out of shit and then back again whenever he pleased.[84] This *anekdot* clearly rang true across the years, for we see it appearing again after the war, now focused on Stalin conjuring and destroying generals, who represented the latest wave of rapid risers.[85] Shitts also recorded a rather sharp joke about upwardly mobile individuals (called the *vydvizhentsy*), in which a *muzhik* (a peasant, or 'good fellow') harnesses a donkey to a carriage, causing some consternation among onlookers. He hushes them, saying 'just wait a bit – he's a *vydvizhenets*. In a couple of weeks he'll be a horse'.[86] Clearly, for those who shared and enjoyed this joke, the rising stars in Soviet society were little more than laughable frauds.

We find similarly creative disdain aimed at the 'heroes of the *Cheliuskin*'. The *Cheliuskin* was a steamship which, in an attempt to navigate the Northern Sea Route without an icebreaker, was caught in an ice floe and sank in February 1934. The crew escaped onto the ice and, from a makeshift camp, used shovels to build and rebuild an airstrip. The pilots who eventually rescued them were awarded the newly-minted title of Hero of the Soviet Union and were widely and loudly fêted. But while the craze for pilots, Arctic exploration and heroic rescues undeniably caught the imaginations of many Soviet citizens, another widespread response was mockery and derision, as we find captured in the lines of a song recorded time and time again in late 1934 and early 1935.[87]

Здравствуй Ляпидевский	Hey there, Liapidevskii,
Летчик Леваневский	And pilot Levanevskii,
Здравствуй лагерь Шмидта и прощай	Hey there Camp Schmidt, and farewell
Вы зашухерили ледокол Челюскин	You ratted out icebreaker *Cheliuskin*
А теперь червонцы огребай.	But now you're raking in the gold.
Если-бы не Мишка, Мишка Водопьянов	If it weren't for Misha, Misha Vodop'ianov
Не видать-бы больше Вас Москва.	Moscow would see you no more.
Плавали-б на льдине	You'd float on the ice floe
Как в своей малине	Like in your den [of thieves]
Стал-бы по медвежьи завывать.	You'd begin to howl like a bear.
Вы теперь герой, как пчелы в рое	Now you're heroes, like bees in a swarm
Зажужжали по родной стране.	Buzzing in your native country.
Деньги поделили	The money's divvied up,
В Крым Вы укатили	You roll off to Crimea
А Челюскин плавает на дне.	But *Cheliuskin* floats at the bottom.
Вам теперь нескучно	You're having a great time now,
Весело живется, песня, вечеринка	Life is joyous: songs, parties
И гульба.	And revelry.
Денежки в кармане	Money in your pocket,
Рожа на экране	Your mug on the screen,
Вот, что экспедиция дала.	That's what the expedition brought.

Rather like the jokes about Stakhanovites, the song gives particular attention to the arbitrariness of success and failure in the Soviet Union: although the *Cheliuskin* was lost, the mission was reimagined as a sparkling, heroic success. The pilots and survivors became 'heroes', but the song makes it plain that this is empty celebrity: 'Money in your pocket / Your mug on the screen' was all the expedition truly achieved.

More tellingly, the song is actually a loose parody of a ditty called 'Murka', which recounts the tale of a thief's bride sentenced to death for betraying the thieves' code of honour.[88] Associating these heroic pilots with the criminal milieu of Murka pointedly linked their achievements with theft and subterfuge, and, as with the Stakhanovites, thereby delegitimised them and their rewards, as well as implicitly elevating the ordinary, honest citizen above them.

Other contemporary *anekdoty* describe a more complex and nuanced breakdown of how ordinary people saw society and their place within it. Take, for example, an *anekdot* relating specifically to the end of rationing in 1935:

> There are four categories [of people]: (1) *Torgsiane* (2) *Krasnozvezdiane* (3) *Zaerkane* (4) *Koe-kane* [roughly: the Torgsiners, the Red Stars, the Closed Workers' Cooperative people, the Somehow-or-Others].[89]

Clearly, the majority of citizens are identified as separate from the listed organisations (all of which gave their members variously privileged levels of access to food, housing and consumer goods). Everyone else is not only lumped into one general category, but a category which is defined by the struggle to get by and make ends meet.

The railway attendant I.G. Orobinskii told a joke which made this even clearer:

> Power to the Soviets, stars to the cadets, money to the Bolsheviks, and a fuck you to the rest.[90]

In both jokes, the majority's social identity is defined by a *lack* of privileges, and everyone sharing in the joke could feel a grim sense of camaraderie in their mutual suffering. In this second example it's hammered home by the profanity; by the suggestion that the majority receive absolutely nothing; and by the specific references not just to goods, but to power, honours and money. These distinctions closely mirror what the economic historian Elena Osokina has since named 'hierarchies of distribution' or 'hierarchies of poverty' (бедности). These are key themes in her view of prewar Soviet society but, clearly, when contemporaries identified and described those hierarchies, they did so with rather more colourful language and emotional investment.[91]

They also used wordplay, as a note posted to the local Dolinskii Party committee in Ukraine shows:

They've built all these co-ops and claim it's freedom, but I don't think it's much of a commune if some can 'come-on-in', but for others it 'commune-*isn't*'.[92]

Dispensing with subcategories amongst the privileged minority, this withering note derides the very principle of communist egalitarianism and inclusiveness. In fact, it distills what all these jokes are, in essence, about: 'haves' and 'have nots' – those who can 'come-on-in' and join the party (pun intended), and those who cannot.

If official labels like 'Stakhanovite' could be reappropriated and inverted to become vulgarities, here we see contemporaries going much further: they were also creating their own classifications of Soviet society at the grassroots level. They could identify, structure and then share their perceptions of the society in which they lived without simply inverting or mirroring official propaganda and values. Even if inflected by the latter, they were also simply but creatively describing their world as they saw it. Moreover, by sharing these interpretations through the social medium of humour, these interpretations could gain increasing weight and reality through repetition.

All this evidence of a broad co-identification between ordinary citizens appears to support Sarah Davies's view that in everyday discourse we find a strong sense of 'us', the poor or '*nizy*', set against 'them', the powerful or privileged '*verkhi*'. Davies's sources present much the same resentments we find in humour, including the 'moral superiority of the toiler', compared to those in power, as well as the 'negative quality' of these acts of self-identification, because they were primarily '*against* more than identification *with*' particular groups.[93]

On the other hand, Harvard Project respondents highlight a more positive kind of self-identification, defined by the word '*svoi*', meaning 'one's own'. As one respondent put it, 'Among the workers there were *svoi liudi* ['our people'] – non-party members, *lishentsy* [people deprived of civil rights]…'; or, as another respondent recounted, 'for most of the people an ordinary worker is *svoi chelovek*' ['our person'], which describes much the same 'us' intimated by the negative jokes and sarcasm we've examined.[94]

Although these respondents make it sound rather simple, being '*svoi*' could be quite a complex affair. A factory committee (Fabkom) chairman might be seen as *svoi*, for example, but Party officials might not. A factory director, who, despite his rank, clearly considered himself to be one of the boys, rather than allied with Party authorities, made a point of addressing the Fabkom chairman by his first name, but always addressed the Party Organiser very formally because, as he summed up,

'[The Fabkom] is "one of our own" [*svoi*],' whereas 'The Partorg is not; he is an alien'.[95]

So, even if '*svoi*' often seemed to evoke large-scale loyalties, in practice the distinction operated on a person-by-person basis. Once again, this closely resembles the way criminals have to communicate: just as two *mafiosi* are unable to introduce themselves openly to one another and must be vouched for by a third party who knows both, so it might require a middleman to connect someone into a *blat* network, a trust group in which people could speak critically, or for them to be considered *svoi*.[96]

Unlike the mafia, trust in the 1930s USSR might still be established in the way we explored above, with a careful exchange of increasingly dangerous trust tokens, without the need for a mediator or matchmaker. But being accepted into broader networks or other trust groups often turned on character assessments made by people you already trusted. This practice lies somewhere between what we'd consider the 'normal' introductions made by a mutual friend, and the practices of the criminal underworld. It remains rather closer to the latter, however, because although Soviet contemporaries who shared critical opinions were hardly *mafiosi*, they were still perpetrating acts deemed criminal by the state.

All the same, as Alexei Yurchak has argued of the later Soviet period, deciding whom to trust and who was *svoi* did not simply involve a binary distinction of 'the people' versus 'the state'.[97] This is already plain from the Harvard Project respondents describing their ties between family and friends – bonds that were clearly far more defined by interpersonal factors than by the looming presence of the suspicious state. Just because you didn't trust someone, didn't mean they were an agent of Soviet power. But if decisions about whom to trust and who was *svoi* were made at the individual level, the *idea* of much broader social identities often provided the frame of reference or terminology for these distinctions.

As with reactions to disasters and states of emergency, people's individual actions are often quite different to how they imagine 'people' or 'society' to think or feel. In this instance, although trust was developed at the micro level, it toyed all the while with ideas of broader 'us' and 'them' categories which couldn't be readily and safely activated between strangers. Instead, these were evoked between individuals or within small groups. By doing so, a given trust group imagined itself to be part of a whole constellation of similar groups, potentially linked by the multiple memberships each person might hold. Even though it was never actualised on a grand scale, this was the group-level equivalent of an individual person's urge to escape isolation (and a sense of powerlessness) by finding a commonality of interests and outlooks with other people: simply put, to find a shared identity and not to live or to suffer alone.

These acts of identity affirmation gave individuals a sense of meaning through association. The macro-level group identity of 'us' versus 'them' didn't constitute a practical or actualised social force in the 1930s, but its flickering existence in the minds of contemporaries who shared the idea (or hope) that such a broad shared identity *might* exist was an important factor in encouraging people to risk an exchange of trust tokens in the first place. This was, to use Jochen Hellbeck's term, a process of 'self-fashioning', by which contemporaries attempted to understand and find their place within the new realities of the 1930s. But, in contrast to Hellbeck's focus on diarists, what we see here is a process of *social* self-fashioning carried out within trust groups and reflecting their shared sense of place within, and relationship to, broader society. When we joke, we're often discovering who 'we' are.

While studies of Soviet subjectivity like Hellbeck's have largely focused on diarists, and hence have given us valuable insight into the self-fashioning of introspective, often solitary individuals, most citizens were not as alienated, insular, or given to depressed reflections in written form. The majority were, instead, engaged in social, shared processes of self-fashioning which, although no doubt distinct for each individual, were nevertheless founded upon membership of particular trust groups, or of broader, latent social groupings that were evoked within those trust groups.

So how might we interpret this imagined constellation of trust groups or particular identities? It seems a truism to say that there was no 'public sphere' in the Soviet Union in which critical and unorthodox speech could take place, but is it fair to understand 'imagined' identities as 'unreal' because they couldn't flourish openly?

When elaborating his influential definition of 'the public sphere' – that roughly-distinguished 'space' where civil society happens – Jürgen Habermas allowed that 'A portion of the public sphere is constituted in every conversation in which private persons come together to form a public'. If they do so not to conduct business or trade, these gatherings and discussions, he argues, constitute part of a social whole – like cells of a larger organism. Habermas emphatically limited this to gatherings free from all state influence or coercion, so he would doubtless deny that trust groups in Stalin's 1930s could possibly be considered a 'public sphere'.[98]

But I think the image of the small social gathering being just one part of a greater body still works here. In jokes and critical comments, people could imagine themselves to be part of a greater whole, just as cells contain a rough recipe for the larger organism of which they are a part. And in a sense they truly were – there were many, many other people across the country sharing similar jokes and opinions – but these common perceptions were, thanks to the repressive state and the need for trust to be established before the strongest unorthodox views could be revealed, limited in their ability to connect with one another or to become a self-aware, civil society. Soviet society in the 1930s was certainly fragmented, but it was patently not atomised.

* * *

If the broader structures of societal trust – trust in institutions, customs, strangers, or leaders – faltered or fell in this decade, smaller configurations of citizen-citizen trust persisted and could even grow stronger in the face (or in light) of shared difficulties. It was always a challenge and a risk to foster and maintain these relationships, but a challenge that many seized upon naturally and passionately. Families might have been the most secure trust groups, but they were far from the only ones. Like a mafia family, trust and shared culpability extended well beyond blood relations, and could remain secure even in the face of mass repressions and the fear that walls had ears.

'The various insufficiencies and misfortunes' a Cossack bookkeeper insisted to his interviewers, actually 'solidified them more [...] It made friendships more firm'.[99] Just as Solnit writes of disasters and emergencies, closer study 'makes it clear that there are plural and contingent natures – but the prevalent human nature in disaster is resilient, resourceful, generous, empathic, and brave.'[100] In our period, disastrous as it was in so many ways, this nature was far from indiscriminate: trust groups were *trust* groups because of the risks involved in being honest and open with others, but these were also 'networks of affinity and affection',[101] founded on shared interests, shared activities, personal or physical attraction, or, essentially, any reason for establishing a friendship we might think of in 'normal' societies. Trust groups provided protection for critical speech, but also more fundamental psychological and personal rewards: they served a basic human need to share difficulties and understandings of the Soviet world – to get by and to find a way to live and to share that life with other people.

In her study of street gangs in modern Russia, Svetlana Stephenson argues that the 'contrast between [...] the shadow and nonshadow worlds is far less stark than it seems. Both are parts of the same social reality; they overlap and coalesce, taking a variety of different forms and configurations'. Stephenson directly associates the blurring – or, given their meaning-generating nature, the crosshatching – of these official and unofficial worlds with 'informal networks and ties' between individuals which are not confined to either one or the other world.[102]

For our period, we can move a step further and note that it is the personal interactions within these networks and ties – these trust groups – which actually *facilitate* the crosshatching of the official and unofficial worlds. Because these were the social contexts in which people learnt and explored and pushed those limits – those borders between the shadow and nonshadow worlds – giving each other points of orientation, as well as the mutual confidence to challenge those same limits. This was the space where identity affirmation and shared pictures of social reality were developed and disseminated. As they joked, they discovered who they were and where they stood in this molten new world.

But this process also involved a generous dose of self-deception and misrecognition. People frequently seem to have believed themselves and their confidantes to be the exceptions rather than the rule, whether that meant believing society was atomised, while they were able to trust their own friends and family, or if it meant believing in broad, shared identities of 'us' and 'them', while in practice making careful person-by-person judgements.

In any case, even if individuals are social 'atoms', atoms are never random: they are always situated according to relational forces, many of which we see played out in jokes.

Notes

1. The Harvard Project interview transcripts were written out in English. Throughout, they use the not-entirely-accurate English word 'anecdote' as the translation from 'anekdot', as you'll see in the quotations throughout this chapter. The transcripts are also littered with typos, which I've silently corrected.
2. Rebecca Solnit, *A Paradise Built in Hell: The Extraordinary Communities That Arise in Disaster* (New York, 2010).
3. Stepan Podlubnyi, diary entry of 16 November 1934, Hellbeck (ed. & trans.), *Tagebuch aus Moskau*, 175-6; also cf. 220-21.
4. Jimmy Carr & Lucy Greeves, *The Naked Jape: Uncovering the Hidden World of Jokes* (London, 2007), 5; 33.
5. Freud, *Jokes*, A, II, esp. 81-8. On the social importance of humour, cf. Carr & Greeves, *The Naked Jape*, 26-33; also cf. Levine, *Black Culture*, 320.
6. Chapman, 'Social Aspects', Chapman & Foot (eds.), *Humour and Laughter*, 156.
7. Katherine Hawley, *Trust: A Very Short Introduction* (Oxford, 2012), 3.
8. Geoffrey Hosking, *Trust: A History* (Oxford, 2014), Ch.1.
9. See Hosking, *Trust*, and Hosking (ed.), *Slavonic and East European Review: Trust and Distrust in the USSR*, 91.1 (2013). Note that contributors to this special issue hold a range of views.
10. See in particular Alexey Tikhomirov, 'The Regime of Forced Trust: Making and Breaking Emotional Bonds between People and State in Soviet Russia, 1917-1941', *Slavonic & East European Review*, 91.1 (2013), 78-118.
11. Pope-Hennessy, *Closed City*, 37.
12. Yoram Gorlizki, 'Structures of Trust After Stalin', *Slavonic & East European Review*, 91.1 (2013), 132.
13. Joan P. Emerson, 'Negotiating the Serious Import of Humor', *Sociometry*, 32.2 (1969), 180.
14. Emerson, 'Negotiating the Serious', 169.
15. Ted Cohen, *Jokes: Philosophical Thoughts on Joking Matters* (London & Chicago, IL, 1999), 28-31; on this subject, see also Mel'nichenko, *Sovetskii anekdot*, 24-5; Carroll, *Humour*, 77; Scott, *Weapons of the Weak*, xvii.
16. HPSSS 104/(NY)1492/A/34, p.21. Also cf. 6/A/1, p.65.
17. HPSSS 395/A/20, p.27.
18. HPSSS 127/A/10, p.36.
19. HPSSS 88/A/6, p.15; 100/A/7, p.20.
20. HPSSS 110/A/8, pp.61-2.
21. HPSSS 86/A/6, pp.14, 21.
22. HPSSS 66/A/6, p.13 (seq.79). 'Kidding Stalin' is an Americanism meaning 'to joke about Stalin'.
23. HPSSS 96/A/7, p.24.
24. HPSSS 481/A/24, pp.37-8. ('нескромные анекдоты'.)
25. HPSSS 526/A/27, p.15.
26. HPSSS 433/(NY)1240/A/32, p.44.
27. HPSSS 24/A/3, pp.29, 37.
28. e.g. HPSSS 100/A/7, p.16, 127/A/10, p.29.
29. cf. Fitzpatrick & Lüdtke, 'Energizing the Everyday', 281-92; Thurston, 'The Soviet Family', 563-8.
30. HPSSS 398/A/20, p.34.
31. HPSSS 59/A/5, p.29.

32   HPSSS 14/A/2, p.22. The Harvard Project categorised her as a 'rank and file intellectual' from a 'superior intellectual' family.
33   HPSSS 144/A/11, pp.26-7.
34   e.g. David L. Hoffmann, *Peasant Metropolis: Social Identities in Moscow, 1929-1941* (Ithaca, NY, 1994).
35   HPSSS 9/A/1, p.71.
36   e.g. HPSSS 40/A/4, p.15; 46/A/4, p.18; 107/A/7, p.16; 127/A/10, p.29.
37   Solnit, *Paradise*, 2.
38   Although Solnit, too, seems to be of the opinion that society under Stalin was populated by Winston Smiths: Solnit, *Paradise*, 19.
39   HPSSS 59/A/5, p.7 (seq.70).
40   Solnit, *Paradise*, 7.
41   Rittersporn, *Anguish, Anger, and Folkways*, 196-7.
42   HPSSS 41/A/4, p.12.
43   HPSSS 113/A/9, p.16.
44   HPSSS 62/A/5, p.26.
45   HPSSS 96/A/7, p.24.
46   HPSSS 1/A/1, p.52.
47   cf. Hawley, *Trust*, 13, 17.
48   Gambetta, *Codes of the Underworld*, x.
49   Gambetta, *Codes of the Underworld*, 59.
50   Gambetta, *Codes of the Underworld*, 66.
51   Unless, of course, this was an attempt by someone in a weaker position to gain the trust of a more powerful figure by offering up *kompromat* on themselves.
52   Gambetta, *Codes of the Underworld*, 60. Emphasis original. Gambetta uses the term 'bilateral' with regards to the exchange; I use it here to describe the trust bond the exchange may create.
53   Emerson, 'Negotiating the Serious', 180.
54   e.g. HPSSS 144/A/11, p.25.
55   F.K.M. Hillenbrand identified something similar in Nazi Germany and named it 'the German glance' ('*der deutsche Blick*'). F.K.M. Hillenbrand, *Underground Humour in Nazi Germany, 1933-1945* (London, 1995), xvii.
56   e.g. HPSSS 26/A/3, p.54; 29/A/3, p.86; 33/A/4, p.6.
57   HPSSS, 305/A/15, p.17.
58   HPSSS 144/A/11, pp.27-8.
59   HPSSS 25/A/3, pp.36-7 (seq.159-60).
60   HPSSS 41/A/4, p.21. The interview transcript uses the rather awkward 'talked' rather than 'spoke'. ('по-советски'.)
61   e.g. Nancy Ries, *Russian Talk: Culture and Conversation during Perestroika* (Ithaca, NY, 1997), esp. 21.
62   Katerina Gerasimova, 'The Soviet Communal Apartment', trans. Jakub Lopatko, Jeremy Smith (ed.), *Beyond the Limits: The Concept of Space in Russian History and Culture* (Helsinki, 1999), 116.
63   When some kind of 'private sphere' has been theorised in the early Soviet setting, there has been little sense of *where* it could exist, except within an individual person's mind, yet these were clearly perceptions shared and shaped by social interactions, so the spatial question remains. (On the idea of a 'private life' in this period, see Figes, *The Whisperers*, and Geoffrey Hosking, *A History of the Soviet Union, 1917-1991* (Final Edition, London, 1992), 219.)
64   Katerina Gerasimova, 'Public Privacy in the Soviet Communal Apartment', David Crowley & Susan E. Reid (eds.), *Socialist Spaces: Sites of Everyday Life in the*

Eastern Bloc (Oxford, 2002).
65   Leif Jerram, 'Space: A Useless Category for Historical Analysis?', *History and Theory*, 52.3 (2013), 404.
66   HPSSS, 96/A/7, pp.12-13.
67   Goldman, *Inventing*; Scott, *Behind the Urals*.
68   Figes, *The Whisperers*, 183-4; Gerasimova, 'The Soviet Communal Apartment', 127-8.
69   GARF, f.8131, op.31, d.8782 (1937).
70   Likhachev, Panchenko & Ponyrko, *Smekh*, 3.
71   GARF, f.8131, op.31, d.15636, l.11 (c.1940). 'Sovnarkom' was the contraction for the 'Council of People's Commissars' (*Sovet narodnykh kommissarov*).
72   GARF, f.8131, op.31, d.8782, l.5(ob) (1937).
73   On youth activism and its complex relationship with the Soviet state, see Andy Willimott's excellent study, *Living the Revolution: Urban Communes and Soviet Socialism, 1917-1932* (Oxford, 2017).
74   HPSSS 11/A/2, pp.18-9.
75   TsGAIPD, f.24, op.2v, d.2685, l.26.
76   For a report concerning abuse directed against Stakhanovites in general, cf. TsGAIPD, f.24, op.2v, d.1185, ll.317-21 (November 1935).
77   Sergei Zhuravlev & Mikhail Mukhin, '*Krepost' sotsializma': Povsednevnost' i motivatsiia truda v sovetskom predpriiatii, 1928-1938 gg.* (Moscow, 2004), 122.
78   TsGAIPD, f.24, op.2v, d.1185, l.319 (7 November 1935).
79   GARF, f.8131, op.31, d.15636, l.11 (c.1940).
80   TsGAIPD, f.24, op.2v, d.1200, l.273 (1935). Thanks to Sarah Davies for this reference.
81   TsGAIPD, f.24, op.2v, d.1185, l.318 (November 1935); HPSSS 5/A/1, p.12.
82   Gary Alan Fine, 'Humour in Situ: The Role of Humour in Small Group Culture', Chapman & Foot (eds.), *It's a Funny Thing*, 315.
83   TsGAIPD, f.24, op.2v, d.1185, l.318. Nevertheless, when the local procuracy opened an investigation into the matter, a preliminary report from the oblast' procurator made it plain that all official sympathy continued to lie with the departed regime favourites.
84   Shitts, *Dnevnik*, 2 (1928); see also Mel'nichenko, *Sovetskii anekdot*, 202.
85   HPSSS 133/A/10, p.30 (although here 'dirt' is used rather than 'shit').
86   Shitts, *Dnevnik*, 115 (1929).
87   RGASPI, f.M-1, op.23, d.1072, l.14 (September 1934); other recordings with slight variations: d.1103, l.111 (1935); TsGAIPD, f.24, op.5, d.2291, l.21, quoted in Rimmel, who notes the NKVD also found another version circulating in Arkhangel'sk (*The Kirov Murder*, 112). Also cf. Sarah Davies, *Propaganda and Popular Opinion in Soviet Russia, 1934-1941*, DPhil Thesis, University of Oxford (1994), 144-5, for variations of the song, and that it spread as far East as Novosibirsk.
88   The element of parody accounts for the incongruous use of the slang term 'зашухерили' ('ratted out'), which does not quite make sense in the context of the *Cheliuskin*, but was a memorable part of the original 'Murka' song. In both an archival source (RGASPI f.M-1, op.23, d.1103, l.111 (1935)) and a collection of prison songs (dated as contemporary in 1937-1942), the version recorded replaces 'ratted out' with, more simply and accurately, 'wrecked' (утопили) or 'sank' (потопили), implying that the song was fluid, but also that it was perhaps quite consciously parodying the original 'Murka' song, with different elements of that original retained or discarded as the singer(s) wished. See Iakov Vaiskopf, *Blatnaia lira. Sbornik tiuremnykh i lagernykh pesen* (Jerusalem, 1981), 9, for

the parody, and pp.22-6 for the original 'Murka', including its melody. (See also Davies, *Propaganda and Popular Opinion*, 144-5, for versions with additional parodic verses.) Many thanks to Gleb Albert and David Brandenberger for their help translating and analysing this song, and particularly to Gleb for bringing the 'Murka' connection to my attention.

89   TsGAIPD, f.25, op.5, d.46, l.73 (1934); also cited in Davies, *Popular Opinion*, 142. Translation Davies's. For variations, cf. GARF, f.5451, op.43, d.12, l.146 (1932); HPSSS 64/A/6, p.66.

90   GARF, f.8131, op.31, d.91956, l.6 (1934-5). ('Власть советам, звезда кадетам, деньги большевикам и остальне [*sic*] [нецензурными словами]'.)

91   Elena Osokina, *Za fasadom 'stalinskogo izobiliia': Raspredelenie i rynok v snabzhenii naseleniia v gody industrializatsii 1927-1941* (Moscow, 1999). For specific information on access to particular shops, on canteens and prices, see 110-13.

92   TsDAHOU, f.1, op.20, d.3198, l.8 (1930). ('...а по моему это не коммуна: кому на, а кому нет.') For similar wordplay aimed at activist communes in the 1920s, cf. Willimott, *Living the Revolution*, 136.

93   Davies, '"Us" Against "Them"', 80, 72.

94   HPSSS 492/A/25, p.9; 470/B/20, p.34. (*Lishentsy* were those people formally deprived of their civil rights, usually due to their prerevolutionary backgrounds.)

95   HPSSS 384/B/4, p.26.

96   cf. Gambetta, *Codes of the Underworld*, 189-90; 218-9.

97   Alexei Yurchak, *Everything was Forever Until It was No More: The Last Soviet Generation* (Princeton, NJ, 2006), 103.

98   Jürgen Habermas, 'The Public Sphere', Chandra Mukerji & Michael Schudson (eds.), *Rethinking Popular Culture: Contemporary Perspectives on Cultural Studies* (Berkeley, CA & Oxford, 1991), 398.

99   HPSSS 5/A/1, p.38.

100   Solnit, *Paradise*, 8.

101   Solnit, *Paradise*, 3.

102   Svetlana Stephenson, *Gangs of Russia: From the Streets to the Corridors of Power* (Ithaca, NY, 2015), 1.

CONCLUSION

At some point in the future, when someone is given the difficult task of writing the history of our everyday life, it's difficult to imagine that he will be able to skirt the subject of political jokes. […] Within them, everything is captured in whimsical form: the ordinary citizen's hatred and protest against the cruelty and injustice of state policy; his hope and despair; his laughter and tears. Is there anything, anything at all, that hasn't made it into those jokes? They're openly swapped out-loud among drinking companions while clinking glasses; they're whispered to one another while chuckling at crossroads and tram stops; they're exchanged at work among colleagues while keeping a watchful eye out. Hope, despair, laughter and tears…[1]

Diary of A.G. Man'kov, 24 July 1933.

The Soviet Union was striving in the 1930s to tell a story of incredible progress, of catching and overtaking the capitalist world, and, above all, of building a fundamentally new, better and happier society. Many Soviet citizens could readily and enthusiastically buy into this vision, striving to make themselves into the New Soviet Person. The clashes between this appealing story and the everyday realities that ordinary people experienced in the 1930s were countless and often painful, but for many the master narrative could still give reassuring meaning to their suffering.

When its power was limited or it simply failed to do so, however, unless they despaired completely or became outright opponents, contemporaries had to find other ways for their lives to make sense, other stories to weave for themselves. Jokes played a powerful role in this process, exploring and challenging, relieving tensions and nurturing insights, developing shared identities and grounding regime ideology in lived everyday realities.

As they did so, contemporaries could and naturally still did draw from the wells of prerevolutionary ideas, values and practices, ranging from the traditionally raucous and obscene displays of Kirov's Carnival, to the more subtle persistence of religious assumptions, sexist prejudices, and ideas of basic fairness. They continued to weave these elements into their responses to the new world taking shape around them. They did not arrive in the 1930s as a blank slate and nor could their memories, loyalties and values simply be effaced by state decree.

Society in the 1930s wasn't 'atomised', but trust became a delicate affair, explored and established through mafia-like signalling and mutual self-incrimination. Trust groups might be secure social contexts, but they were *trust* groups because of the risks people faced in speaking openly and critically. Jokes helped to test the waters and establish these groups, but they were also an important element in displaying and cultivating trust. If the level of 'ambient trust' in the Soviet Union was extremely low,[2] this made it all the more valuable and essential for survival, but because trust was therefore established on an individual basis, it was easy for people to believe that their own trust bonds were unique, while society around them huddled in constant fear of denunciation by friends and family.

In this tense atmosphere, contemporaries could certainly learn to speak Bolshevik, but this didn't mean they became trapped within regime ideology, nor that they were merely parroting it. As they spoke, many people also sought to make 'Bolshevik' reflect reality as they experienced it, whether by decoding official acronyms and buzzwords, or by calling the regime out on its own unfulfilled promises. They tried to make Bolshevik speak 'real' and speak sense, and in the process resolve the tensions between ideology and everyday experience.

Humour can certainly be a resolutionary device, but joke-telling is also exploratory, playing with the boundaries of acceptability and challenging assumptions and expectations. Exploring the Soviet world through jokes helped citizens to map out the world as it was, not only as it was supposed to be. This wasn't a clash of 'principle' versus 'practice', however, but an attempt to find out what existed in practice in a life lived along the fault-lines between rhetoric and reality.

It's certainly important to recognise that many joke-tellers thought and felt as though they were kicking back against the regime, but, as we've seen, they usually did so while accepting many of its values, wishing it would work as it was supposed to, rather than simply rejecting it outright. Ultimately, people attacked the Soviet status quo more for its failures than for its promises.

In contemporary western democracies, it would only be radical left-wing analysts who would suggest that biting satires or political jokes about our own difficulties and struggles could equate to a conscious (or unconscious) rejection of capitalism, liberalism, or democracy. Yet this is, in essence, what it means to interpret jokes under Stalinism or Communism as absolute rejections of a vast and complex political system which could appeal in some ways, be rejected in others, and far more often come to seem like 'just the way things are'.

Telling critical jokes could certainly feel like resistance, or even just a powerful, fleeting assertion of personal agency in the face of a regime which sought to define not only what you could do, but also who you could be. It could feel deliciously transgressive, but what joking did for people was not necessarily the same as what it (consciously) meant to them.

Humour could contain and control the tensions and inconsistencies around them, forming a potent placebo to assuage a sense of powerlessness and make frightening and depressing realities feel benign, even if just for a moment. But it wasn't simply a pill which numbed the pain. It could defuse tension and fear, but in the process it enabled people to push on with their lives, rather than falling into despair or being driven to take up arms against the system. It created and sustained trust bonds between people; at times it reasserted a feeling of personal sovereignty; while at others it provided crucial advice on how to get by as best you could.

This book has at its core been an argument against dualism – a rejection of an 'either/or' approach to understanding Soviet society in the 1930s in which the population was either deeply convinced by Soviet ideology (whether brainwashed or through active self-fashioning), or that it was coerced into conformity (albeit with some grumbling). What I've tried to show is that criticism and conformity can exist not only simultaneously, but that they overlap, influence, and are even mutually constitutive of each other.

By interpreting the friction between official and unofficial realities and values as crosshatching, we can avoid the assumption that this was a head-on collision between incompatible worlds, and instead appreciate the ways in which they interacted with and shaped each other. Nothing was clear-cut in this process and so the borderlands between affirmation and dissent have often been described as 'grey zones'; but in the playful, provocative realm of humour we can see they were so much more than 'grey'.

They were vibrant, creative, and in a constant state of change. People were not content to live in a fog of contradictions: studying their humour reveals that they desperately sought to find clarity and escape confusion. As they found their way, the jokes helped them to find themselves. And for them, this was not a zero-sum game, in which either Soviet or traditional values would emerge triumphant. Instead, like the Komsomol members who said their prayers before taking their exams, or the priest who called on fellow believers to become 'Stakhanovites of our belief and religion',[3] contemporaries drew on as wide a repertoire as possible to live and understand their lives to their minimum disadvantage.

The new Soviet ideology and its ruthlessly implemented policies were constantly confronted by alternative popular viewpoints, and the two often seemed utterly incompatible. But this didn't produce Orwell's infamous 'doublethink', in which two contradictory ideas are held hermetically sealed from each other in people's minds, never to interact. Nor did citizens develop a 'permanently schizophrenic vision' of the world and their lives,[4] and even if they – like all people – calibrated their actions and choices of words differently in public to how they spoke within their trust groups, this did not mean a stark separation between 'public' and 'private' worlds.

Soviet citizens strove – as we all do – to find some kind of harmony between the tune they were supposed to sing, and the experiences, hopes and fears they and their loved ones held and shared. People can adapt to almost anything over time and in the process of that adaptation they normalise what first seemed extraordinary. Humour helped them to do so, but their humour also allows us to put ourselves in their shoes and, once there, we begin to realise how familiar their reactions, coping mechanisms, frustrations, social and psychological needs, and the way in which they set about addressing them are to us. These were certainly extraordinary times, but this is also, despite all its unique elements, a fundamentally and recognisably human story.

Notes

[1] Man'kov, *Dnevniki*, 73-4; also cited in Brandenberger, *Political Humor*, 2. Translation Brandenberger's, with my adjustments to British English.
[2] Gorlizki, 'Structures of Trust', 132.
[3] See Chapter 3. Quotation from Davies, *Popular Opinion*, 78.
[4] Martin Malia, *The Soviet Tragedy: A History of Socialism in Russia* (New York, 1994), 269.

SELECT BIBLIOGRAPHY

Archives

Russia

GARF Государственный архив Российской Федерации. State Archive of the Russian Federation.

In the footnotes, I omit the 'R' prefix.

- *fond* R-1235 – Всероссийский центральный исполнительный комитет советов рабочих, крестьянских и красноармейских депутатов (ВЦИК) РСФСР. *All-Russian Central Executive Councils of Workers, Peasants and Red Army Deputies (VTsIK) RSFSR.*
- *fond* R-3316 – Центральный исполнительный комитет СССР (ЦИК СССР). *Central Executive Committee of the USSR (TsIK SSSR).*
- *fond* R-5446 – Совет министров СССР. *Council of Ministers of the USSR.*
- *fond* R-5451 – Всесоюзный центральный совет профсоюзов (ВЦСПС). *All-Union Central Council of Trade Unions (VTsSPS).*
- *fond* R-7522 – Центральные избирательные комиссии по выборам в верховный совет СССР. *Central Electoral Commissions for the Elections to the Supreme Soviet of the USSR.*
- *fond* R-7676 – Центральные комитеты профсоюзов рабочих машиностроения. *Central Councils of Trade Unions for Machine-Building Workers.*
- *fond* R-8131 – Прокуратура СССР. *Procurator [State Prosecutor] of the USSR.*
- *fond* R-9425 – Главное управление по охране государственных тайн в печати при совете министров СССР (ГЛАВЛИТ). *General Directorate for the Protection of State Secrets in the Press, under the Council of Ministers of the USSR (GLAVLIT).*
- *fond* R-9474 – Верховный суд СССР. *Supreme Court of the USSR.*
- *fond* R-9492 – Министерство юстиции СССР. *Ministry of Justice of the USSR.*

NA Народный архив. *The People's Archive*. Previously independent archive in Moscow, now inaccessible and held by RGANI. References are to the microfilmed portion of the archive, under the title *Voice of the People Under Soviet Rule*.

fond 389 – Zotov.

RGASPI Российский государственный архив социально-политической истории. Russian State Archive of Socio-Political History.

fond 17 – Центральный комитет КПСС (ЦК КПСС). *Central Committee of the CPSU (TsK KPSS)*.
fond 74 – Ворошилов Климент Ефремович. *Voroshilov, Kliment Efremovich*.
fond 326 – Радек Карл Бернардович. *Radek, Karl Bernardovich*.
fond 558 – Сталин Иосиф Виссарионович. *Stalin, Iosif Vissarionovich*.
fond 671 – Ежов Николай Иванович. *Ezhov, Nikolai Ivanovich*.
fond M-1 – Центральный комитет ВЛКСМ. *Central Committee of the VLKSM*.
[Formerly *fond* 1 in Центр хранения документов молодежных организаций (ЦХДАМО). *Document Storage Centre of Youth Organisations (TsKhDAMO)*.]

RGALI Российский государственный архив литературы и искусства. Russian State Archive of Literature and Art.

fond 600 – Редакция газеты "Крокодил". *Editors of the Newspaper* Krokodil.
fond 2172 – Личный фонд Афиногенова А.Н. *Personal fond of A.N. Afinogenov*.

TsGAIPD (SPb) Центральный государственный архив историко-политических документов Санкт-Петербурга. Central State Archive of Historico-Political Documents, St Petersburg.

fond 24 – Ленинградский областной комитет ВКП(б). *Leningrad Oblast' Committee of the VKP(b)*.
fond 25 – Ленинградский городской комитет ВКП(б). *Leningrad City Committee of the VKP(b)*.
fond K598 – Ленинградский областной комитет ВЛКСМ. *Leningrad Oblast' Committee of the VLKSM [Komsomol]*.

Ukraine

TsDAHOU   Центральний державний архів громадських об'єднань України. Central State Archive of Public Organisations of Ukraine.

fond 1 – Центральний комітет компартії України. *Central Committee of the Communist Party of Ukraine.*
fond 6 – Центральний комітет комуністичної партії західної України. *Central Committee of the Communist Party of Western Ukraine.*

TsDAVO   Центральний державний архів вищих органів влади та управління України. Central State Archive of the Highest Organs of Government and Administration of Ukraine.

fond 24 – Верховний суд Української РСР Харків, Київ. *Supreme Court of the Ukrainian Socialist Soviet Republic, Kharkhiv, Kyiv.*
fond 288 – Прокуратура Української РСР Харків, Київ. *State Prosecutor of the Ukrainian Socialist Soviet Republic, Kharkhiv, Kyiv.*

HDA SBU   Галузевий державний архів служби безпеки України. Sectoral State Archive of the Security Service of Ukraine.

fond 6 – Уголовные дела на реабилитированных лиц. *Criminal files of rehabilitated persons.*
fond 16 – Секретариат ГПУ-КГБ УССР. *Secretariat of the GPU-KGB of the Ukrainian Socialist Soviet Republic.*

USA

HPSSS   Harvard Interview Project on the Soviet Social System.

Available at <http://hcl.harvard.edu/collections/hpsss/index.html>.

Newspapers & Magazines

Krokodil
Pravda

Published Works

Abramskii, Isaak Pavlovich (ed.), *Vragi i druz'ia v zerkale 'Krokodila'*, *1922-1972* (Moscow, 1972).
Adams, Bruce, *Tiny Revolutions in Russia: Twentieth Century Soviet and Russian History in Anecdotes* (London, 2005).
Afanas'ev, A.N., *Russkie zavetnye skazki* (St Petersburg, 1994 [Geneva, 1872]).
Aleksandrov-Derkachenko, P.P. (ed.), *Russkoe i sovetskoe molodezhnoe dvizhenie v dokumentakh 1905-1937 gg.* (Moscow, 2002).
Alexopoulos, Golfo, Hessler, Julie & Tomoff, Kirill (eds.), *Writing the Stalin Era: Sheila Fitzpatrick and Soviet Historiography* (New York, 2011).
Andreev, N.P., *Ukazatel' skazochnykh siuzhetov po sisteme Aarne* (Leningrad, 1929).
Andreevich, Evgenii, *Kreml' i narod* (Munich, 1951).
Arendt, Hannah, *The Origins of Totalitarianism* (New York, 1973).
Aristotle, *On the Parts of Animals*, trans. James G. Lennox (Oxford, 2001).
Arkhipova, Aleksandra & Mel'nichenko, Mikhail, *Anekdoty o Staline: Teksty, kommentarii, issledovaniia* (Moscow, 2010).
Arzhilovskii, Andrei, Diary published in Véronique Garros, Natalia Korenevskaya & Thomas Lahusen (eds.), *Intimacy and Terror: Soviet Diaries of the 1930s*, trans. Carol A. Flath (New York, 1995).
Attardo, Salvatore, *Linguistic Theories of Humor* (Berlin & New York, 1994).
Augé, Marc, *Non-Places: An Introduction to Supermodernity*, trans. John Howe (2nd edn., London, 2008).
Aurelius, Marcus, *Meditations*, trans. Gregory Hays (New York, 2002).
Bakhtin, M.M., *The Dialogic Imagination. Four Essays*, ed. Michael Holquist, trans. Caryl Emerson & Michael Holquist (Austin, TX, 1981).
Bakhtin, Mikhail, *Rabelais and his World*, trans. Hélène Iswolsky (Bloomington, IN, 1984).
Bakhtin, V., 'Anekdoty nas spasali vsegda', A. Strelianyi, G. Sapgir, V. Bakhtin & N. Ordynskii (eds.), *Samizdat veka* (Moscow/Minsk, 1997).
Baldaev, D.S. (ed.), *Russian Criminal Tattoo Encyclopaedia*, 3 Vols. (London, 2003-8).
Banc, C. & Dundes, Alan, *You Call This Living? A Collection of East European Political Jokes* (Athens, GA, 1990).
Bauer, Raymond A., Inkeles, Alex & Kluckhohn, Clyde, *How the Soviet System Works: Cultural, Psychological & Social Themes* (New York, 1960).
Beard, Mary, *Pompeii: The Life of a Roman Town* (London, 2008).
Beard, Mary, *Laughter in Ancient Rome: On Joking, Tickling, and Cracking Up* (Oakland, CA, 2014).
Beaumont, Matthew & Freeman, Michael (eds.), *The Railway and Modernity: Time, Space, and the Machine Ensemble* (Oxford, 2007).
Benton, Gregor, 'The Origins of the Political Joke', Chris Powell & George E.C. Paton (eds.), *Humour in Society: Resistance and Control* (Houndmills, 1988).
Bergson, Henri, *Laughter: An Essay on the Meaning of the Comic*, trans. Cloudesely Brereton & Fred Rothwell (Rockville, MD, 2008).

Bernstein, Frances Lee, *The Dictatorship of Sex: Lifestyle Advice for the Soviet Masses* (DeKalb, IL, 2011).
Blium, V., 'Vozroditsa li satira?', *Literaturnaia gazeta*, 6 (27 May 1929).
Bogomolov, N. (ed.), *Anti-mir russkoi kul'tury. Iazyk. Fol'klor. Literatura.* (Moscow, 1996).
Bolton, Jonathan H., 'Writing in a Polluted Semiosphere: Everyday Life in Lotman, Foucault, and de Certeau', Andreas Schonle (ed.), *Lotman and Cultural Studies: Encounters and Extensions* (Madison, WI, 2006).
Borev, Iurii, *Istoriia gosudarstva sovetskogo v predaniiakh i anekdotakh* (Moscow, 1995).
Bourdieu, Pierre, *Distinction: A Social Critique of the Judgement of Taste*, trans. Richard Nice (London, 2010).
Brandenberger, David, *Political Humor under Stalin: An Anthology of Unofficial Jokes and Anecdotes* (Bloomington, IN, 2009).
Brandenberger, David, *Propaganda State in Crisis: Soviet Ideology, Indoctrination, and Terror under Stalin, 1927-1941* (New Haven, CT, 2011).
Bronckart, Jean-Paul & Bota, Cristian, *Bakhtine démasqué: Histoire d'un menteur, d'une escroquerie et d'un délire collectif* (Geneva, 2011).
Brooks, Jeffrey, *Thank You, Comrade Stalin! Soviet Public Culture from Revolution to Cold War* (Princeton, NJ, 2001).
Brown, Kate, *A Biography of No Place: From Ethnic Borderland to Soviet Heartland* (Cambridge, MA, 2004).
Buckley, Mary, 'The Untold Story of the *Obshchestvennitsa* in the 1930s', *Europe-Asia Studies*, 48.4 (1996).
Bulgakov, M., *Dnevnik. Pis'ma, 1914-1940* (Moscow, 1997).
Bulgakov, Mikhail, *The Heart of a Dog*, trans. Michael Glenny (London, 2005 [1925]).
Bulgakov, Mikhail, *The Master and Margarita*, trans. Michael Glenny (London, 2003 [1967]).
Bulgakowa, Oksana, 'Der erste sowjetische Filmstar', Jan Plamper & Klaus Heller (eds.), *Personality Cults in Stalinism / Personenkulte im Stalinismus* (Göttingen, 2004).
Burleigh, Michael, *Sacred Causes: Religion and Politics from the European Dictators to Al Qaeda* (London, 2006).
Cameron, Keith (ed.), *Humour and History* (Oxford, 1993).
Carr, Jimmy & Greeves, Lucy, *The Naked Jape: Uncovering the Hidden World of Jokes* (London, 2007).
Carroll, Noël, *Humour: A Very Short Introduction* (Oxford, 2014).
Carse, James P., *Finite and Infinite Games: A Vision of Life as Play and Possibility* (New York, 1986).
Certeau, Michel de, *The Practice of Everyday Life*, trans. Steven Rendall (Berkeley & Los Angeles, CA, 1988).
Chamberlin, William Henry, *Russia's Iron Age* (London, 1935).
Chamberlin, William, 'The "Anecdote": Unrationed Soviet Humor', *Russian Review*, 16.3 (1957).
Chapman, Anthony J., 'Social Aspects of Humorous Laughter', Anthony J.

Chapman & Hugh C. Foot (eds.), *Humour and Laughter: Theory, Research and Applications* (London, 1976).

Chatterjee, Choi, 'Everyday Life in Transnational Perspective: Consumption and Consumerism, 1917-1939', Choi Chatterjee, David L. Ransel, Mary Cavender & Karen Petrone (eds.), *Everyday Life in Russia Past and Present* (Bloomington, IN, 2015).

Chesterton, G.K., *The Collected Works of G.K. Chesterton*, Vol.1, ed. David Dooley (San Francisco, CA, 1986).

Clements, Barbara Evans, 'The Birth of the New Soviet Woman', Abbot Gleason, Peter Kenez & Richard Stites (eds.), *Bolshevik Culture: Experiment and Order in the Russian Revolution* (Bloomington, IN, 1985).

Clements, Barbara Evans, *A History of Women in Russia: From Earliest Times to the Present* (Bloomington, IN, 2012).

Cochran, Robert, '"What Courage!": Romanian "Our Leader" Jokes', *The Journal of American Folklore*, 102.405 (1989).

Cohen, Ted, *Jokes: Philosophical Thoughts on Joking Matters* (London & Chicago, IL, 1999).

Critchley, Simon, *On Humour* (London, 2002).

Dal', Vladimir, *Tolkovyi slovar' zhivogo velikoruskogo iazyka* (2nd edn., St Petersburg & Moscow, 1882).

Dale, Robert, 'The Valaam Myth and the Fate of Leningrad's Disabled Veterans', *Russian Review*, 72.2 (2013).

Daniels, Robert Vincent, *The Rise and Fall of Communism in Russia* (New Haven, CT, 2007).

Danilov, V.P., 'Vvedenie', V. Danilov, R. Manning & L. Viola (eds.), *Tragediia Sovetskoi derevni: Kollektivizatsiia i raskulachivanie. Dokumenty i materialy v 5 tomakh, 1927-1939*. Tom 1 (Moscow, 1999).

David-Fox, Michael, 'Whither Resistance?', *Kritika*, 1.1 (2000).

Davies, Christie, *The Mirth of Nations* (New Brunswick, 2002).

Davies, Christie, 'Humour and Protest: Jokes Under Communism', Marjolein 't Hart & Dennis Bos (eds.), *Humour and Social Protest*, International Review of Social History Supplements, 15 (Cambridge, 2007).

Davies, Christie, *Jokes and Targets* (Bloomingtom, IN, 2011).

Davies, R.W. & Wheatcroft, Stephen G., *The Years of Hunger: Soviet Agriculture, 1931-1933* (Houndmills, 2004).

Davies, Sarah, *Popular Opinion in Stalin's Russia: Terror, Propaganda, and Dissent* (Cambridge, 1997).

Davies, Sarah, '"Us Against Them": Social Identity in Soviet Russia, 1934-41', *Russian Review*, 56.1 (1997).

Davies, Sarah, 'The "Cult" of the Vozhd': Representations in Letters, 1934-1941', *Russian History*, 24.1-2 (1997).

Davies, Sarah, 'The Crime of "Anti-Soviet Agitation" in the Soviet Union in the 1930s', *Cahiers du Monde russe*, 39.1-2 (1998).

Davies, Sarah, '"A Mother's Cares": Women Workers and Popular Opinion in Stalin's Russia, 1934-41', Melanie Ilič (ed.), *Women in the Stalin Era* (Houndmills, 2001).

Dmitriev, A.V., Latynov, V.V. & Khlop'ev, A.T., *Neformal'naia politicheskaia kommunikatsiia* (Moscow, 1997).
Dmitriev, A.V., *Sotsiologiia politicheskogo iumora* (Moscow, 1998).
Dobrenko, Evegeny, 'The Singing Masses and the Laughing State in the Musical Comedy of the Stalinist 1930s', Lesley Milne (ed.), *Reflective Laughter: Aspects of Humour in Russian Culture* (London, 2004).
Dolgopolova, Zhanna, 'The Contrary World of the Anecdote', *Melbourne Slavonic Studies*, 15 (1981).
Dolgopolova, Zhanna, *Russia Dies Laughing* (London, 1983).
Douglas, Mary, *Implicit Meanings: Selected Essays in Anthropology* (2nd edn., London, 1999).
Draitser, Emil A., *Taking Penguins to the Movies. Ethnic Humor in Russia* (Detroit, MI, 1998).
Edele, Mark, 'Soviet Society, Social Structure, and Everyday Life: Major Frameworks Reconsidered', *Kritika*, 8.2 (2007).
Eidelman, Natan, 'Under Stalin's Spell', *Moscow News*, 30 (1988).
Ellman, Michael, 'The Soviet 1937 Provincial Show Trials: Carnival or Terror?', *Europe-Asia Studies*, 53.8 (2001).
Emerson, Joan P., 'Negotiating the Serious Import of Humor', *Sociometry*, 32.2 (1969).
Fayet, Jean-François, *Karl Radek (1885-1939) Biographie politique* (Bern, 2004).
Figes, Orlando & Kolonitskii, Boris, *Interpreting the Russian Revolution: The Language and Symbols of 1917* (New Haven, CT, 1999).
Figes, Orlando, *The Whisperers: Private Life in Stalin's Russia* (London, 2007).
Fine, Gary Alan, 'Humour in Situ: The Role of Humour in Small Group Culture', Antony J. Chapman & Hugh C. Foot (eds.), *It's a Funny Thing, Humour* (Oxford, 1977).
Fitzpatrick, Sheila, *Stalin's Peasants: Resistance and Survival in the Russian Village After Collectivization* (New York, 1994).
Fitzpatrick, Sheila, *Everyday Stalinism: Ordinary Life in Extraordinary Times* (New York, 1999).
Fitzpatrick, Sheila, 'Blat in Stalin's Time', Stephen Lovell, Alena Ledeneva & Andrei Rogachevskii (eds.), *Bribery and Blat in Russia: Negotiating Reciprocity from the Middle Ages to the 1990s* (Houdmills, 2000).
Fitzpatrick Sheila & Slezkine, Yuri (eds.), *In the Shadow of Revolution: Life Stories of Russian Women from 1917 to the Second World War* (Princeton, NJ, 2000).
Fitzpatrick, Sheila, 'A Response to Michael Ellman', *Europe-Asia Studies*, 54.3 (2002).
Fitzpatrick, Sheila, 'Revisionism in Soviet History', *History and Theory*, 46.4 (2007).
Fitzpatrick, Sheila, 'Popular Opinion in Russia under Pre-War Stalinism', Paul Corner (ed.), *Popular Opinion in Totalitarian Regimes: Fascism, Nazism, Communism* (Oxford, 2009).
Fitzpatrick, Sheila & Lüdtke, Alf, 'Energizing the Everyday: On the Breaking and Making of Social Bonds in Nazism and Stalinism', Michael Geyer &

Sheila Fitzpatrick (eds.), *Beyond Totalitarianism: Stalinism and Nazism Compared* (Cambridge, 2009).

Fitzpatrick, Sheila, 'Afterword', Choi Chatterjee, David L. Ransel, Mary Cavender & Karen Petrone (eds.), *Everyday Life in Russia Past and Present* (Bloomington, IN, 2015).

Foucault, Michel, *A History of Sexuality Vol.1: The Will to Knowledge*, trans. Robert Hurley (London, 1998).

Frankl, Viktor E., *Man's Search for Meaning: An Introduction to Logotherapy*, trans. Ilse Lasch (4th edn., Boston, MA, 1992 [1946]).

Freud, Sigmund, *Jokes and their Relation to the Unconscious*, trans. James Strachey (London, 2001).

Freud, Sigmund, *The Future of an Illusion, Civilization and its Discontents and Other Works*, trans. James Strachey (London, 2001).

Froese, Paul, *The Plot to Kill God: Findings from the Soviet Experiment in Secularization* (Berkeley, CA, 2008).

Fürst, Juliane, 'Prisoners of the Soviet Self? – Political Youth Opposition in Late Stalinism', *Europe-Asia Studies*, 54.3 (2002).

Fürst, Juliane, 'Re-examining Opposition under Stalin: Evidence and Context – A Reply to Kuromiya', *Europe-Asia Studies*, 55.5 (2003).

Geldern, James von & Stites, Richard (eds.), *Mass Culture in Soviet Russia* (Bloomington, 1995).

Gerasimova, Katerina, 'The Soviet Communal Apartment', trans. Jakub Lopatko, Jeremy Smith (ed.), *Beyond the Limits: The Concept of Space in Russian History and Culture* (Helsinki, 1999).

Gerasimova, Katerina, 'Public Privacy in the Soviet Communal Apartment', David Crowley & Susan E. Reid (eds.), *Socialist Spaces: Sites of Everyday Life in the Eastern Bloc* (Oxford, 2002).

Gérin, Annie, 'On rit au *NarKomPros*: Anatoli Lounatcharski et la théorie du rire soviétique', *RACAR Revue d'art canadienne/Canadian Art Review*, 37.1 (2012).

Getty, J. Arch & Naumov, Oleg V. (eds.), *The Road to Terror: Stalin and the Self-Destruction of the Bolsheviks, 1932-1939* (New Haven, CT, 1999).

Gilbert, Daniel, *Stumbling on Happiness* (London, 2007).

Glassman, L.M., 'The Bolsheviki as Humorists', *Current History*, 32.4 (1930).

Goldman, Wendy Z., *Women, the State and Revolution: Soviet Family Policy and Social Life, 1917-1936* (Cambridge, 1993).

Goldman, Wendy Z., 'Babas at the Bench: Gender Conflict in Soviet Industry in the 1930s', Melanie Ilič (ed.), *Women in the Stalin Era* (Houndmills, 2001).

Goldman, Wendy Z., *Women at the Gates: Gender and Industry in Stalin's Russia* (Cambridge, 2002).

Goldman, Wendy Z., *Terror and Democracy in the Age of Stalin: The Social Dynamics of Repression* (Cambridge, 2007).

Goldman, Wendy Z., *Inventing the Enemy: Terror and Denunciation in Stalin's Russia* (Cambridge, 2011).

Gorlizki, Yoram, 'Structures of Trust After Stalin', *Slavonic & East European Review*, 91.1 (2013).

Graham, Seth, 'Varieties of Reflexivity in the Russo-Soviet *Anekdot*', Lesley Milne (ed.), *Reflective Laughter: Aspects of Humour in Russian Culture* (London, 2004).

Graham, Seth, *Resonant Dissonance: The Russian Joke in Cultural Context* (Evanston, IL, 2009).

Griesse, Malte, 'Soviet Subjectivities: Discourse, Self-Criticism, Imposture', *Kritika*, 9.3 (2008).

Griffin, Roger (ed.), *Fascism, Totalitarianism and Political Religion* (London, 2005).

Grossman, Vasily, *Life and Fate*, trans. Robert Chandler (London, 2006).

Habermas, Jürgen, 'The Public Sphere', Chandra Mukerji & Michael Schudson (eds.), *Rethinking Popular Culture: Contemporary Perspectives on Cultural Studies* (Berkeley, CA & Oxford, 1991).

Hagenloh, Paul, *Stalin's Police: Public Order and Mass Repression in the USSR, 1926-1941* (Washington DC, 2009).

Halfin Igal & Hellbeck, Jochen, 'Rethinking the Stalinist Subject: Stephen Kotkin's "Magnetic Mountain" and the State of Soviet Historical Studies', *Jarbücher für Geschichte Osteuropas*, 44.3 (1996).

Halfin, Igal, *From Darkness to Light: Class, Consciousness, and Salvation in Revolutionary Russia* (Pittsburgh, PA, 2000).

Halfin, Igal, *Terror in My Soul: Communist Autobiographies on Trial* (Cambridge, MA, 2003).

Halfin, Igal, 'The Bolsheviks' Gallows Laughter', *Journal of Political Ideologies*, 11.3 (2006).

Harari, Yuval Noah, *Sapiens: A Brief History of Humankind* (London, 2015).

Harris, James (ed.), *The Anatomy of Terror: Political Violence under Stalin* (Oxford, 2013).

Havel, Václav et al., *The Power of the Powerless: Citizens Against the State in Central-Eastern Europe* (London, 1985).

Hawley, Katherine, *Trust: A Very Short Introduction* (Oxford, 2012).

Healey, Dan, *Homosexual Desire in Revolutionary Russia* (Chicago, IL, 2001).

Healey, Dan, 'The Disappearance of the Russian Queen, or How the Soviet Closet was Born', Barbara Evans Clements, Rebecca Friedman & Dan Healey (eds.), *Russian Masculinities in History and Culture* (Houndmills, 2002).

Hellbeck, Jochen (ed. & trans.), *Tagebuch aus Moskau 1931-1939* (Munich, 1996).

Hellbeck, Jochen, 'Fashioning the Stalinist Soul: The Diary of Stepan Podlubnyi (1931-9)', *Jahrbücher für Geschichte Osteuropas*, 44.3 (1996).

Hellbeck, Jochen, 'Working, Struggling, Becoming: Stalin-Era Autobiographical Texts', *Russian Review*, 60.3 (2001).

Hellbeck, Jochen, *Revolution on My Mind: Writing a Diary Under Stalin* (Cambridge, MA, 2006).

Henry, Stuart, *The Hidden Economy: The Context and Control of Borderline Crime* (London, 1978).

Herstein, William, 'Confabulations about Personal Memories, Normal and Abnormal', Suzanne Nalbantian, Paul M. Matthews & James L. McClelland (eds.), *The Memory Process: Neuroscientific and Humanistic Perspectives* (Cambridge, MA, 2011).

Higgonet, Margaret & Patrice, 'The Double Helix', Higgonet et al. (eds.), *Behind the Lines: Gender and the Two World Wars* (New Haven, 1987).

Hille, Nicola, 'Der Führerkult im Bild. Die Darstellung von Hitler, Stalin und Mussolini in der politischen Sichtagitation der 1920er bis 1940er Jahre', Benno Ennker & Heidi Hein-Kircher (eds.), *Der Führer im Europa des 20. Jahrhunderts* (Marburg, 2010).

Hillenbrand, F.K.M., *Underground Humour in Nazi Germany, 1933-1945* (London, 1995).

Hoffmann, David L., *Peasant Metropolis: Social Identities in Moscow, 1929-1941* (Ithaca, NY, 1994).

Hoffmann, David L., *Stalinist Values: The Cultural Norms of Soviet Modernity, 1917-1941* (Ithaca, NY, 2003).

Holiday, Ryan, *The Obstacle is the Way: The Ancient Art of Turning Adversity to Advantage* (London, 2014).

Holquist Michael & Clark, Katerina (eds.), *Mikhail Bakhtin* (Cambridge, MA, 1984).

Hobbes, Thomas, *The Elements of Law, Natural and Politic*, ed. Ferdinand Tönnies (London, 1889 [1640]).

Hobbes, Thomas, *Leviathan*, ed. Richard Tuck (Cambridge, 2010 [1651]).

Holmes, Larry E., 'A Symbiosis of Errors: The Personal, Professional and Political in the Kirov Region, 1931-1941', Lewis Siegelbaum (ed.), *Borders of Socialism: Private Spheres of Soviet Russia* (Houndmills, 2006).

Holmes, Larry E., *War, Evacuation, and the Exercise of Power: The Center, Periphery, and Kirov's Pedagogical Institute, 1941-1952* (Lanham, MD, 2012).

Hooper, Cynthia, 'Terror of Intimacy: Family Politics in the 1930s Soviet Union', Christina Kiaer & Eric Naiman (eds.), *Everyday Life in Early Soviet Russia: Taking the Revolution Inside* (Bloomington, IN, 2006).

Hooper, Cynthia, 'Trust in Terror? The Search for a Foolproof Science of Soviet Personnel', *Slavonic & East European Review* 91.1 (2013).

Hopkin, David, *Voices of the People in Nineteenth-Century France* (Cambridge, 2012).

Hosking, Geoffrey, *A History of the Soviet Union, 1917-1991* (Final Edition, London, 1992).

Hosking, Geoffrey, *Trust: A History* (Oxford, 2014).

Huizinga, Johann, *Homo Ludens: A Study of the Play Element in Culture* (New York, 1949).

Husband, William B., 'Soviet Atheism and Russian Orthodox Strategies of Resistance, 1917-1932', *Journal of Modern History*, 70.1 (1998).

Husband, William B., *'Godless Communists': Atheism and Society in Soviet Russia, 1917-1932* (DeKalb, IL, 2000).

Il'f, Il'ia & Petrov, Evegenii, *Sobranie sochinenii v piati tomakh*, tom 5 (Moscow, 1961).

Il'f, Il'ia & Petrov, Evgenii, *Polnoe sobranie sochnenii v odnom tome* (Moscow, 2009).

Ilic, Melanie, 'The Great Terror in Leningrad: Evidence from the *Leningradskii martirolog*', James Harris (ed.), *The Anatomy of Terror: Political Violence under Stalin* (Oxford, 2013).
Inkeles, Alex & Bauer, Raymond A., *The Soviet Citizen: Daily Life in a Totalitarian Society* (Cambridge, MA, 1959).
Jacobson, Howard, *Seriously Funny: From the Ridiculous to the Sublime* (London, 1997).
Jerram, Leif, 'Space: A Useless Category for Historical Analysis?', *History and Theory*, 52.3 (2013).
Johnston, Timothy, *Being Soviet: Identity, Rumour, and Everyday Life under Stalin, 1939-1953* (Oxford, 2011).
Jung, Carl Gustav, *Modern Man in Search of a Soul*, trans. W.S. Dell & Cary F. Baynes (Abingdon, 2001 [1933]).
Kane, Thomas R., Suls, Jerry & Tedeschi, James T., 'Humour as a Tool of Social Interaction', Antony J. Chapman & Hugh C. Foot (eds.), *It's a Funny Thing, Humour* (Oxford, 1977).
Kelly, Catriona, *Comrade Pavlik: The Rise and Fall of a Soviet Boy Hero* (London, 2005).
Kershaw, Ian, *Popular Opinion and Political Dissent in the Third Reich: Bavaria 1933-1945* (Oxford, 1984).
Kharkhordin, Oleg, 'Reveal and Dissimulate: A Genealogy of Private Life in Soviet Russia', Jeff Weintraub & Krishnan Kumar (eds.), *Public and Private in Thought and Practice: Perspectives on a Grand Dichotomy* (Chicago, IL, 1997).
Khaustov, Vladimir N., 'Razvitie sovetskikh organov gosudarstvennoi bezopastnosti: 1917-1953 gg.', *Cahiers du Monde russe*, 42.2-4 (2001).
Khlevniuk, Oleg, *The History of the Gulag: From Collectivization to the Great Terror* (New Haven, CT, 2004).
Kiaer, Christina & Naiman, Eric (eds.), *Everyday Life in Early Soviet Russia: Taking the Revolution Inside* (Bloomington, IN, 2006).
Kirpotin, V.Ia., speech in *Pervyi vsesoiuznyi s"ezd sovetskikh pisatelei, 1934: Stenograficheskii otchet* (Moscow, 1934).
Kizenko, Nadieszda, 'Sacramental Confession in Modern Russia and Ukraine', Catherine Wanner (ed.), *State Secularism and Lived Religion in Soviet Russia and Ukraine* (New York, 2012).
Klinghoffer, Arthur Jay, *Red Apocalypse: The Religious Evolution of Soviet Communism* (Lanham, MD, 1996).
Kobo, Kh. (ed.), *Osmyslit' kul't Stalina* (Moscow, 1989).
Koestler, Arthur, *The Act of Creation* (London, 1964).
Koestler, Arthur, *The Invisible Writing* (London, 2005 [1954]).
Kolasky, John, *Laughter Through Tears: Underground Wit, Humor and Satire in the Soviet Russian Empire* (Bullsbrook, 1985).
Kolonitskii, Boris, '*Tragicheskaia erotika*': *Obrazy imperatorskoi sem'i v gody pervoi mirovoi voiny* (Moscow, 2010).
Komissarov, D.S. (ed.), *Persidskie narodnye anekdoty* (Moscow, 1990).
Kon, Igor', *Klubnichka na berezke: Seksual'naia kul'tura v Rossii* (Moscow, 2010).

Kostyrchenko, Gennadii, *Stalin protiv 'kosmopolitov'. Vlast' i evreiskaia intelligentsiia v SSSR* (Moscow, 2009).

Kotkin, Stephen, *Magnetic Mountain: Stalinism as a Civilization* (Berkeley, CA, 1997).

Kowalsky, Sharon A., *Deviant Women: Female Crime and Criminology in Revolutionary Russia, 1880-1930* (DeKalb, IL, 2009).

Kravchenko, Victor, *I Chose Freedom. The Personal and Political Life of a Soviet Official* (London, 1947).

Krongauz, M.A., 'Bessilie iazyka v epokhu zrelogo sotsializma', *Znak: Sbornik statei po lingvistike, semiotike i poetike pamiati A.N. Zhurinskogo* (Moscow, 1994).

Krylova, Anna, 'Saying "Lenin" and Meaning "Party": Subversion and Laughter in Soviet and Post-Soviet Society', Adele Marie Barker (ed.), *Consuming Russia: Popular Culture, Sex, and Society since Gorbachev* (London, 1999).

Krylova, Anna, 'The Tenacious Liberal Subject in Soviet Studies', *Kritika*, 1.1 (2000).

Krylova, Anna, *Soviet Women in Combat: A History of Violence on the Eastern Front* (New York, 2010).

Kundera, Milan, *The Joke*, trans. Michael Henry Heim (London, 1992).

Kundera, Milan, *The Book of Laughter and Forgetting*, trans. Aaron Asher (London, 1996).

Landmann, Salcia, *Der Jüdische Witz* (Olten, 1960).

Larsen, Egon, *Wit as a Weapon: The Political Joke in History* (London, 1980).

Leatherby, Gayle & Reynolds, Gillian, *Train Tracks: Work, Play and Politics on the Railways* (Oxford, 2005).

Lebina, N.B., *Povsednevnaia zhizn' sovetskogo goroda 1920-1930 gody* (St Petersburg, 1999).

Lebina, Nataliia, *Sovetskaia povsednevnost': Normy i anomalii ot voennogo kommunizma k bol'shomu stiliu* (Moscow, 2015).

Ledeneva, Alena V., *Russia's Economy of Favours: Blat, Networking and Informal Exchange* (Cambridge, 1998).

Lenoe, Matthew, *The Kirov Murder and Soviet Society* (New Haven, CT, 2010).

Levine, Lawrence W., *Black Culture and Black Consciousness: Afro-American Folk Thought from Slavery to Freedom* (New York, 1977).

Levine, Lawrence W., 'William Shakespeare and the American People: A Study in Cultural Transformation', *American Historical Review*, 89.1 (1984).

Lewis, Ben, *Hammer & Tickle: A History of Communism Told Through Communist Jokes* (London, 2008).

Likhachev, D.S., Panchenko, A.M. & Ponyrko, N.V., *Smekh v drevnei Rusi* (Leningrad, 1984).

Likhachev, D.S., 'Smekh kak mirovozzrenie', D.S. Likhachev, *Istoricheskaia poetika russkoi literatury. Smekh kak mirovozzrenie i drugie raboty* (St Petersburg, 1997).

Lipman, Steve, *Laughter in Hell: The Use of Humor During the Holocaust* (Northvale, NJ, 1993).

Livshin, Aleksandr & Orlov, Igor', *Vlast' i obshchestvo: Dialog v pismakh*

(Moscow, 2002).
Livshin, A.Ia., Orlov, I.B. & Khlevniuk, O.V. (eds.), *Pis'ma vo vlast', 1928-1939: Zaiavleniia, zhaloby, donosy, pis'ma v gosudarstvennye struktury i sovetskim vozhdiam* (Moscow, 2002).
Livshin, Alexander, 'Bridging the Gap: Government-Society Dialogue via Letters', *Slavonic and East European Review*, 91.1 (2013).
Lüdtke, Alf, *The History of Everyday Life: Reconstructing Historical Experiences and Ways of Life*, trans. William Templer (Princeton, NJ, 2005).
Lukes, Steven & Galnoor, Itzhak, *No Laughing Matter: A Collection of Political Jokes* (London, 1987).
Lunacharskii, A.V., 'O smekhe', *Literaturnyi kritik*, 4 (1935).
Lunacharskii, A.V., 'Budem smeiat'sia', *Sobranie sochinenii v vos'mi tomakh* (Moscow, 1963-7).
Lur'e, V.F., 'Shkol'naia khronika', A.F. Belousov (ed.), *Russkii shkol'nyi fol'klor – Ot 'vyzyvanii' Pikovoi damy do semeinykh rasskazov* (Moscow, 1998).
Lyons, Eugene, *Modern Moscow* (London, 1935).
McDonald, Tracy, *Face to the Village: The Riazan Countryside under Soviet Rule, 1921-1930* (Toronto, 2011).
McGraw, Peter A. & Warren, Caleb, 'Benign Violations: Making Immoral Behavior Funny', *Psychological Science*, 21.8 (2010).
McGraw, Peter & Warner, Joel, *The Humor Code: A Global Search for What Makes Things Funny* (New York, 2014).
Malia, Martin, *The Soviet Tragedy: A History of Socialism in Russia* (New York, 1994).
Man'kov, A.G., *Dnevniki tridtsatykh godov* (St Petersburg, 2001).
Matza, David, *Delinquency and Drift* (New York, 1990).
Mauss, Marcel, *The Gift: The Form and Reason for Exchange in Archaic Societies* (London, 2002).
Mayr, Andrea, *Prison Discourse: Language as a Means of Control and Resistance* (Houndmills, 2004).
Medvedev, Roy, *Let History Judge: The Origins and Consequences of Stalinism*, revised & expanded edition, trans. George Shriver (Oxford, 1989).
Megrelidze, K.R., *Osnovnye problemy sotsiologii myshlenniia*, ed. A. T. Bochorisheli (Moscow, 2007).
Mehnert, Klaus, *The Anatomy of Soviet Man*, trans. Maurice Rosenbaum (London, 1961 [1958]).
Mel'nichenko, Mikhail, 'Fenomen frontovogo anekdota: narodnoe tvorchestvo ili instrument agitatsii', *Rossiiskaia istoriia*, 6 (2009).
Mel'nichenko, M., *Sovetskii anekdot: Ukazatel' siuzhetov* (Moscow, 2014).
Merziger, Patrick, 'Totalitarian Humour'? National Socialist Propaganda and Active Audiences in Entertainment, *History Workshop Journal*, 79 (2015).
Miéville, China, *The City and the City* (London, 2009).
Mikes, George, *Humour in Memoriam* (London, 1970).
Milne, Lesley (ed.), *Reflective Laughter: Aspects of Humour in Russian Culture* (London, 2004).
Mironenko, S.V. & Werth, N. (eds.), *Istoriia stalinskogo Gulaga*, Tom 1, *Massovye*

repressii (Moscow, 2004).
Mochulsky, Fyodor Vasilevich, *Gulag Boss: A Soviet Memoir*, ed. & trans. Deborah Kaple (New York, 2011).
Montagu, Ivor & Marshall, Herbert (eds.), *The Crocodile Album of Soviet Humour* (London, 1943).
Morreall, John (ed.), *The Philosophy of Laughter and Humor* (Albany, NY, 1987).
Muschard, Jutta, 'Jokes and their Relation to Relevance and Cognition or "Can Relevance Theory Account for the Appreciation of Jokes?"', *Zeitschrift für Anglistik und Amerikanistik*, 47.1 (1999).
N., A. et al, *Russia Dies Laughing: Jokes from Soviet Russia* (London, 1983).
Naiman, Eric, *Sex in Public: The Incarnation of Early Soviet Ideology* (Princeton, NJ, 1997).
Neumann, Matthias, *The Communist Youth League and the Transformation of the Soviet Union, 1917-1932* (Abingdon, 2011).
Nikanorova, E.K., *Istoricheskii anekdot v russkoi literature XVIII veka. Anekdoty o Petre Velikom* (Novosibirsk, 2001).
Obrdlik, Antonin J., '"Gallows Humor" – A Sociological Phenomenon', *American Journal of Sociology*, 47.5 (1942).
Orwell, George, 'Funny but not Vulgar', *The Collected Essays, Journalism and Letters of George Orwell*, Vol. III: *As I Please, 1943-45*, ed. Sonia Orwell & Ian Angus (London, 1968).
Osokina, Elena, *Ierarkhiia potrebleniia: O zhizni liudei v usloviiakh stalinskogo snabzheniia 1928-1935 gg.* (Moscow, 1993).
Osokina, Elena, *Za fasadom 'stalinskogo izobiliia': Raspredelenie i rynok v snabzhenii naseleniia v gody industrializatsii 1927-1941* (Moscow, 1999).
Osokina, Elena, 'Economic Disobedience under Stalin', Lynne Viola (ed.), *Contending with Stalinism: Soviet Power and Popular Resistance in the 1930s* (Ithaca, NY, 2002).
Pascal, Blaise, *Les Provinciales* (1656-7; freely available online).
Paulos, John Allen, *I Think, Therefore I Laugh: The Flip Side of Philosophy* (London, 2000).
Perfetti, Lisa, *Women and Laughter in Medieval Comic Literature* (Ann Arbor, MI, 2003).
Petrone, Karen, *Life has Become More Joyous, Comrades: Celebrations in the Time of Stalin* (Bloomington, IN, 2000).
Petrushevskaia, Liudmila, 'O chem rech'', Maksim Blant (ed.), *Istoriia glazami Krokodila XX vek: Slova 1922-1937gg.* (Moscow, 2014).
Peukert, Detlev J.K., *Inside Nazi Germany: Conformity, Opposition and Racism in Everyday Life*, trans. Richard Deveson (London, 1987).
Pi-Sunyer, Oriol, 'Political Humor in a Dictatorial State: the Case of Spain', *Ethnohistory*, 24.2 (1977).
Plamper, Jan, 'Abolishing Ambiguity: Soviet Censorship Practices in the 1930s', *Russian Review*, 60.4 (2001).
Plamper, Jan, 'Introduction: Modern Personality Cults', Jan Plamper & Klaus Heller (eds.), *Personality Cults in Stalinism / Personenkulte im Stalinismus* (Göttingen, 2004).

Plamper, Jan, *The Stalin Cult: A Study in the Alchemy of Power* (New Haven, CT, 2012).
Plato, *Laws*, Books 7 & 11 (freely available online).
Platonov, Andrei, *The Foundation Pit*, trans. Robert & Elisabeth Chandler, & Olga Meerson (London, 2010).
Podlubnyi, Stepan, Diary published in Véronique Garros, Natalia Korenevskaya & Thomas Lahusen (eds.), *Intimacy and Terror: Soviet Diaries of the 1930s*, trans. Carol A. Flath (New York, 1995).
Poliakov, Iu.A. (ed.), *Vsesoiuznaia perepis' naseleniia 1937 goda: obshchie itogi. Sbornik dokumentov i materialov* (Moscow, 2007).
Pope-Hennessy, Una, *The Closed City: Impressions of a Visit to Leningrad* (London, 1938).
Pratchett, Terry, *A Slip of the Keyboard: Collected Non-Fiction* (London, 2014).
Priestland, David, *Stalinism and the Politics of Mobilization: Ideas, Power, and Terror in Inter-war Russia* (Oxford, 2007).
Propp, Vladimir, *Morphology of the Folktale*, trans. Laurence Scott & Louis A. Wagner (2nd edn., London, 1968).
Provine, Robert R. & Fischer, Kenneth R., 'Laughing, Smiling, and Talking: Relation to Sleeping and Social Context in Humans', *Ethology*, 83.4 (1989).
Provine, Robert R., *Laugher: A Scientific Investigation* (London, 2000).
Ramachandran, V.S., 'The Neurology and Evolution of Humor, Laughter, and Smiling: The False Alarm Theory', *Medical Hypotheses*, 51.4 (1998).
Rancour-Laferriere, Daniel, *The Slave Soul of Russia: Moral Masochism and the Cult of Suffering* (London, 1995).
Ransel, David L., 'The Scholarship of Everyday Life', Choi Chatterjee, David L. Ransel, Mary Cavender & Karen Petrone (eds.), *Everyday Life in Russia Past and Present* (Bloomington, IN, 2015).
Rapaport, Lynne, 'Laughter and Heartache: The Functions of Humor in Holocaust Tragedy', Jonathan Petropoulos & John K. Roth (eds.), *Gray Zones: Ambiguity and Compromise in the Holocaust and Its Aftermath* (New York, 2005).
Rees, E.A., 'Leader Cults: Varieties, Preconditions and Functions', Balázs Apor et al. (eds.), *The Leader Cult in Communist Dictatorships: Stalin and the Eastern Bloc* (Houndmills, 2004).
Ries, Nancy, *Russian Talk: Culture and Conversation during Perestroika* (Ithaca, NY, 1997).
Rimmel, Lesley A., 'Another Kind of Fear: The Kirov Murder and the End of Bread Rationing in Leningrad', *Slavic Review*, 56.3 (1997).
Rittersporn, Gábor T., 'Formy obshchestvennogo obikhoda molodezhi i ustanovki sovetskogo rezhima v predvoennom desiatiletii', Timo Vihavainen (ed.), *Normy i tsennosti povsednevnoi zhizni: stanovlenie sotsialiticheskogo obraza zhizni v Rossii, 1920-1930-e gody* (St Petersburg, 2000).
Rittersporn, Gábor T., 'Perevernutyi mir sovetskogo smekha', I.V. Narskii et al (eds.), *Ot velikogo do smeshnogo... Instrumentalizatsiia smekha v rossiiskoi istorii XX veka* (Cheliabinsk, 2013).
Rittersporn, Gábor T., *Anguish, Anger, and Folkways in Soviet Russia* (Pittsburgh,

PA, 2014).

Rolf, Malte, 'The Leader's Many Bodies: Leader Cults and Mass Festivals in Voronezh, Novosibirsk and Kemerovo in the 1930s', Jan Plamper & Klaus Heller (eds.), *Personality Cults in Stalinism / Personenkulte im Stalinismus* (Göttingen, 2004).

Rolf, Malte, *Soviet Mass Festivals, 1917-1991*, trans. Cynthia Klohr (Pittsburgh, PA, 2013).

Ruksenas, Algis, *The World's Best Russian Jokes* (London, 1987).

Ryan, Karen L., *Stalin in Russian Satire, 1917-1991* (London, 2009).

Saussure, Ferdinand de, *Course in General Linguistics*, trans. Wade Baskin (London, 1974).

Schlögel, Karl, *Moscow 1937*, trans. Rodney Livingstone (Cambridge, 2012).

Schrand, Thomas G., 'Socialism in One Gender: Masculine Values in the Stalin Revolution', Barbara Evans Clements, Rebecca Friedman & Dan Healey (eds.), *Russian Masculinities in History and Culture* (Houndmills, 2002).

Scott, James C., *Weapons of the Weak: Everyday Forms of Peasant Resistance* (New Haven, CT, 1985).

Scott, James C., *Domination and the Arts of Resistance* (New Haven, CT, 1990).

Scott, John, *Behind the Urals: An American Worker in Russia's City of Steel*, ed. Stephen Kotkin (Bloomington, IN, 1989).

Seneca, *Letters from a Stoic*, ed. & trans. Robin Campbell (London, 1969).

Serge, Victor, *From Lenin to Stalin* (London, 1937).

Shearer, David R., *Policing Stalin's Socialism: Repression and Social Order in the Soviet Union, 1924-1953* (New Haven, CT, 2009).

Shitts, I.I., *Dnevnik 'Velikogo pereloma' (mart 1928-avgust 1931)* (Paris, 1991).

Shklovskii, Viktor, 'K teorii komicheskogo', *Epopeia*, 3 (1922).

Shmeleva, E.Ia. & Shmelev, A.D., *Russkii anekdot: Tekst i rechevoi zhanr* (Moscow, 2002).

Shturman, Dora & Tiktin, Sergei, *Sovetskii Soiuz v zerkale politicheskogo anekdota* (London, 1985).

Siegelbaum, Lewis H., & Suny, Ronald Grigor (eds.), *Making Workers Soviet: Power, Class, and Identity* (Ithaca, NY, 1994).

Skradol, Natalia, 'Laughing with Comrade Stalin: An Analysis of Laughter in a Soviet Newspaper Report', *Russian Review*, 68.1 (2009).

Skradol, Natalia, '"There is Nothing Funny About It": Laughing Law at Stalin's Party Plenum', *Slavic Review*, 70.2 (2011).

Sloterdijk, Peter, *Critique of Cynical Reason*, trans. Michael Eldred (London, 1988).

Smith, S.A., 'The Social Meanings of Swearing: Workers and Bad Language in Late Imperial and Early Soviet Russia', *Past and Present*, 160 (1998).

Smith, S.A., 'Heavenly Letters and Tales of the Forest: "Superstition" against Bolshevism', *Forum for Anthropology and Culture*, 2 (2006).

Smith, Steve, 'Fear and Rumour in the People's Republic of China in the 1950s', *Cultural and Social History*, 5.3 (2008).

Sokolov, A.K. (ed.), *Obshchestvo i vlast' 1930-e gody. Povestvovanie v dokumentakh* (Moscow, 1998).

Sokolova, Nataliia, 'V zerkale smekha', *Voprosy Literatury*, 3 (1996).
Solnit, Rebecca, *A Paradise Built in Hell: The Extraordinary Communities That Arise in Disaster* (New York, 2010).
Solomon, Jr., Peter H., *Soviet Criminal Justice under Stalin* (Cambridge, 1996).
Stephenson, Jill, *Hitler's Home Front: Württemberg under the Nazis* (London, 2006).
Stephenson, Svetlana, *Gangs of Russia: From the Streets to the Corridors of Power* (Ithaca, NY, 2015).
Stites, Richard, *The Women's Liberation Movement in Russia: Feminism, Nihilism and Bolshevism, 1860-1930* (Princeton, NJ, 1991).
Taleb, Nassim Nicholas, *The Black Swan: The Impact of the Highly Improbable* (London, 2007).
Telesin, Iulius, *1001 Izbrannyi sovetskii politicheskii anekdot* (Tenafly, NJ, 1986).
Thurston, Robert W., 'Social Dimensions of Stalinist Rule: Humor and Terror in the USSR, 1935-1941', *Journal of Social History*, 24.3 (1991).
Thurston, Robert W., *Life and Terror in Stalin's Russia, 1934-1941* (London, 1996).
Tikhomirov, Alexey, 'The Regime of Forced Trust: Making and Breaking Emotional Bonds between People and State in Soviet Russia, 1917-1941', *Slavonic & East European Review*, 91.1 (2013).
Trivers, Robert, *Deceit and Self-Deception: Fooling Yourself the Better to Fool Others* (London, 2013).
Tumarkin, Nina, *Lenin Lives! The Lenin Cult in Soviet Russia* (Cambridge, MA, 1983).
Ulam, Adam B., *Stalin: The Man and his Era* (London, 1989).
Uspenskii, B., '"Zavetnye skazki" A.N. Afanas'eva', N. Bogomolov (ed.), *Anti-mir russkoi kul'tury. Iazyk. Fol'klor. Literatura.* (Moscow, 1996).
Vaiskopf, Iakov, *Blatnaia lira. Sbornik tiuremnykh i lagernykh pesen* (Jerusalem, 1981).
Vasil'ev, Valerii, '30-e gody na Ukraine', *Kommunist*, 17 (1990).
Vatlin, Alexander & Malashenko, Larisa (eds.), *Piggy Foxy and the Sword of Revolution: Bolshevik Self-Portraits* (New Haven, CT, 2006).
Vernadskii, V.I., *Dnevniki 1935-1941 v dvukh knigakh* (Moscow, 2006).
Viola, Lynne, 'Visions of Apocalypse in the Soviet Countryside', *Journal of Modern History*, 62.4 (1990).
Viola, Lynne, *Peasant Rebels under Stalin: Collectivization and the Culture of Peasant Resistance* (Oxford, 1996).
Viola, Lynne, 'Popular Resistance in the Stalinist 1930s: Soliloquy of a Devil's Advocate', *Kritika*, 1.1 (2000).
Viola, Lynne (ed.), *Contending with Stalinism: Soviet Power and Popular Resistance in the 1930s* (Ithaca, NY, 2002).
Vogel, Susan C., *Humor: A Semiogenetic Approach* (Bochum, 1989).
Volkogonov, Dmitri, *Stalin: Triumph and Tragedy*, trans. Harold Shukman (London, 2000).
Voloshinov, V.N., *Marxism and the Philosophy of Language*, trans. Ladislav Matejka & I.R. Titunik (New York & London, 1973).

Waterlow, Jonathan, 'Intimating Trust: Popular Humour in Stalin's 1930s', *Cultural and Social History*, 10.2 (2013).

Waterlow, Jonathan, 'More than Resistance: Political Humour under Stalin in the 1930s', Elisabeth Cheauré & Regine Nohejl (eds.), *Humour and Laughter in History: Transcultural Perspectives* (Bielefeld, 2014).

Waterlow, Jonathan, 'Sanctioning Laughter in Stalin's Soviet Union', *History Workshop Journal*, 79 (2015).

Waterlow, Jonathan, 'Speaking More than Bolshevik: Humour, Subjectivity, and Crosshatching in Stalin's 1930s', Matthias Neumann & Andy Willimott (eds.), *Rethinking the Russian Revolution as Historical Divide* (Abingdon, 2017).

Waterlow, Jonathan, '*Babushka*, Helper, Harlot, Joker: Women and Gender in 1930s Political Humour', Melanie Ilic (ed.), *The Palgrave Handbook of Women and Gender in Twentieth-Century Russia and the Soviet Union* (London, 2018).

Whitson, Jennifer A. & Galinsky, Adam D., 'Lacking Control Increases Illusory Pattern Perception', *Science*, 322 (2008).

Willimott, Andy, 'Everyday Revolution: The Making of the Soviet Urban Communes', C. Read, A. Lindenmeyr & P. Waldron (eds.), *Russia's Great War and Revolution, 1914-1922: The Home Front* (Bloomington, IN, 2015).

Willimott, Andy, *Living the Revolution: Urban Communes and Soviet Socialism, 1917-1932* (Oxford, 2017).

Wilson, Christopher, *Jokes: Form, Content, Use and Function* (London, 1979).

Winter, Ella, *Red Virtue: Human Relationships in the New Russia* (London, 1933).

Yekelchyk, Serhy, *Stalin's Citizens: Everyday Politics in the Wake of Total War* (New York, 2014).

Yurchak, Alexei, 'The Cynical Reason of Late Socialism: Power, Pretense, and the *Anekdot*', *Public Culture*, 9 (1997).

Yurchak, Alexei, *Everything was Forever Until It was No More: The Last Soviet Generation* (Princeton, NJ, 2006).

Zamyatin, Evgeny, *We*, trans. Natasha Randall (London, 2007).

Zhiromskaia, V.B., Kiselev, I.N. & Poliakov, Iu.A. (eds.), *Polveka pod grifom "sekretno": vsesoiuznaia perepis' naseleniia 1937 goda* (Moscow, 1996).

Zhuravlev, Sergei & Mukhin, Mikhail, *'Krepost' sotsializma': Povsednevnost' i motivatsiia truda v sovetskom predpriiatii, 1928-1938 gg.* (Moscow, 2004).

Online Sources

Arkhipova, Alexandra, 'Laughing About Stalin: The Formation and Evolution of Soviet Uncensored Jokelore', available on the website of the conference, *Totalitarian Laughter: Cultures of the Comic Under Socialism* <http://slavic.princeton.edu/events/calendar/detail.php?ID=1921>.

Arkhipova, A.S. & Mel'nichenko, M.A., '"Vot protsenty na vash kapital!" K voprosu o genezise i evoliutsii politicheskogo anekdota' <http://www.ruthenia.ru/document/545661.html>.

Arosev, A.Ia., diary archived at <www.prozhito.org>.

Brandenberger, David, 'A Background Guide to Working with the HPSSS Online', <http://hcl.harvard.edu/collections/hpsss/working_with_hpsss.pdf>.

Multiple Authors, 'Political Humor from North Korea', <http://www.rfa.org/english/news/korea/koreanjokes-09102008183510.html>.

Nikolaev, Lev Petrovich, diary archived at <www.prozhito.org>.

Watts, Alan, 'Our Image of the World', lecture available at <https://www.alanwatts.org/>.

Unpublished

Belokowsky, Simon, 'Laughing on the Inside: Gulag Humor in Terms of a Gulag Society' (article, forthcoming).

Bernstein, Seth, *Communist Upbringing under Stalin: The Political Socialization and Militarization of Soviet Youth, 1934-1941*, PhD Thesis, University of Toronto (2013).

Davies, Sarah, *Propaganda and Popular Opinion in Soviet Russia, 1934-1941*, DPhil Thesis, University of Oxford (1994).

Graham, Seth, *A Cultural Analysis of the Russo-Soviet* Anekdot, PhD Thesis, University of Pittsburgh (2009).

Healey, Dan, 'Forging Gulag Sexualities: Penal Homosexuality and the Reform of the Gulag after Stalin', conference paper delivered at the British Association for Slavonic and East European Studies Conference, April 2014.

Rimmel, Lesley Ann, *The Kirov Murder and Soviet Society: Propaganda and Popular Opinion in Leningrad, 1934-1935*, PhD Thesis, University of Pennsylvania (1995).

www.ingramcontent.com/pod-product-compliance
Lightning Source LLC
Chambersburg PA
CBHW070129080526
44586CB00015B/1616